Power and Ceremony in European History

Cultures of Early Modern Europe

Series Editors: Beat Kümin, Professor of Early Modern European History, University of Warwick, and Brian Cowan, Associate Professor and Canada Research Chair in Early Modern British History, McGill University

Editorial Board: Adam Fox, University of Edinburgh, UK
Robert Frost, University of Aberdeen, UK
Molly Greene, University of Princeton, USA
Ben Schmidt, University of Washington, USA
Gerd Schwerhoff, University of Dresden, Germany
Francsesca Trivellato, University of Yale, USA
Francisca Loetz, University of Zurich, Switzerland

The 'cultural turn' in the humanities has generated a wealth of new research topics and approaches. Focusing on the ways in which representations, perceptions and negotiations shaped people's lived experiences, the books in this series provide fascinating insights into the past. The series covers early modern culture in its broadest sense, inclusive of (but not restricted to) themes such as gender, identity, communities, mentalities, emotions, communication, ritual, space, food and drink, and material culture.

Published:

Food and Identity in England, 1540–1640, Paul S. Lloyd (2014)
The Birth of the English Kitchen, 1600–1850, Sara Pennell (2016)
Vagrancy in English Culture and Society, 1650–1750, David Hitchcock (2016)
Angelica's Book and the World of Reading in Late Renaissance Italy, Brendan Dooley (2016)
Gender, Culture and Politics in England, 1560–1640, Susan D. Amussen and David E. Underdown (2017)
Food, Religion, and Communities in Early Modern Europe, Christopher Kissane (2018)
Religion and Society at the Dawn of Modern Europe, Rudolf Schlögl (2020)
Power and Ceremony in European History: Rituals, Practices and Representative Bodies since the Late Middle Ages, Anna Kalinowska and Jonathan Spangler (eds.)

Power and Ceremony in European History

Rituals, Practices and Representative Bodies since the Late Middle Ages

Edited by
Anna Kalinowska and Jonathan Spangler,
with the assistance of Paweł Tyszka

BLOOMSBURY ACADEMIC
LONDON · NEW YORK · OXFORD · NEW DELHI · SYDNEY

BLOOMSBURY ACADEMIC
Bloomsbury Publishing Plc
50 Bedford Square, London, WC1B 3DP, UK
1385 Broadway, New York, NY 10018, USA
29 Earlsfort Terrace, Dublin 2, Ireland

BLOOMSBURY, BLOOMSBURY ACADEMIC and the Diana logo are
trademarks of Bloomsbury Publishing Plc

First published in Great Britain 2021
Paperback edition first published 2023

Copyright © Anna Kalinowska and Jonathan Spangler, 2021

Anna Kalinowska and Jonathan Spangler have asserted their right under the
Copyright, Designs and Patents Act, 1988, to be identified as Editors of this work.

Cover image: Coronation Procession of Charles II MET DP165316 361499
(© Cultural Archive / Alamy Stock Photo).

All rights reserved. No part of this publication may be reproduced or transmitted
in any form or by any means, electronic or mechanical, including photocopying,
recording, or any information storage or retrieval system, without prior
permission in writing from the publishers.

Bloomsbury Publishing Plc does not have any control over, or responsibility for,
any third-party websites referred to or in this book. All internet addresses given in
this book were correct at the time of going to press. The editors and publisher
regret any inconvenience caused if addresses have changed or sites have
ceased to exist, but can accept no responsibility for any such changes.

Every effort has been made to trace copyright holders and to obtain their permissions
for the use of copyright material. The publisher apologizes for any
errors or omissions and would be grateful if notified of any corrections that
should be incorporated in future reprints or editions of this book.

A catalogue record for this book is available from the British Library.

A catalog record for this book is available from the Library of Congress.

ISBN: HB: 978-1-3501-5218-2
PB: 978-1-3502-6886-9
ePDF: 978-1-3501-5219-9
eBook: 978-1-3501-5220-5

Typeset by RefineCatch Limited, Bungay, Suffolk

To find out more about our authors and books visit www.bloomsbury.com
and sign up for our newsletters.

Contents

List of Illustrations   vii
List of Contributors   ix

Introduction *Anna Kalinowska and Jonathan Spangler*   1

Part 1 Coronation and Enthronement

1. Where exactly is the throne? Locating sovereignty in sixteenth-century Ottoman succession rituals *N. Zeynep Yelçe*   19
2. Proclamations and coronations in Palermo (1700–1735): Performing kingship and celebrating civic power *Pablo González Tornel*   33
3. The evolution of the British coronation rite, 1761–1953 *Nicholas Dixon*   49

Part 2 Ceremonial of Royal Courts

4. The daily court ceremonial of the French queen in the reign of Henry III *Vladimir Shishkin*   69
5. Courtly and ceremonial spaces in Spanish royal sites: An evolution from the renaissance to the baroque *José Eloy Hortal Muñoz*   87
6. Royal baptism in the Spanish court: Art and ritual from the sixteenth to the eighteenth century *Inmaculada Rodríguez Moya*   105
7. From marshal to monarch: State ceremonies and Jean-Baptiste Bernadotte in post-napoleonic Sweden *Mikael Alm*   121

Part 3 Ceremonial of Institutions and Representative Bodies

8. Not the ruler, but the land: Estates and ceremonial order at the diet of besztercebánya, 1620 *Gábor Kármán*   143
9. Oath-taking and hand-kissing: Ceremonies of sovereignty in a 'Monarchia composita', the states of the house of savoy from the sixteenth to the nineteenth century *Andrea Merlotti*   157

Part 4 Tangible and Intangible Elements in Staging Ceremonies

10   Jagiellonians and habsburgs: Heraldic dynastic representation in Central
     Europe from the fifteenth to the seventeenth century *Géza Pálffy*   171
11   Operas and masquerades: Court rituals and entertainments under
     Ernest Augustus and George I of Brunswick-Lüneburg (1660–1727)
     in the electorate of Hanover and Great Britain *Babara Arciszewska*   193
12   Public staging, visualization and performance of eighteenth-century
     danish absolutism: Queen Caroline Mathilde's journey across funen
     as ritual *Michael Bregnsbo*   213

Select Bibliography   229
Index   241

Illustrations

Figures

2.1	Giovanni Battista Ragusa, *Coronation of Vittorio Amedeo of Savoy*, 1713	37
2.2	Giuseppe Vasi, Royal entry of Charles of Bourbon in Palermo, 1735	43
5.1	*Map of the Royal Sites around Madrid ca. 1600*	91
5.2	*Map of the Royal Sites in the south of the Iberian Peninsula ca. 1600*	92
6.1	Teodoro Ardemans, *Plan of the Royal Chapel*, 18th century drawing	109
6.2	Teodoro Ardemans, *Plan of the convoy for the prince's baptism*, 18th century drawing	110
9.1	F. Festa, *The Oath of allegiance to Charles Felix of Savoy, King of Sardinia, in the Cathedral of Turin 14 March 1822*	162
10.1	Coats of Arms of the Central European Lands and Provinces ruled by the Hungarian King Matthias Corvinus from *Chronica Hungarorum of Johannes Thuróczy*, 1488	173
10.2	Hungarian Royal Double Seal of King Władysław II Jagiellon, 1493	174
10.3	Royal Oratory in the Saint Vitus Cathedral in Prague	174
10.4	Silver Schaumünze of Bernhard Beheim with Coats of Arms of the Hungarian and Bohemian Lands, 1525, Kremnica	175
10.5	Flag of Silesia in funeral procession of Ferdinand I, 1565	180
10.6	Triumphal Chariot of Liberalitas in funeral procession of Archduke Albert of Austria from Jacob Franquart, *Pompa Funebris Alberti*, Brussels, 1623	180
10.7	Coronation of Leopold I as Hungarian King in Pozsony, 27 June 1655	181
10.8	Flags of the ten Lands of the Hungarian Crown in the Coronation Ordinance of Ferdinand II in Pozsony, 1618	183
10.9	Hungarian Royal Double Seal of Emperor Rudolph II, 1607	184
10.10	Hungarian Coronation Medal of King Ferdinand II with Coats of Arms of the ten Lands of the Hungarian Crown, 1618	185
11.1	William Hogarth, *The Bad Taste of the Town* (also known as *Masquerades and Operas*), 1724	194
11.2	Chariot of Neptune, a float in grand regatta, from Giovanni Matteo Alberti, *Giuochi festiui, e militari, danze, serenate, machine, boscareccia artificiosa, regatta solenne, et altri sontuosi apprestamenti di allegrezza esposti alla sodisfattione uniuersale dalla generosità dell'A. S. d'Ernesto Augusto duca di Brunsuich...*, 1686	196
11.3	Herrenhausen design, attributed to Elector Ernest Augustus of Hanover, c. 1690	197
11.4	Cross-section of the opera house in the Leine Palace, Hanover, 1746	197

11.5	Frontispiece of *The Architecture of A. Palladio; In Four Books*, ed. Giacomo Leoni, John Watts for the Author, 1715	199
11.6	Frontispiece of *The Designs of Inigo Jones, Consisting of Plans and Elevations for Publick and Private Buildings*, William Kent, 1727	200
11.7	William Hogarth, *Berenstadt, Cuzzoni, and Senesino*, 1724	201
11.8	Water festivities organized on the canal in Piazzola sul Brenta to mark the visit of Ernest Augustus of Brunswick-Lüneburg in 1685, Francesco Maria Piccioli, *L'orologio del piacere*, part II, *Il Vaticinio della Fortuna*, 1685	203
11.9	William Hogarth, *Taste: The Gate of Burlington House*, 1731	204

Tables

10.1	Coats of arms of lands and provinces paraded in the funeral processions of German King Albert II and Emperor Frederick III of Habsburg (in the order in which they processed)	176
10.2	Reconstruction of the twelve flags on the funeral of Matthias Corvinus in 1490	177
10.3	Flags of lands and provinces paraded in the funeral processions of Albert II, Frederick III, Ferdinand I, and Maximilian II of Habsburg (in the order in which they processed)	179

Contributors

Editors

Anna Kalinowska is Assistant Professor in The Tadeusz Manteuffel Institute of History, Polish Academy of Sciences. Her research interests focus mainly on diplomacy and news networks in early modern Europe, and she has published extensively on both subjects. Formerly Head of Historical Research at the Royal Castle in Warsaw, she is currently Head of the Publications and Digital Resources Department in the Polish History Museum. She has been a Fulbright Scholar, and recipient of awards from the British Academy, the National Science Centre Poland, as well as the Royal Society of Edinburgh.

Jonathan Spangler is a specialist of the court and higher nobility of Early Modern France. He has published on both the court of Louis XIV and on the smaller court and dynasty of the Duchy of Lorraine, including his first book, *The Society of Princes* (2009), and a second book on the role of the second son in the French monarchy (forthcoming). Jonathan is a Senior Lecturer in History at Manchester Metropolitan University (UK), and Senior Editor of *The Court Historian*, the journal of the Society for Court Studies.

Paweł Tyszka is Head of Historical Research at the Royal Castle in Warsaw. He is a historian of the early modern period, with special interest in court and patronage. He has coordinated a number of international conferences and educational projects, and authored and co-edited a number of books and exhibition catalogues.

Authors

Mikael Alm is Senior Lecturer in History at Uppsala University. His research focus is on the political and social culture of late eighteenth- and early nineteenth-century Europe. His latest book is on *Sartorial Practices and Social Order: Fashioning Difference in Late Eighteenth-Century Sweden* (2021).

Barbara Arciszewska is Associate Professor in the Institute of Art History, University of Warsaw. Her work focuses on theory and practice of architecture in early modern Europe, and her publications include books such as *Classicism and Modernity: Architectural Thought in Eighteenth-Century Britain* (2011), as well as numerous articles and book chapters (recently 'The Office of the King's Works and Modernization of Architectural Patronage in 18th-Century England' and 'Chiswick House' in *Companion to Architecture in the Age of the Enlightenment* (2017). She is currently engaged in the international research project PALAMUSTO, which develops multi-disciplinary approaches to study of early modern court residences.

Michael Bregnsbo is Associate Professor in the Department of History, University of Southern Denmark at Odense. His research interests concentrate on the Danish absolutist regime (1660–1848), often in European comparison. He has published books in Danish and articles in Danish, English, German or French about various aspects of Danish absolutism, as well as a biography of Queen Caroline Mathilde and a source edition of her correspondence with her brother, King George III. His latest project is a book co-authored with Kurt Villads Jensen *The Danish Empire's Glory and Fall* (forthcoming).

Nicholas Dixon is a UK-based independent scholar. His historical research focuses on religion, politics and education in modern Britain. He is a member of the executive committee of the Ecclesiastical History Society and an external contributor to the History of Parliament project. He has also undertaken a visiting fellowship at the Lewis Walpole Library, Yale University. In 2019, he was awarded a PhD in History by the University of Cambridge for his thesis, 'The Activity and Influence of the Established Church in England, c. 1800-1837'. His articles have appeared in *Studies in Church History* and the *English Historical Review*.

Gábor Kármán is a Research Fellow of the Research Centre for the Humanities (until recently of the Hungarian Academy of Sciences), Institute of History, Budapest. He has published widely on the history of Transylvania in various contexts, confessional politics in the seventeenth century, and Ottoman tributary states. His recent works include *A Seventeenth-Century Odyssey in East Central Europe: The Life of Jakab Harsányi Nagy* (2015), and *Confession and Politics in the Principality of Transylvania, 1644–1657* (2020).

Andrea Merlotti is Director of the Centro studi delle Residenze Reali Sabaude (Reggia di Venaria). He has published many studies on the history of the Sabaudian States and on the court of the House of Savoy. His most recent books are: *Storia degli Stati Sabaudi (1416–1831)*, written with P. Bianchi (2017) and *The Shroud at Court: History, Usages, Places and Images of a Dynastic Relic*, co-edited with P. Cozzo and A. Nicolotti (2019). He has been curator of several exhibitions, including *Dalle regge d'Italia. Tesori e simboli della regalità sabauda*, with S. Ghisotti (Reggia di Venaria, 2017).

Inmaculada Rodríguez Moya is Associate Professor of History of Art and Vice-Rector of Students and Social Commitment at Universitat Jaume I of Castellón (Spain). Her research has followed four lines of investigation: iconography of power, colonial art, emblem studies and urbanism history. She was the Principal Investigator of two research projects funded by the Spanish Scientific Ministry, and has authored *El retrato en México: 1781–1867. Héroes, emperadores y ciudadanos para una nueva nación* (2006), and co-authored *El Tiempo de los Habsburgo. La configuración iconográfica de un linaje en el Renacimiento* (2020), and *The Seven Ancient Wonders in the Early Modern World* (2017).

José Eloy Hortal Muñoz is Associate Professor of Early Modern History at the University Rey Juan Carlos, Madrid. His main research interests are the Royal Households of the Spanish Habsburgs and the Royal Sites. His major works include *Las guardas reales de los Austrias hispanos* (2013); and the co-edited volumes *A Constellation of Courts: The Households of Habsburg Europe, 1555–1665* (2014, with R. Vermeir and D. Raeymaekers); and *El ceremonial en la Corte de Bruselas del siglo XVII. Los manuscritos de Francisco Alonso Lozano* (2018, with A. Espíldora and P.-F. Pirlet), which was awarded the Henri Pirenne Prize in 2019.

Géza Pálffy is Research Professor and Leader of the *Holy Crown of Hungary Research Group* in the Research Centre for the Humanities, Institute of History, Budapest. His research interests focus on the early modern history of the Ottoman and the Habsburg Empires, with the special regard to nobility, rituals and ceremonies. He is author of *The Kingdom of Hungary and the Habsburg Monarchy in the Sixteenth Century* (2009), and co-author of *Crown and Coronation in Hungary 1000–1916 A.D.* (2020), as well as numerous books in Hungarian, German, and other languages.

Vladimir Shishkin is a Professor at the North-West Institute, a branch of the Russian Presidential Academy of National Economy and Public Administration, in the Department of Historical Studies, Saint Petersburg State University. His research interests focus on French medieval and early modern history, specifically royal and diplomatic correspondence of the fifteenth to seventeenth centuries. His most recent book is *Frantzuzski korolevski dvor v XVI veke. Istoria instituta* ('The Court of France in the 16th Century. History of an Institution') (2018).

Pablo González Tornel is Associate Professor of Art History at the Universitat Jaume I and Director of the Fine Arts Museum of Valencia (Spain). His scholarship examines early modern Spanish art and its European connections, and the cultural configuration of the early modern Spanish monarchy. He has been awarded grants and fellowships by the Mellon Foundation, the Università degli Studi Palermo and the Bogliasco Foundation. His research has been published in *The Sixteenth Century Journal*, *Hispanic Research Journal*, *I Tatti Studies*, and *Renaissance Studies*, and he has published the monographs *Roma hispánica. Cultura festiva española en la capital del Barroco* (2017), and *Unblemished Mary: Politics and Religiosity in Baroque Spain* (2017).

N. Zeynep Yelçe is a Researcher and Instructor at the Foundations Development Directorate and Coordinator for Humanities Courses at Sabanci University, Istanbul. Her PhD dissertation, 'The Making of Sultan Süleyman: A Study of Process/es of Image-Making and Reputation-Management' (2009) focuses on political propaganda. Her research interests include early modern power structures, formation and representation of authority, legitimation, court studies, and ritual studies. She is currently working on News and Information Networks in the Mediterranean in the first half of the sixteenth century.

Introduction

Anna Kalinowska and Jonathan Spangler

In July 1633 Thomas Wentworth, the future earl of Strafford, arrived in Dublin as a new Lord Deputy, or viceroy, of Ireland. The post had been vacant for several years, since the relationship between the Irish and Wentworth's predecessor, Lord Falkland, had been complicated to say the least, and he had been recalled to England in the summer of 1629. The new viceroy's aim was, therefore, to stabilize the situation and to strengthen Stuart rule on the island. As a savvy politician, Wentworth decided that what would be instrumental in achieving these goals was, as described by Dougal Shaw, 'a more sophisticated ritual strategy for the articulation of his viceregal authority'.[1]

The new Lord Deputy decided to implement this strategy straight away. There was no official ceremonial entry to the city of Dublin organized, but within days of his arrival Irish elites were invited to participate in an inauguration, a ceremony that proved to be packed with elements reflecting the most typical monarchical rituals. During a solemn ceremony in Dublin Castle, Wentworth received the Sword of State, was installed into the Chair of Estate (seated on a dais, under a canopy – both symbolizing royal power), and knighted a number of members of his new administration, thereby performing the very same rituals that would normally accompany royal coronations throughout early modern Europe.

Another step was taken soon after, when new regulations for the Lord Deputy's household were announced. For his contemporaries, and for later historians, it was clear that the viceregal residence was set up to mirror Charles I's Whitehall court, in regards to matters of etiquette, access and the use of space. Together with his programme of improvements in Dublin Castle and plans to build an impressive stately residence in Kildare, plus other undertakings notably in visual culture and performance, this can be interpreted as just another element in the process of creating a new ceremonial system intended to serve his purposes, namely to demonstrate his status and to control his non-verbal communication with Irish elites.

Finally, in July 1634, Wentworth participated in the opening of the Irish Parliament. His focus was not, however, solely only on politics and taxes, which were the core aims of the assembly. Rather, as seen in his letter to the Secretary of State, Sir John Coke, the Lord Deputy clearly indicated that he took interest in the ceremonial side of the opening too, and even sent him some materials presenting details on a procession being planned as part of the event. Despite the absence of a number of the Irish lords,

Wentworth deemed the opening to be a success – he proudly described its splendour in his letters to England, and provided Coke with a copy of the ceremonial order that showed the placement of the Sword of State (carried just in front of Wentworth) in the procession, and stressed that in St Patrick's Church 'all the Lords did stand till the Lord Deputy was placed in his State'.[2]

All of these elements of Wentworth's strategy were typically presented in historical scholarship only two generations ago as simply the decisions or acts of a controversial Caroline politician – described, in detail and with precision, but without any analytical weight given to them.[3] However, historians' approaches to ceremony and ritual have changed significantly over the last several decades. No longer are these seen as the objects of merely 'antiquarian' interest, in meticulous, lengthy description, or as quaint activities connected to historical tradition but separate from the real work of governing; instead, they are now analysed, contextualized and identified as integral elements of political culture, and important markers for social and cultural interactions on various levels.

This is precisely the approach adopted by Shaw in his argument that Wentworth's inauguration ceremonies should be looked at as a transformative ritual event, one that was – by making use of carefully selected elements of the royal coronation – designed to help the new Lord Deputy exercise his power by establishing and highlighting his status as the most important person in the Kingdom of Ireland, second only to Charles I. At the same time it can be also treated as a form of communication between the new viceroy and the Irish people, though clearly not the most successful one as Wentworth focused his attentions only on the elite. This enraged other social groups who were not satisfied with the extent to which they were included in this communication process. Similarly, the changes made to the everyday functioning of the Lord Deputy's residence, including limiting access to his person – thereby aiming to create ceremonial situations and spatial arrangements that were as similar as possible to those Wentworth knew from Whitehall or other Stuart royal residences – should not be identified only as having a strictly practical meaning, but rather as a calculated means of underlining and maintaining his special status. Finally, the attention he paid to the procession that constituted part of the parliamentary ritual suggests that he was eager to treat it as another performance and another opportunity to act as a stand-in for the actual monarch.

As we can see, all these interpretations of Wentworth's actions have very little in common with a purely descriptive approach that treats the history of ceremonies and rituals as, at best, secondary to political history, and demonstrate that this situation has evolved in the scholarship of the last few decades. At the heart of this evolution stood the social sciences. The important, far-reaching step of incorporating the methodologies of these disciplines into historical research as it pertained to ceremonies and rituals was taken up by two German scholars, Ernst Kantorowicz and Norbert Elias, who examined, respectively, medieval monarchical rituals and the functionality of ceremonial at the court of Louis XIV at Versailles.[4]

First published in 1957, Kantorowicz's *The King's Two Bodies* examined the key role of ritual for understanding kingship by exploring a monarch's 'body politic' and 'body natural' and the way this concept functioned in developing the political theory behind royal power. The book resonated strongly not only with medievalists, but also with early modernists focusing on the study of monarchy and political rituals, despite Stephen Greenblatt's quip that 'Renaissance scholars rarely know more than the opening chapters, some 34 pages out of the 506 that constitutes its learned heft'.[5]

In the meantime, Elias's *The Court Society* became one of the most fundamental works and influential narratives for historians dealing with early modern courts. His vision of Louis XIV's court, presented as a social system, especially the notion of the King's success in 'domesticating' his courtiers (the famous 'gilded cage' concept) and the parallel argument that ceremonies and rituals became a key element in exercising royal power over the nobility, who in turn transformed their behaviour into a much more controlled (or 'civilized') one, served – at least for some time – as the go-to model for studying princely courts in general.

Both Kantorowicz and Elias were to be contested by the following generations of historians, but their contribution is undeniable, as they did pave the way for the far wider interpretations and new approaches to the materials that scholars of ceremonial and rituals have at their disposal.[6] They also made it much easier to bring another discipline, anthropology, including studies by Clifford Geertz and Don Handelman, into the picture. As a result, the simply descriptive approach to the issue of monarchical or political rituals and ceremonies, whether courtly, institutional or civic, is today no longer adequate or justified.

However, this variety of external influences has resulted in clear differences in the approaches applied by historians in dealing analytically with rituals and ceremonies. For instance some scholars prefer to concentrate on the role rituals and ceremonies played in the management of power and 'high politics' and the manner in which it was utilized by various participants in political life and political processes. For others, these are rather the elements or building blocks of a social and cultural system within a certain court or state, and can be best understood as instruments of royal propaganda. Still others opt to look at this issue from the perspective of political thought and treat rituals and ceremonies as tangible elements of the incarnation of state or monarchical ideology.

As a result, if one looks at the diverse developments in the study of rituals and ceremonies, no uniform definitions – including those for ritual or ceremonial themselves – or coherent methodologies can be offered or agreed upon. Thus scholars have little choice but to decide themselves what definitions they find most accurate. For example, for the editors of this volume, that given by Edward Muir of a 'ritual' simply as 'a social activity that is repetitive, standardized, a model or a mirror, and its meaning is inherently ambiguous',[7] stresses all the most important roles it played. When it comes to 'ceremonial', we prefer Jeroen Duindam's definition that focuses on the fact that it 'was a product of the tradition of kingship, and it served to protect the monarch. At the same time, it structured and codified the contacts between the dynasty and the people, thus also providing possibilities for displaying the monarch's power to his subjects.'[8] We add the proviso here that it should refer not only to monarchy or dynasty, but also to the government (e.g. civic authorities) and the governed (individuals and groups) more generally.

This necessity to choose between various understanding of these two terms means that historians often find it difficult to distinguish precisely whether they are dealing with a ritual or a ceremony,[9] especially since these could be, and often were, interrelated or complementary, as one can see in the case of Wentworth's inauguration when the transformative ritual was the culmination of an extended ceremonial situation involving various participants. Therefore one can only agree with Wolfgang Reinhard, when he observes that: 'The terms "ceremonial" and "ritual" can hardly be clearly separated. Through stereotypical repetition, ritual offers behavioural security; it is primarily action, not representation. Ceremonial turns action into a spectacle, as an aestheticized, visually accentuated ritual. One could distinguish between the coronation as ritual and the crown-wearing as ceremony.'[10]

In general, however, historians whose primary interests have been linked to state formation, its constitutional development or royal ideology, lean towards a ritual and its role as a key element of their scholarship, while those interested more in social or sociopolitical aspects, and especially in the history of a court, are in their approach more ceremonial oriented, although they treat 'court rituals' as an important element of their study. In other words some tend to follow the path originally laid out by Kantorowicz, while the others prefer rather to build on the interest awakened by Elias, though they frequently dismiss and contest the specifics of his findings. It is not our intention here to provide a complete historiographical survey of these parallel movements, but a few examples will help relate these developments to the case studies on ritual and ceremonies included within this volume, and allow us to draw relevant conclusions.

The first name that needs to be mentioned here – again – is that of Edward Muir, though a relationship between ritual and power was not his main interest *per se*. His work is relevant, however, due to his efforts to straighten out the terminology and to coin a clearer definition of 'ritual' in a historical context. In his *Ritual in Early Modern Europe*, which dealt with a wide typology of rituals, for example, 'rituals of the body', Muir stressed that political rituals were key elements in state formation, as they help to 'mask or legitimate hegemony, thereby creating the necessary fiction of government'.[11] He further differentiated between regal rituals that 'enacted' kingship (transformative 'rites of enactment'), and the ones that 'represented' kingship, often in a performative way, and thus helped to introduce some more precision into the understanding of their role. Muir also suggested that, despite the perception of political ritual having become 'a dirty word' by the eighteenth century, it had in fact evolved, and remained an important element of social life, albeit in altered form.[12]

David Cannadine, in turn, rather than focusing on continuity, instead explained how rituals reflect the processes of political change, and took up the fight himself for the irrelevant – in some historians' opinion – 'theatre of power'. Indeed, he opened his essay on 'divine rites of kings' (being also an introduction to the important volume *Rituals of Royalty: Power and Ceremonial in Traditional Societies*) with a statement that 'Power is like the wind: we cannot see it, but we all feel its force. Ceremonial is like the snow: the insubstantial pageant soon melted into thin air'.[13]

Cannadine's argument presented in this text – by now widely shared by numerous historians – is that by making use of a diversity of examples and reaching outside the traditional range of historians' interests, often limited by a Eurocentric perspective, historians can better understand the complexity of relations between power and rituals and ceremonies, while spectacle and pageantry should be treated as an integral part of any comprehensive analysis of political power.¹⁴ Other important reminders he offers are that, regardless of the historical period or geographic scope, ceremonies usually are composed of various already known elements, and that one needs to be very careful about the meaning of the terms 'power' and 'ceremonial' as their meaning could be very different in different societies and times, and thus they could have little in common despite their perfunctory resemblance.¹⁵

A final, and certainly no less important, historiographical milestone, is the work of Barbara Stollberg-Rilinger, who in her research approaches the topic of ritual and ceremonial via the interplay between the cultural history of politics and the functioning of the state.¹⁶ Building upon the case study of a representative institution, namely the Imperial Diet in the early modern period, Stollberg-Rilinger offered the concept of ritual and ceremonial as the important elements of symbolic-expressive communication in more general terms. She convincingly argues, for example, that the constitutional symbolic language enacted in rituals and ceremonies became one of the fundaments for the functioning of the Holy Roman Empire, and therefore cautions that they must not be treated separately from the traditional histories of the political structures of the Imperial state that were based on written texts rather than visual or performative sources. Because the key element of communication is reciprocity, that is, the message must be both sent *and* understood, rituals and ceremonies became part of a wider process of communicating the key attributions of political culture by the involved parties. Another theme present in Stollberg-Rilinger's research is the issue of change in the role of rituals over time. This was connected in her opinion to the bureaucratization of the early modern state, which had a significant impact on the protagonists within a constitutional relationship, namely the ruler and his people, and resulted in Imperial rituals of state becoming by the eighteenth century more a spectacle than a 'constitution' in practice, as it had been earlier in the early modern period.¹⁷

Similar to the ideas formulated by Muir, Cannadine and Stollberg-Rilinger, important approaches and ideas have been presented, developed or redeveloped by historians who focused their attention on the princely court, its practices and the ceremonial aspects of its functioning. The field of court studies has been undeniably one of the most successful in recent decades, in particular because its leading scholars, for example Marcello Fantoni, have adopted the notion that the court is 'an entity in constant evolution, in a close dialectical relationship with political theory, religious doctrine and cultural forms'.¹⁸ As early as the 1980s the court – mainly thanks to David Starkey – started to be treated as a pivotal element in the analysis of politics, not merely a colourful sideshow. Starkey, long before the famous 'spatial turn',¹⁹ used the English court as a model to stress the issue of access, and therefore also space, and the importance of both of these for political process within a monarchical state. By recalling Hugh Murray Baillie's observations on relations between palace spaces and ceremonial, he stressed that 'palace buildings create a more binding framework for behaviour than any ordinance'.²⁰

With time, the ways in which the physical spaces of the court were being used and arranged, and which persons and under what conditions were able to enjoy access to the ruler, have become a popular subject of analysis and useful conceptual tools,²¹ even though it has been also pointed out that access needs to be treated as only one of a number of factors in the analysis of political power. Building on this argument it is now, rightly, claimed that more comprehensive insight into the functioning of courtly 'culture of access' is still needed, and that it could be achieved by focusing more on 'the ways in which the idea of access was visualized, ritualized, symbolized, negotiated and performed'.[22]

This brings us to Jeroen Duindam's research. He has been one of the scholars most actively – and successfully – working on formulating alternatives for Elias's model, as he stressed that Elias's vision of a monarch's omnipotence with regards to ritual and the use of ceremonial for his own purposes was far too exaggerated. Instead Duindam argues that the position of the nobility continued to be strong, even in the face of the so-called rise of absolutism, while the king's options were in many respects limited, and indeed that 'the ceremonial facade of the court served the interests of both the monarch and the nobility'.[23] Both sides had to negotiate and re-negotiate their positions. Duindam's work has also been instrumental in helping historians better comprehend the ceremonial practices of the court in general, as not only applied a comparative approach in his analysis of the subject, but also, especially in recent years, pushed the scope of research far beyond traditionally dominant Eurocentric borders.[24] His significant contribution is also an attempt – similar to Edward Muir's effort in regards to ritual – to provide more precision in understanding the concept of ceremonial itself and its role in the early modern court and society.[25]

Duindam's successful attempts to revisit the issues that had been for some time dominated by an approach that treated careful analysis of various types of primary sources (always a crucial element of any historian's work) as secondary to developing models or concepts supported often only by scarce source material, gave a boost to another field of study, one that is important for anyone dealing with courts, ceremonial and ritual, that is, the importance of patronage and faction. This approach was present in the academic discourse as early as in 1980s, but with time became one of the most promising trends in court studies in the following decades. It focused scholarly interest on informal groups (factions, parties), often constructed around or by royal favourites, and the role these played at various courts, including their influence on the distribution of royal patronage and on the policy-making processes of monarchical government.[26] While taking advantage of the methodologies and terminologies of the social sciences, recent scholars of the court have managed, however, to find some balance between theoretical and practical approaches in the way they analyse the interactions of favour, patronage and power. Still, although this trend is now well established and is treated as an important element in the studies of the functioning of the court, the multi-faceted relationships between court factions and court ceremonial have not been adequately analysed. This is crucial, as the issues involved in the organizational structure of the court and the coexistence of different factions – recently pointed out as key for the study of court politics[27] – can also find their reflection in the various elements of court ceremonial and ritual practice. A holistic approach to court studies will allow scholars to understand the relationships between political and ceremonial, power and tradition, written and unwritten, theoretical and practical, that defined the centres of social and cultural authority across Europe for much of its history.

* * *

The emergence of these concepts put forward by the scholars discussed above pushed historical research on rituals and ceremonies in new directions and made it possible to assemble this collection of essays. Practically all of the papers – to a lesser or larger degree – deal with the issue of using ceremonial and ritual as a form of communication, whether it was to be the means of communication between a ruler and all of his or her subjects in general or with just one select group (court elites, representatives of a specific territory, etc.); direct or indirect communication; or the processes of decision making between the forging of new elements, strategies and traditions or retaining the old ones. In some cases the focus has been shifted more to the 'receiving end' as authors like Kármán and Bregnsbo focus on the way in which the ceremonial system, usually constructed around royal power, was adopted and performed by its non-monarchical participants, though often still closely linked to the ruler. To do this, Kármán uses the case study of the Diet of the Kingdom of Hungary organized in Besztercebánya in the summer of 1620 and attended by a variety of foreign ambassadors, and discusses the ceremonial conflicts this body had to deal with while in session, namely the issue of the Austrian representatives' claims for pre-eminence before the Moravians. This case study offers a peculiar opportunity to show that mostly the same cultural patterns were used when it was not the rulers, but the territories who struggled for the acknowledgement of their rights and reputation at an event of international diplomatic relevance. The use of extensive archival documentation of the precedence struggle that took place between the representatives of the estates of Upper Austria, Styria, Carinthia and Carniola in the years leading up to this Diet, permits the author to show how ceremonial practices could have been linked to the institutions of a composite monarchy. Michael Bregnsbo's essay examines Queen Caroline Mathilde's 1766 journey across the Danish island of Funen on the way to her marriage, and the ways used to stage this journey as a royal absolutist ritual. The author argues that this journey should not be looked at as merely a king's new bride being transported from England to Copenhagen, but as a ritual whereby Danish royal power and the Danish absolutist system of government were being staged and visualized for the benefit of royal subjects. Bregnsbo does this by applying the details of the specific case to existing research about Danish absolutism and its court culture, and on political culture in general. The journey was organized in such a way as to permit both the royal person and her courtiers, as well as the local population, to play their respective roles, in a reciprocal conversation. The locals participated in the absolutist system, either as spectators, as participants of the royal meals in their capacities as local officials, or as providers of horses, carriages and wagons and other goods or services to the royal retinue. Thus, the local population was being given an opportunity to perform its role as obedient, but also grateful, loyal and obliging subjects, and the absolutist regime was confirmed and consolidated.

Another of these themes is the transformative role of the rituals and ceremonies, especially of coronations and enthronement ceremonies. This is most clearly present in all of the texts in the first section. In her chapter, Zeynep Yelçe uses the events surrounding of the accession of Sultan Selim II in 1566 to discuss the enthronement ritual as an integral part of the accession ceremonies, a generic process more or less applicable to any Ottoman ruler as narrated by contemporary sources, and the process that marked the transformation of the 'felicitous prince' into the 'blessed sovereign'. Her chapter aims to understand the rationales behind the ritual and what these implied about the transference of sovereign authority through ritual, by answering the question of whether it is possible to define a single moment or a single ceremony that inaugurated the reign of a new sultan. The Ottoman sultan did not ascend the throne with a coronation rite; he was not vested with a sacred and/or dynastic object by a single religious and/or temporal authority. Yet his accession to sovereignty was unchallenged and legitimized through a number of symbolic and ritual elements. So when and how did a young prince become a sultan? Was enthronement enough? These questions help uncover the dynamics underlying the process of legitimate succession whereby the new ruler personified the state through various 'state ceremonials', and the use of ritual in constituting power rather than just reflecting what already existed.

Pablo González Tornel, in turn, takes us from the sixteenth-century Ottomans to early eighteenth-century Sicily where, after the death of Charles II – the last Spanish Habsburg – with no appointed heir, four kings came to the throne between 1700 and 1735: Philip V of Bourbon, Victor Amadeus of Savoy, Charles VI of Habsburg, and Charles of Bourbon. Each of these transitions in power was accompanied by lavish ceremonies and festivals in the capital of the kingdom, Palermo, where all the arts and resources of Baroque culture were brought together to exalt the new king. González Tornel's text argues that the rapid changes of dynasty in Sicily and the coronations of the new kings were to prove a trial for the capacity of the ceremonial and the resources allotted to it for the exaltation of royalty. The proclamations and coronations of the four monarchs tested the capacity of the kingdom and its capital to acclaim princes of very different origins and conditions whose legitimacy, nevertheless, was never called into question. This trial, however, was overcome with enormous success, interweaving history, religion, allegory and mythology into a kind of swan song of a way of understanding power, and the relation between a prince and his subjects, one that would fall into decline just a few decades later. Among the analysed aspects are the articulation of the ritual, its iconographic configuration as propaganda and the involvement of the civic authorities in the festival. As those great festivities of the first decades of the century, especially the coronations, were regarded as a virtual monopoly of the municipal powers of Palermo, the king needed the collaboration of the city authorities. Since it was the members of the Senate who retrieved and modernized the ritual, and who established the iconographic programmes for royal exaltation (and of course paid for their execution), this body managed to transform the festival into a triumph of civic power.

In a third case study of the transformative power of ritual, Nicholas Dixon looks at the evolution of the British coronation rite in the period between the coronations of George III and Elizabeth II. He argues that historians have long displayed a tendency to view the post-1689 British coronation rite as a fixed and inflexible ceremony, unsusceptible to change. Where modern alterations to the rite have been acknowledged, these have usually been dismissed as damaging and unfaithful to medieval archetypes. Such assumptions have impeded meaningful study of the extensive revisions that were made to the British coronation ceremony after the seventeenth century. The modern process of revision began in 1761, when the Archbishop of Canterbury, Thomas Secker, rephrased many of the prayers for King George III's coronation, bringing these into line with the Anglicanism of his time. Secker had a primary aim to harmonize the coronation rite with Protestant soteriology, constitutional conventions of limited monarchy stemming from the Glorious Revolution and an overarching belief in Providence. In the early nineteenth century, Secker's successors Charles Manners-Sutton and William Howley continued his work, abridging the service considerably and making additional alterations to the prayers for the coronations of King George IV, King William IV and Queen Victoria. This chapter charts this complex series of reforms and restorations, dividing it into two distinct phases: Protestant reformation during the eighteenth and nineteenth centuries and Anglo-Catholic restoration during the twentieth. Dixon argues that the modern British coronation liturgy was a far more protean phenomenon than previously imagined. The chapter also addresses the broader political and religious implications of liturgical revision, suggesting that developments in the coronation ritual reflected the evolving self-conception of the British monarchy and of the Church of England. More specifically, the rise and fall of Protestant confessionalism may be traced in these revisions, as can the gradual circumscription of the monarchy's political role. Above all, the coronation ritual in Britain was never static, immovable or anachronistic; it became a product of the modern era as much as of the medieval and early modern periods, and it may therefore be viewed as an evolving tradition.

The transformative elements of ceremonies and their ritual meanings are also present in the chapters by Merlotti and Alm, which deal respectively with ceremonial interactions between the rulers of the House of Savoy and representatives of their domains, and court ceremonies in Sweden at the start of the reign of the Bernadotte dynasty. Merlotti discusses the issue of the participation of representatives of the *Stati sabaudi*, the domains ruled by the House of Savoy, in princely funerals, acclamations, and in particular in oath-taking and hand-kissing ceremonies. All these ceremonies were closely linked to the concept of 'Monarchia composita', but evolved over time. For example, until the mid-fifteenth century, the accession to the throne by a Sabaudian ruler was marked by the funeral ceremony for the previous sovereign, while from this point onwards, the public funeral was replaced by the acclamation of a new prince before the *assemblea dei ceti* (the gathering of the different orders or classes). At the same time, another practice increased in importance: the *entrée*, similar to those which characterized other ruling houses. In the States of Savoy it allowed the sovereign to receive, town by town, the oaths of allegiance of all the Pays and Patriae that made up the Sabaudian possessions. These ceremonies were regulated under Duke Carlo Emanuele I (1580–1630), when practices and rituals were set up that would last, at least in part, until the early nineteenth century. Carlo Emanuele I initially maintained the tradition of the *entrée*, but progressively concentrated this ceremony, among others, in Turin – the capital of the States since 1563. It was around that time that the States of Savoy embraced a new tradition, whereby the duke would no longer travel to the capitals of his Pays for the oath-taking (and to confirm privileges), but instead the representatives of the Pays would congregate in Turin to participate in a solemn – and singular – ceremony to take their oath in the Cathedral of Turin. It is clear that all these changes can be looked at in the context of relations between a ruler and his people, especially as they were partly transmitted into the nineteenth century and were foundational for the creation of the Kingdom of Italy in 1861. In a similar manner, Mikael Alm's chapter focuses on the transformative rituals and ceremonies of the Swedish royal court that were designed to confirm the status of the first Bernadotte king, Charles XIV John (Jean-Baptiste Bernadotte), and his new dynasty in the first half of the nineteenth century. Despite his invitation by the Swedish people to inherit the throne from the last king from the House of Holstein-Gottorp, as a foreigner and a man of non-royal birth, he faced serious challenges. By means of specific rituals and ceremonies encompassing both old traditions and new practices the new crown prince assumed his place in the extant royal family and then as head of state and founder of a new dynasty. Alm examines several of these rituals and ceremonies: Bernadotte's entry to Stockholm and his first interactions with his new family and subjects in 1810, his coronation in 1818 and his funeral in 1844. What stands out here is the persistence of royal traditions and an effort to claim continuity from the past, but also some new elements, such as recalling the King's martial accomplishments and stressing more democratic ideals than those typically seen in a traditional monarchy.

The chapters by Shishkin and Hortal Muñoz explore court ceremonial in the context of space, access and, to some extent, the relation between court and government, both in the daily life of the royal court and during the most important monarchical rituals. Vladimir Shishkin portrays the ceremonies of the sixteenth-century French female households, a segment of court culture often overlooked and difficult to research as royal legislation in general says very little about these ceremonies, and the royal ordinances and regulations concerning the court mainly define positions of men only within the queen's entourage. The chapter argues that the mixing of regulations traditionally used in the French court with those more 'modern' foreign practices and ideas of ceremonial, and further combined with the professionalization of service within the household of the queen, created over time a new ceremonial space for the queen of France that was finally regulated and made law by Henry III in 1585. The chapter also defines the limits of this female space and relates these to the active involvement of prominent French royal women in the difficult political manoeuvres of the period, even taking on the role of sovereign itself in cases of absence or minority of the monarch. Forced to deal with political affairs and having received the appropriate authority from kings, these queens of France created their own political space in the court. This apparent female expansion and change of the power structures of the royal court were then formalized, largely due to the autonomous organization of the ceremonial aspects of the queen's household, as well as its own hierarchy of posts, and integrated into the hierarchy and ceremonial of the court of men. The regulations of Henry III from the 1570s and 1580s not only accorded the highest rank to the queen in the curial system, sharing the divinely sanctioned power of her crowned husband, but also entered the queens of France into the absolutist order, of which they became an unshakeable foundation of monarchical power, while at the same time being positioned as the first of the 'most humble and most obedient servants and subjects'. José Eloy Hortal Muñoz focuses on the use of ceremonial space at the Spanish court and its evolution in more general terms. He argues that the so-called 'spatial turn' in court studies has changed the way that political interactions, cultural symbols and institutional structures within the court are understood, therefore introducing new possibilities for research on Spanish Royal Sites of the seventeenth century. As a result, he presents how various Royal Sites, such as Valladolid, El Pardo, Buen Retiro, Aranjuez, Alcázar de Madrid and San Lorenzo de El Escorial, were adapted in the seventeenth century in order to meet the needs of the Spanish court after certain key changes were made in court ceremonial. The text analyses the evolution of ceremonial customs and etiquette in the Spanish monarchy, resulting in the gradual transfer of festivities to the interior of the royal palaces from the last decades of the sixteenth century onwards, so that they were in full view of the courtiers but beyond the reach of the general public.

Some authors, especially Moya and Pálffy, elaborate also on various aspects linking ceremonial and material culture, mostly the symbolism of related objects, while still treating them in connection to the process of communication between the ruler and his subjects. Inmaculada Rodríguez Moya delivers a detailed presentation of the role played by the christenings of royal children in the Spanish court. Historically it was a public demonstration of a king's power and its continuity. But the baptism was also a significant occasion for noble courtiers since the baptism procession, celebrated inside or outside the Royal Palace, was conceived as a mirror of the hierarchy in the court. The godparents were usually relatives of the child, of royal rank, but sometimes could be members of the high nobility, chosen for that honour, and, for that reason, had to be prominent. It was crucial that the person who would carry the ritual objects would be selected from amongst the *Grandes de España*. The decoration for the palace and the church where the baptism took place was also carefully curated, with its rich furniture and textiles. This chapter examines the processions and entertainments following the baptism, and in particular, the ritual and decorative objects that were central to these ceremonial occasions in Spain, from the sixteenth to the eighteenth century. It demonstrates how these occasions were used by the courtiers to highlight their proximity to the monarch, in a physical and political sense, but also shows how these ritual objects acquired a sacred value for the monarchy, one which would be preserved for centuries. Géza Pálffy concentrates on a previously neglected aspect of the field of dynastic representation and symbolic communication, the heraldic representation of ruling dynasties (in this case, Jagiellonian and Habsburg) in late medieval and early modern coronations and funerals. He demonstrates that from the fifteenth century onwards, coats of arms and heraldic flags (banners) played an increasingly prominent role in dynastic representation in Central Europe, as shown in the built spaces and ceremonial activities in the residences of the Luxembourg, Jagiellonian and Habsburg monarchs. Moreover, these dynasties influenced and competed with each other in this area of dynastic representation and identity establishment. Later on, from the mid-sixteenth century in funerals of the Habsburg emperors, the coats of arms represented especially the structure and power of their dynastic composite monarchy, but in coronations they simultaneously fulfilled a function of symbolizing the sovereignty and political significance of the particular kingdoms, duchies and lordships themselves within that composite monarchy.

Finally, several texts present the evolution or a shift in ritual and ceremonial that resulted from the introduction of new or different elements incorporated and used for the sake of achieving specific goals, for instance enhancing dynastic legitimacy. It is an important element in the articles already discussed by Dixon and Alm, but it dominates in Arciszewska's paper, as she explores court culture and ritual under George Louis of Brunswick-Lüneburg, Elector of Hanover and, from 1714, King of Great Britain. The chapter focuses on ways in which the Hanoverians exploited their family's glorious past, especially its medieval connections to the Veneto through a distant kinship with the Este dynasty. She argues that the lasting impact of Venetian culture on Hanoverian patronage affected all forms of artistic expression, most notably architecture, but that more attention should be paid to opera and masquerades and their place in the rituals of Hanoverian rulership. The chapter's title consciously refers to the famous 1724 print by William Hogarth, which aimed to highlight the controversial role of the new court culture in contemporary society. The author's contention is that – rather paradoxically – some aspects of these court entertainments propelled the processes of modernization and social mobility in contemporary Britain, while the growing popularity of these court-supported entertainments became a lightning rod for a wide-ranging debate questioning the cultural prerogatives of the court and ultimately the limits of royal power. The impact of Venetian culture on ritual and patronage in Hanover proved (not surprisingly) to be very significant. Like their counterparts in Venice, the Hanoverian elite enjoyed in their homeland a life divided between the city and the country. The demand for fashionable opera and masquerading began to transcend traditional upper class boundaries, aiding the widespread circulation of cultural patterns associated with the new regime.

The volume's wide geographical and chronological scope – it covers not only Western but also Central Europe and Turkey, from the mid-fifteenth to the mid-twentieth century – is designed primarily to provide readers with material covering a variety of rituals and ceremonies from different geographical areas and periods, as the main idea behind this book was to produce a number of interesting case studies regarding ceremonial and ritual based on new research, presenting specific aspects that were important for the functioning of a state and/or a court and dynasty. This allows historians and students to look at these issues from a comparative angle; and even though there are no direct comparisons made, still many similarities and differences can be easily identified and recognized, as some common themes are very much present across the chapters, regardless of their actual location in the volume's structure.

The fact that many of these chapters explore multi-faceted topics, such as ritualized communication between multiple protagonists or the complex evolution of a particular ceremony, makes them much richer for the reader, but also forced the editors to consider a variety of options for the volume's structure. Finally, it emerged that – for the benefit of clarity – the structure should reflect to some extent the pattern visible so evidently in the strategy seen at the start of this introduction in Wentworth's initial arrival in Ireland: taking advantage of traditional rituals of monarchical power (as seen during his inauguration), the usage of courtly ceremonies and space (new regulations for the viceregal household), and finally the ceremonial interaction with representatives of the people (the opening of the Irish Parliament) to establish, demonstrate and sustain status, often with the use of the visual arts or performance. This structure is also designed to emphasize the mechanisms behind the specific types of events and the system of ceremonial and ritual communication and interactions in general.

As a result, the book comprises four parts. The first deals with coronations and enthronement and the evolution of this transformative ritual and its various forms. The second discusses the strategies behind the use of court ceremonial, spaces within a royal residence or its surroundings, as well as family ceremonies performed for the sake of dynasty and monarchical interests, with cases from France and Spain, but also Sweden. The third section concentrates on the ceremonies and rituals aiming at or performed by the representatives of specific groups or territories, while the final part of the volume focuses on the performative or performance-related elements of ceremonial, including the ways of exploiting various forms and components of dynastic and royal representation in the 'spectacles' of power, whether it was to be the use of heraldry during monarchical rituals and ceremonies, the employment of court entertainment or some form of royal progress.

Collectively, the following chapters aim to provide the readers with concrete descriptions of specific rituals and ceremonies that were important for the functioning of the state, the court, and for relations between a ruler and his people, but also a detailed analysis of them, in a manner that situates these ceremonies and rituals in a wider political, social and artistic context. This allows us to see how they were transformed into and utilized as the most visible means of communication between different participants in political and courtly life, the rulers and the ruled. In this way the volume contributes to the ongoing debate about the governing practices, courtly rituals, and expressions of power prevalent in Europe and the Ottoman Empire from the medieval age to the modern era.

Notes

1   Dougal Shaw, 'Thomas Wentworth and Monarchical Ritual in Early Modern Ireland', *The Historical Journal* 49, no. 2 (2006): 345.
2   Ibid., 345–53.
3   For the classic example: V.C. Wedgwood, *Thomas Wentworth: First Earl of Strafford 1593-1641. A Revaluation* (London: Phoenix Press, 2000), 137, 150. Originally published in 1961.
4   Ernst Kantorowicz, *The King's Two Bodies: A Study in Mediaeval Political Theology* (Princeton: Princeton University Press, 1957); Norbert Elias, *The Court Society* (Oxford: Blackwell, 1983), written in the 1930s, published originally in German in 1969 and in English in 1983. Another important German scholar providing a significant contribution to the field was Percy Ernst Schramm, who introduced the concept of 'political theatre' and the modern study of monarchical images. On Schramm and his research, see Antti Matikkala, 'Percy Ernst Schramm and Herrschaftszeichen', *Mirator* 13 (2012): 37–69.
5   Stephen Greenblatt, 'Introduction: Fifty Years of The King's Two Bodies', *Representations* 106, no. 1 (2009): 63. See also works by Ralph Giesey (Kantorowicz's pupil): *The Royal Funeral Ceremony in Renaissance France* (Geneva: Droz, 1960, reprinted in 1983; idem, 'Models of Rulership in French Royal Ceremonial', in *Rites of Power: Symbolism, Ritual and Politics Since the Middle Ages*, ed. Sean Wilentz (Philadelphia: University of Pennsylvania Press, 1985), 41–64; idem, 'Inaugural Aspects of French Royal Ceremonials', in *Coronations: Medieval and Early Modern Monarchic*

Ritual, ed. János M. Bak (Berkeley: University of California Press, 1990), 35–45; and also a key work by Sarah Hanley, *The 'Lit de Justice' of the Kings of France: Constitutional Ideology in Legend, Ritual, and Discourse* (Princeton: Princeton University Press, 1983).

6 *Theorizing Rituals: Annotated Bibliography of Ritual Theory*, vol. 2, *1966–2005*, ed. Jens Kreinath, Jan Snoek and Michael Stausberg (Leiden–Boston: Brill, 2007), lists 442 examples of primary literature on the subject.

7 Edward Muir, *Ritual in Early Modern Europe* (Cambridge: Cambridge University Press, 2005, 2nd revised edn), 6. For explanation of 'models' and 'mirrors' see pp. 4–5.

8 Jeroen Duindam, *Myths of Power: Norbert Elias and Early Modern European Court* (Amsterdam: Amsterdam University Press, 1995), 133.

9 See Stéphane van Damme and Janet Dickenson, 'Court and Centres', in *The European World 1500-1800: An Introduction to Early Modern History*, ed. Beat Kumin (London: Routledge, 2017), 348–57.

10 Wolfgang Reinhard, *Geschichte der Staatsgewalt: Eine vergleichende Verfassungsgeschichte Europas von den Anfängen bis zur Gegenwart* (Munich: C.H. Beck, 2000), 91. For the concept of 'crown-wearing' (German: *Unter-der-Krone-Gehen*), see Ernst Kantorowicz, *Laudes Regiae: A Study in Liturgical Acclamations and Mediaeval Ruler Worship* (Berkeley–Los Angeles: University of California Press, 1958), 92–6. We are grateful to Dr. Kolja Lichy for his help regarding this reference.

11 Muir, *Ritual in Early Modern Europe*, 254.

12 Ibid., 294.

13 David Cannadine, 'Introduction: Divine Rites of Kings', in *Rituals of Royalty: Power and Ceremonial in Traditional Societies*, ed. David Cannadine and Simon Price (London: Past and Present Society, 1987), 1.

14 In the past ten years there have been a number of excellent publications that incorporate analysis of specific elements of ceremonial pageantry and music into the narrative of the history of princely courts, diplomatic and civic ceremonial, for example: *Music at German Courts, 1715–1760. Changing Artistic Priorities*, ed. Samantha Owens, Barbara M. Reul and Janice B. Stockigt (Woodbridge: Boydell Press, 2015); *Les foyers artistiques à la fin du règne de Louis XIV (1682-1715). Musique et spectacles*, ed. Anne-Madeleine Goulet et al. (Turnhout: Brepols, 2019); Arne Spohr, 'Concealed Music in Early Modern Diplomatic Ceremonial', in *Music and Diplomacy from the Early Modern Era to the Present*, ed. Rebekah Ahrendt, Mark Ferraguto and Damien Mahiet (New York: Palgrave, 2014), 19–43; and Ian Fenlon, 'Theories of Decorum: Music and the Italian Renaissance Entry', in *Ceremonial Entries in Early Modern Europe: The Iconography of Power*, ed. J.R. Mulryne, Maria Ines Aliverti and Anna Maria Testaverde (London: Routledge, 2015), 135–48; and Matthias Range, *Music and Ceremonial at British Coronations: From James I to Elizabeth II* (Cambridge: Cambridge University Press, 2012).

15 Cannadine, 'Introduction: Divine Rites of Kings', 15, 18.

16 Among her numerous works, the most important in this context are: Barbara Stollberg-Rilinger, 'Zeremoniell, Ritual, Symbol: Neue Forschungen zur symbolischen Kommunikation in Spätmittelalter und Früher Neuzeit', *Zeitschrift für Historische Forschung* 27, no. 3 (2000), 389–405; 'Symbolische Kommunikation in der Vormoderne. Begriffe – Forschungsperspektiven – Thesen', *Zeitschrift für Historische Forschung* 31, no. 4 (2004): 489–527; and 'Rituals of Decision Making? Early Modern European Assemblies of Estates as Acts of Symbolic Communication', in *Political*

Order and the Forms of Communication in Medieval and Early Modern Europe, ed. Yoshihisa Hattori (Rome: Viella, 2014), 63–95.
17 *Des Kaisers alte Kleider. Verfassungsgeschichte und Symbolsprache des Alten Reiches* (Munich: C.H. Beck 2008; 2nd edn, 2013); English edn: *The Emperor's Old Clothes: Constitutional History and the Symbolic Language of the Holy Roman Empire*, trans. by Thomas Dunlap (New York–Oxford: Berghahn Books, 2015).
18 Marcello Fantoni, 'The Future of Court Studies: The Evolution, Present Successes and Prospects of Discipline', *The Court Historian* 16, no. 1 (2011): 5.
19 Felix Driver, Raphael Samuel, 'Rethinking the Idea of Place', *History Workshop Journal* 39, no. 1 (1995): v–vii.
20 David Starkey, 'Introduction: Court History in Perspective', in *The English Court: From the Wars of Roses to the Civil War*, ed. David Starkey (London–New York: Longman, 1987), 2. Some of the recent publications sponsored by the Society for European Festivals Research stress once again the physicality of the spaces used for ceremonial and ritual purposes, for example: *Architectures of Festival in Early Modern Europe. Fashioning and Re-fashioning Urban and Courtly Space*, ed. J.R. Mulryne et al. (Abingdon: Routledge, 2018).
21 *The Politics of Space: European Courts, ca. 1500-1750*, ed. Marcello Fantoni, George Gorse and Malcolm Smuts (Roma: Bulzoni, 2009); *The Key to Power? The Culture of Access in Princely Courts, 1400–1750*, ed. Dries Raeymaekers and Sebastiaan Derks (Leiden: Brill, 2016), including, for example, the chapter by Jonathan Spangler, 'Holders of the Keys: The Grand Chamberlain the Grand Equerry and Monopolies of Access at the Early Modern French Court', 155–77.
22 Dries Raeymaekers and Sebastiaan Derks, 'Repertoires of Access in Princely Courts, 1400–1750', in *New Perspectives on Power and Political Representation from Ancient History to the Present Day*, ed. Harm Kaal and Daniëlle Slootjes (Leiden: Brill, 2019), 83.
23 Duindam, *Myths of Power*, 134.
24 Jeroen Duindam, *Vienna and Versailles. The Courts of Europe's Dynastic Rivals, 1550-1780* (Cambridge: Cambridge University Press, 2003); idem, *Dynasties: A Global History of Power, 1300-1800* (Cambridge: Cambridge University Press, 2015).
25 Duindam, *Myths of Power*, chapter V, 'Ceremonial and "Politesse"', especially 102–5, 133–7.
26 *The World of the Favourite*, ed. J.H. Elliott, L.W.B. Brockliss (New Haven, CT- London: Yale University Press, 1999); *Klientelsysteme im Europa der Frühen Neuzeit*, ed. Antoni Mączak (Munich: Oldenbourg Verlag, 1988); Roger Mettam, *Power and Faction in Louis XIV's France* (Oxford: Blackwell, 1988); Sharon Kettering, *Patrons, Brokers, and Clients in Seventeenth-Century France* (Oxford: Oxford University Press, 1986); Alan Marshall, *The Age of Faction: Court Politics, 1660-1702* (Manchester: Manchester University Press, 1999).
27 Rubén González Cuerva and Alexander Koller, 'Photography of a Ghost: Factions in Early Modern Courts', in *A Europe of Courts, a Europe of Factions: Political Groups at Early Modern Centres of Power (1550-1700)*, ed. Rubén González Cuerva and Alexander Koller (Leiden: Brill, 2017), 10–11.

Part One

Coronation and Enthronement

1

Where exactly is the throne? Locating sovereignty in sixteenth-century ottoman succession rituals

N. Zeynep Yelçe

As Prince Selim rode hurriedly to Istanbul with a small retinue to claim the throne of his recently deceased father Süleyman I in 1566, his men inquired about their new appointments. Selim asked them: 'Have we yet arrived and ascended the throne, and have we yet met the officials of the state and learned about our situation, and has the House of Osman ever disregarded anyone's toil and services? Is there none among you who knows how to behave?' His scolding – or rather what the late sixteenth-century historian and statesman Mustafa Selaniki Efendi makes him utter in his account of these events – underlines the fact that the Prince was not Sultan just yet.[1] Unlike in some western monarchies where the tradition was that the moment one monarch died his successor immediately became a king, Ottoman tradition required the successor to go through some transformational steps before his sovereignty was recognized and he could claim the title. It is the intention of this chapter to explore when and how precisely Prince Selim became Sultan Selim II.

The 'long sixteenth century' for the Ottoman Empire, usually considered to begin with the conquest of Istanbul in 1453 and lasting up to either the accession of Ahmed I in 1603 or the treaty of Zsitvatorok with the Habsburg Monarchy in 1606,[2] is marked by the reigns of eight sultans. The first Ottoman sultan to be enthroned in Istanbul was Bayezid II in 1481. Residents of sixteenth-century Istanbul witnessed five enthronement ceremonies: Selim I in 1512, Süleyman I in 1520, Selim II in 1566, Murad III in 1574, and Mehmed III in 1595. We can give the exact date of enthronement for all except one, namely Selim II. As the only surviving heir to the throne, Selim did not have to worry about or compete with rival siblings as his forebears Bayezid II and Selim I did. Unlike his successors Murad III and Mehmed III, he did not have to worry about the notorious custom of fratricide where he would need to kill his siblings to ensure the 'order of the world' (*nizâm-ı 'âlem*).[3] His succession, under normal circumstances, should have resembled his father's accession, as Süleyman I, too, was a sole heir to the throne without any dynastic competition. However, the fact that the army, accompanied by the Grand Vizier, was on campaign far from the centre of power, renders Selim's accession a rather unusual case, as the very people whose presence – and submission – were required in the rituals recognizing the successor as legitimate sovereign, were far from the seat of the throne. This chapter is an exercise to understand the reasons why and what they imply about the transference of sovereign authority through ritual.

Among the questions steering this discussion, the most urgent would be: is it possible to define a single moment or a single ceremony that inaugurates the reign of a new sultan? The Ottoman sultan did not ascend the throne with a coronation rite; he was not vested with a sacred and/or dynastic object by a single religious and/or temporal authority. Yet once free of dynastic competition, a prince's accession to sovereignty was unchallenged by the establishment and was then legitimized through a number of symbolic and ritual elements. But was a ritual act like enthronement enough? In a monarchic regime founded on dynastic continuity, would the only living male member of the dynasty not automatically become sultan the moment his father died? In the absence of other candidates to the throne, was ritual succession of sovereignty really necessary to assume authority? These questions help uncover the dynamics underlying the process of legitimizing succession whereby the new ruler personifies the state through various 'state ceremonials'[4] and the use of ritual in constituting power rather than simply reflecting what already exists.[5]

Generic concept of enthronement

Enthronement was an integral part of the accession ceremonies, a generic process more or less applicable to any Ottoman ruler as narrated by contemporary sources. The process marked the transformation of the 'felicitous prince' into the 'blessed sovereign'. Contemporary accounts begin narrating the accession of a new sultan upon the death of the former sultan, the father. As a first step, the grand vizier informs the heir while keeping the news secret. Accounts continue with the prince-to-be-sultan receiving the news and hurrying on the journey to take over the throne. The next phase is the arrival and entry of the prince in Istanbul as the seat of the throne. All of these phases can be categorized as pre-accession phases that bring the prince to the locus of actual transformation; that locus is where the throne is. The actual accession ceremonial seems to involve three stages at this location: the funeral of the deceased ruler; the enthronement itself; and the presentation of obedience by various echelons of the Ottoman military-administrative system.

The complete ceremonial accession of a new sultan would normally last two days, starting with his arrival in Istanbul and ending with the council (*divan*), presumably held the day after his father's funeral. The ceremonial observed signified not only the taking over of the ruling authority, but also the symbolic meanings and the titles attached to that authority. The heir would first arrive at Üsküdar, the point where the military usually camped when embarking on or returning from eastern campaigns. The site is on the other side of the Bosphorus, across from the Imperial Palace. Boarding the galley prepared for him there, the prince would come ashore near the Imperial Palace. There he would be greeted by the Janissaries and other servants of the royal household, along with the various religious groups and inhabitants of Istanbul. At this point in time, the death of the former sultan was finally made public. The procession would make its way through the spectators who came to see the new sultan, then the prince would enter the palace in the company of the Janissaries. This generic flow presents us with three subsequent stages which can be considered as constituting the first ceremonial phase of accession: the revelation of the death of the ruler, the acceptance of the dynastic successor, and the appropriation of the abode of power. These stages can be identified in a physical sense with the arrival of the prince, the procession and the entry into the palace.

After its conquest in 1453, being enthroned in Istanbul seems to have become a must for any sultan-to-be. Before then, sultans were enthroned in Bursa or Edirne. Until the candidate appeared in the city, the news of the demise of his predecessor would be kept secret. The main reason behind such secrecy was the fear of insurrection and chaos. The Janissary corps was, in theory, a slave army loyal only to the reigning sultan. The death of the monarch, therefore, technically freed the Janissaries of their bound status until they proclaimed loyalty to a new master. In a similar sense, the realm could be considered a 'no man's land' until the rightful heir claimed the throne. Unrest, even if small in scale, has been observed on previous occasions, especially in incidents involving plunder of non-Muslim inhabitants of the city.[6] In 1481, Mehmed II died around Gebze, allegedly at the outset of a new eastern campaign. He had two living sons, namely Bayezid and Cem. The central court faction seems to have favoured Bayezid over his younger brother, evidenced by this prince's young son Korkud being put briefly on the throne to secure it until his father arrived. In the meantime, the viziers kept the death as discreet as possible. Although Cem eventually did revolt and create long-lasting trouble for Bayezid II, the enthronement ceremony was performed smoothly in Istanbul.[7]

The enthronement of Selim I in 1512 posed an anomaly in that this prince challenged his father and took the throne while he was still alive. Although Selim I was first enthroned outside the palace precincts as a demonstration of respect to his father, he had to enter Istanbul and gain control of the seat of the throne before the accession process was completed with the traditional homage ceremony involving hand-kissing and distribution of accession gratuities.[8] Selim's act of stationing his son Süleyman in Istanbul as guardian of the throne, while he went after his older brother and arch-rival Ahmed, is yet another signifier of the importance of Istanbul as the physical location of the throne and therefore the seat of sovereignty.[9] Selim I died near Çorlu, on the way to Edirne, not far from Istanbul. The grand vizier immediately sent a messenger to Süleyman who hurried to Istanbul. Until he arrived, his father's death was kept secret for fear of sedition among the soldiers. He attended his father's funeral the next day and was subsequently enthroned at the imperial palace.[10] The locations of the deaths of sultans is also relevant. Whereas, as we have seen, Mehmed II and Selim I died away from the capital, and Süleyman died during campaign in Hungary, far from home, his successors Selim II, Murad III and Mehmed III all died at the imperial palace in Istanbul. Their sons were at their assigned posts as provincial governors and had to return. In contrast, when Mehmed III died in 1603, his oldest heir was Prince Ahmed who had not yet been assigned a governorship in Anatolia as he was not yet old enough. This unexpected situation brought about a change in Ottoman accession ceremonial. As the prince-to-be-sultan was already in Istanbul, the entry was now redundant and would remain so, as the practice of sending princes to provinces was abandoned.

The succession of 1566

If everything had gone so smoothly in most sixteenth-century successions, what made Selim II's enthronement in 1566 peculiar? Luckily, we have two eye-witness accounts of the process. Contemporary courtier and Grand Vizier Sokollu Mehmed Pasha's personal secretary, Feridun Ahmed Beğ, devotes a large portion of his campaign chronicle *Nüzhet-i Esrârü'l-Ahyar Der-Ahbâr-i Sefer-i Sigetvar* (Pleasures of the Secrets of Auspicious Men from the News of the Szigetvar Campaign) to the enthronement process of Selim II.[11] Feridun Beğ was present on this campaign as Mehmed Pasha's secretary. As confidante of the Grand Vizier, he was not only in a privileged position to witness the subsequent events but also to influence the strategy adopted during the succession.[12] Another viewpoint comes from Selaniki Mustafa Efendi, a well-connected man in court circles and a protégé of the above-mentioned pasha-secretary faction. As another eye-witness to the Szigetvar campaign in his capacity as Quran-reciter, he dedicates numerous pages to the events following the death of the Sultan.[13] While a deliberate attempt at eulogizing the Grand Vizier can be observed in Feridun Beğ's work, Selaniki's longer chronicle, spanning the years between 1563 and 1595, was not intended to please any state official. In other words, Selaniki seems to provide us with a more matter-of-fact account. His chronicle is also quite rich in its descriptions of ritual occasions and celebrations, thus rendering it an exceptionally effective source for our purpose.[14]

Using both sources, the events unfold as follows: when Sultan Süleyman died in 1566 at Szigetvar in Hungary, far away from home, the efforts of Grand Vizier Sokollu Mehmed Pasha not only to keep the Sultan's death a secret but also to keep the government administration going are impressive. As Feridun Ahmed Beğ writes, the Grand Vizier saw it as a matter of honour to transfer sovereignty to 'Sultan Selim Han' the rightful heir to the throne.[15] An accompanying poem reveals that it was his aim and desire to keep 'the order of religion and state' intact until 'Sultan Selim Han the owner of the throne, came in haste and ascended on the throne'.[16]

Sokollu Mehmed Pasha wrote a letter to inform the Prince of the death of Sultan Süleyman and to invite him to take over the realm. In the attempt to keep the matter confidential, the letter was disguised as a proclamation of victory upon the conquest of Szigetvar.[17] In the letter, Selim – at the time hunting at Kütahya, in central Anatolia, his princely seat of governorship – was instructed to keep the news secret and to get to the army in Hungary in haste. The Grand Vizier also emphasized that those who might wish to create a disturbance should not be privy to this news lest they put their mischievous schemes into action. He stresses that keeping the death secret was vital until the sultan reached 'the abode of noble sultanate and the site of eminent caliphate, the accepted [desirable] seat of the throne the city of Istanbul'. Thus, the first step towards becoming sultan is coming to Istanbul, which is pointed out as the seat of the throne. The letter continues to explain what would happen next, namely the accession ceremonies. Selim should ascend the throne at 'the site of the sultanate and the place of the caliphate and take over the duty of sovereignty'. Only then would the news be publicized.[18]

This letter resembles a bold letter of instruction rather than a humble notification. While the urgency of claiming the seat of the throne is clearly a pressing issue, Sokollu's role in Selim's princely career thus far should not go unnoticed. During the years of conflict in the previous decade between Selim and his brother Bayezid, Sokollu Mehmed Pasha was involved in Sultan Süleyman's efforts to reconcile the two princes who already had begun competing for the throne. To initiate negotiations in 1558, he had been sent to Selim in his capacity as third vizier, while fourth vizier Pertev Pasha was sent to Bayezid. In 1559, when tension worsened between the two royal brothers, Sokollu sided with Selim against the by-then 'rebellious' Bayezid upon the request of Sultan Süleyman. The cooperation between the vizier and the Prince culminated in Sokollu marrying Selim's daughter İsmihan with great pomp in 1562.[19] Thus, the tone of the letter written by the Grand Vizier summoning the Prince to claim not only the throne, but the army should not be surprising.

Selim seems to have taken the instructions seriously and acted in haste as requested. However, his first destination was Istanbul instead of Belgrade where the grand vizier hoped to meet him. Based on the advice of his own councillors in opposition to those of his now deceased father, this move 'can be interpreted as an assertion of independence from the grand vizier', as Emine Fetvacı suggests based on comparative examination of contemporary sources.[20] As the messenger found the Prince and gave him Sokollu's letter, Selim summoned his advisers to ask for their opinion. As agreed, a small retinue accompanied the Prince riding in haste towards, in Feridun Beğ's words, 'the throne of sovereignty and the site of caliphate'. It took Selim and his party three stops to reach 'the abode of noble sultanate and the site of eminent caliphate the city of Constantinople', from Kütahya.[21] Selaniki tells a similar story. However, in his account Selim is not as discreet as he should have been. As Selaniki has it, he not only informed the imam, the local clerical leader in Kütahya, that his father had passed away, but he ordered the imam 'to inform the congregation of Muslims through praying in his own name the exalted *khutbah*'.[22] This act of indiscretion on the part of Selim helps explain the rumours that reached Istanbul and made Grand Vizier Sokollu more and more worried as he awaited the arrival of the heir.[23]

Eight days after receiving the news, Selim and his retinue arrived on the Asian coast of the Bosphorus. According to Feridun Ahmed Beğ, he crossed to the Imperial Palace in a boat prepared for him and there he ascended the throne. A poem marking the moment reads 'today our Sultan became the ruler of the world felicitously'.[24] Selim then stayed a few days in Istanbul 'to dignify the throne of caliphate with the dignity of sultanate'.[25] Selaniki's version of the story is a bit more detailed and explains the shock of the palace staff on the sight of the Prince. While Selim, not seeing any preparations, wondered why no one had come to receive him, the governor-general of Anatolia, İskender Pasha, the appointed guardian of Istanbul, wondered why the Prince arrived unannounced in the capital: 'We have no knowledge of this, nothing good has come out of such an act, what good could come to him?'[26] Apparently, for İskender Pasha, who was not aware of the death of Süleyman I, Selim's arrival in Istanbul meant revolt. A prince was not allowed to set foot in Istanbul while his father was alive. Thus, the presence of a prince in the city meant only two things: open revolt by the prince or the death of his father.

In previous successions, for example in 1520, the death of Sultan Selim I had been kept secret until the arrival of his son Süleyman in Istanbul. But accounts imply that some kind of preparation had been made in Istanbul for the latter's arrival, implying knowledge of Selim's death. Mid-sixteenth-century author Sa'di reports instant preparations by the commander of the Janissaries on his own initiative with no one being aware of the situation until Süleyman appeared on the shores of Üsküdar.[27] Contemporary statesman Celalzade Mustafa, on the other hand, mentions orders being sent to the palace for preparations for the arrival of the Sultan.[28] Since no name was mentioned, those who were to proceed with the preparations probably thought they were meant for Sultan Selim I.

The insight Selaniki provides on how the preparation mechanism worked in the case of Selim II's entry in Istanbul upon Sultan Süleyman's death resembles this example. According to his account, a letter was sent to the Chief Gardner (*Bostancıbaşı*) – the head of the palace guards – ordering cleaning and preparations at the Imperial Palace. The letter commanded that the palace should be handed over to its owner in good shape when he arrived (... *hidmetinde kusûr itmeyüb sâhibi geldükde teslim eyleyesiz*). The letter also gave instructions to put everything in order at the other side of the Bosphorus because the Sultan wished to cross to his gardens there when he came back. It was in the context of these preparations that Selim II arrived, and crossed to the Imperial Palace by boat. Although cannons were fired, and heralds announced that it was 'the era of Sultan Selim' (*Devr-i Sultân Selim Hândır*), he had a difficult time entering the Palace because the guards there were still not aware of the death of Sultan Süleyman.[29]

It is at this point that problems start rising at the court of Selim II. The first one to arrive at the palace by boat was Selim's Master of the Horse. The guards of the Imperial Palace looked down on him as they asked for his identity and condescendingly asked whether he knew where he was. His answer is instructive: 'I know well. It is the garden of the throne of the rule of our Padishah Sultan Selim Han, the son of Sultan Süleyman. You are the guards and servants. I am the Master of the Horse.'[30] A second quarrel followed as Selim himself disembarked. This time it was over issues of precedence between the head of the Imperial Palace guards and the Master of the Horse. The latter believed that it was his right to lead the way now that his master was sultan, while the head of the guards claimed this right as being within his jurisdiction, as imperial territory. Selim found a middle ground in requesting the head of the guards to lead the way as he knew the palace grounds better.[31] After this, Selim was finally inside the palace and ready for enthronement; however, he needed money to distribute during the ceremony. Although he asked his Master of the Horse to find the necessary amount, his powerful sister Mihrimah Sultan advised him against opening up the treasury and lent him the money herself.[32] Mihrimah's prudence indicates hesitance in recognizing the sovereign rights of the successor, including financial, before he has gone through all the ritual phases of accession, including the submission of the army.

Selim II stayed in Istanbul for three days before leaving for Edirne, during which time he visited the tomb of Ayyub al-Ansari, a revered Muslim saint, as well as the tombs of his ancestors. Once these customary visits were performed, he left Istanbul and hastened to reach the army to take over its command and loyalties.[33] Meanwhile, the Grand Vizier, still in the field, was anxious to receive the new sultan at the head of the army. He sent another letter in the guise of yet another proclamation of victory, urging Selim to hurry. Reminding him of the previous letter, he informed him that the army had been kept under control so far with maintenance work at the castle of Szigetvar.[34] Sokollu Mehmed Pasha's anxiety brings forth the second vital aspect of the enthronement process: the claiming of the army through the homage ceremony. Miniatures illustrating late sixteenth-century chronicles reveal that the enthronement ceremonies of all sultans prior to Ahmed I in 1603 were characterized by depictions of a soldier of some rank kneeling before the new sultan.[35] It was clear, therefore, that loyalty of the military took precedence before government or representative bodies (or even religious ones).

Thirty-three days after the death of Süleyman, Sokollu Mehmed Pasha still expected some sort of news, with the urgent expectation of uniting the new sultan with his army for a definite transfer of sovereignty. Two days later, finally, a letter arrived from Selim notifying the Grand Vizier of his arrival at Istanbul and his ceremonial ascension onto the throne. He also informed the anxious Grand Vizier about his departure from the city, after staying for a couple of days, to reach the army.[36] Mehmed Pasha's reply demonstrates a continuing concern about possible unrest in the army. The Grand Vizier highlights two main problems that were making it harder to maintain order among the soldiers as Selim's arrival became delayed. First, the army had been stationed at Szigetvar for a long time, causing shortage in food supplies. Second, and more importantly, rumours of Selim's accession in Istanbul had spread through individuals travelling from there. As such, the Grand Vizier once more stresses the urgency of the situation:

> However, it is not possible to silence the news relating to the royal accession on the felicitous throne brought by those coming from [those lands]. It is thus acknowledged that the arrival [of your Majesty] in haste and hurry is for the best interest of the religion and the state (...) There should be no doubt that haste in heading toward and steering for [the army] is an important kingly matter.[37]

The Grand Vizier was hesitant to move the army into the heart of the Ottoman lands before the new sultan could arrive to take up leadership of the household troops. As soon as he learned that Selim had reached Plovdiv, he decided to take the army back to Belgrade to meet him.[38] Receiving Sokollu Mehmed Pasha's letter, Selim wrote to him from Sofia informing him that he had received the letters and was very much aware of the urgency of the situation.[39] Selim's concern also is reflected in the official letter sent to Shah Tahmasp to notify the Safavid ruler in Persia of his accession. Feridun Beğ has included a copy of this letter in his famous compilation, *Münşeatü's-selatin* (Correspondences of the Sultans). The relevant part of the letter, in loose translation, reads:

> As soon as the truth of the matter was made known to my person, we departed for our sovereign seat and we were able to ascend our auspicious throne. However, since this exceptionally important situation came into being while our victorious army was within the realms of the cursed infidels beyond the borders of the Abode of Islam, the duty of protection is doubtlessly a most important royal obligation

dictated by the honour of sovereignty. Therefore, we have departed from our felicitous throne to ride toward our victory-bringing army.[40]

The army was around Sotin (in today's eastern Croatia, on the Danube) when news of Selim's arrival in Belgrade reached Sokollu, who sent the banners and the military band to Belgrade at night, gave leave to the soldiers, and summoned the Quran reciters to surround the late sultan's funeral cart. At this point, Feridun Beğ informs us that the imperial guards realized the truth and fell into violent demonstrations of grief.[41] On 24 October 1566, the imperial tent was set up and the next day the funeral cart was brought in. Selim met the cart in mourning attire. Funeral prayers (*meyyid namazı*) were performed with the presence of Selim, the Grand Vizier, the other viziers, high ranking officials, soldiers and others.[42] Following the prayers, the new sultan walked to the imperial tent as he saluted the crowd. As he entered the tent, those in attendance first presented their condolences and then congratulated him for ascending to the 'throne of sultanate and the abode of caliphate'. The funeral cart was then sent to Istanbul accompanied by vizier Ahmed Pasha. Once the funeral cart left, the officials came back to the imperial tent and kissed the hand of the Sultan who was still in mourning attire.[43] Under normal circumstances, this hand kissing ritual may have been considered as the homage ceremony, as Selim held court in Belgrade during his six-day stay there.[44] By the time he left Belgrade, Selim seems to have been officially Sultan in the eyes of all his subjects be they civilians or high-ranking members of the military establishment, as attested by a letter sent around this time to Ferdinand I by the governor of Buda, Mustafa Pasha, referring to the new sultan as 'Our Exalted Sultan Selim'.[45]

Happily commencing a new reign?

Sultan Selim arrived back in Edirne on 24 November, only to leave for Istanbul after a four-day stay.[46] Normally, this would have been the end of the story and Selim would have commenced his reign. He had been enthroned in Istanbul, then received the obedience of the army and received the homage of his chief officers. However, this was not the case. When they returned to Istanbul the Janissaries created unrest and the cavalry followed their example. There seemed to be two problems: one was the rivalry between the officials of the imperial centre, namely the household officers of the deceased Sultan Süleyman, and the provincial officials, namely the men of the new Sultan Selim, who now claimed positions in the central imperial hierarchy.[47] Part of the problem was that some of the men accompanying Selim from Kütahya were of peasant origin, therefore taxpayers to the provincial governors of the deceased Sultan Süleyman. When these newcomers were elevated to military status, their previous tax debts were left unpaid. In other words, the conflict between these two groups of men was not only a matter of precedence but also a financial matter. This was resolved only after their military status was confirmed on the condition that they paid accrued taxes up to the date of conscription into Selim's army.[48]

The second issue brings us back to the central question, 'where is the throne'? Feridun Beğ's eyewitness account reads:

> The Sultan camped and held court for six days in Belgrade. The Janissaries were to be given accession gratuities by the order of the Sultan. The amount to be given to each man was unknown. When they asked how much had been given when the late sultan had ascended the throne, no one was able to pronounce a correct amount because forty-eight years had passed. Thus, an order was given for the treasury registers to be consulted. But the registers of those years had not been brought along on campaign but left in Istanbul. With the truth of the matter unresolved, both the infantry and the cavalry were given a thousand aspers each for the moment. The registers of the old times would be consulted when they arrived in Istanbul. If the registers showed a higher amount, the remaining amount would be paid to each man. This was how the gratuities matter was seemingly solved on the spot. However, it turned out that some of the Janissaries had made a plot and started to talk seditiously saying: 'The thousand aspers we received at Belgrade is the campaign gratuity of the deceased sultan. And if the registers pertaining to the time of our deceased sultan's accession show that a thousand aspers were given per person, we want two thousand aspers each from our Sultan.' Such were the bandits who knew nothing of the honour of the state and religion.[49]

The whole affair, in Feridun Beğ's version of the story, ends with Selim II giving one thousand aspers in the end, and finally entering the Imperial Palace through the Imperial Gate.[50]

Conclusion

What does this story tell us? In looking at the succession processes as a whole, we see that, after hearing of his father's death, Selim II came to Istanbul, which he and his contemporaries regarded as the 'seat of the throne', as his predecessors had before him. He was enthroned in Istanbul and gave gratuities to those present, again, as his predecessors had done. He even disregarded his own counsellors to an extent and rode to Belgrade to receive the oath of the army. Further to this, he brought along a throne from Istanbul and was enthroned again in Belgrade to further make the point. On his return to Istanbul, these previous enthronements seem to have been lost on the lower echelons of the military establishment. The ensuing unrest may have been caused by the greed of lower ranking Janissaries or by the competitive conflict between the old household officers and the new or by the tension between the central imperial faction and the newly prominent provincial princely faction. Regardless of the complexity of reasons, it underlines one central factor about the location of the throne in the accession ceremonial: the throne is where the imperial army is. The entire episode about the accession of Selim II seems to confirm an allegedly ancient saying reiterated by Selaniki: 'The House of Osman cannot ascend the throne of the Sultanate, unless they pass under the sword of the Janissaries.'[51]

Notes

1. Selaniki Mustafa Efendi, *Tarih-i Selaniki*, ed. Mehmet İpşirli (Ankara: Türk Tarih Kurumu Yayınları, 1999), 41: '...varub tahta cülus eyledük mi ve erkan-ı devletle mülakat eyleyüb ahvalimüz nice olduğın bildük mi ve Al-i Osman şimdiye dek kimsenin emeğin ve hakk-ı hidmetin zayi eylemiş müdür? İçünüzde bir edeb bilür söz anlar adem yok mudur?'.
2. For a brief discussion of the 'long sixteenth century', see Kate Fleet, 'The Ottomans, 1451–1603: A Political History Introduction', in *The Cambridge History of Turkey: Vol. 2, The Ottoman Empire as a World Power, 1453–1603*, ed. Suraiya N. Faroqhi and Kate Fleet (Cambridge–New York: Cambridge University Press, 2013), 21.
3. Transferred to Ottoman political thought from Persian theories of statecraft, the notion of *nizam-ı 'âlem* signifies an unchangeable universal order without which security and stability cannot be achieved. The sultan is ultimately responsible for the protection of this order whose alternative is chaos. For a thorough discussion on this notion, see Gottfried Hagen, 'Legitimacy and World Order', in *Legitimizing the Order: The Ottoman Rhetoric of State Power*, ed. Hakan T. Karateke and Maurus Reinkowski (Leiden: Brill, 2005), 53–83.
4. For 'state ceremonials' personifying the Crown/State, see Ralph Giesey, 'Inaugural Aspects of French Royal Ceremonials', in *Coronations: Medieval and Early Modern Monarchic Ritual*, ed. János M. Bak (Berkeley: University of California Press, 1990), 35–6.
5. David I. Kertzer, *Ritual, Politics, and Power* (New Haven, CT: Yale University Press, 1988), 25.
6. Cemal Kafadar, 'Janissaries and Other Riffraff of Ottoman Istanbul: Rebels without a Cause?', in *Identity and Identity Formation in the Ottoman World: A Volume of Essays in Honour of Norman Itzkowitz*, ed. Baki Tezcan and Karl K. Barbir (Wisconsin: Wisconsin University Press, 2007), 113–34. Also see Sergio Bertelli, *The King's Body* (University Park: Pennsylvania State University, 2001), 41. For some contemporary views, see İbn Kemâl [Kemalpaşazâde], *Tevârih-i Âl-i Osmân: X. Defter*, ed. Şefaettin Severcan (Ankara: Türk Tarih Kurumu, 1996), 19; Celâlzâde Mustafa Çelebi, *Selim-nâme*, ed. Ahmet Uğur and Mustafa Çuhadar (Ankara: Kültür Bakanlığı, 1990), 220; Marino Sanuto, *I Diarii di Marino Sanuto*, vol. 29, *1520–1521* (Bologna: Forni Editore, 1969), 306; *Letters and Papers, Foreign and Domestic, Henry VIII*, vol. 3, *1519–1523* ed. John Sherren Brewer (London: Her Majesty's Stationery Office, 1867), 388.
7. Franz Babinger, *Mehmed the Conqueror and His Time*, ed. William C. Hickman, trans. Ralph Manheim (Princeton: Princeton University Press 1992), 406; also see İbn Kemâl [Kemalpaşazâde], *Tevârih-i Âl-i Osmân: VIII. Defter*, ed. Ahmet Uğur (Ankara: Türk Tarih Kurumu, 1997), 531–4.
8. In the Ottoman context, the 'seat of the throne' (*pay-i taht*), denotes the physical location where the throne is. The Ottomans during this period did not use the term 'capital city'; for them, the centre of the Empire was wherever the throne of the sultan was situated.
9. For Selim I's enthronement see, for example, Celâlzâde Mustafa Çelebi, *Selim-nâme*, 98–9, and Zeynep Tarım Ertuğ, 'The Depiction of Ceremonies in Ottoman Miniatures: Historical Record or a Matter of Protocol', *Muqarnas* 27, no.1 (2010): 256.

10 For a brief overview of the arrival and entry of Süleyman I, for example, see Nevin Zeynep Yelçe, 'The Making of Sultan Süleyman: A Study of Process/es of Image-Making and Reputation Management' (PhD Dissertation, Sabanci University, 2009), 112.
11 Feridun Ahmed Bey, *Nüzhet-i Esrârü'l-Ahyâr der-Ahbâr-i Sefer-i Sigetvar: Sultan Süleyman'ın Son Seferi*, ed. H. Ahmet Arslantürk and Günhan Börekçi (İstanbul: Zeytinburnu Belediyesi, 2012). This critical edition is based on the Topkapı Palace Museum Library's (hereafter: TSMK) manuscript of Feridun Ahmed Beğ's work. The manuscript under the archive number TSMK H.1339 has been comparatively used along with the critical edition throughout this paper.
12 For more information on Feridun Ahmed Beğ, see J.H. Mordtmann, 'Ferîdûn Beg', in *Encyclopaedia of Islam*, 2nd edn, ed. P. Bearman, Th. Bianquis, C.E. Bosworth, E. van Donzel, and W.P. Heinrichs (accessed 9 April 2021) http://dx.doi.org/10.1163/1573-3912_islam_SIM_2354. First published online: 2012. First print edn: ISBN: 9789004161214, 1960-2007; Abdülkadir Özcan, 'Feridun Ahmed Bey (ö. 991/1583)', in *TDV İslam Ansiklopedisi*, vol. 12 (İstanbul: Türkiye Diyanet Vakfı, İslâm Ansiklopedisi Genel Müdürlüğü, 1995), 396–7.
13 For more information on Selaniki Mustafa Efendi, see Mehmet İpşirli, 'Selânîkî Muṣṭafâ Efendi', in *Encyclopaedia of Islam*, 2nd edn, ed. P. Bearman, Th. Bianquis, C.E. Bosworth, E. van Donzel, W.P. Heinrichs, http://dx.doi.org/10.1163/1573-3912_islam_SIM_6701 (accessed 9 April 2021). First published online: 2012. First print edn: ISBN: 9789004161214, 1960-2007; Mehmet İpşirli, 'Selaniki Mustafa Efendi', *TDV İslam Ansiklopedisi*, vol. 36 (İstanbul: Türkiye Diyanet Vakfı, İslâm Ansiklopedisi Genel Müdürlüğü, 2009): 357–9.
14 For these aspects of Selaniki's work, see Metin Kunt, 'A Prince Goes Forth (Perchance to Return)', in *Identity and Identity Formation in the Ottoman World: A Volume of Essays in Honor of Norman Itzkowitz*, , 63, and Ertuğ, 'The Depiction of Ceremonies in Ottoman Miniatures': 251.
15 Feridun Ahmed Bey, *Nüzhet-i Esrâr*, 51b.
16 Ibid., 52a.: 'Ki tahtın sahibi Sultan Selim Han cülus ide gelüb tahta şitaban'.
17 Ibid., 55b–56a.
18 Ibid., 57a–58a.: 'Erbab-ı fitne fesaddan şurü ifsada kasd idenlerin hakikat-ı hale ıttılaları ve vukufları olmamağla fikr-i fesadları batıl-ı hayal kasidleri atıl ola ve bil cümle saadetlü padişah hazretleri devlet-ü ikbal ve azamet-ü iclalle darü's-saltanatü's-seniye ve medera-ül hilafetü's-semiye tahtgah-ı makbul mahmiye-i İstanbula duhül kılmayınca ve serir-i saltanat-ı izzet-rütbet ve mesned-i hilafet-i saadet- menziletde cülus-u hümayun müyesser ve nigin-i devlet rehin-i hatem-i Süleymani karin-i şayikan-ı hüsrevani nöbet-i devlet-i saltanat-destgahi ele geçirmeyince kimesneye ifşa-yı esrar eylemekten ihtiraz üzere olasızdiye nasihat etti.' Selaniki, on the other hand, does not give a comparable description of the letter's tone and content, see Selaniki, *Tarih-i Selaniki*, 40.
19 For more information on Sokollu Mehmed Pasha, see G. Veinstein, 'Soḳollu Meḥmed Pasha,' in *Encyclopaedia of Islam*, 2nd edn, ed. P. Bearman, Th. Bianquis, C.E. Bosworth, E. van Donzel, W.P. Heinrichs http://dx.doi.org/10.1163/1573-3912_islam_SIM_7090 First published online: 2012 (accessed 9 April 2021). First print edn: ISBN: 9789004161214, 1960-200
20 Emine Fetvacı, 'The Production of the Şehnâme-i Selim Ḫân', *Muqarnas* 26, no.1 (2009): 265.
21 Feridun Ahmed Bey, *Nüzhet-i Esrâr*, 70b–71a.

22 Selaniki, *Tarih-i Selaniki*, 40. The khutbah refers to the sermon delivered at the congregational Friday prayer; having his name recited during the sermon was a prerogative of the Muslim ruler.
23 Ibid., 39–40.
24 Printed in Feridun Ahmed Bey, *Nüzhet-i Esrâr*, 71b.
25 Ibid., 74a: '... şeref-i saltanatla serir-i hilafeti müşerref eylemek...'.
26 Selaniki, *Tarih-i Selaniki*, 41.
27 TSMK, R.1277, Sa'dî b. Abd el-Mute'al, *Selimnâme*, Aleppo:1055 [1645], 108a: '...Üsküdar'dan dîde-i halka 'ayân oldı. Henüz ol hâdise-i 'azmi agâh değillerdi. Nâgâh sâye salıcak halka bir mikdâr ızdırâb irişdi. Bunlar deryâ-yı fikre düşüb girdâb-ı tevehhümde ser-gerdân iken yeniçeri ağası mütenebbih olub şeref-i kûdüm ve şahîs-i vürûd-ı hümâyûn idiği ıttılâ' idicek...'.
28 Celâlzâde, *Selim-nâme*, 221.
29 Selaniki, *Tarih-i Selaniki*, 41–2.
30 Ibid., 42.
31 Ibid., 42–3.
32 Ibid., 43.
33 Feridun Ahmed Bey, *Nüzhet-i Esrâr*, 74b; Selaniki, *Tarih-i Selaniki*, 43.
34 Feridun Ahmed Bey, *Nüzhet-i Esrâr*, 75a–7b.
35 For a comparative examination, see Ertuğ, 'The Depiction of Ceremonies in Ottoman Miniatures': 257–8.
36 Feridun Ahmed Bey, *Nüzhet-i Esrâr*, 80a–b.
37 Feridun Ahmed Bey, *Mecmua-yı Münşeat-ı Feridun Bey* (Istanbul: Takvimhane-yi Âmire, 1265-1274/1848-1858), 477–8.
38 Feridun Ahmed Bey, *Nüzhet-i Esrâr*, 86a–7b.
39 Ibid., 85a–b. For Selim's journey to Belgrade, also see Selaniki, *Tarih-i Selaniki*, 44.
40 Feridun Ahmed Bey, *Münşeat*, 469–70.
41 Feridun Ahmed Bey, *Nüzhet-i Esrâr*, 105a–6a. Also see Selaniki, *Tarih-i Selaniki*, 47–8.
42 Feridun Ahmed Bey, *Nüzhet-i Esrâr*, 108b.
43 Ibid., 109b–10a. Selaniki mentions a new throne being brought from Istanbul. Selaniki, *Tarih-i Selaniki*, 48.
44 Feridun Ahmed Bey, *Nüzhet-i Esrâr*, 111b–12b. For a thorough analysis of the significance of the ceremony in Belgrade, see Fetvacı, 'The Production of the Şehnâme-i Selîm Ḫân'.
45 Alpertunga Altaylı and Yasemin Altaylı, 'Macarların Sigetvar Destanı: Szigeti Veszedelem (Siget Tehlikesi) ve Zrínyiler', *Modern Türklük Araştırmaları Dergisi* 6, no. 4 (2009): 96.
46 Feridun Ahmed Bey, *Nüzhet-i Esrâr*, 114a–b.
47 Selaniki, *Tarih-i Selaniki*, 51, 54–8. This issue has been discussed in its various perspectives by notable scholars. See, for example, Fetvacı, 'The Production of the Şehnâme-i Selîm Ḫân': 263–316, and Ertuğ, 'The Depiction of Ceremonies': 251–75, esp. 269–70, for discussions built around art historical evidence.
48 Kunt, 'A Prince Goes Forth', 63–71, especially 67–9.
49 Feridun Ahmed Bey, *Nüzhet-i Esrâr*, 115b–16b: 'Sabıka mahruse-i Belgradda ki altı gün oturak ve divan-ı hümayun olmuşdı, cülus-ı saltanat-ı şerif teşrifi kul taifesine bahşiş verilmek ferman olunmuşdı. Adem başına ne kadar akçe virileceği malum olmayub merhum padişah-ı gazi cülus itdükde ne kadar virildiği sual olundukda ol zemandan beri kırk sekiz yıl mürur edüp tül zeman olmağıla sıhhat üzre kimsne haber virmeye kadir olmayıp ve 'hazine-i amire defterleri görilsün' diyü ferman

olundukda, 'ol zemanun defatir-i seferde bile olmayub İstanbulda hızane-i amirede kalmışdur.' diye cevab olunduğı ecilden hakikat-i hal malum olmamağla adem başına atluya ve yayaya biner akçe virilüb saadetle İstanbul'a geründükde ol zemanın defterleri görilüb daha ziyade virilmiş mukayyet bulınursa adem başına yine ne kadar ziyade virilmek lazım gelürse virilecek olub bahşiş hususı fasl olmuşdı. Bu hususda taife-i mezbure (yeniçeriler) meğer ki ittifak eylemişler imiş. İçlerinde güft ü gu olmağa başlayub 'Belgradda aldığumuz biner akçe merhum gazi padişahun sefer bahşişidir ve merhum padişah cülus ittüği zemanun defteri görilüb ol zemanda biner akçe virildüği mukayyet bulındığı takdirce dahi bu defa biz padişahımuzdan ikişer bin akçe isterüz' diyü söyleşürek giderlerdi ve içlerinde anlar ki eşkıyadur ırz-ı din ü devlet bilmezlerdi.'

50 Ibid., 116b–18b.
51 Selaniki, *Tarih-i Selaniki*, 49: 'Al-i Osman saltanat tahtına geçmez madem ki kulun kılıcı altından geçmeye.'

2

Proclamations and coronations in Palermo (1700–1735): Performing kingship and celebrating civic power

Pablo González Tornel

During the first decades of the eighteenth century, the Kingdom of Sicily went through a period of great political instability. Ever since the Habsburgs had secured their rule in the early sixteenth century, kings of the island had always been born as such, and it had been enough for their predecessor to die for the heir to become king automatically. However, this was not the case between 1700 and 1735. Following the death without an heir of Charles II (III of Sicily), the last of the Spanish Habsburgs, the succession, according to his last will and testament, was to pass to Philip of Bourbon (numbered King Philip V of Spain, IV of Sicily). The refusal by the Austrian branch of the Habsburg dynasty to accept any transfer to a Bourbon of Spanish possessions – including those in Italy: Sicily, Naples, Milan, Sardinia – led to the start of a great war involving all the powers of Europe. After the conflict, the Peace of Utrecht put Sicily into the hands of Victor Amadeus II of Savoy (I of Sicily), who then exchanged it for Sardinia under the terms of a new treaty seven years later, in 1720. This new treaty granted the island to Charles VI of Habsburg (IV of Sicily). But the situation changed yet again in 1734, after the military expedition into Southern Italy by Philip V's son, Charles of Bourbon (V of Sicily), Duke of Parma, which led to the expulsion of the Habsburgs once more. An independent Kingdom of Sicily was reborn – after an absence of about three hundred years – which, joined to the mainland kingdom of Naples, was known as 'the Kingdom of the Two Sicilies', and which would survive up to the unification of Italy in 1861.

The main objective of this study is to foreground the exceptional nature and meaning of the celebrations orchestrated to hail the four new kings of Sicily, in this extraordinary succession of dynastic claims.[1] In Palermo, the essential difference between the four transitions of power was the purely proclamatory nature of the festivals held for Philip V of Bourbon and Charles VI of Habsburg, in contrast with the elaborate ceremonial displays arranged for Victor Amadeus of Savoy and Charles of Bourbon. The key factor was the physical presence of the dukes of Savoy and Parma in the capital of Sicily at the time of their recognition as kings, a presence which facilitated open expressions of loyalty to the new monarch and the recovery of a ceremony that had been abandoned for centuries: the coronation ritual in the Cathedral of Palermo.

The characteristics of the coronation ritual, together with the physical presence of the new kings on the island, brought about a peculiar symbiosis of the arts that was immediately made visible in the publication of luxurious illustrated volumes. Four different kings were elevated to the throne of Sicily in only thirty-five years, and three different lineages were crowned as rulers of the island. This chapter presents the ideological content of these successive enthronements according to the official accounts, analyses the main rituals recovered for the ceremonies and finally, determines the level of responsibility of the different actors involved and reveals the leading role of the local Senate of Palermo in these four transitions of power. As I shall show, in eighteenth-century Palermo, the ancient ritual of the Sicilian coronation was recovered after two centuries of oblivion under the Habsburg regime. In a scenario of seemingly unending dynastic change, the Senate's actions secured the stability of the institution – the Sicilian monarchy – through the use of ritual, and organized some of the most astonishing festivals ever seen in the island.

Four kings for one kingdom

The first transition of power in eighteenth-century Sicily, from Charles II of Habsburg to Philip V of Bourbon, took place without question in 1700 and stressed the continuity between the last Spanish Habsburg and the first Spanish Bourbon. The royal exequies of Charles II at Palermo Cathedral and the printed record of the occasion, written by Diego de Loya, bear testimony to the idea of a seamless change of dynasties.[2] One of Loya's allegorical texts eulogized the peace between Spain and France forged by Charles's will, and praised the choice of a Bourbon for the Spanish (and thus the Sicilian) throne.[3] An illustration included in the book shows Charles on his deathbed handing a golden lily to the allegorical figure of Peace, while the accompanying emblem exhibits the closed temple of Janus, a Roman sign of peaceful times, bearing the text *Amoris Impero*. A further allegory represented the love of the Spanish monarchy for Philip V, welcoming the Bourbon lilies and suggesting that Spain should no longer envy the lilies that crowned the temple of Solomon.[4] Like Solomon, Philip was presented as a fair and peaceful man, and the pictorial scene chosen to illustrate this idea was the image of Philip V on the throne with an allegorical figure of the Spanish monarchy at his feet, offering the new king a heart, that of Charles II.

The funeral held on Monday 18 April 1701, was preceded by the proclamation of the new king, the true core of the ceremony of transition.[5] Philip V, as the Habsburg king's legitimate heir, was proclaimed a lily of Christianity and Catholicism. The day established for the proclamation of Philip V by the Viceroy of Sicily, the Duke of Veragua, was 30 January 1701, and the events in the city of Palermo were recorded in several pamphlets authored by Antonino Mongitore and printed by order of the Senate.[6] In addition, a marble statue of the King was sculpted by Giambattista Ragusa and erected for the occasion in the Piazza Marina, at the start of the ceremonial route along the main avenue of Palermo, the Cassaro.[7]

As recounted by Diego de Loya, the proclamation parade of the Bourbon prince passed by the façade of the Jesuit College, whose profuse decoration included an image of the Pillars of Hercules, on which it was intended Philip V would inscribe the sacred laws of the Bible, thus keeping alive the symbolic language of emblems that had been used by the Habsburgs since the sixteenth century.[8] However, the continuity was maintained not only in the language employed, but in the chosen symbols themselves, in that the Pillars of Hercules immediately identified the new king with the Emperor Charles V.[9] Philip of Bourbon would adopt Habsburg imperial imagery, and like a new Solomon, would write on the mythological two columns of Hercules and make them Christian, as if they were the biblical pillars of Boaz and Jachin. Moreover, when the entourage left the Royal Palace, passing by the marble sculpture of Philip IV, the marble embodiment of the new king was greeted with cheers hailing him as the new Solomon: 'vivat rex Salomon'.[10]

Continuity with the past was a constant concern during the transitions of power in early eighteenth-century Palermo, and an effort was made to transmit a sensation of total normality. The Viceroy, who organized the proclamation of Philip V, had held the same position under the Habsburg Charles II, and the erection of a new sculpture was a continuation of the policy of displaying public effigies of all the monarchs in place ever since the reign of Emperor Charles V.[11] Therefore, Philip V and Charles II were both symbolically and ichnographically aligned as links in the same chain, and the traditional symbols of the Habsburg dynasty, from King Solomon to the lion or the eagle, were unhesitatingly adopted for the Bourbon king.[12] This was the general state of affairs during the early years of Philip's reign, when the sole objective appeared to be stability, but as we shall see, the accession ceremonies connected to all four of the island's successive kings retained in every case this link with the Spanish past. There were instances when all memory of the immediate predecessor was obliterated from the festivities, but the union with the Spanish monarchy, which had governed the island for two centuries, was used on every occasion as a symbol of continuity and stability.

The outbreak of the War of the Spanish Succession between those supporting the claims of Philip of Bourbon and those of the Archduke Charles of Austria for the inheritance of Charles II, was a major setback to the stability sought by the Bourbon regime. Milan was taken by Austrian troops in 1706, and Naples in 1707, removing Italy from Spanish control.[13] In addition, Pope Clement XI recognized the Archduke in 1709, making the situation of the Spanish possessions in Italy increasingly precarious.[14] Sicily remained loyal to the Bourbon cause, and as late as 1711 still greeted Philip's victories at Brihuega and Villaviciosa with enthusiasm.[15] However, just two years later, in 1713, the island was handed over to the House of Savoy as a consequence of the complicated diplomacy of the Treaties of Utrecht.

As a result of the 1713 peace, Sicily was ceded by Philip V to Victor Amadeus II, Duke of Savoy. This raised the Duke to the rank of a king, and made Turin the capital of a monarchy that was territorially divided between the House of Savoy's hereditary possessions in the north of the Italian peninsula and the island of Sicily.[16] The new situation thus awarded the House of Savoy its long-craved royal crown,[17] but also implied that Sicily might finally have a king residing on the island that had given him his royal title. Accordingly, Victor Amadeus travelled to Palermo to be solemnly crowned in the Cathedral, bringing about the recovery of an almost forgotten ceremony and unleashing a veritable explosion of celebrations and festivities.

Elisabeth Wünsne-Werdehausen observantly underlined the polysemic nature of the encounter between the Savoyard king and his new capital, which went far beyond that of a simple festive ritual.[18] The *adventus-triumphus* of Victor Amadeus combined Sicilian and Savoyard traditions in the staging of a pact aimed at legitimizing a new and untested monarchy. For centuries Sicily had shown a relative degree of obedience to distant kings represented by their viceroys, but Victor Amadeus was a much closer king who people probably hoped would transfer his residence in 1713 to Palermo. Therefore, at his coronation, references to earlier kings were manipulated and the immediate Sicilian past was ignored in order to consecrate a foreign dynasty, the House of Savoy.[19]

The coronation of the new king and the festivals and decorations prepared in Palermo to celebrate the occasion were described in lavish detail in a luxurious tome printed by order of the Senate of Palermo to commemorate the event, written by its secretary, Pietro Vitale, and illustrated by the Sicilian engraver Francesco Cichè.[20] Over the days that followed his arrival, right up to the coronation ceremony, Victor Amadeus, whom some may have considered an upstart king, did all he could to curry favour with his Sicilian subjects. In an effort to display an image of continuity, he granted audiences in the palace and visited different churches in the city to attend mass and the adoration of the Eucharist. Moreover, on various occasions, according to Pietro Vitale, on encountering a priest on his way to administer the Last Rites, the king-to-be descended from his carriage and offered it up for the sacrament of the Viaticum, transforming the *pietas austriaca*, the characteristic virtue propagated by the Habsburg dynasty, into a new form of Savoyard piety.[21] The gaining of a kingdom for the House of Savoy and the royal dignity that could now be attributed to the dynasty merited the adoption of certain external symbols of the House of Austria.[22]

Six triumphal arches marked the route to be followed by the monarch from the shore beyond the city walls right up to the Cathedral and the Royal Palace. The icons employed for their decoration freely combined allegories of the cardinal virtues, emblems, and figures of the kings of Sicily from different dynasties. All of these, together with the crowned effigies of the emperor and the kings of France, Spain and Portugal, were intermingled with pictorial scenes portraying King Victor Amadeus. Moreover, in the open area opposite the Royal Palace, an enormous triangular firework assembly was erected in honour of the three-legged symbol of Sicily, the Trinacria.

The solemn entry of Victor Amadeus into Palermo was arranged for 21 December 1713, and the coronation for Christmas Eve. When the King was ready to enter the Cathedral, Archbishop Gasch, accompanied by the bishops of Syracuse, Mazzara and Cefalù, left the sacristy and proceeded to the main altar. Once inside, Victor Amadeus was led to the presbytery, where he kneeled before the Archbishop of Palermo (see Figure 2.1). The attendant bishops read out the ritual affirmation of the worthiness of the candidate for the crown, upon which the king-to-be recited the profession of faith. Monsignor Gasch then anointed him with holy oil on his arm and shoulders and the Savoyard became king of Sicily.

Baroque rhetoric was fundamental to the 1713 coronation, since the traditional instruments of royal exaltation, such as heraldry, allegory, and historical and dynastic components, had to be manipulated to adapt them to a king who was atypical in that

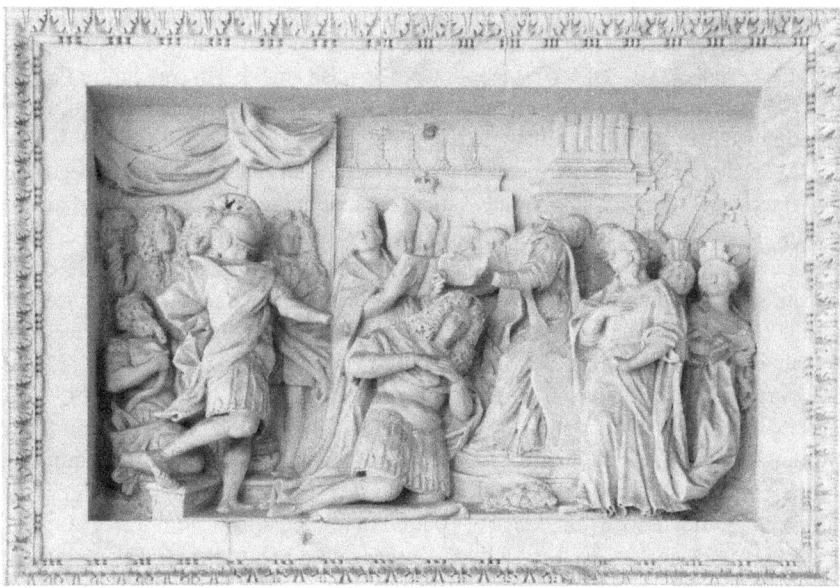

Figure 2.1 Giovanni Battista Ragusa, *Coronation of Vittorio Amedeo of Savoy*, 1713 in the Palermo Cathedral. © Pablo González Tornel.

he was the first monarch of his lineage: his paternal ancestors were not crowned heads, and his family had no prior relation to the Sicilian monarchy. In spite of this, the heterogeneous selected images deliberately gave no sense of incoherence in identifying the new Piedmontese prince with Normans, Aragonese or Habsburgs, or in pairing Victor Amadeus with antagonistic rulers such as Charles VI of Austria, Philip V or Louis XIV. Everything was valid for a ceremony which did not in essence extol the monarch so much as the institution he represented, the Sicilian monarchy, which was celebrating the coronation of a king for the first time in centuries, since the Habsburgs had never visited Sicily to be crowned as kings.

On the return of Victor Amadeus II and his queen, Anne-Marie d'Orléans, to Turin, the Savoyards' rapid loss of control over Sicily was largely brought about by Philip V of Spain, who launched an expedition in 1718 to reconquer the island. After two years of war, the Treaty of The Hague placed the island instead in the hands of the Emperor Charles VI of Habsburg, the traditional rival of the Spanish Bourbons. In order to retain the royal dignity he had gained by his coronation in Palermo, Victor Amadeus ensured that he received the kingdom of Sardinia, a mostly empty title in terms of power and prestige, but a territory with a historic royal crown, and, practically, one much closer to his Piedmontese possessions.

The result of this third transition of power was the return of Sicily to the domains of the House of Habsburg. In 1720, Charles VI still harboured a desire to recover the entirety of the Spanish Monarchy for his dynasty, but his rise to the imperial throne in 1711 had undermined support for his cause in the War of the Spanish Succession, and he had been obliged to renounce Spain itself by the Treaty of Utrecht in 1713.[23] However, his renunciation of the throne in Madrid did not prevent him from attempting to gain the Italian possessions of the splintered Spanish empire. His conquests of Milan in 1706 and Naples in 1707 were guaranteed at Utrecht, so now he followed up by retaking Sicily in 1720.[24]

The festivities to celebrate the official proclamation of the new monarch began on 29 September 1720, and the decorative and iconographic programme prepared for the occasion had the clear objective of emphasizing the continuity of the Habsburg dynasty – from the Spanish branch to the Austrian branch – on the throne of Sicily.[25] In doing so, the recent history of the island was conveniently ignored, and, for instance, the façade of the Palazzo Pretorio (the seat of the Senate) was decorated with a series of overtly dynastic images centred on a portrait of Charles VI. The Emperor's likeness was surrounded by the names and simulacra of his ancestors: Rudolf I the Glorious, Ferdinand I the Wise, Maximilian II the Clement, Matthias I the Just, Ferdinand II the Strong, Ferdinand III the Pacific, Leopold I the Pious, and Joseph I the Magnanimous. Moreover, on the lower level of the façade, six gilded statues represented the uninterrupted dynasty of the kings of Spain: Philip I, Charles V, Philip II, Philip III, Philip IV and Charles II. Therefore, the programme of the Senate Palace showed Charles VI as the sole descendant of two monarchies, Spain and the Holy Roman Empire, and one family, the Habsburgs. In addition, the strong dynastic content of the celebrations was underlined by the Jesuit College in the Cassaro, which funded a publication, by Domenico Turano, to record the embellishment of its building.[26] The decorative scheme was guided by the idea of the embodiment in Charles VI of all the virtues of the emperors of the Habsburg dynasty and the excellence of the House of Austria, represented on the front of the Jesuit College by a monumental figure of Charles VI surrounded by medallions of the fifteen previous Habsburg emperors.

But this too did not last. After fifteen years of Austrian government, the expulsion of the Habsburgs from the throne of Sicily and the return of the Bourbons to the kingdom were the result of a war of conquest. Charles of Bourbon, younger son of Philip V, had become Duke of Parma and Piacenza in 1732 (the inheritance of his mother), and retook Naples and Sicily in 1734 with the support of his father.[27] Once the island had been pacified, at the start of 1735, the new king of the Two Sicilies (the united kingdoms of Naples and Sicily) began his journey from Naples towards his coronation in Palermo, a ceremony that was duly recorded by the printing of yet another exquisite coronation book.[28] This time, the text of the publication was entrusted to Pietro La Placa, chancellor of the Senate, and the plates illustrating it to Antonio Bova, Francesco Cichè and Giuseppe Vasi.

As with the coronation of Victor Amadeus, according to La Placa, the route of the procession was ornamented by six triumphal arches: three of these, erected in the Strada Colonna, the Porta Felice and the Piazza Vigliena, were commissioned by the Senate, and three by the Neapolitans, Genoese and Milanese (the most important merchant communities in the city). These six structures laid emphasis on the idea of continuity between Philip V and Charles of Bourbon, father and son, staging a new and creative genealogy for the kingdom of Sicily. Therefore, the architect Nicolò Palma decorated the aisles of the Cathedral with eighteen paintings of only the kings of Sicily who had been crowned, from Roger I to Victor Amadeus of Savoy, ignoring the fifteen years of Austrian government. Special prominence was accorded to nine scenes showing the story of King David placed on the ceiling of the nave. In the same way as Solomon had been employed as the chief symbol in the proclamation of his father Philip V, the iconography selected for Charles cleverly made use of the story of King David to proclaim the renewed pact between divinity and monarchy, and legitimized his accession to the throne.[29]

The long-awaited arrival of Charles of Bourbon in Palermo occurred on Wednesday, 18 May, and on the following day the King entered the city for the first time, albeit privately, while the date of the public entry and acclamation was set for 30 June, and the ensuing coronation for 3 July. On the day of the coronation, the procession took the King from the Royal Palace to the Cathedral, where Archbishop Matteo Basile sat at the high altar with the Roman Pontifical (the liturgical book that contains the rites performed by bishops) on his knees, upon which Charles of Bourbon swore to observe the laws of the Kingdom. The Duke of Arión exposed the right arm and shoulder of the King so that the Archbishop could anoint him with holy oils and this prelate, who was also Primate of Sicily, then laid the crown upon his head and placed the sceptre in his right hand while, as recorded by Pietro la Placa, the multitude broke into applause. Just a few days later, on the evening of 8 July Charles boarded a ship and set sail for Naples, never to return. However, by contrast with the earlier celebrations, the coronation of this prince marked the beginning of a long reign that placed a stable new dynasty, the House of Bourbon, upon the Sicilian throne.

A Deo coronatus?

One aspect inherent to any proclamation but necessarily underlined in the Palermo coronations was the duality of the monarchic institution versus the individual king. In Sicily, the heterogeneous protagonists of the proclamations and coronations of the eighteenth century made the dual nature of the monarchy especially prominent, a fact that had already been made evident under the Spanish domination by the dissemination of royal images around the city.[30] Through those effigies, the Sicilian people had paid homage for nearly two centuries to kings they had no physical knowledge of, and the personality of the individual thus disappeared and faded into the institution he represented. However, it was the physical presence of Victor Amadeus of Savoy and Charles of Bourbon amidst their subjects that tested their loyalty to and reaffirmed the supremacy of the monarchy over the individual prince, demonstrating the independence of the monarchical concept from dynasties or lineages.

This rift between the individual and the concept of the monarchy was signalled by Kantorowicz with reference to French royalty.[31] In that case, the dual corporality of the monarch, with one physical body and another of a mystic or politic nature, was made manifest during funerals, and, as Giesey analysed in depth, such bodily duality was justified by the need to legitimize the successor.[32] In early modern Europe, a prince's validity was generally based on his belonging to a series, and on his ability to present himself before his subjects as part of an institution that transcended him. However, in most royal polities, the concept of the dual corporality of the monarchy was susceptible to dilution by lineage, since the infinite succession of members of a dynasty, and the almost complete absence of interregna, blurred the distinction between power and the individual, strengthening the institution. Nevertheless, some non-hereditary monarchies provide perfect illustrations of the dual nature of sovereignty and of the existence of a political power superior to the succession of individuals, something absolutely necessary in eighteenth-century Sicily.

In Rome, for instance, the figure of the pontiff, with the duality of his spiritual and temporal power, was at once the representative of a dignity that did not die with his own physical extinction and his perishability as a human being.[33] Here, as occurred in Central Europe with the imperial title, the elective kingship established a clear separation between the physical entity and the body politic, and the annulment of the dynastic element minimized the value of the successive princes enhancing the exaltation of a political, theological and philosophical structure that remained immutable. Therefore, for non-dynastic monarchies – those that tended to ignore the individual – ceremonial was fundamental in order to maintain the sacred image of the institution, and the recovery of the coronation ritual in eighteenth-century Sicily responded to this necessity.

The Sicilian coronation ritual is partially known from the study of the *ordines*, compilations of the etiquette to be employed for specific ceremonies. While all of these share a common ground, one that has been especially widely studied, since several manuscript copies have been preserved, is that drawn up for the ascent to the throne of Roger II during the Christmas festival of 1130.[34] The coronation ceremony in the kingdom of Sicily was based on the *Ordo Romanus* and was one of very long-standing tradition linked to Byzantium and its divine conception of monarchy. The sacred character granted to the Sicilian monarchy by the coronation ritual was portrayed later on in the mosaics of Monreale Cathedral (outside Palermo), where King William II is shown as being crowned by Jesus Christ himself.[35] The Monreale mosaic presents implications that run far deeper than the simple exaltation of the Norman king, and it incorporates the text taken from the Book of Psalms, where the God of Israel appoints David as his executor on earth.[36] According to the Bible, God anointed and crowned him as king, declaring him to be the chosen one and promising to ensure his victories, and thereby making him a *deo coronatus*.[37]

The image of King William II being crowned by Christ largely reflects the overlap between religion and state present in a coronation ritual that tended towards a definition of the prince as someone elected by the hand of God and, consequently, indisputable.[38] This union of *rex* and *sacerdos* had held firm after Antiquity in the Holy Roman Empire, and its restoration on the island by the Norman dynasty in the eleventh century largely explains the coronation ceremonies of the eighteenth.[39] It should also be considered that up to 1713, the kingdom of Sicily had formed part of the conglomerate of states of the Spanish empire, whose monarchy had been a prime example of the identification between religion and state.[40] In his triumphant passages through Italy, Charles V had taken on the mantle of a new Constantine, the author of a new pact between the Papacy and the Empire that ensured a Catholic world.[41] Afterward, the identification between politics and religion, the sacralization of civil power, and the complex relations between church and state would remain constant in Europe through the seventeenth century – and no monarchy took the identification of the king with Catholicism as far as Spain's.[42]

This digression regarding the more or less sacred character of the institution of the monarchy in Sicily is pertinent in that it is directly bound to the legitimacy of the monarch on the throne. The identification of royalty with divinity was a creation of late Antiquity that evolved and reached its apotheosis in medieval times, before the progressive secularization of European politics from the mid-seventeenth century onwards. However, early eighteenth-century Sicily appeared well suited to this renewal of the sacred connotation of the monarchy because the legitimacy of the two kings crowned in Palermo was dubious and totally incongruent as far as any dynastic continuity was concerned. Victor Amadeus of Savoy arrived in Palermo as a result of a peace treaty, and Charles of Bourbon did so after a war of conquest. Therefore, in this restless Europe where kingdoms were constantly changing hands, it was necessary to maintain the loyalty of the subjects to a crumbling institution by reminding the Sicilians that a king was established as such by the grace of God.

The face-to-face meeting between the new princes and their Sicilian subjects put the identification of the individual with the institution to the test, and it is this situation of uncertainty that largely explains the retrieval of the coronation ceremonial. The successive unstable situations were overcome thanks to the mystification of the princes through anointment, which transformed them into God's elected. This explains the disregard of lineage, the constant changes of content, and the iconographic adaptations of a monarchy that appeared both immutable and flexible at the same time. Victor Amadeus of Savoy and Charles of Bourbon were not marble statues, but real foreigners, and needed to be crowned in order to transcend their individuality and become part of the Sicilian monarchy. But who decided to recover the forgotten rituals in order to ensure the stability of the monarchy? Was it the dukes of Savoy and Parma, or it was Palermo's Senate, the guardian of the thousand-year-old traditions of the capital of the Kingdom?

A monarchic celebration or a civic festival?

The four Sicilian royal celebrations, especially the coronations, crystallized the ideological and symbolic construction of the successive kings in the early part of the eighteenth century. The enthronements of these monarchs tested the capacity of the Kingdom and its capital, Palermo, to acclaim princes of very different origins and conditions whose legitimacy was never officially called into question, and this trial was overcome with enormous success thanks to the recovery of the sacred character of the Sicilian monarchy through the coronation ritual. In order to understand the importance of Palermo coronations it is fundamental to underline that these ceremonies were not a manifestation of power but the action or set of actions which created that power structure.[43] In Palermo, then, the king was unable to reign without a coronation, and so needed the collaboration of the city authorities in order to create the power structure. Therefore, it is time to face the problem of who was really responsible for the success of these extraordinary transitions of power and the ceremonies orchestrated to celebrate them in the Sicilian capital.

To determine if the eighteenth-century Palermo coronations were the responsibility of the kings-to-be or of the municipal Senate, it may be useful to analyse their printed records, because, as Helen Watanabe-O'Kelly has shown, the festival book did not merely chronicle an event but formed an integral part of it.[44] The Sicilian festival books, conceived from the outset as one more manifestation of the organization of the spectacle, moreover had a dual value.[45] On the one hand, they functioned as memory, fixing an event in an oscillation between historical narrative and commemoration. On the other, they were an exaltation of the protagonist of the festival, and as such they were often far from objective. Fortunately, these books are characterized by a rich text and an abundance of engravings and allow the festivals to be reconstructed in detail, especially through the chorographic views of the city of Palermo in the printed records of the coronations of Victor Amadeus of Savoy and Charles of Bourbon, engraved by Antonio Bova, Francesco Cichè and Giuseppe Vasi.[46]

The festival book's very constitution as an integral part of the festivity implies its link with the organizer of the event, who was generally also the patron of the publishing venture and the one that designated for whom the book was intended. The court festival book was destined in most cases for one of two types of reader.[47] If it was the prince himself who orchestrated the festival, the book was usually conceived as a propaganda element destined for a wide circulation. However, when the patronage of the event fell to the host city, and it was the civic authorities who were responsible for the book's publication, the volume tended to be a homage to the protagonist of the festival, the prince himself.

A search through the contents of Europe's principal libraries allows us to form various hypotheses concerning the circulation of the Sicilian books, directly linked with those they were intended for, and to determine who took control of the festivals. In the case of the records of the Palermo festivities, the circulation and intended recipients of the books are by no means homogeneous. Both the text by Mongitore on the acclamation of Philip V and the editions printed in 1720 to celebrate the proclamation of Charles VI are modest works produced under the patronage of the Senate that seem intended for local circulation only. In the case of the book produced by Turano in 1720 under the patronage of the Jesuits, the work, despite its two magnificent engravings and its cultured programme, was published by and for the congregation itself, with no involvement of external authorities. Therefore, all these books and pamphlets seem to have been intended as chronicles aimed at recording the festival rather than genuine propaganda articles. On the contrary, the books by Pietro Vitale for the coronation of Victor Amadeus of Savoy and by Pietro La Placa for that of Charles of Bourbon present a different picture (see Figure 2.2). Both volumes have a similar structure characterized by abundant text and numerous large-format engraved illustrations executed with considerable care. The patron of both publications, and also of the coronation rituals, was the Senate of Palermo, and, in this case, the prince himself was not only the object of the ceremony but also the intended recipient of its printed record.

The circulation of the festival books relevant to this study was fairly restricted and this reinforces the hypothesis of the Senate being the only protagonist of the enterprises. Those relating to Philip V were not found by Helen Watanabe-O'Kelly in either the British Library or the Bibliothèque Nationale de France.[48] Neither was the book by

Figure 2.2 Giuseppe Vasi, Royal entry of Charles of Bourbon in Palermo, 1735, engraving from Pietro La Placa, *La Reggia in Trionfo per l'acclamazione, e coronazione della Sacra Real Maestà di Carlo Infante di Spagna, Re di Sicilia, Napoli e Gerusalemme, Duca di Parma, Piacenza, e Castro, Gran Principe Ereditario della Toscana ordinata dall'Eccellentissimo Senato Palermitano* (Palermo: Regia Stamperia di Antonino Epiro, 1735). (Palermo, Biblioteca Centrale della Regione Siciliana 'Alberto Bombace', Rari Sic 658. © Biblioteca Centrale della Regione Siciliana 'Alberto Bombace') Su concessione dell' Assessorato regionale dei Beni Culturali et dell'Identitá Siciliana, Departamento dei Beni Culturali et dell'Identitá Sciciliana.

Pietro Vitale on Victor Amadeus of Savoy to be found in either library.[49] Only the record of the coronation of Charles of Bourbon had some diffusion, since copies have been located in both the French and British libraries, but the responsibility for this probably lies with the court of the king of Naples and Sicily, who in 1735 was beginning a long reign and may well have used the book as a further instrument for his legitimization after the Sicilian coronation.[50]

In spite of their irregular circulation, however, the importance of the intended royal recipient of the festival books for the two coronations led to their presence in the principal libraries of Turin and Naples, respectively the Savoyard and Bourbon capitals. This makes both printed records, and also the festivals they narrate, part of a concrete ritual. With the proclamations of Philip V and the Emperor Charles, the Senate fulfilled its obligation of celebrating a ceremony while at the same time demonstrating the city's might and pomp in a kind of self-celebration. However, with Victor Amadeus of Savoy and Charles of Bourbon, the capital and the realm were also paying homage to their prince: they first crowned him while celebrating his reign, and then reminded him with a luxurious book of Palermo's love and fidelity.

As I have explained, the success of the Sicilian coronations of Victor Amadeus of Savoy and Charles of Bourbon and the printed records of the festivities were the direct responsibility of the Senate of Palermo. It is also significant that Pietro Vitale, the author of the texts that relate the proclamations of the Savoyard king as well as that of the Emperor Charles in 1720, was the secretary to the Senate, and that Pietro La Placa, who wrote the festival book exalting Charles of Bourbon, was the chancellor of the same institution. Considering that these books were part of the ceremony, are the coronations then to be seen as a monarchic or a civic rite? Apparently, the main beneficiary of the ritual and its exploitation as political propaganda was the king himself, particularly in a situation of dubious legitimacy. However, as in the case of their printed records, the exceptional nature of the coronation festivals in Palermo can only be explained by the implication of the civic authorities, necessary in an unstable situation and fundamental for the success of both the festive and the editorial enterprises.

Laurie Nussdorfer described in a number of publications a power arrangement in seventeenth-century Rome that can usefully be extrapolated to eighteenth-century Palermo. She distinguished clearly between the power of the prince and that of the citizens' Senate, showing how the power of the Pope was imposed in the Roman case upon that of the city.[51] This contrast of the different authorities also found expression in urban planning, and in Rome, the two great public squares destined for the representation of power, the Capitoline and Saint Peter's Square, were the result of papal initiative.[52] The two powers had a similar coexistence in Palermo, but, as it is appreciable in the course followed by the festive ceremonial, the urban prominence was divided between the Royal Palace and the Senate Palace, a civic urban initiative.[53] Spanish Habsburg monarchs of Sicily had always been distant, and, therefore, although these kings had always been represented in Palermo during their absence by a viceroy, the prominence of the Senate was far greater.

Conclusion

In Palermo, as in Rome during a situation of *Sede Vacante*, the transitional phase between two rulers also led to the temporary assumption of power by the civic authorities.[54] Until the coronation of Victor Amadeus of Savoy, the Spanish viceroy had acted as the *alter ego* of the monarch, becoming the principal promoter of all royal proclamations. Nevertheless, the presence of a king on Sicilian soil, the change of dynasty, and the instability of a viceroy who had sworn allegiance to the previous monarch permitted the Senate of Palermo to take the reins of the festival. For this reason, the great festivities in the city during the first decades of the century, and especially the coronations, must be regarded as a virtual monopoly of the municipal powers. It was the members of the Senate who retrieved and modernized the ritual of the *ordo*, it was the senators who established the iconographic programmes for royal exaltation, it was the finest writers in Palermo who composed the printed narratives of the ceremony, and it was the Senate that assumed the cost of printing them, so transforming the festival into a triumph of civic power. It was only the determination of the Senate that ensured the continued vigour of the monarchy in spite of the constant changes of king, but those kings, probably, were less important for Palermo than the monarchy itself, a symbol and embodiment of Sicily.

Notes

1 For general information on the royal festivities of eighteenth-century Sicily, see Francesco Maria Villabianca, *Le feste reali di Sicilia nel secolo XVIII* (Palermo: Giada,

1991); Maria Sofia Di Fede, 'La festa barocca a Palermo: città, architetture, istituzioni', *Espacio, Tiempo y Forma. Serie VII. Historia del Arte* 18–19 (2005–6): 49–75; and the section 'Sicilia e Sardegna', in *Le capitali della festa: Italia centrale e meridionale*, ed. Marcello Fagiolo (Rome: De Luca, 2007), 377–406.

2   Diego De Loya, *Ocaso del mejor sol en el occidente de Iberia: Noticias fúnebres en el ocaso de Carlos II* (Palermo: Real Estampa de Felix Marmio, 1701).

3   Ibid., 659.

4   Ibid., 662–9.

5   Ibid., 393 and ff.

6   Antonino Mongitore, *Il trionfo palermitano nella solenne acclamnazione del católico re delle Spagne, e di Sicilia. Filippo V. festeggiata in Palermo a 30 di Gennaro 1701* (Palermo: Felice Marino, 1701); *La felicità in trionfo per l'acclamazione di Filippo V. re delle Spagne, e di Sicilia portata su'l cuore della felice e fedelissima città di Palermo dall'illustrissimo Senato* (Palermo: Felice Marino, 1701). Palermo's Senate was a government institution composed of representatives elected from amongst the aristocratic families of the city.

7   Engraving in Mongitore, *Il trionfo*.

8   See Fernando Rodríguez de la Flor, *Emblemas: Lecturas de la imagen simbólica* (Madrid: Alianza, 1995).

9   Earl Rosenthal, '"Plus Ultra, Non Plus Ultra", and the Columnar Device of Emperor Charles V', *Journal of the Warburg and Courtauld Institutes* 34 (1971): 204–28; Earl Rosenthal, 'The Invention of the Columnar Device of Emperor Charles V at the Court of Burgundy in Flanders in 1516', *Journal of the Warburg and Courtauld Institutes* 36 (1973): 198–230; and Sandra Sider, 'Transcendent Symbols for the Habsburgs: "Plus Ultra" and the Columns of Hercules', *Emblemática* 4 (1989): 247–71.

10 This identification with Solomon takes up a traditional Sicilian form of royal representation. See Ernst Kitzinger, 'The son of David: A note on a mosaic in the Cappella Palatina in Palermo', *Studies in Late Antique, Byzantine and Medieval Western Art* 2 (2003): 1147–57.

11 Diane H. Bodart, 'La piazza quale "teatro regio" nei regni di Napoli e di Sicilia nel Seicento e nel Settecento', in *Platz und Territorium: Urbane Struktur gestaltet politische Räume*, ed. Alessandro Nova and Cornelia Jöchner (Berlin-Munich: Deutscher Kunstverlag, 2010), 223–48.

12 For a study of this Hispanicization of the image of the monarch, see José Miguel Morán Turina, ¿Felipe V de Habsburgo?, in *Sevilla y corte: Las artes y el lustro real (1729-1733)*, ed. Nicolás Morales and Fernando Quiles García (Madrid: Casa de Velázquez, 2010), 179–83. For a broader approach to the iconographic approximation of the Bourbons to the image of the Spanish Habsburgs, see *¿Louis XIV espagnol?:Madrid et Versailles, images et modèles*, ed. Gérard Sabatier and Margarita Torrione (Versailles: Centre de recherche du château de Versailles, 2009).

13 Pere Molas Ribalta, ¿Qué fue de Italia y Flandes?, in *La pérdida de Europa: La guerra de Sucesión por la Monarquía de España*, ed. Antonio Álvarez-Ossorio Alvariño et al. (Madrid: Fundación Carlos de Amberes, 2007), 693–715.

14 Stefano Tabacchi, 'L'impossibile neutralità: Il Papato, Roma e lo Stato della Chiesa durante la Guerra di Successione Spagnola', *Cheiron* 39–40 (2003): 223–43, and David Martín Marcos, 'Ideología e historiografía en torno al papel del Papado en la Guerra de Sucesión española', *Anuario Historia de la Iglesia* 19 (2010): 361–72.

15 Pietro Vitale, *Le simpatie dell'allegrezza tra Palermo capo del Regno di Sicilia e la Castiglia regia capitale della cattolica monarchia: manifestate nella presente relazione*

delle massime pompe festive de'palermitani descritta dal dottor d. Pietro Vitale (Palermo: Agostino Epiro e Forte, 1711).

16 See Geoffrey Symcox, *Victor Amadeus II: Absolutism in the Savoyard State, 1675-1730* (Berkeley: University of California Press, 1983) and Christopher Storrs, *War, Diplomacy and the Rise of Savoy, 1690-1720* (New York: Cambridge University Press, 1999).

17 Robert Oresko, 'The House of Savoy in Search for a Royal Crown in the Seventeenth Century', in *Royal and Republican Sovereignty in Early Modern Europe*, ed. Robert Oresko et al. (New York: Cambridge University Press, 1997), 272-350.

18 Elisabeth Wünsche-Werdehausen, '"La felicità in trono": L'entrata di Vittorio Amedeo II a Palermo nel 1713', *Artes* 13 (2005-2007): 361-88.

19 An interesting analysis of the Savoyard period, and particularly the early days of the reign of Victor Amadeus as King of Sicily, is found in *Sicilia 1713: Relazioni per Vittorio Amedeo di Savoia*, ed. Salvo Di Matteo (Palermo: Fondazione Lauro Chiazzese, 1994), 7-50.

20 Pietro Vitale, *La felicità in trono sull'arrivo, acclamatione, e coronationne delle reali maestà di Vittorio Amedeo Duca di Savoja, e di Anna d'Orleans da Francia, ed Inghilterra. Re', e Regina di Sicilia Gerusalemme, e Cipro: Celebrata con gli applausi di tutto il Regno tra' le pompe di Palermo reggia, e capitale descritta per ordine dell'Illustrissimo Senato palermitano dall'abbate Don Pietro Vitale secretario di esso* (Palermo: Regia Stamperia di Agostino Epiro, Stampatore di S.S.R.M., 1714).

21 Enrique Rodrigues-Moura, 'Religión y poder en la España de la Contrarreforma: Estructura y función de la leyenda de los Austria devotos de la Eucaristía', in *Austria, España y Europa: Identidades y diversidades*, ed. Manuel Maldonado Alemán (Seville: Universidad de Sevilla, 2006), 11-30.

22 Anna Coreth, *Pietas Austriaca* (West Lafayette, IN: Purdue University Press, 2004). For a further enlightening examination of the image of the pious king within the Spanish monarchy, see Antonio Álvarez-Ossorio Alvariño, 'Virtud coronada: Carlos II y la piedad de la Casa de Austria', in *Política, religión e inquisición en la España moderna: Homenaje a Joaquín Pérez Villanueva*, ed. Pedro Fernández Albadalejo et al. (Madrid: Universidad Autónoma de Madrid, 1996), 29-57.

23 Friedrich Polleross, 'Hispaniarum et Indiarum Rex: Zur Repräsentation Kaiser Karls VI. als König von Spanien', in *Denkmodelle*, ed. Jordi Jané (Tarragona: Universitat Rovira i Virgili, 2000), 121-73.

24 *Dilatar l'Impero in Italia: Asburgo e Italia nel primo Settecento*, ed. Marcello Verga (Rome: Bulzoni, 1995).

25 *Il festino della felicità nel cuore, nella bocca, en ella pompa di Palermo, sulla trionfal acclamazione di Carlo VI Imperatore, III Re delle Spagne, e di Sicilia: Stretto in breve relazione d'ordine dell'Illustrissimo Senato Palermitano* (Palermo: Regia Stamperia di Antonino Epiro, 1720).

26 Domenico Turano, *Apparato fatto in Palermo nel Collegio Imperiale di Studi da' PP. Della Compagnia di Giesu l'anno 1720 in occasione della solenne acclamazione dell'Imperatore Carlo VI, e III Re delle Spagne, e di Sicilia, descritto dal P. Domenico Turano della medesima Compagnia, cogli epigrammi, ed emblemi dell'istesso autore* (Palermo: Cristoforo d'Anselmo, 1720).

27 Giuseppe Senatore, *Giornale storico di quanto avvenne ne' due reami di Napoli, e di Sicilia l'anno 1734, e 1735: Nella conquista che ne fecero le invitte Armi di Spagna sotto la condotta del glorioso nostro Re Carlo Borbone in qualità di Generalissimo del gran monarca cattolico* (Naples: Stamperia Blasiana, 1742).

28 Pietro La Placa, *La Reggia in Trionfo per l'acclamazione, e coronazione della Sacra Real Maestà di Carlo Infante di Spagna, Re di Sicilia, Napoli e Gerusalemme, Duca di Parma, Piacenza, e Castro, Gran Principe Ereditario della Toscana ordinata dall'Eccellentissimo Senato Palermitano* (Palermo: Regia Stamperia di Antonino Epiro, 1735). See Giuseppe Lanza Tomasi, *Le feste di Carlo III (Palermo 1735 e 1738)* (Palermo: Esse, 1970), and Víctor Mínguez and Pablo González Tornel, 'La reggia in trionfo, 1735: La coronación de Carlos de Borbón en Palermo y "gli splendori della magnificenza"', *Reales Sitios*, 188 (2011): 50–67.

29 See Ernst H. Kantorowicz, '"Deus per Naturam, Deus per Gratiam": A Note on Mediaeval Political Theology', in Ernst H. Kantorowicz, *Selected Studies* (Locust Valley, NY: J.J. Augustin Publisher, 1965), 121–37.

30 Bodart, 'La piazza quale teatro regio', 223–48.

31 Ernst H. Kantorowicz, *The King's Two Bodies: A Study in Mediaeval Political Theology* (Princeton: Princeton University Press, 1957).

32 Ralph E. Giesey, *The Royal Funeral Ceremony in Renaissance France* (Geneva: Droz, 1960); and idem, *Le roi ne meurt jamais: Les obsèques royales dans la France de la Renaissance* (Paris: Flammarion, 1987).

33 Agostino Paravicini Bagliani, *Il corpo del papa* (Turin: Einaudi, 1994), 147–253.

34 Reinhard Elze, 'The Ordo for the Coronation of King Roger II of Sicily: An Example of Dating from Internal Evidence', in *Coronations: Medieval and Early Modern Monarchic Ritual*, ed. János M. Bak (Berkeley: University of California Press, 1990), 165–78.

35 See Thomas Dittelbach, *Rex imago Christi: Der Dom von Monreale: Bildsprachen und Zeremoniell in Mosaikkunst und Architektur* (Wiesbaden: Reichert Verlag, 2003).

36 Ps.88.22

37 Mirko Vagnoni, 'Evocazioni davidiche nella regalità di Guglielmo II di Sicilia', in *Hagiologica: Studi per Réginald Grégoire*, ed. Alessandra Bartolomei Romagnoli et al. (Fabriano: Monastero San Silvestro Abate, 2012), 771–87.

38 Regarding the proclamations and the cult of the sovereign in the Middle Ages, see Ernst H. Kantorowicz, *Laudes Regiae: A Study in Liturgical Acclamations and Mediaeval Ruler Worship* (Berkeley–Los Angeles: University of California Press, 1946).

39 See, with a respective bibliography for each case, for the Carolingians, Ildar Garipzanov, 'David, Imperator Augustus, Gratia Dei Rex: Communication and Propaganda in Carolingian Royal Iconography', in *Monotheistic Kingship: The Medieval Variants*, ed. Aziz Al-Azmeh and János M. Bak (Budapest: Central European University, Department of Medieval Studies, 2004), 89–118; and for the Ottonians, Ludger Körntgen, 'König und Priester: Das sakrale Königtum der Ottonen zwischen Herrschaftstheologie, Herrschaftsraxis und Heilssorge', in *Die Ottonen: Kunst, Architektur, Geschichte*, ed. Klaus Gereon Beuckers, Johannes Cramer and Michael Imhof (Petersberg: Michael Imhof, 2006), 51–61. For an approach to the sacralization of the monarchy, see Marc Bloch, *Les rois thaumaturges: Étude sur le caractère surnaturel attribué à la puissance royale particulièrement en France et en Angleterre* (Paris: Gallimard, 2002) and *Per me reges regnant: La regalità sacra nell'Europa medieval*, ed. Franco Cardini and Maria Saltarelli (Rimini: Il Cerchio, 2002).

40 Adelina Sarrión Mora, 'Identificación de la dinastía con la confesión católica', in *La monarquía de Felipe III: La Casa del Rey*, ed. José Martínez Millán and Maria Antonietta Visceglia (Madrid: Fundación Mapfre, 2008), 246–302.

41 Thomas J. Dandelet, 'Searching for the New Constantine: Early Modern Rome as a Spanish Imperial City', in *Embodiments of Power*, ed. Gary B. Cohen and Franz A. J. Szabo (New York: Berghahn Books, 2008), 191–202. The image of Constantine

remained very much alive in early modern Rome. See Jack Freiberg, 'In the Sign of the Cross: The Image of Constantine in the Art of Counter-Reformation Rome', in *Piero della Francesca and his legacy*, ed. Marilyn Aronberg Lavin (Hanover: University Press of New England, 1995), 67–87.

42 Paul Kléber Monod, *The Power of Kings: Monarchy and Religion in Europe, 1589–1715* (New Haven, CT: Yale University Press, 1999).

43 Helen Watanabe-O'Kelly, 'Early Modern European Festivals: Politics and Performance, Event and Record', in *Court Festivals of the European Renaissance. Art, Politics and Performance*, ed. John R. Mulryne and Elizabeth Goldring (Aldershot: Ashgate, 2002), 15–25.

44 Ibid.

45 Marie-Claude Canova-Green, 'Preface', in *Writing Royal Entries in Early Modern Europe*, ed. Marie-Claude Canova-Green et al. (Turnhout: Brepols, 2013), xi–xviii.

46 On Bova, see Teresa Augello, *La Sicilia nelle incisioni del Bova* (Palermo: Giada, 1983). On Vasi, see Martine Boiteux, 'L'effimero e il servizio del principe: Giuseppe Vasi: Palermo-Napoli-Roma', in *Il Settecento e il suo doppio: Rococò e Neoclassicismo: Stili e tendenze europee nella Sicilia dei viceré*, ed. Mariny Guttilla (Palermo: Kalós, 2008), 375–405.

47 Helen Watanabe-O'Kelly, 'The Early Modern Festival Book: Function and Form', in *Europa Triumphans: Court and Civic Festivals in Early Modern Europe*, vol. 1, ed. John R. Mulryne, Helen Watanabe-O'Kelly and Margaret Shewring (Aldershot: Ashgate, 2004), 3–17.

48 *Festivals and Ceremonies: A Bibliography of Works Relating to Court, Civic and Religious Festivals in Europe, 1500 – 1800*, ed. Helen Watanabe-O'Kelly and Anne Simon (London: Mansell, 2000).

49 Ibid., 118–20.

50 Ibid., 120.

51 Laurie Nussdorfer, 'Politics and the People of Rome', in *Rome, Amsterdam: Two Growing Cities in Seventeenth-Century Europe*, ed. Peter van Kessel and Elisja Schulte (Amsterdam: Amsterdam University Press, 1997), 165–78. See also Laurie Nussdorfer, *Civic Politics in the Rome of Urban VIII* (Princeton: Princeton University Press, 1992).

52 Laurie Nussdorfer, 'The Politics of Space in Early Modern Rome', *Memoirs of the American Academy in Rome* 42 (1997): 161–86.

53 Maria Luisa Madonna, 'Palermo nel '500, la rifondazione della "Città Felice"', *Psicon* 7 (1976): 40–65, and Marcello Fagiolo and Maria Luisa Madonna, *Il Teatro del Sole: La rifondazione di Palermo nel cinquecento e l'idea della città barocca* (Rome: Officina Edizioni, 1981).

54 Laurie Nussdorfer, 'The Vacant See: Ritual and Protest in Early Modern Rome', *The Sixteenth Century Journal* 18 (1987): 173–89.

3

The evolution of the British coronation rite, 1761–1953

Nicholas Dixon

British coronation ceremonial has long been presented by its defenders and critics alike as an elaborate vestige of a long-departed era. In 1821, the clergyman George Croly celebrated King George IV's coronation as a 'Ritual bequeathed through a thousand years', while the Unitarian writer Harriet Martineau wrote that the rites for Queen Victoria's coronation of 1838 were 'offensive as offered to the God of the nineteenth century in the western world'.[1] The notion that the ritual performed in Westminster Abbey, originating as it did in the tenth century, was essentially anachronistic was also promoted by historians throughout the twentieth century. Percy Schramm, in his seminal *History of the English Coronation* of 1937, ended his account by considering the alterations made for William and Mary's coronation in 1689 by Bishop Compton of London, the most important of which was the addition of a presentation of a Bible to the monarchs as the culmination of the service. Schramm wrote, 'With these alterations ... we may close our survey of the history of the coronation rite, for the *ordo* of 1689 has remained in use until to-day.' He added, 'The only subsequent changes concern details of minor importance, on which there is no need to linger now.'[2] Yet the history of British coronation ritual did not end in 1689, and is not the product of medieval and early modern centuries alone. Nor were subsequent changes minor. From the mid-eighteenth century, successive generations of clergy continued to revise the liturgy, gradually altering its religious and political import.

Within a European context, this modern process of liturgical revision was unusual. Possibly the closest parallel was the Danish coronation rite, which was discontinued after 1840 following 'considerable alterations and omissions'.[3] In other European monarchies, ancient rites were generally maintained intact before their disappearance. Leopold II was crowned Holy Roman Emperor in 1790 in eighth-century robes, the emperor adapting 'his coiffure and beard to the style of Charlemagne'.[4] Likewise, the late medieval French coronation rite was retained 'with small and unimportant variations' until the French Revolution.[5] However, when the rite was revived for the

---

* I am most grateful to Brian Young, Andrew Thompson and Jonathan Spangler for their helpful comments and suggestions.

coronation of Charles X in 1825, there were, as Richard Jackson notes, significant omissions and abridgements.[6] Comparative studies of coronations have seldom taken notice of the eighteenth, nineteenth and twentieth centuries, as the majority of European monarchies dispensed with or declined to adopt such rites in these centuries. Accordingly, János Bak's volume *Coronations* focuses on the medieval and early modern periods.[7] The British coronation rite represents a significant case study in the response of monarchies to the shifting political and religious climate of the post-eighteenth-century period.

In a British context, historians of royal ritual have tended to belittle the liturgical contribution of the Anglican clergy. The standard account of changes to British royal ritual in the modern era remains David Cannadine's 1983 contribution to a volume of essays entitled *The Invention of Tradition*. Cannadine makes two significant claims: that the 'meaning' of a ritual was primarily dependent on its broader social and political context as opposed to its actual content, and that rituals such as coronations were inept and farcical for most of the nineteenth century. Underplaying the religious element of these occasions, Cannadine also argues that prior to the later nineteenth century there was 'a lack of interest in ritual on the part of the clergy, who were either indifferent or hostile'. He represents the coronation as a pageant that constituted a 'repeated ritual' with a 'basic text' that was 'essentially unaltered'. Thus, for Cannadine, the coronation liturgy itself and its evolution do not merit notice; what matters most is the '"thick" descriptive context' in which liturgy and ceremonial were 'performed'.[8] A more recent historian, Roy Strong, does acknowledge the work of the modern revisers of the liturgy, but only in so far as they 'cheerfully butchered' an 'ancient liturgical rite' before some of the resulting damage was gradually undone during the twentieth century.[9]

This chapter takes a different approach, viewing the coronation liturgy as an evolving tradition not beholden to any ancient archetype, and affected but by no means defined by its modern context. Instead of judging the efforts of modern revisers by rigid ecclesiological standards, it seeks to understand why they made the changes they did and with what effects. Focusing on the texts of coronation rituals as opposed to their outward aspect, the chapter describes a complex process of liturgical transformation. This process may broadly be divided into two phases: one of Protestant reformation during the eighteenth and nineteenth centuries, and one of Anglo-Catholic restoration during the twentieth. These phases are minutely recorded in the papers of various archbishops at Lambeth Palace Library. Of particular interest are a series of coronation orders with handwritten emendations by successive archbishops and a significant body of correspondence bearing upon the process of revision. From these sources, it is possible to trace the modern evolution of the rite, and to consider its implications for the evolving self-conception of monarchy and church.[10]

Protestant Reformation

In 1761, many elements of the medieval English coronation rite survived in the British rite. The English rite originated in the coronation of Athelstan in 924, and was largely preserved after the Norman Conquest. Significant revisions were made in the twelfth and fourteenth centuries, the latter revision being contained in the *Liber Regalis*, a liturgical manuscript preserved in Westminster Abbey.[11] Among the principal features of the *Liber Regalis* liturgy were the recognition of the monarch by the acclamations of the congregation; the monarch's oath to rule justly and uphold the Church's privileges; the anointing of the monarch in five places; their symbolic investiture with a robe, a sword, bracelets, a mantle, a ring, a sceptre and a rod; and the crowning of the monarch.[12] The Latin prayers that accompanied this series of rituals were translated into English for the 1603 ceremony, and heavily abridged for the coronation of James II in 1685.[13] In 1689, the ceremony was inserted into an Anglican communion service liturgy, and the oath rendered distinctively Protestant in character.[14] Despite such changes, and the Acts of Union between England and Scotland (1706-7), the translated medieval prayers and rituals of anointing and investiture largely remained. On the whole, the coronation liturgy represented a conspicuous survival from the pre-Reformation era.

By convention, the archbishop of Canterbury adapted the liturgy for each coronation, subject to the approval of the Privy Council. The archbishop would consult orders for previous coronations and make handwritten amendments to them. The first major revision to the rite after 1689 was undertaken in advance of King George III's coronation in 1761 by Archbishop Thomas Secker, who was especially diligent in studying older liturgies. By his own account, he obtained 'several former Coronation Offices, which was difficult, because none had been printed, till that of Geo[rge] 2[nd] & compared them with each other, & with printed Accounts of Coronations, & with such Extracts from m[anu]s[cript]s, as I could get.' Secker also cursorily set out his understanding of the previous history of the rite: 'The Offices after the Reformation were taken, with some necessary changes, from those before, but leaving as in [James] 1[st] the Latin Beginnings in the Margin. At the Revolution great Alterations were made, much for the better: & the Delivery of the Bible was added.' Hence for Secker the coronation was not immutable tradition; it was an evolving entity susceptible of improvement. Regarding his own changes, Secker only wrote of having 'endeavoured to shorten the prayers a little' and 'to avoid ungraceful Repetitions of the same words'.[15] But Secker's changes were not simply stylistic, and accorded with the religious and political orthodoxies of the time. In many respects, he was belatedly reconciling the coronation rite with the principles of the Protestant Reformation of two centuries earlier, as well as the Glorious Revolution of 1688.

First, Secker removed references to the Roman Catholic doctrine of justification by works, replacing them with affirmations of the Anglican belief in justification by faith. Before 1761, the prayer accompanying the delivery of the ring had addressed monarchs thus: 'as You are this day Consecrated Head of this Kingdom and People, so being Rich in Faith and abounding in good works, You may reign with Him who is the King of Kings'. After Secker's revision, which derived from Ephesians 1:13–14, it read: 'as You are this day solemnly invested in the Government of this earthly kingdom, so may You be sealed with that spirit of Promise, which is the Earnest of an heavenly Inheritance, and reign with Him who is the blessed and only Potentate'.[16] Justification by faith was now the promoted belief, and a clear distinction between divine and kingly authority was made. In the coronation of Queen Charlotte, an allusion to her 'piety and good works' was superseded by a reference to the 'powerful and mild Influence of her Piety and Virtue'.[17] The new phraseology was redolent of contemporary funerary epitaphs, and the counterbalancing of the adjectives 'powerful' and 'mild' reflected the eighteenth-century Anglican belief that religious sentiment was most beneficial when it was moderate, reasonable and devoid of 'enthusiasm'.[18]

Second, Secker magnified the role of Providence in proceedings. This accorded with Anglicans' general scepticism concerning post-apostolic miracles and their belief in a distant, indirect divine overruling of human affairs. In their application to the monarchy, these assumptions militated against the seventeenth-century belief that kings were directly appointed and given absolute power by God, and instead were consonant with constitutional ideas of limited monarchy deriving from the Glorious Revolution.[19] As Bishop Robert Lowth put it, '[g]overnment in general is the ordinance of God: the particular Form of Government is the ordinance of man'.[20] Hence, at the investiture of the monarch with the sword, the phrase 'sanctify and bless thy servant King GEORGE' became 'direct and support thy servant King GEORGE'.[21] Similarly, at the crowning, the petition to 'Bless and Sanctifie this thy Servant GEORGE' was superseded by '[l]ook down upon this thy Servant GEORGE'.[22] Most intriguingly, an invocation of 'the gracious Assistance of God's infinite goodness' was replaced with the phrase 'the merciful Superintendency of the Divine Providence'.[23] These words appear to have derived from a work of 1701 by the nonconformist botanist Nehemiah Grew entitled *Cosmologia Sacra*, which was partially dedicated to Secker's predecessor Thomas Tenison and stated that '[t]he Divine Providence, which hath a visible respect to the Being, and Condition of every Man: is yet more observable, in its Superintendency over Societies or Publick States.'[24] The probable interpolation of nonconformist natural theology in a medieval prayer by Secker, who had himself been educated in a dissenting academy, indicates the extent to which he was prepared to alter the import of the coronation.

A further change reflected the eighteenth-century Anglican concern for the extrinsic utility of the established church. In the benediction, Secker added a prayer for 'a pious and learned and useful Clergy'.[25] This emphasis was characteristic of contemporary Anglican thought, which downplayed *a priori* justifications for institutional Christianity such as the apostolic succession. Bishop Warburton of Gloucester had famously argued that 'THE TRUE END FOR WHICH RELIGION IS ESTABLISHED IS, NOT TO PROVIDE FOR THE TRUE FAITH, BUT FOR CIVIL UTILITY'.[26] William Paley would write, in a similar vein, that '[t]he authority ... of a church-establishment is founded in its utility', and that its 'single end' was 'the preservation and communication of religious knowledge'.[27] Taken together, Secker's revisions reflected a new emphasis on the beliefs that distinguished Anglicans from Roman Catholics: justification by faith rather than justification by works, a providential as opposed to a miraculous understanding of divine intervention and a utilitarian, rather than apostolic, basis for clerical authority. In making such alterations, Secker represented a Protestant confessional church and state that remained anti-Catholic to the point of excluding Roman Catholic peers from the coronation ceremony.[28]

The period following the death of George III in 1820 witnessed three coronations in quick succession: George IV's in 1821, William IV's in 1831 and Victoria's in 1838.

The most significant modification that occurred during this period was the shortening of the rite. In 1821, George IV held the most lavish coronation ever recorded, having stipulated that 'the same rules & regulations sh[oul]d be as closely as possible observ'd, as at the last Coronation'.[29] However, Archbishop Charles Manners-Sutton abridged three prayers accompanying the investiture of the monarch with various items of regalia. In so doing, he adhered to the contemporary Anglican concern for an enlightened but limited mode of kingship regulated by religious duty, what might be termed a 'divine responsibility' monarchy.[30] Thus, at the presentation of the sceptre, a violent exhortation to the King to 'Break the Jaws of the Wicked, and pluck the Spoil out of his Teeth' was excised and replaced by the milder words 'Punish the Wicked, protect the Oppressed'.[31] Manners-Sutton also removed passages which suggested that the King was directly, as opposed to providentially, appointed by God. The words at the crowning 'may You be also a Crown of Glory in the hand of the Lord, and a Royal Diadem in the hand of Your God' disappeared. So too did a lengthy comparison between the British monarch's coronation and the presentation of 'the Book of the Law' to the Old Testament King of Judah, Jehoash, that had accompanied the presentation of a Bible since the ceremony of 1689 in order to emphasize the monarchy's adherence to biblical precedent.[32] Interestingly, the devisers of the liturgy for the coronation of King Charles X of France in 1825 adopted a similar approach, abridging prayers and removing passages that drew parallels with Old Testament kingship.[33]

The process of abridgement accelerated with Archbishop William Howley's revisions of 1831, which also incorporated one important textual change. At the investiture with the sword, a petition that the monarch would 'represent our Lord Jesus Christ in this Life' was altered to a prayer that he would 'faithfully serve our Lord Jesus Christ in this life'.[34] Thus, the monarch was now Christ's servant rather than his representative, a providential agent as opposed to a ruler by divine right. This alteration coincided with the modification of the anointing of both king and queen, which was now on the head and hands only, and no longer on the breast.[35] Additionally, the king was no longer girded with a sword representing justice or a priestly stole.[36] These drastic changes to the anointing and investiture belied a lack of interest in the full array of medieval regalia, which was amplified by William IV's wearing of an admiral's uniform under his coronation robe.[37] When viewed in the light of Howley's textual revision, they indicate a concurrence with the circumscribed vision of kingship suggested by Manners-Sutton's abridgements. The order for the coronation of Queen Victoria in 1838, which essentially followed the liturgy of 1831, was in large part the product of the early nineteenth-century Anglican attachment to Protestant doctrine and limited monarchy.[38]

Such revision had not gone unnoticed in an era when many Anglicans were becoming increasingly hostile to any prospect of liturgical innovation.[39] The *Christian Remembrancer*, a periodical established by Anglican clergymen, complained that the liturgy had now '*deteriorated* from that performed at the coronation of ... William IV.; as the service then used was a departure *for the worse* from that of the preceding monarch, which was *the ancient rite* in all its fulness and majestic beauty'.[40] In this spirit, Strong describes Victoria's coronation as 'the last of the botched coronations, rituals put together by those who had no knowledge of its evolution, nor had any idea of correct liturgical structure'.[41] But the coronation of 1838 is better seen as the last of the reformed coronations, rituals devised by clergy who were perfectly aware of the history and structure of the rite, but believed it possible to render it more compatible with the Anglican tradition as they saw it.

Anglo-Catholic restoration

The ecclesiological gulf that separated the coronation of 1838 from the next coronation, that of Edward VII in 1902, was considerable. Victoria's reign had witnessed a revival in Catholic-inspired belief and liturgical practice in the Church of England in the form of the Oxford or Tractarian movement, leading to the formation of an influential Anglo-Catholic wing within the Church. Anglo-Catholics laid great emphasis on those aspects of the Anglican tradition that indicated continuity with a pre-Reformation, medieval past. As the nineteenth century progressed, many pressed for the revival of pre-Reformation Catholic ritual as a component of Anglican worship.[42] Hence the coronation rite was an object of their particular interest, and received significant attention from liturgical scholars for the first time.[43] In 1847, the Tractarian clergyman William Maskell, later a convert to Roman Catholicism, edited the texts of a series of coronation orders in the third volume of his *Monumenta Ritualia Ecclesiae Anglicanae*. He wrote, 'I cannot in candour pretend to conceal my regret, that some changes, scarcely called for, were introduced upon the occasion of K. William IV. But that was a time when the outcry was extreme against any thing which bore the impress of antiquity; and it is moreover probable that there were then reasons, why certain alterations should be made, which now might not be regarded as of much weight or value.'[44] To another liturgical scholar, H.A. Wilson, writing half a century later, the coronation was like 'some ancient fabric, which has suffered much from the work of ignorant builders, destroying where they sought to improve, but which yet remains a monument of singular interest, demanding not only taste and skill, but regard for its whole past history in any architect to whose care it can safely be committed'.[45]

By this time, John Wickham Legg and his son Leopold were emerging as the pre-eminent British scholars of coronations. John Wickham Legg was an eminent medical doctor who retired prematurely following an attack of rheumatism in the 1880s. For the rest of his life, he devoted himself to liturgical studies, which was a burgeoning field towards the end of the nineteenth century. Among his published editions were *Three Coronation Orders* (1900) and *The Coronation Order of King James I* (1902).[46] Leopold Wickham Legg was equally interested in coronations, and pursued his enquiries concerning them as a fellow of New College, Oxford. In 1901, he published *English Coronation Records*, a comprehensive – and still unsurpassed – edition of surviving coronation orders. While John Wickham Legg was resistant to liturgical revision and ritualist revivalism, his son took a resolutely Anglo-Catholic attitude.[47] Leopold Wickham Legg saw the pre-Reformation coronation orders as constituting an archetype that the revisions of recent centuries had only served to mutilate. He wrote that '[t]he coronation of Queen Victoria shows the ceremonies at the lowest ebb they have yet reached', and, in response, published a proposed new order in advance of Edward VII's coronation, intended as 'a scheme of restoring to this ancient and magnificent pageant some of its pristine splendours'.[48] This proposal undid most of the changes of the eighteenth and nineteenth centuries, restoring the older form of many prayers.[49]

However, in 1902, the liturgists' moment had not yet come.[50] The ageing liberal Archbishop Frederick Temple had little sympathy for Anglo-Catholic revivalism, and, according to his successor, 'in his rugged way, disregarded, or despised history, tradition or precedent'.[51] Temple proposed a change to the anointing more drastic than any hitherto made by his post-Reformation predecessors. He suggested that, following biblical precedent, the monarch should be anointed on the head only, complaining that '[t]he multiplied anointing is really a part of that ceremonialism which ... wearied our forefathers before the Reformation.'[52] Temple's wishes were not fulfilled because King Edward VII, an admirer of Roman Catholic ritual, desired the restoration of the triple anointing.[53] In the event, the coronation of 1902 was abridged on account of the King's illness, and eccentrically combined piecemeal restorations of ancient usage with some drastic departures from precedent. Temple reinstated a medieval introit, collect and prayer at the crowning as well as the girding of the monarch with a sword. But he also relinquished his medieval right to crown the Queen to the archbishop of York, removed the sermon and omitted the Litany and Ten Commandments.[54] The disjointed result pleased neither Protestant nor Anglo-Catholic opinion. Lodges of the Orange Order, a pan-Protestant fraternity, protested against the lack of the Ten Commandments, a key element in the post-Reformation Anglican communion service.[55] Additionally, Leopold Wickham Legg deplored the unprecedented crowning of the Queen by an Archbishop of York.[56] The more advanced Anglo-Catholics lamented the absence of bishops' mitres and incense from proceedings.[57] Revisions to the coronation order were no longer the province of a small group of clergymen; they were now a matter of public debate, carried on in newspapers, pamphlets and letters to high-ranking clergy.[58] However, public interest in revisions to the rite appears to have waned at subsequent coronations.

With George V's coronation in 1911, the tide began gradually to turn in favour of restoration, as archbishops increasingly left the task of revising the liturgy to Anglo-Catholic scholar-clergymen. A key figure in this process was Claude Jenkins, the librarian at Lambeth Palace. Temple's successor as archbishop, Randall Davidson, asked Jenkins to study the history of the ceremony and devise suggestions for its improvement. Jenkins shared Leopold Wickham Legg's view that Victoria's coronation was the 'nadir' of the rite. According to his own account, his proposals were 'constructed largely with a view to undoing B[isho]p Compton's work for William & Mary & A[rch]b[isho]p Secker's for George III; Compton an ex Guards officer having subintroduced [sic] almost every military passage in the New Testament & Secker preferring the English of Nehemiah Grew & Samuel Johnson to that of the Seventeenth century.' Yet Jenkins's bold attempt to remove all traces of Secker's revisions from the liturgy met with opposition from the Dean of Westminster, J. Armitage Robinson, who was charged by Davidson with reviewing Jenkins's proposals. He told Jenkins:

[T]his Coronation Rite, like the Abbey, is part of the history of England and the result of a process of growth. In a proposed 'restoration' we must not remove all the date-markings of the centuries. Thus ... you point out that Archbishop Secker substituted 'the merciful superintendency of the Divine Providence' for 'the gracious assistance of God's infinite goodness' and you wish to put back the old. There is no liturgical point at issue, and it must not be done. You don't want to take the monuments out of the Abbey, do you?

Robinson, who had also been consulted in 1902, further stated, 'I managed to get back some of the old last time and we are getting back some more of it now. But we must not disturb people more than is necessary, and we may be quite content to leave something to our successors'.[59] Accordingly, the 1911 rite incorporated modest restorations such as an ancient prayer at the crowning, but largely left eighteenth- and nineteenth-century revisions intact.[60]

The two remaining coronations of the twentieth century, those of George VI and Elizabeth II, bore the imprint of Edward Ratcliff, Ely Professor of Divinity at the University of Cambridge, who was consulted by both Archbishop Cosmo Lang in 1937 and Archbishop Geoffrey Fisher in 1953.[61] Ratcliff was more steeped in Anglo-Catholicism than the Wickham Leggs or Jenkins, so much so that he eventually came to abandon any pretence of conventional Anglicanism. According to a fellow liturgical scholar, A.H. Couratin:

> As a schoolboy [Ratcliff] attended a church in South London which was notoriously 'Anglo-Catholic'. Here the Communion service of the Book of Common Prayer was celebrated with all the ceremonial of High Mass of the Roman rite, and the *Canon Missae* was silently interpolated under the cover of the elaborate music. Whatever may have been the devotional value of such a performance, it could not fail to arouse the intellectual curiosity of a highly intelligent schoolboy. Ratcliff never escaped from the influence of this upbringing. [...] His wide and unprejudiced study of Anglican history and theology convinced him that the traditional Anglo-Catholic case was indefensible; and at the end of his life he confessed that he had never really been an Anglican at all. He felt no theological attachment to the Church of England, and was indeed preparing to leave it, and to seek communion with the Orthodox, when he died.[62]

Ratcliff's lack of sympathy with the Protestant aspects of Anglicanism was reflected in his revisions. His attitude to the Protestant accretions in the coronation ritual may be gleaned from his comments on the presentation of the Bible added in 1689. This, in his view, was 'clearly an anti-Roman Catholic gesture', which could be delegated to a 'non-Anglican minister', separated from the investiture and made a mere coda to the oath-taking. Ratcliff stated, 'Should there be any protest at such a change of place on the part of "the Protestant underworld" (as the late Bishop Henson termed it) the answer is obvious: the first thing presented to the Queen at her Coronation is the Bible.'[63]

In 1937, in the wake of the Abdication Crisis, there was little time for Ratcliff to undertake a thorough restoration, and he managed only to restore the ancient practice of anointing the monarch's hands, breast and head in that order, signifying glory, knowledge and strength.[64] The ceremony made a strong impression on George VI, who wrote to Archbishop Lang of how, though it was an 'ordeal', he felt that he was 'being helped all the time by Someone Else'.[65] The *Times* newspaper, in an editorial, laid emphasis on the spiritual dimension of the ceremony, and especially the anointing:

> As the golden canopy was held over King Edward's chair, and the Archbishop went in under it to the King, bearing the consecrated oil, as into a tabernacle, it seemed that these two men were alone with God, performing an act greater than they knew, more solemn than any person present could hope to understand.[66]

In 1953, with greater time at his disposal, Ratcliff was able to devote his efforts to expunging all traces of the eighteenth century from the coronation. A number of prayers were restored to their original medieval form, while the medieval ritual of presenting bracelets or 'armills', signifying sincerity and wisdom, to the monarch was revived. The presentation of the Bible was moved to an earlier point in the service, and unprecedentedly given to the Moderator of the Church of Scotland. A reference to 'good works' removed by Secker was restored, while his invocation of 'the merciful superintendency of the divine Providence' finally disappeared.[67] Of the latter phrase, Ratcliff wrote: 'The phrase is post-Compton; it is somewhat pompous; and the series of sibilants gives it a distressing sound!'[68] In the benediction, post-Reformation prayers for 'a faithful Senate' and an 'obedient commonalty' were replaced by petitions for 'faithful Parliaments' and 'dutiful citizens'.[69] Here the liturgy was uncharacteristically modern. The term 'citizen', in the egalitarian sense, would have been anathema to the Church of Manners-Sutton and Howley's time, which deplored the French Revolution and expressed grave reservations concerning the Reform Bill of 1832.[70]

Nevertheless, the coronation of 1953 represented the apex of Anglo-Catholic restorationism. Ratcliff wrote with satisfaction, 'How closely related to the classical English Coronation rite the modern Service, in its latest revision, continues to be, may be seen from a comparison of it with the rubrical directions of *Liber Regalis*'.[71] In spite of this the monarch's coronation oath, as amended in 1937, contained an undertaking to 'maintain in the *United Kingdom* the Protestant Reformed Religion established by law'.[72] Yet this form of words rendered the precise nature of the obligations imposed by the oath ambiguous, given that there were no longer established churches afforded legal privileges by the state in Wales or Northern Ireland.[73] Moreover, comparatively few distinctively Protestant elements of the service remained intact. The main concern of twentieth-century revisers had been to restore medieval prayers, items of regalia and forms of anointing. Concomitantly, post-Reformation forms of prayer, the Ten Commandments, the Litany and the Sermon had all disappeared, while the presentation of the Bible had been made less prominent.

This dramatic reordering was made possible by the demise of the Protestant confessional assumptions that had underpinned the rite during the eighteenth and nineteenth centuries. By the 1950s, bishops considered themselves far less bound than their predecessors to the principles of the Royal Supremacy and the Reformation. Under the influence of Anglo-Catholicism, the Church hierarchy had, during the first half of the twentieth century, gradually come to favour the looser relationship with the state manifested in the formation of the Church Assembly in 1919. They also generally supported liturgical reforms that would restore pre-Reformation prayers and rituals to the Anglican tradition, as exemplified by the new Prayer Book rejected by Parliament in 1928.[74] Furthermore, many of the Church hierarchy now hesitated to characterize the Church of England as 'Protestant'.[75] The British monarchy and state, for their part, were no longer wedded to the promotion of an exclusive Protestant Anglicanism.[76] This was not only because of the disestablishment of the Church in Ireland and Wales but also due to the advent of self-governing British dominions and Commonwealth realms, whereby the Queen became the head of state of a more religiously diverse group of nations than ever before.[77] Although Protestantism had contributed much to the coronation rite's development, it was now increasingly obscured at such occasions of national importance.

By 1953, monarchy, with all of its ancient regalia restored, had recovered the transcendence denied it by eighteenth- and nineteenth-century revisers, not in the seventeenth-century sense of possessing absolute power but rather in its absolute detachment from temporal concerns and identification with the nation as a community. In an influential article of 1953, the sociologists Edward Shils and Michael Young argued that the coronation of Elizabeth II was an 'act of national communion' whereby the monarch had promised to 'abide by the moral standards of society', and the service had reinforced 'their supremacy above the personality of the Sovereign'. The monarchy was 'protected from the full blast of destructiveness by its very *powerlessness*'.[78] From a contrasting vantage point, Archbishop Fisher advanced a similar interpretation of the rite in a sermon of 1953:

> The great solemnity of the Coronation means that the Queen comes to accept her temporal kingdom, power, and glory from God.... The executive power, the power to rule and govern, to order and compel, has been steadily taken from our monarchs. But this diminution of temporal power has given to the Sovereign the possibility of a spiritual power far more exalted and far more searching in its demands ... She comes to seek a consecration to the hardest and loveliest of all forms of power: 'lo, I am among you as one that serveth' – to that ministry of sacrifice she gives herself.
>
> And there is the glory of her temporal kingdom, which is at once the Queen's glory and ours, ours because it is hers and hers because it is ours. It comes from the interaction, under God, of Queen and people in a joint pursuit of all things true and lovely and of good report.[79]

Conclusion

This chapter has described two important phases of revision to the British coronation rite: Protestant reformation in the eighteenth and nineteenth centuries, and Anglo-Catholic restoration in the twentieth century. Both of these phases left their mark on the coronation rite, demonstrating the capacity of the tradition to evolve after 1689. At the heart of such successive revisions were the questions of whether the Church of England was to be conceived of primarily in Protestant or pre-Reformation terms, and whether monarchy was to be seen as transcendent or limited. The solutions to these questions arrived at by successive revisers tell us much about how the leadership of the Church of England understood both itself and the state. In Secker's revisions of 1761, a concern to harmonize the coronation rite with Protestant theology as well as a providential and limited understanding of monarchy was apparent. Such an approach was also adopted, more in abridgement than innovation, by Manners-Sutton and Howley in the early nineteenth century. But in the twentieth century, Protestant accretions were dramatically reversed as the concerns of Anglo-Catholic liturgical scholarship took priority, lending a more determinedly antiquated character to the service.

We may trace in this continuous liturgical rearrangement not only the ascendancy and decline of Protestant confessionalism in Britain, but also the gradual circumscription of the monarchy's political role. Instead of remaining a protean phenomenon responsive to political and religious change, as the coronation rite had been in the eighteenth century, the ceremony came to be considered essentially static and immovable, a self-conscious anachronism. As such, it contributed to the modern perception of monarchy as an upholder of tradition devoid of genuine political power. Whether this antiquarian and Anglo-Catholic approach to the rite will satisfy the devisers of the next coronation remains to be seen. We may, however, be certain that their revisions will reflect the concerns of their time, and contribute to a continuous, and often contradictory, process of evolution.

Notes

1 George Croly, *The Coronation: Observations on the Public Life of the King* (London: J. Warren, 1821), 56; Harriet Martineau, *Autobiography*, vol. 2 (London: Smith, Elder, 1877), 128.
2 Percy Ernest Schramm, *A History of the English Coronation*, trans. Leopold G. Wickham Legg (Oxford: Clarendon Press, 1937), 102–3. Paul Bradshaw writes that from 1689 to 1838 'changes in the rite were relatively few, apart of course from the disappearance of the '"joint" character' of William and Mary's coronation: Paul Bradshaw, 'Coronations from the Eighteenth to the Twentieth Centuries', in *Coronations Past, Present and Future*, ed. Paul Bradshaw et al. (Cambridge: Grove Books, 1997), 22.
3 Reginald Maxwell Woolley, *Coronation Rites* (Cambridge: Cambridge University Press, 1915), 149.
4 Ibid., 125.
5 Ibid., 105.
6 Richard A. Jackson, *Vive le Roi! A History of the French Coronation from Charles V to Charles X* (Chapel Hill: University of North Carolina Press, 1984), 193–7.
7 *Coronations: Medieval and Early Modern Monarchic Ritual*, ed. János M. Bak (Berkeley: University of California Press, 1990).
8 David Cannadine, 'The Context, Performance and Meaning of Ritual: The British Monarchy and the "Invention of Tradition", c. 1820–1977', in *The Invention of Tradition*, ed. Eric Hobsbawm and Terence Ranger (Cambridge: Cambridge University Press, 1983), 103–20. For a critique of Cannadine's argument, see Walter L. Arnstein, 'Queen

Victoria opens Parliament: The Disinvention of Tradition', *Historical Research* 63, no. 151 (1990): 178–94.
9   Roy Strong, *Coronation: A History of Kingship and the British Monarchy* (London: Harper Collins, 2005), 378, 471, 481, 486–8. Cf. David Sturdy, '"Continuity" versus "Change": Historians and English Coronations of the Medieval and Early Modern Periods', in *Coronations*, 243; Bradshaw, 'Coronations from the Eighteenth to the Twentieth Centuries', 27–30.
10 On the non-liturgical aspects of British coronations in the period up to 1838, see Nicholas Dixon, 'The Church of England and the Coronation Rite, 1761-1838', *Church History* 90, no. 1 (2021): 98–116.
11 *English Coronation Records*, ed. Leopold G. Wickham Legg (Westminster: Archibald Constable, 1901), xviii–xix, 3–42; Christopher E. Hohler, 'Some Service-Books of the Later Saxon Church', in *Tenth-Century Studies: Essays in Commemoration of the Millennium of the Council of Winchester and Regularis Concordia*, ed. David Parsons (London: Phillimore, 1975), 67–9.
12 *English Coronation Records*, 81–130.
13 *The Coronation Order of King James I*, ed. John G. Wickham Legg (London: F.E. Robinson, 1902); *English Coronation Records*, 287–316.
14 *English Coronation Records*, 317–42.
15 Lambeth Palace Library, London (hereafter: LPL), Thomas Secker Papers, MS 1130, fol. 172, Thomas Secker's account of the coronation of George III. On Secker, see Robert G. Ingram, *Religion, Reform and Modernity in the Eighteenth Century: Thomas Secker and the Church of England* (Woodbridge: Boydell & Brewer, 2007).
16 LPL, MS 1082, 45, Order of George II's coronation amended in Thomas Secker's hand; *The Form and Order of the Service that is to be Performed, and of the Ceremonies that are to be Observed, in the Coronation of Their Majesties King George III. and Queen Charlotte, in the Abbey Church of S. Peter, Westminster on Tuesday the 22d of September, 1761* (London: Mark Baskett, 1761), 45. Cf. Ephesians 1:13–14, 'In whom ye also trusted, after that ye heard the word of truth, the gospel of your salvation: in whom also after that ye believed, ye were sealed with that holy Spirit of promise, Which is the earnest of our inheritance until the redemption of the purchased possession, unto the praise of his glory.'
17 LPL, MS 1082, 68; *Form and Order* (1761), 68.
18 Michael Heyd, *'Be Sober and Reasonable': The Critique of Enthusiasm in the Seventeenth and Early Eighteenth Centuries* (Leiden: Brill, 1995), 165–90, 196–203; John G.A. Pocock, 'Enthusiasm: The Antiself of Enlightenment', in *Enthusiasm and Enlightenment in Europe, 1650-1850*, ed. Lawrence E. Klein and Anthony J. La Vopa (San Marino, CA: Huntington Library, 1998), 7–28; William Gibson, *The Church of England 1688-1832: Unity and Accord* (London: Routledge, 2001), 232–6.
19 Heyd, *'Be Sober and Reasonable'*, 173–5; Gibson, *Church of England*, 36–48; Jane Shaw, *Miracles in Enlightenment England* (New Haven, CT: Yale University Press, 2006), 21–33; Ingram, *Religion, Reform and Modernity*, 100, 110–13, 164.
20 Robert Lowth, *A Sermon preached before the Lords Spiritual and Temporal, in the Abbey-Church, Westminster; on Friday, January 30, 1767: being the Day appointed to be Observed as the Day of the Martyrdom of King Charles I* (London: A. Millar, T. Cadell and J. Dodsley, 1767), 14. Cf. Charles James Blomfield, *A Sermon preached at the Coronation of Their Most Excellent Majesties King William IV. and Queen Adelaide in the Abbey Church of Westminster September VIII. MDCCCXXXI* (London:

B. Fellowes, 1831), 4–5. See Robert Hole, *Pulpits, Politics and Public Order in England, 1760–1832* (Cambridge: Cambridge University Press, 1989), 14–15.
21 LPL, MS 1082, 40; *Form and Order* (1761), 40.
22 LPL, MS 1082, 48; *Form and Order* (1761), 48.
23 LPL, MS 1082, 55; *Form and Order* (1761), 55.
24 'The New Coronation Service: An Historical Account', *The Times*, 29 March 1911, 9; Nehemiah Grew, *Cosmologia Sacra or a Discourse of the Universe as it is the Creature and Kingdom of God* (London: W. Rogers, S. Smith and B. Walford, 1701), 105. Bishop Potter of Oxford, preaching at George II's coronation in 1727, had referred to 'the superintendency of Divine Providence': John Potter, *A Sermon preach'd at the Coronation of King George II. and Queen Caroline, in the Abbey-church of Westminster, October 11. 1727* (London: R. Knaplock, 1727), 4.
25 LPL, MS 1082, 53; *Form and Order* (1761), 53.
26 William Warburton, *The Alliance between Church and State, or, the Necessity and Equity of an Established Religion and a Test-Law Demonstrated, From the Essence and End of Civil Society, upon the Fundamental Principles of the Law of Nature and Nations* (London: Fletcher Gyles, 1736), 154.
27 William Paley, *The Principles of Moral and Political Philosophy* (London: R. Faulder, 1785), 555.
28 College of Arms, London, 'Coronation of George. III 1761', 1, Order of 'the Lords of the Committee of Council appointed to consider of his Majesty's Coronation', 14 July 1761.
29 LPL, Fulham Papers (Howley), vol. 47, 101, Charles Knyvett to William Howley, 16 May [1820]; E.A. Smith, *George IV* (New Haven, CT: Yale University Press, 1999), 187.
30 Nicholas Dixon, 'Church and Monarchy in England, 1811–1837' (MPhil thesis, University of Cambridge, 2015), 27–32.
31 LPL, MS 1312, 51, Order of George III's coronation amended in Charles Manners-Sutton's hand; *The Form and Order of the Service that is to be performed, and of the Ceremonies that are to be observed, in the Coronation of His Majesty King George IIII. in the Abbey Church of S. Peter, Westminster, on Thursday, the 19th of July 1821* (London: George Eyre and Andrew Strahan, 1821), 39.
32 LPL, MS 1312, 54, 57; *Form and Order* (1821), 41–3; *English Coronation Records*, 317, 334.
33 Jackson, *Vive le Roi!*, 196–7.
34 LPL, MS 1083b, 41, Order of George III's coronation amended in William Howley's hand; *The Form and Order of the Service that is to be Performed and of the Ceremonies that are to be Observed, in the Coronation of their Majesties King William IV. and Queen Adelaide, in the Abbey Church of S. Peter, Westminster, on Thursday, the 8th day of September 1831* (London: George Eyre and Andrew Strahan, 1831), 34.
35 LPL, MS 1083b, 37, 65; *Form and Order* (1831), 31, 51. According to William Maskell, the anointing of the king on the breast had already been omitted in 1821, as indicated by its deletion in a copy of the coronation order 'corrected *as it was used on the occasion*, by the then York Herald, C.G. Young, Esq.': William Maskell, *Monumenta Ritualia Ecclesiae Anglicanae or Occasional Offices of the Church of England according to the Ancient Use of Salisbury the Prymer in English and other Prayers and Forms with Dissertations and Notes*, vol. 3 (London: William Pickering, 1847), 108. However, the copy used by Archbishop Manners-Sutton at the ceremony does not contain this deletion: LPL, KA113 1821 [**], 31, Order of George IV's coronation used by Charles Manners-Sutton.

36 LPL, MS 1083b, 41-3.
37 'The Coronation', *The Times*, 9 September 1831, 1.
38 *The Form and Order of the Service that is to be performed, and of the Ceremonies that are to be observed, in the Coronation of Her Majesty Queen Victoria, in the Abbey Church of St. Peter, Westminster, on Thursday, the 28th of June 1838* (London: George Eyre and Andrew Spottiswoode, 1838); Dixon, 'Church and Monarchy', 22-6.
39 Andrew Braddock, *The Role of the Book of Common Prayer in the Formation of Modern Anglican Church Identity* (Lewiston, NY: Edwin Mellen Press, 2010), 109-17.
40 *Christian Remembrancer*, November 1838, 650-1. This perception had little basis in fact, as although significant changes had been made in 1831, the same was not the case in 1838. Aside from the curtailment to the anointing, the only example quoted to support the assertion was the line 'And warm them with thy heavenly fire' in the hymn *Veni Creator Spiritus*, a deviation from the version in the *Book of Common Prayer* attributed to 'the *improving* hand of Whig-Radicalism': ibid., 651. But the writer was unaware that this version had been in use since 1689: *English Coronation Records*, 317.
41 Roy Strong, 'Queen Victoria's Coronation' (Essay) in Royal Archives, VIC/MAIN/QVJ (W), http://qvj.chadwyck.com/info/QueenVictoriasCoronation.do.
42 Nigel Yates, *Anglican Ritualism in Victorian Britain 1830-1910* (Oxford: Oxford University Press, 1999).
43 Sturdy, '"Continuity" versus "Change": Historians and English Coronations', 228-31; Peter Hinchliff, 'Frederick Temple, Randall Davidson and the Coronation of Edward VII', *Journal of Ecclesiastical History* 48, no. 1 (1997): 74-7; Strong, *Coronation*, 469-71.
44 Maskell, *Monumenta Ritualia*, 3: lxv.
45 H.A. Wilson, 'The English Coronation Orders', *Journal of Theological Studies* 2, no. 8 (1901): 504.
46 Anthony Ward and Cuthbert Johnson, 'John Wickham Legg (1843-1921): A Contribution towards the Rediscovery of British Liturgical Scholarship', *Ephemerides Liturgicae* 97 (1983): 70-84.
47 Eidem, 'A Forgotten Liturgical Scholar: John Wickham Legg', *Notitiae* 21 (1985): 119.
48 *English Coronation Records*, 263; Leopold G. Wickham Legg, *Suggestions for the Reconstruction of the Coronation Ceremonies: A Paper read before St. Paul's Ecclesiological Society on December 11, 1901, together with a Revised Form and Order of the Coronation Service of the Kings and Queens of England* (London: SPCK, 1902), 6.
49 Wickham Legg, *Suggestions*, 35-55.
50 For a more complete account of the revisions of 1902, see Hinchliff, 'Frederick Temple, Randall Davidson and the Coronation of Edward VII'. These are also described (along with later twentieth-century changes) in Strong, *Coronation*, 471-90.
51 LPL, Randall Davidson Papers (hereafter: Davidson Papers), vol. 280, fol. 60r, Randall Davidson to Cosmo Lang, 27 December 1910.
52 LPL, Frederick Temple Papers (hereafter: Temple Papers), vol. 58, fol. 72r, Memorandum by Frederick Temple, 4 January 1902. Cf. LPL, Davidson Papers, vol. 278, fol. 80, Frederick Temple to Randall Davidson, 13 December 1901.
53 LPL, Davidson Papers, vol. 278, fol. 166, Frederick Temple to Randall Davidson, 10 February 1902; Temple Papers, vol. 58, fol. 87, Francis Knollys to Frederick Temple, 16 February 1902. On Edward VII's appreciation of Roman Catholicism, see Edward Legge, *King Edward in his True Colours* (London: Eveleigh Nash, 1912), 215-25; Sigmund Münz, *King Edward VII at Marienbad: Political and Social life at the Bohemian Spas* (London: Hutchinson, 1934), 16, 288-95. The King also wished the

bishops to wear mitres: LPL, Davidson Papers, vol. 278, fol. 227, Francis Knollys to Randall Davidson, 6 May 1902.

54 LPL, Temple Papers, vol. 58, fols. 69–74, Memorandum by Frederick Temple, 4 January 1902; *The Form and Order of the Service that is to be performed, and of the Ceremonies that are to be observed, in the Coronation of Their Majesties King Edward VII. and Queen Alexandra, in the Abbey Church of S. Peter, Westminster, on Thursday, the 26th day of June, 1902* (London: Eyre and Spottiswoode, 1902), 11–12, 27, 33, 45–8; LPL, Geoffrey Fisher Papers (hereafter: Fisher Papers) vol. 123, fols. 78–9, Memorandum by Edward Ratcliff, 13 June 1952.

55 LPL, Temple Papers, vol. 58, fols. 145–7, William Groves to Frederick Temple, 20 May 1902; ibid., fols. 148–9, F.R. Allen to Frederick Temple, 9 June 1902. T.D. Bernard, the octogenarian evangelical Chancellor of Wells, complained to *The Times* that the omission 'touches the very heart of the occasion, and is a grave deduction from its most serious meaning', adding, 'I believe that I am expressing what will be a common feeling in classes which are the firmest support of the stability of the Throne; and it may be allowed to one, whose recollections now extend through five reigns, to plead that the inauguration of the fifth shall not be marked by so significant and ill-omened an omission': T.D. Bernard, letter to the editor, *The Times*, 1 May 1902, 3. The Ten Commandments had first appeared in the coronation order for George II: *The Form and Order of the Service that is to be performed, and of the Ceremonies that are to be observed, in the Coronation of Their Majesties King George II. and Queen Caroline in the Abby Church of S. Peter, Westminster, on Wednesday the 11th of October, 1727* (London: John Baskett, 1727), 21–3.

56 Leopold G. Wickham Legg, *On the Right of the Archbishop of York to Crown the Queen Consort* (London: Harrison and Sons, 1902); LPL, Davidson Papers, vol. 280, fol. 3, Leopold G. Wickham Legg to William Spooner, 22 July 1910; ibid., fol. 1, William Spooner to Randall Davidson, 23 July 1910; Leopold G. Wickham Legg, letter to the editor, *The Times*, 16 November 1910, 12.

57 LPL, Temple Papers, vol. 57, fols. 208–11, George Pollard to Frederick Temple, 15 March 1902; ibid., fols. 212–5, George Pollard to Frederick Temple, 17 March 1902; Davidson Papers, vol. 278, fols. 253–4, John Sheepshanks to Randall Davidson, 26 May 1902; Temple Papers, vol. 57, fols. 228–9, E.G. Coventry Pocock to Frederick Temple, 12 June 1902; ibid., fol. 276, George Gregory to Frederick Temple, 19 June 1902.

58 Sturdy, '"Continuity" versus "Change": Historians and English Coronations', 231–3; Hinchliff, 'Frederick Temple, Randall Davidson and the Coronation of Edward VII', 89–90. See e.g. (besides the examples cited above) LPL, Davidson Papers, vol. 278, fols. 1–3, Lord Halifax to Randall Davidson, 27 April 1901; Temple Papers, vol. 58, fols. 152–4, John Steel to Frederick Temple, 3 October 1901; Herbert Thurston, *The Coronation Ceremonial: Its True History and Meaning* (London: Catholic Truth Society, 1902); 'The New Coronation Service', *The Times*, 5 May 1902, 5.

59 LPL, Fisher Papers, vol. 123, fols. 126r–127r, Memorandum by Claude Jenkins, 10 September 1952. Archbishop Davidson referred to Jenkins as '[t]he man who has been at work on this [the coronation service] with me, and who is really responsible for many of the researches and their outcome': LPL, Davidson Papers, vol. 280, fol. 155, Randall Davidson to George Earle Buckle, 20 March 1911.

60 *The Form and Order of the Service that is to be performed and of the Ceremonies that are to be observed in the Coronation of Their Majesties King George V and Queen Mary in the Abbey Church of S. Peter, Westminster, on Thursday, the 22nd day of June, 1911* (London: Eyre and Spottiswoode, 1911), 29–30.

61 See the correspondence between Edward Ratcliff and Cosmo Lang in LPL, Cosmo Lang Papers, vol. 21, and an undated memorandum by Cosmo Lang, ibid., fol. 180. See also the correspondence between Edward Ratcliff and Geoffrey Fisher in LPL, Fisher Papers, vols. 123–4. In 1953, Ratcliff was part of a 'Coronation Service Committee' convened by Fisher to discuss revisions at Lambeth Palace, which also included Claude Jenkins and Leopold Wickham Legg as well as Norman Sykes, Dixie Professor of Ecclesiastical History at the University of Cambridge: LPL, Fisher Papers, vol. 123, fols. 143–51, 234–42, Minutes of 'Coronation Service Committee', 7 October 1952 and 21 November 1952.
62 Arthur H. Couratin, 'E. C. Ratcliff as Liturgist', in Edward Ratcliff, *Liturgical Studies*, ed. Arthur H. Couratin and David H. Tripp (London: SPCK, 1976), 12.
63 LPL, Fisher Papers, vol. 123, fols. 88r–89r, Memorandum by Edward Ratcliff, 13 June 1952.
64 *English Coronation Records*, xxxv; *The Form and Order of the Service that is to be performed and of the Ceremonies that are to be observed in the Coronation of Their Majesties King George VI and Queen Elizabeth in the Abbey Church of S. Peter, Westminster, on Wednesday, the 12th day of May, 1937* (London: Eyre and Spottiswoode, 1937), 16; LPL, Fisher Papers, vol. 123, fols. 79–80, Memorandum by Edward Ratcliff, 13 June 1952.
65 Robert Beaken, *Cosmo Lang: Archbishop in War and Crisis* (London: I.B. Tauris, 2012), 134–5.
66 Quoted in *The Coronation Service of Her Majesty Queen Elizabeth II with a Short Historical Introduction, Explanatory Notes and an Appendix,* ed. Edward Ratcliff (London: SPCK, 1953), 19.
67 *English Coronation Orders*, 260; *Coronation Service of Her Majesty Queen Elizabeth II*, 20–3, 39, 46–8, 50. Christopher Chavasse, Bishop of Rochester, deplored the new positioning of the presentation of the Bible. Evoking a time in the sixteenth century when 'England became the people of a Book, and that Book the Bible', Chavasse suggested that 'the introduction of the presenting of the Holy Bible at the coronation of William and Mary was in response to the national will'. He further quoted the words of the Queen Mother, who had stated at the Festival of Britain in 1951 that 'the King and I long to see the Bible back where it ought to be, as a guide and comfort in the homes and lives of our people'. Chavasse surmised, 'In view of our chief national need, thus proclaimed from the Throne itself, it cannot but be disturbing to learn that the presenting of the Holy Bible is to be displaced from its "crowning" position at the Coronation, to become a side issue in the administration of the Coronation Oath': Christopher Chavasse, letter to the editor, *The Times*, 19 March 1953, 9.
68 LPL, Fisher Papers, vol. 123, fol. 90r, Memorandum by Edward Ratcliff, 13 June 1952.
69 *Form and Order* (1937), 27; *Coronation Service of Her Majesty Queen Elizabeth II*, 50.
70 Edward R. Norman, *Church and Society in England 1770–1970: A Historical Study* (Oxford: Clarendon Press, 1976), 19–21, 83–9; Jakob Evertsson, *Bishops, Politics and Anti-clericalism in Nineteenth Century England and Sweden: An Analysis of the Debate on the Political Role of the Anglican Bishops during the 1830s Parliamentary Reform Debate in comparison to Sweden* (Falun: Högskolan Dalarna, 2005), 51–63.
71 *Coronation Service of Her Majesty Queen Elizabeth II*, 23.
72 *Form and Order* (1937), 5; *Coronation Service of Her Majesty Queen Elizabeth II*, 38. This undertaking derived from the form of the oath settled by Parliament in 1689 and modified following the Act of Union with Ireland of 1801: Dixon, 'Church and Monarchy', 98.

73 C.L. Berry, 'The Coronation Oath and the Church of England', *Journal of Ecclesiastical History* 11, no. 1 (1960): 100–1.
74 Norman, *Church and Society*, 272–8, 341–4; Owen Chadwick, *Hensley Henson: A Study in the Friction between Church and State* (New York: Clarendon Press of Oxford University Press, 1983), 182–218; Adrian Hastings, *A History of English Christianity 1920–2000* (London: SCM Press, 2001), 49–64, 193–212; John Maiden, *National Religion and the Prayer Book Controversy, 1927–1928* (Woodbridge: Boydell & Brewer, 2009).
75 Berry, 'The Coronation Oath', 103–4; Edward Carpenter, *Archbishop Fisher: His Life and Times* (Norwich: Canterbury Press, 1991), 252.
76 John Wolffe, 'Protestantism, Monarchy and the Defence of Christian Britain 1837–2005', in *Secularisation in the Christian World: Essays in Honour of Hugh McLeod*, ed. Callum G. Brown and Michael Snape (Farnham: Ashgate, 2010), 57–74.
77 Carpenter, *Archbishop Fisher*, 248–53; Wolffe, 'Protestantism', 65–6.
78 Edward Shils and Michael Young, 'The Meaning of the Coronation', *Sociological Review* 1, no. 2 (1953): 63–81.
79 Geoffrey Fisher, *I Here Present Unto You. . .: Addresses interpreting the Coronation of Her Majesty Queen Elizabeth II* (London: SPCK, 1953), 21–3.

Part Two

Ceremonial of Royal Courts

4

The daily court ceremonial of the French queen in the reign of Henry III

Vladimir Shishkin

The writer Christine de Pisan, apparently for the first time in French literature, mentions the expression 'a royal ceremony' in French, modified from Latin and adopted from the prevalent liturgical lexicon, in her *Book of the Deeds and Good Character of King Charles V the Wise* (1404). But she was using a phrase already in use by contemporaries of the period for the established solemn ritual and ordering of royal representation: 'Royal ceremonies were made not because of the inclination [of the king] for pleasure, but in order to keep, support and demonstrate an example to his future successors; in fact, only thanks to a solemn order can there be a crown of France in a place of high honour.'[1]

According to Ralph Giesey's research, the word *cérémonial* in the fifteenth to sixteenth centuries in France was applied only in relation to important acts of state that testified and emphasized the exclusive position of the royal person and the sacred nature of his powers.[2] Following the definition of André Duchesne, the royal historiographer of the first half of the seventeenth century, there are the ceremonies of consecration, coronation, solemn entries and for the presence of the king at sessions of the Parlement of Paris, the so-called *lit-de-justice*. Duchesne adds to these various 'public festivals' that involved the participation of 'their Majesties', royal christenings and weddings, receptions of ambassadors and so forth, as well as the funerary ceremonies of monarchs.[3]

Besides the grand state ceremonial regulations, which all kings had to follow to maintain tradition and the foundations of the political body, there were, according to Giesey's definition, also separate ceremonials for court festivals and performances, plus the daily rituals of the royal court including the smaller courts of the different members of the royal family (widows, sisters, sons) whose norms became part of public law over time.[4] Of these, the daily ceremonial rituals that regulated the Queen's Household are the focus here. This chapter will examine ceremonies that involved the queen of France – the lesser bearer of the sovereign crown, according to contemporary thinking – and which were often organized by her. In fact, little is known about these in detail, so much of the description here is at times sketchy. The reason for such a state of affairs is the nature of our sources: in general, royal legislation says very little about ceremonial specifically for the queen and her court, and the extant relevant royal *ordonnances* and *règlements* mainly define the position of men in her entourage.[5] Of course, in the Early Modern period, as it had been in the Middle Ages, the royal court was first of all a society of men. Even a noble court lady of the sixteenth century was considered by representatives of the opposite sex merely as an object of pleasant and prestigious pastimes, favourable marriages, and a motivation for their interests in objects of art, games, hunting and duels.[6]

Kings therefore set the tone, having given their favourites official status at court starting with Agnès Sorel (1422–1450), the mistress of Charles VII.[7] However, the same century became a period of a noticeable transformation of the socio-political situation and a strengthening of the influence of French queens, as well as the ladies in their company. Attempts to create a special place at court, and to play a political role were characteristic of many medieval queens of France. But from the thirteenth and fourteenth centuries, and even earlier, all of them faced a real 'constitutional' barrier: the socio-political limit forbidding women to inherit the throne, which demeaned their status. This was the Salic Law (*Lex Salica*), which called their right to rule the kingdom into doubt when necessity arose.[8]

This chapter will illustrate the significance of the Salic Law in relation to the political place of the queen of France in the sixteenth century, which is directly connected with the organization of curial ceremonies of the Queen's Household (her place in processions and other public events, access to her rooms, and so on), and finally, how the kings of France constituted these ceremonies within the greater royal ceremonial practices and envisioned the new higher position of the queen in the changing world of the Renaissance. I will demonstrate that, instead of desiring to claim or threaten the dominance of male power, French queens became one of its greatest supports. This is shown through ritual and ceremony, not only in the great ceremonies of state – the coronation, royal weddings, etc. – but also in the smaller ceremonies of daily life at court.

Salic Law and the limitation of the power of the queen

The Salic Law was considered by French jurists to be one of the fundamental laws of the Kingdom. It was firmly established in legal practice in the fifteenth century and indicated, primarily, the denial of royal women and their descendants of any rights of inheritance to the French crown. Salic Law was justified by contemporary ideas of female inconstancy, which affected women of any rank and position, as well as a fear of the prospect of foreign rule (almost all queens-consort being born abroad) or that the crown would pass into the hands of a weak woman (*tomber en quenouille*). It also had an impact on the position of the queen in government and at court. The original sense of the *Lex Salica* from the sixth century, however, regulated only the inheritance of private property (land, moveable goods), but its reinterpretations by lawyers of the fourteenth to sixteenth centuries – especially regarding the question of the Valois succession in the early fourteenth century – allowed the French monarchy to exclude even a possibility of discussion about the accession of a woman to the French throne.[9] St Paul's first letter to the Corinthians always allowed medieval theologians to justify the power of the husband over the wife: 'I want you to understand that Christ is the head of every man, and the man is the head of a woman, and God is the head of Christ.'[10] At the same time, experts in Roman Law could easily prove that in legal texts, Roman and Byzantine empresses had been known only as 'the emperors' wives', their first subjects, without having any imperial administrative rights or duties of their own.[11] Nevertheless, very few people could deny the real power and influence that these queens potentially could possess. Yet every time a queen-consort or dowager queen needed to assume regency duties, there were political forces, mainly led by the princes of the blood, which challenged her powers and competencies.[12]

The Renaissance and Reformation epoch was characterized by the secularization of consciousness; its scholars looked again to ancient texts and examples to enable them to rethink and re-shape attitudes regarding the role of the monarch's consort in society, fixing for her a more significant place. Despite the disappearance of the knightly cult of the beautiful lady, and as one of the consequences, the growth of anti-feminism in clerical circles and partly among the judicial nobility (the *noblesse de robe*), society continued to consider men's wives as their property, including the goal of complete control over their changeable nature (as, with some cynicism, wrote Montaigne).[13] Thus a more mundane veneration of women was gradually asserted in the Renaissance spirit, where marriage was seen as a spiritual and corporal union, and where, in addition to marital duties, a woman was recognized as having the right to gain intellectual and moral knowledge, previously reserved only for men. This right was first announced openly by Christine of Pisan in her *The Book of the City of Ladies*, and these thoughts were picked up by humanists of later times.[14] The royal court was an ideal space where the main political and cultural threads of the kingdom converged and which provided some freedom for women's activism, because the kings themselves maintained it. Moreover, in the sixteenth century the court of France began to be associated more closely with queens and noble ladies. Thus, the well-known historian of court life, Pierre de Brantôme, wrote: 'Whoever has seen the court of our kings Francis, Henry II and his sons and successors, will admit that, whoever he is and however much of the world he has seen, he will never have seen anything so beautiful as the women of their court, and in the courts of our queens, their wives, mothers and sisters.'[15]

King Francis I (1515–1547), like no other, contributed to the appearance at court of a new cult of the *règne des femmes*. His mother, Louise de Savoie, and his sister Marguerite de Navarre, were both actively involved in the processes of public administration and diplomatic affairs, as well as his favourite, the duchesse d'Étampes. According to the reports of the Venetian ambassador, Marino Giustiniano (1535), the King spent lavishly on gifts, pensions and jewellery for his favoured ladies, up to a hundred thousand *écus* – more money than was allocated for the construction of royal palaces.[16] As the century progressed, the model of the ideal queen was established: above all, she fully shared the rank (*dignité*) of her spouse and therefore claimed similar honours. She would be devoted to his interests during his reign and after his death, and at the same time, being his main counsellor, would keep her thoughts and emotions to herself, without expressing them publicly. As an early example, Anne de Beaujeu, Regent of France for her brother Charles VIII, instructed her daughter Susanne in this spirit, in her famous *Enseignements à sa fille* (1504–1505).[17] Thierry Wanegffelen considers that this model is a consequence of the conclusion of an implicit 'absolutist pact' between the king and the queen, which appeared around the time of the marriage of Charles VIII and Anne of Brittany (1491), created to best guarantee social and political order at the court and in the kingdom, by establishing a clear algorithm of monarchical continuity, simultaneously defining the hierarchy of women in the royal family, and also protecting the privileges and property of noble families and estates.[18]

The queen-consorts and queen-regents of France, as shown by the studies of Éliane Viennot and Fanny Cosandey, were able to ensure the continuity of women's power, creating and using different forms of solidarity. A key concern was the organization of the education and upbringing at court of noble girls, including foreign ones, as potential future royal brides. They also considered the importance of giving them regular gifts, annuities and everything that could bring their income to the level worthy of their status, and also of creating women's offices for a number of functions previously reserved for men. They directly intervened in changes made to the grand ceremonies of the court, and even in the evolving manifestations of the regular patronage of the monarchs themselves.[19] Paradoxically, the approval of the laws of succession to the throne, involving the unconditional exclusion of women and the strengthening of the personal power of kings, allowed them to make use of the female factor in politics more usefully and productively than before. The ladies' segment of the court, led by its queens, became firmly embedded in the royal system of public administration and the representation of power, now appearing as an obligatory part of the state mechanism. Challenging political situations, which touched the lives of all queens of France in the sixteenth century, could thus bring royal women into pre-eminent positions of power in the state.

The example of the regency and active participation in public affairs of Catherine de Medici (1519–1589), mother of the last three kings of the Valois dynasty, is the best demonstration of this possibility of the use of female power in the context of a weakening of the monarchy. Playing the role of guardian of the family and guarantor of the safety of her young sons, Catherine, following in the footsteps of her female predecessors as regents, made use of divine and dynastic rights to make decisions which before had been reserved only for kings. Again, according to Brantôme: 'I heard a story told when I was at court, that the Queen Mother gave orders to visit the chambers and closets of all those who had lodgings in the Louvre, with no exception, ladies and young women included, in order to ensure that there were no hidden weapons, even small pistols, during our time of troubles.'[20]

No member of the royal family, even as an adult, could leave the king's residence without the Queen Mother's permission or notifying her of their intentions. Catherine's daughter Marguerite de Valois, queen of Navarre (1553–1615), in her memoirs emphasizes particularly: 'Even I always maintained this respect for the Queen my mother, for all the time I was living near her, either as a girl or a married woman, to never leave any place without first requesting permission.'[21]

Ceremonial alone became the main administrative instrument of power, which allowed royal women to create an autonomous political space for the queens of France, also to permit them completely to dominate the female side of the court, and through that, to influence that of the men. The representative performance that was played by these queens, partly in imitating the ceremonial of the king's masculine court, thus found its own niche within the larger arena of ceremonial prestige: henceforth male courtiers would have to look for protection and favour not only from the king, but also the queen.[22] Catherine de Medici had pushed out the boundaries of the ceremonial space of the French queen. Nevertheless, she did not violate the 'absolutist pact', and through the use of this space managed to strengthen the ceremonial and organizational ordering of the entire court, while at the same time stressing the claims of the exclusivity of French royal blood: in one of her letters to the French ambassador in Rome, Henri Clutin de Villeparisis (1564), she asked him to make it clear to Pope Pius IV that any claims to ecclesiastical jurisdiction in France did not extend over those who had the title of king or queen, as French monarchs did not receive their crown and sceptre from papal hands.[23]

The ceremonial of the court of the queen: tradition and influence

The foundations of French court ceremonial lie in the historical depths of the Capetian monarchy. The first royal *ordonnance* – the act regulating court services and everyday life in the royal residence – appeared in the middle of the thirteenth century. It discusses the separate services required to provide for the needs of the queen of France and called for an organized daily routine.[24] During the Hundred Years War (1337–1453) the initiative in revising court ceremonial was taken up by the Burgundian court – a junior branch of the French royal house – whose brilliant organization gained considerable development and subsequently had a huge impact on most European courts, including its 'parent' in France.[25] The memoirs of the Burgundian noblewoman Alienor (Eléonore) de Poitiers (1480s) describe for us the difficult and detailed organization of the everyday life of the duchess of Burgundy, the duties of her ladies-in-waiting, and the obligatory behaviour of all nobles of either gender at court, or *etiquette*.[26] With the disappearance of an independent Burgundian court (1477), the ceremonial legislator became Spain, and in general, the dynasty of the Habsburgs, successors of the Burgundian dukes. Despite their ongoing rivalry, Spanish cultural and political influence, including norms of court ceremonial, made a significant impact on the daily ceremonial of the French court, including the ladies' court. It should not be forgotten that two representatives of the Habsburg family were wives of the kings of France in the sixteenth century: Eléonore and Elisabeth of Austria, the spouses of Francis I and Charles IX.[27]

In general, all the queens of France in the sixteenth century had foreign origins, and came from countries where the Salic Law did not apply, and therefore potentially had certain sovereign rights or, at least, claims to these rights. One might mention in this regard, Catherine de Medici's (quite tenuous) claims put forward for the throne of Portugal in 1580.[28] These non-French brides arrived in France with their own foreign entourages and ideas about a queen's rights and prerogatives, as well as about the ceremonies most fitting for their natural dignity. Most of these princesses did not see themselves as the obedient and faceless wives of a king, as his shadow hidden in distant rooms of the castle whose mission was limited to giving birth and occasionally attending state ceremonies and regency councils. Renaissance ideas began to recognize the right for self-expression for women, including in the sphere of political decisions.[29] Anne of Brittany (1477–1514), wife of Charles VIII then of Louis XII, summoned women and girls of noble birth into her entourage. However, unlike her predecessors as queen-consort, she herself made political decisions, having fashioned these women into a professional court, because for the first time they were allocated official positions and duties, a regular status at court, and a corresponding annual salary.[30]

The influence at the court of a reigning queen with foreign origins in many respects depended on the importance for the French crown of her potential hereditary and sovereign rights – the most notable example being Mary Stuart, already a sovereign queen in her own right when she married the Dauphin François – and, accordingly, on the role that the king trusted her to perform, since, depending on the circumstances, this role could be reduced to nothing at all. Thus, Charles IX and his brother Henry III did not give their wives, Elisabeth of Austria and Louise of Lorraine, respectively, any opportunity to make political decisions, relying more on women of their own family – their mother, Catherine de Medici, and their sister, Marguerite de Valois – to perform numerous royal ceremonial duties and diplomatic missions in the 1570s–80s. The logic of royal policy was that French tradition did not attach sacred significance to blood of foreign females, even if it was the 'noble blood of the Caesars' as was the case for princesses from the House of Habsburg. Instead, the main purpose given to foreign princesses on the French throne was to transmit the sacral royal blood of France through childbirth – to give birth to heirs of the male sex. It is no coincidence that in the seventeenth century, after the birth of his long-awaited son (in 1638), Louis XIII would devote his kingdom to the Virgin Mary, and accordingly, ideologists of the Kingdom would draw parallels between the Virgin Mary and the queens of France.[31] The Virgin was seen here as merely the vessel that carried God's gift to humankind.

On the other hand, the status of a queen-mother, as a widow, and thus no longer ideologically and legally subject to her husband, completely changed her position and allowed her to assume regency powers and public authority, even sometimes after the king's majority.[32] However, as it turned out, most decisions emanating from the queen, a woman and a foreigner, were passionately criticized in society, especially during periods of state difficulties, together with challenging her authority and her right to speak on behalf of the whole kingdom.[33] In face of this opposition, one of the main mechanisms for settling the domestic political situation remained the royal court and its rules for functioning.

The mixing together of ancient French and modern rules, traditions and ideas from abroad concerning ceremonial rights and responsibilities in the female side of the court, combined with the transformation of service in the household of the queen into a profession, forged over time a new ceremonial space for the queen of France, which was finally decreed as law by Henry III in 1585. The next section seeks to define the limits of this space.

Queenship in the regulations of Henry III, 1570s–1580s

Queens of France have long been essential participants in important state ceremonies. André Duchesne, speaking about the rights and powers of queens, writes that, among other things, queens participate alongside the king in solemn entrances and public feasts, are crowned, participate in sessions of the Estates General and sessions of the Parlement of Paris, and 'accept ambassadors with honour great and small, depending on the rank of the sovereign who sent them'.[34] It should be noted that, at the same time, all these ceremonies displayed an essential distinction between the dignity of the king and that of the queen, always emphasizing the superiority of the first. Accordingly, queens were crowned in the Abbey of Saint-Denis, outside Paris, not in the traditional coronation city of Reims. They received at their coronations a special ring symbolizing the Trinity, and were charged with the duty to strive against heresy and to care for the poor.[35] During the ceremony, the queen's crown was held by barons, while at the king's coronation, his crown was given to him by the peers of France – exclusively dukes and counts. The ceremony of the queen's *Sacre* (sacralizing) was carried out through anointing with special oils designed to promote fertility, which differed from the unction given in kings' coronations, using the Sacred Ampoule with its wonder-working ability to cure scrofula, a power given only to men.[36] The queen's throne, crown and other royal insignia were smaller in size; in solemn processions the queen was never next to, but behind the monarch.[37] However, as with her spouse, she was accorded the privileged style used in legal and diplomatic documents of *Très-Chrétienne* (Most Christian) queen of France; she could generate and sign royal acts, and in accordance with the commands of the king, could make decisions in public affairs in case of need.[38] Such ceremonial acts of state, while not frequent, were based on both liturgical and public law, and testified to the political and familial character of the status, corresponding duties and powers of the queen of France, and also to the gradual formation of 'the queen's two bodies' in the sixteenth century.[39]

All grand state ceremonial was closely connected with daily court ceremonial. The evolution of this ceremonial has been analysed by Ralph Giesey and Fanny Cosandey, who demonstrated that the court rituals that were repeated daily with participation of the monarch and members of his family gradually became part of the public space of France, and in the reign of Louis XIV (1643–1715), absorbed other types of ceremonial, having turned into a united ceremonial space.[40]

However, the first attempt to make ceremonial the main control lever for the court, and therefore for the whole of France, was made by Henry III, governing in the midst of civil wars between Catholics and Huguenots. The regulations of the 1570–1580s, which were issued on his initiative, though based on the rules and experiences of the organization of the court of his predecessors, allowed queens to become part of the court ceremonial space *de jure*.[41] In general, all these royal regulations concerning the court (which, it should be noted, were written personally by the King) can be divided into two parts. The first concerned the general rules of everyday conduct at court and a new order for the royal ceremonies of the king's morning rising and dressing (the *lever*), his movement within his residences, attendance of mass, eating the midday meal (the *dîner*), working in councils, giving audiences, hosting festivals, eating the evening meal (the *souper*), attending vespers and finally, retiring again for sleep (the *coucher*). From the start of each day, each category of courtiers, depending on their particular public state function or place in court service, was required to be in one of three rooms in front of the royal bedchamber, and during ceremonies, to assume their special position as specified by the Grand Master of Ceremonies – a role created in 1585.[42] These rules were specially printed in printing presses based in the Louvre and distributed among the courtiers.[43]

The second part of these regulations, unlike the first, remained unprinted, appearing instead as a manuscript book. It stated in detail the rights and duties of particular court officials, in the form of separate instructions (*Ordres*), including those for the queen's male staff. Undoubtedly, these were the result of the strengthening of the influence of consorts and their courts, the result of the conditional political bargaining of men and women of the royal family, as well as the desire of the king to put under control and to found common rules of conduct for all who served or lived at the royal court – to reach a compromise from a position of strength.

The National Library of Russia in Saint Petersburg holds a copy of these manuscripts of *Règlements*.[44] Using this unique source, we can recreate one day in the life of a French queen in the 1580s in the Louvre, the main royal residence of the ruling Valois family in Paris. Here, the reigning queen-consort (Louise de Vaudémont) lived on the first floor, and her apartments consisted of five main rooms: a bedroom, an adjoining wardrobe and a cabinet connecting to a similar cabinet of the king; plus two audience rooms near the wardrobe, known as the *antichambre* and the *salle*.[45] The Queen Mother (Catherine de Medici) lived in another wing of the palace, on an upper floor.

Specifically focusing on Catherine, we see some particular differences. The secretary to the Papal Nuncio, Cardinal Alessandrini, noted in 1570 that the daily ceremonial of the King's mother was similar to the ceremonial of the King himself, as it repeated the same compulsory rituals, including a *lever* and a *coucher*, at which both ladies and gentlemen were present.[46] This is confirmed in the memoirs of Catherine's daughter, Marguerite de Valois, who reports that her husband, Henry of Navarre, was always present at his mother-in-law's *lever*.[47] It is interesting to note Henry's presence here, since, in contrast, for the king's bedroom the regulations specified that only men were allowed. Marguerite also mentions her own participation in a *coucher* ceremony of her mother, during which she was permitted, as a Daughter of France, to sit on a *coffre* (while most everyone else stood); at the end of the ceremony, she was required to do an obligatory reverence to her mother.[48] On one occasion in 1571, Catherine was working late and broke the rule that ordered daily bedtime at ten o'clock in the evening, prompting Jeanne d'Albret (the mother of Henry of Navarre) to complain to her son that she had been unable to converse with Marguerite in any way alone, because her future daughter-in-law had left the apartments of the Queen Mother 'in those hours which are inconvenient for conversation'.[49]

The *Règlement* of 1585, distributed for common acquaintance, clearly states that the captain of the honour guard (*chevalier d'honneur*), both for the Queen Mother and the Queen-Consort, participates in the ceremony of the *lever* of the King, and, being considered among the most honourable persons at court, was allowed in the King's audience room, and afterwards in the royal bedroom.[50] At the same time, another royal *Ordre* from the manuscript booklet orders the same captain and the ten noblemen under him to arrive by eight o'clock in the morning to the Queen's rooms, in an antechamber room:

> His Majesty wishing henceforth that the Queen his wife would be followed and accompanied with dignity and honour, orders that thirty gentlemen will be chosen, ten per quarter, changing every four months, to start the first quarter up to the first of January, either in whatever room they follow her into from 8 in the morning, or if the queen has not ordered otherwise, in the *salle* or *antichambre* of said Lady.[51]

This passage is revealing: there is no mention that in the bedroom of the King's wife the men of her guard or suite were allowed. Apparently, they waited for the orders of the Queen in her audience room. By the beginning of the *lever*, captains of the Queen's Guards and other men of her suite left her apartments, because the King was already awoken at five o'clock and finished his first ceremonial procedures within an hour or two.[52] The Queen and her ladies then got up an hour or two later.

In contrast, the Queen Mother did allow men in her bedroom, as an exception. Having rendered the required signs of honour and attention, after a few minutes the gentlemen departed for the adjoining room, an audience chamber. We have no information suggesting that men were admitted to the morning or evening ceremonies of the other queens residing in the Louvre, that is, the Queen-Consort, Louise de Vaudémont, or the sister of the King, Marguerite de Valois, Queen of Navarre. In mentioning her own ceremony of the *coucher*, Marguerite in her memoirs speaks only about 'the ladies and maids of honour'.[53] The fact is that the bedroom of a married queen was perceived differently from the bedroom of a widowed queen: the former was visited by the king at night, using a secret private door in their adjacent cabinets, and he surely left it before her *lever*.[54] Thus the queen-consort's bedroom at certain times was off-limits for men and was considered a sacral space.

The details of the procedures for the morning *toilette* of the queen of France for this period are almost unknown, but it is possible to assume that it lasted no less than two hours. One of the few sources, Brantôme's memoirs, does tell us how Marguerite de Valois was dressed and coiffed (though this only applied to solemn festivals), but he lists only the details of the clothes that were evident and remained in his memory after many years.[55] One interesting detail is reported by Marguerite herself: in her relation of events of the Saint Bartholomew's Day Massacre (24 August 1572), in the midst of describing how she saved from certain death a Huguenot nobleman in her bedroom in the Louvre, then hurried to the King's rooms to rescue her husband as well, she does not forget to inform the reader that chambermaids dressed her in the special clothes (*manteau de nuit*) intended for going out at night.[56] Etiquette must always be observed even under extraordinary circumstances.

Every morning, the queen would have a light breakfast, and then attend mass. According to regulations, mass and vespers could be celebrated with the participation of the king, queen and the whole royal court, and would take place in the royal chapel on Sundays, and other religious feast days such as Christmas, Easter, Pentecost, All

Saints, Trinity Sunday, the six feasts of the Virgin (Annunciation, Visitation, Assumption, etc.), and so on.[57] The *Règlement* of 1578 specified the time of this mass as nine o'clock in the morning, and it could last until noon. At other times, the queen would pray together with the court in the chapel adjoining the audience chamber. We know that the Tuileries – the palace connected to the Louvre where Catherine de Medici lodged in the 1580s, had its own large chapel, where services were accompanied by choral singing.[58] Each queen (wife, mother, sister) had an almoner – as a rule at the rank of bishop – as the head of her ecclesiastical household.

In one example where we certainly see the influence of Burgundian and Spanish ceremonial, the *Règlements* of 1585 ordered that no crowned woman could move alone in a public space, within the royal residence or beyond its limits, without an armed honour guard. Henry III in these regulations delegated to the Queen the right to organize this guard independently, in other words, he conditionally shared with her part of the political body and royal majesty. During processions the Queen-Consort and her ladies paraded after the King and the Queen-Mother together, among royal guardsmen joined by noblemen of her honour guard.[59] The captain of her guard had to obey the orders of the Queen: 'They will not move until she comes out and will then accompany her either to mass or wherever she will go in public and will not leave the side of said Lady until she returns to enter her *chambre*,' that is, to her bedroom or cabinet. During these movements the queen's noblemen were ordered:

> whenever the said Lady goes out with the King or with the Queen His Majesty's Mother (…) they will stand in front without approaching too near, marching in front of those who would be more qualified and will place themselves amongst the other gentlemen of His Majesty, and if they process in a ceremonial fashion, that they will be ordered in the same manner.[60]

Noblemen of this honour guard were obliged to protect the queen during any forays outside the royal residence, and also to accompany her during grand court ceremonies, 'needing to accompany said Lady whenever she goes outside, whether on foot or on horseback, and to be of better service for accompanying her when she goes outside, will have at least two horses each and whatever they need for their luggage, both horses being shown at the start of their period of service to the *chevalier d'honneur*'.[61]

The queen's carriage (in which, as a rule, she was accompanied by several ladies) was permitted to go into the courtyard of the Louvre or other royal residences, as could the carriage of the king, his mother, brothers and sisters.[62] In contrast, even the most notable gentlemen and ladies of the court, if arriving independently, were obliged to enter the royal residence on foot, having dismounted or left their carriages.[63]

As with her honour guard, the queen of France could form her ladies' entourage according to her own choice, though always with the consent of the king, her husband; in contrast, the posts in her household that were reserved only for men, whether for domestic, ecclesiastical or military services, were filled personally by the king, without her participation.[64] Sertorio Loschi, the ambassador to Paris from the small Italian principality of Mirandola, confirms the significance of the female household, to which he even dedicated a special section in his description of the French court (c. 1580). He emphasizes its special ceremonies and the main male and female posts (sometimes with names of the courtiers) of the courtiers who were at the head of various departments of the ladies' court, giving premier place to the captain of her honour guard and the *dame d'honneur*.[65]

The important and ancient social ceremony of the midday meal, or *dîner*, was enjoyed free of charge at the royal table by anyone on duty, emphasizing the king's special connection with his servants.[66] According to the *Règlement* of 1582, the *dîner* lasted about two hours and was arranged separately for the king and queen, but was almost identical in form.[67] The queen's tables were portable and set up in her audience room. A separate table was reserved for the queen herself, though, unlike the king's table, it was not separated by barriers from the others dining in the room. All of the ladies on duty and various guests (men and women) could not be seated at one table in the limited space of the audience chamber, so their number was controlled personally by the head of the queen's household, the *dame d'honneur*, and also by the queen's steward of the household, responsible for arrangements for her table.[68] The queen (either queen consort or queen mother) always personally approved the list of guests, which included men. Thus, it became the practice that, at the request of the king, Catherine de Medici would receive foreign ambassadors during a dinner before they were allowed to have an audience with the monarch.[69] As with the king's table, musicians were invited by the queen and sacred music was played. In this way it was emphasized that the meal was sacred, a collective communion where the central figure of the queen imitated that of the king.[70]

Similarly the evening meal, or *souper*, was organized after vespers (at four o'clock and lasting two hours).[71] Unlike the *dîner*, the regulations of 1582 and 1585 obliged the queen to have her *souper* publicly, together with the king, except on Fridays and Saturdays, when the monarch preferred to dine without her or alone.[72] Marguerite de Valois tells us that every time such a public ceremony was coming, when all the royal family gathered and demonstrated its unity, the queen must be solemnly dressed.[73] At the royal table, all the queens (mother, wife, sister) sat near the king, and only the reigning queen had an exclusive right to give a napkin to her husband, which, in turn, she received from the hands of *Grand Maître de France* (the duke of Guise).[74] This right was observed by the English diplomat Richard Cook who left a description of the French court in 1584. The *souper* also took place with the participation of courtiers and foreign guests and lasted about two hours. Musicians also played at the evening meal.[75]

Between the midday meal and vespers, the bedroom of the queen became a public space open to courtiers from the royal households or other invited persons. The memoirs of Marguerite de Valois cite Catherine de Medici, who recalled the era of Francis I, the 1530 and 1540s, as remembering that this king had resolved that ladies from his family would be free to go into the apartments and even the bedrooms of court men, who conversed with them, read and played music.[76] Francis I's sister, Marguerite de Navarre, in her *Heptaméron* also writes about platonic forms of court relationships between noble men and women, and describes the situations in which men entered the rooms of maids of honour and the queen's private spaces without permission.[77] In a letter to Henry III from 1574, which urged the King to reform the court, including its ceremonial practices, Catherine de Medici strongly recommends that her son not forego his daily visit to the rooms of his wife and her ladies: 'After the *dîner*, at least two times a week, give an audience which is something that makes your subjects the most contented. Afterwards, withdraw and come to my rooms or those of the Queen so that one would understand the sort of court this is, something that infinitely pleases the French since they have become accustomed to it.'[78] Cook confirms the execution of this rule: he writes that Henry III adhered to his mother's recommendations and regularly visited the Queen and her social circle in the afternoon, including for the purpose of monitoring the courtiers' behaviour.[79] Provisions were made for these visits: the *Règlement* of 1582 ordered a steward of the household to send twelve dishes to the queen's rooms in the afternoon together with wine: six dishes with fruit 'according to season', and six with sweets.[80]

At the opposite end of the spectrum were the grand semi-public court festivals, and these too needed to be regulated. According to the regulations of 1582 and 1585, grand balls were scheduled with precise details:

> All Sunday and Thursday evenings, if there is no great annual event or in Lent or if it would be otherwise ordered by the King, will be illuminated with torches in the ballroom, and all the instrument players will be summoned for the ball, and their Majesties' thrones will be brought along with twenty other seats, whether *tabourets* or *scabeaux* [stools or folding chairs] for those men and women who have the right to sit, and this before the fruit would be served before His Majesty, and the *maître d'Hôtel* will order the *valet de fourrière* to take care of it, and for the instrumentalists, the *maître d'Hôtel* then in service will alert the equerry about them.[81]

Such large gatherings were held in a special hall intended for balls in the Louvre (about 600 square meters),[82] and they are depicted in several paintings such as *Le bal de noces du duc de Joyeuse* in which we see Henry III sitting with Catherine de Medici next to him, and next to her the reigning queen, Louise of Lorraine.[83] As queen mother, Catherine was allocated independent power, as regent in the court from time to time and as a 'natural royal counsellor', and so held first place after the King in some ceremonies, as her predecessor, Louise de Savoie, had done. Subsequent female regents of France – Marie de Medici and Anne of Austria – would also enjoy the same privileges. In compensation, the reigning queen, unlike the queen mother, was the centre of attention at larger events such as a ball, and had the right of the first dance with the King, as Richard Cook has shown.[84] He writes that the Queen could accept the invitation to dance from another man only with her spouse's permission. However, in the case of Louise of Lorraine, her own brother, the duke of Mercoeur was the only person to invite her.[85]

For Sertorio Loschi the organization and ceremonial of the French court was a model to follow, and he describes in detail the strict rules of the balls held in the Louvre, where the invited courtiers were seated according their rank and title, and adhered to hierarchy and order in paired dancing. The diplomat tells us, for example, that the dances themselves followed a certain order: first a *pavane*, then an *allemande*, a *branle*, and then moving on to the more active *courante*, *volte* and *gaillarde*.[86]

Conclusion

By never disputing the existence of the Salic Law, nor encroaching on the prerogatives of kings, queens of France in the sixteenth century were actively involved in the wielding of power in order to navigate the difficult political waters of the French court. They could take on the role of regent when needed, in the absence or minority of the ruling monarch. Less obviously, having received the appropriate rights and powers from kings, they also created their own political spaces within the court, where they alone could make decisions and control aspects of ceremonial behaviour. This expansion and change of the power vectors in the royal court underwent an important formalization in the later decades of the century, largely due to the autonomous organization of the ceremonial of the queen's household, as well as her own hierarchy of posts, integrated within the hierarchy and ceremonial regulations of the court in general. The regulations of Henry III of the 1570s–80s not only placed within the curial system the highest ranking persons of the queen's household in a practical sense, they also symbolically shared out the divine power of the crowned monarch to the person of the queen of France, and brought her into the absolutist system of rule within which she formed an unshakeable base for monarchical power.

Notes

1 Christine de Pisan, 'Mémoires ou livre des faits et bonnes moeurs du sage Roi Charles V', in *Nouvelle collection des memoires pour servir à l'histoire de France*, vol. II, ed. Michaud et Poujoulat (Paris: L'éditeur du Commentaire analytique du Code civil, 1836), 51.
2 Ralph E. Giesey, *Cérémonial et puissance souveraine: France, XVe–XVIIe siècles* (Paris: A. Collin, 1987), 49.
3 André Duchesne, *Les Antiquitez et recherches de la grandeur et Majesté des Roys de France* (Paris: Jean Petit-Pas, 1609), 339–549.
4 Giesey, *Cérémonial et puissance souveraine*, 68–72.
5 Robert J. Knecht, *The French Renaissance Court, 1483–1589* (New Haven, CT: Yale University Press, 2008), pp. 70–4.
6 Robert Mandrou, *Introduction to Modern France, 1500–1640: An Essay in Historical Psychology*. Translated by R.E. Hallmark (New York: Holmes & Meier, 1976), chapter V.
7 Jehanne d'Orliac, *The Lady of Beauty, Agnes Sorel: First Royal Favourite of France*. Translated by Maida C. Darnton (Philadelphia: J.B. Lippincott, 1931).
8 Éliane Viennot, 'Masculinité et francité du monarque des lis: le débat sur la loi salique et la construction du consensus national pendant la dernière guerre du XVIe siècle', *Proslogion: Studies in Medieval and Early Modern Social History and Culture*, 13, no 1 (2016): 212–29; Ralph E. Giesey, *Le rôle méconnu de la loi salique. La succession royale, XIVe–XVIe siècles* (Paris: Les Belles Lettres, 2007).
9 Fanny Cosandey, 'De Lance en Quenouille: La place de la reine dans l'État moderne (14e–17e siècles)', *Annales: Histoire, Sciences Sociales* 52, no. 4 (1997): 799–820.
10 1 Corinthians 11:3.
11 Maria Teresa G. Medici, 'Les femmes, la famille et le pouvoir: Comment les jurists s'accommodent des réalités, et autres observations', in *Femmes de pouvoir, femmes*

politiques durant les derniers siècles du Moyen Âge et au cours de la première Renaissance, ed. Eric Bousmar, Jonathan Dumont, Alain Marchandisse, Bertrand Schnerb (Brussels: De Boeck Université, 2012), 622–3; Joëlle Beaucamp, 'La situation juridique de la femme à Byzance', *Cahiers de Civilisation Médievale* 20, no. 78–9 (1977): 149.
12 Thierry Wanegffelen, *Le pouvoir contesté: Souveraines d'Europe à la Renaissance* (Paris: Payot, 2008), 101 ff.
13 Madeleine Valette-Fondo, 'Le fourgon et la pelle: Discours sur les femmes et discours du féminin dans les Essais de Montaigne', *Sens public* (October 2003), available online at http://sens-public.org/article53.html?lang=fr.
14 Christine de Pisan, *The Book of the City of Ladies*. Translated by Rosalind Brown-Grant (London: Penguin Classics, 1999).
15 Pierre de Bourdeille [Abbé de Brantôme], *Les Dames galantes,* ed. Pascal Pia (Paris: Gallimard, 1981), 281: 'Qui aura veu la cour de nos rois François, Henry second, et autres rois ses enfans, advouera bien, quel qu'il soit, et eust-il veu tout le monde, n'avoir rien veu jamais de si beau que nos dames qui sont estées en leur cour, et de nos reines, leur femmes et meres et soeurs' (translations from the French by Jonathan Spangler).
16 *Relations des ambassadeurs vénitiens sur les affaires de France au XVIe siècle*, vol. I, ed. M.N. Tommaseo (Paris: Imprimerie Royale, 1838), 100–3: 'Per li piaceri minuti, nelli quali intra ancorala compra di gioje, e massime diamanti e presenti publici che si fanno a dame di corte ai quali sono deputati scudi novantaseimila, ne spende centoimila, e cencinquantamila'.
17 Anne de France, *Enseignements à sa fille: Histoire du siège de Brest*, ed. Tatiana Clavier and Éliane Viennot (Saint-Etienne: Publications de l'Université de Saint-Étienne, 2006).
18 Wanegffelen, *Le pouvoir contesté*, 131.
19 Éliane Viennot, *La France, les femmes et le pouvoir: L'invention de la loi salique (V^e–XVIe siècles)* (Paris: Perrin, 2006), 485–6; Fanny Cosandey, 'Les préséances à la cour des reines de France', in *Femmes et pouvoir politique: Les princesses d'Europe, XVe–XVIIIe siècle*, ed. Isabelle Poutrin and Marie-Karine Schaub (Paris: Éditions Bréal, 2007), 275.
20 Brantôme, *Les Dames galantes,* 196: 'J'ay ouy faire un conte, moy estant à la cour, que, la reine mere ayant fait commandement de visiter un jour les chambers et coffres de tous ceux qui estoient logez dans le Louvre, sans espargner, dames et filles, pour voir s'il n'y avoit point d'armes cachées et mesmes des pistolets, durant nos troubles.'
21 Marguerite de Valois, *Mémoires et autres écrits, 1574–1614*, ed. Éliane Viennot (Paris: Honoré Champion, 1999), 113: 'Moi, ayant toujours gardé ce respect à la reine ma mere, tant que j'ai été auprès d'elle, fille ou mariée, de n'aller en un lieu sans lui en demander congé'.
22 Thierry Wanegffelen, *Catherine de Médicis: Le pouvoir au feminine* (Paris: Payot, 2005), 195–228.
23 *Lettres de Catherine de Médicis*, vol. II, ed. Hector de la Ferrière-Percy (Paris: Hector de la Ferrière-Percy, 1885), 191–4.
24 *Comptes de l'hôtel des rois de France aux XIVe et XVe siècles*, ed. Louis Claude Douët d'Arcq (Paris: Jules Renouard, 1865), notices V–VI.
25 Philippe Contamine, 'Les cours de France, d'Angleterre et d'Écosse dans leurs rapports avec la cour de Bourgogne', in *La cour de Bourgogne et l'Europe: Le rayonnement et les limites d'un modèle culturel*, ed. Werner Paravicini (Ostfildern: Thorbecke, 2013), 405–19.

26 Jacques Paviot, 'Les honneurs de la cour d'Eléonore de Poitiers', in *Autour de Marguerite d'Ecosse. Reines, princesses et dames du XVe siècle*, ed. Geneviève and Philippe Contamine (Paris: Honoré Champion, 1999), available online since 4 April 2009 at http://cour-de-france.fr/article961.html.

27 Aline Roche, '"Une perle de pris": la maison de la reine Eléonore d'Autriche', article published online in October 2010 at http://cour-de-france.fr/article1646.html.

28 Eudes de Mézeray, *Abregé chronologique de l'histoire de France*, vol. V (Amsterdam: Antoine Schelte, 1696), 238–9.

29 Évelyne Berriot-Salvadore, *Les femmes dans la société française de la Renaissance* (Geneva: Librairie Droz, 1990).

30 'Estat de la maison de la reine Anne de Bretagne', in *Histoire de Charles VIII*, ed. Denis Godefroy (Paris: De l'Imprimerie Royale par Sebastien Mabre-Cramoisy, 1684), 706; Antoine Le Roux de Lincy, 'Détails sur la vie privée d'Anne de Bretagne, femme de Charles VIII et de Louis XII', *Bibliothèque de l'École de Chartes* 11 (1850): 148–71.

31 Jean-François Dubost, 'Le corps de la reine, objet politique: Marie de Médicis', in *Femmes et pouvoir politique: Les princesses d'Europe, XVe–XVIIIe siècle*, ed. Isabelle Poutrin and Marie-Karine Schaub (Paris: Éditions Bréal, 2007), 235.

32 Fanny Cosandey, 'Puissance maternelle et pouvoir politique: La régence des reines mères', *Clio. Histoire, Femmes et Sociétés* 21 (2005): 69–90.

33 *Discours sur ce qu'aucuns seditieux ont temerairement dit et soutenu que pendant la minorité des Rois de France, leurs meres ne sont capables de la Regence dudict Royaume, ains qu'elle appartient seulement aux Princes masles qui sont plus proches et habiles a succeder a la Couronne* (Paris: Nicolas Roffet, 1579).

34 Duchesne, *Les Antiquitez et recherches de la grandeur et Majesté des Roys de France*, 565–91.

35 Murielle Gaude-Ferragu, *Queenship in Medieval France, 1300–1500* (New York: Palgrave Macmillan, 2016), 40–52.

36 Marc Bloch, *Les Rois thaumaturges: Étude sur le caractère surnaturel attribué à la puissance royale particulièrement en France et en Angleterre* (Paris: Gallimard, 1983), 172–83

37 Nicolas Russell and Hélène Visentin, 'Introduction: The Multilayered Production of Meaning in Sixteenth Century French Ceremonial Entries', in *French Ceremonial Entries in the Sixteenth Century: Event, Image, Text*, ed. Nicolas Russell and Hélène Visentin (Toronto: Centre for Reformation and Renaissance Studies, 2007), 15–26.

38 Duchesne, *Les Antiquitez et recherches de la grandeur et Majesté des Roys de France*, 565–91; Théodore Godefroy, *Le Ceremonial François: Contenant Les Ceremonies Observées en France aux Sacres & Couronnemens de Roys, & Reynes, & de quelques anciens Ducs de Normandie, d'Aquitaine, & de Bretagne . . .* , vol. I (Paris: Sébastien Cramoisy, 1649), 470–2, 681, etc; Fanny Cosandey, *La reine de France: Symbole et pouvoir, XVe–XVIIIe siècles* (Paris: Gallimard, 2000), 129.

39 *The Body of the Queen: Gender and Rule in the Courtly World, 1500-2000*, ed. Regina Schulte (New York–Oxford: Berghahn Books, 2006).

40 Fanny Cosandey, 'Participer au cérémonial: De la construction des normes à l'incorporation dans les querelles de préséances', in *Trouver sa place: Individus et communautés dans l'Europe moderne*, ed. Antoine Roullet, Olivier Spina and Nathalie Szczech (Madrid: Casa de Velazquez Editions, 2011), 135–52; Giesey, *Cérémonial et puissance souveraine*, 76.

41 Fanny Cosandey, 'Préséances et sang royal à la cour de France à l'époque moderne', *Cahiers de la Méditerranée*, no 77 (2008): 19–26.

42 Nicolas Le Roux, *La faveur du roi: Mignons et courtisans au temps des derniers Valois (vers 1547–vers 1589)* (Seyssel: Éditions Champ Vallon, 2000), 184–5.

43 'Les Règlemens faict par le Roy (1585)', in *Archives curieuses de l'histoire de France, depuis Louis XI jusqu'à Louis XVIII*, series 1, vol. 10, ed. Louis Cimber and Félix Danjou (Paris: Beauvais, 1836), 315–31.

44 National Library of Russia, Saint Petersburg, Department of Manuscripts, Fr. F. II, no 29, *Règlement de la maison du Roi et des principaux officiers servans en icelle* (France, after 1749) (hereafter: *Règlement de la maison du Roi*). Another version, now in the National Library of France in Paris, has been published in electronic form on the website of the Centre de recherche du château de Versailles: *Règlements de la Maison du roi (1551–1625)*: http://chateauversailles-recherche.fr/francais/ressources-documentaires/corpus-electroniques/corpus-raisonnes/l-etiquette-a-la-cour-de-france/reglements-de-la-maison-du-roi.html (accessed: 11 September 2019).

45 Monique Chatenet, *La cour de France au XVIᵉ siècle: Vie sociale et architecture* (Paris: Picard, 2002), 208–9.

46 Knecht, *The French Renaissance Court*, 71.

47 Marguerite de Valois, *Mémoires et autres écrits*, 127.

48 Ibid., 98.

49 *Recueil des lettres missives de Henri IV*, vol. I, *1562–1584*, ed. Jules Berger de Xivrey (Paris: Imprimerie Royale, 1843), 32.

50 'Les Règlemens faict par le Roy (1585)', 315–20: 'Les chevaliers d'honneur des Reynes mère et femme de Sa Majesté entreront aussi en ladite chambre [d'audience], pour l'honneur qu'ils ont d'avoir ledit etat chez icelles.'

51 *Règlement de la maison du Roi*, 80–1, 'L'Ordre que tiendront et observeront les gentilshommes d'honneur que le Roi a honnoré de ce titre pour servir et suivre la Reine femme de Sa Majesté comme aussi l'Etat et gages qu'ils auront': 'Sa Majesté voulant dorenavant que la Reine sa femme soit dignement et honnorablement suivie et accompagnée, avisé faire election de trente gentilshommes qui seront dix par quartier de quatre mois en quatre mois, à commancer [sic] le premier quartier jusqu'a le 1er janvier, si l'endroit, à savoir ceux de chacun quartier assidus ainsi qu'il s'ensuit depuis les huit heures du matin, si plutôt par la Reine ne leur etoit ordonné autrement, en la salle ou antichambre de ladite Dame.'

52 Ibid., 57–8.

53 Marguerite de Valois, *Mémoires et autres écrits*, 190.

54 Chatenet, *La cour de France au XVIe siècle*, 194.

55 Pierre de Bourdeille [Abbé de Brantôme], *Marguerite, reyne de France et de Navarre*, in *Oeuvres completes de Pierre de Bourdeille, abbé séculier de Brantôme*, vol. II, ed. Jean-Alexandre C. Buchon (Paris: Auguste Desrez, Imprimeur-Éditeur, 1848), 159.

56 Marguerite de Valois, *Mémoires et autres écrits*, 99.

57 *Règlement de la maison du Roi*, 44r.

58 Chatenet, *La cour de France au XVIe siècle*, 210–14.

59 David Potter, 'La cour de France sous Henri III vue par un Anglais (1584–1585)', *Proslogion: Studies in Medieval and Early Modern Social History and Culture* 13, no 1 (2016): 329 –30.

60 *Règlement de la maison du Roi*, 80–1: '. . .lors que ladite Dame ira avec le Roy ou avec la Reine Mère de Sa Majesté (…) se tiendront devant aussy sans s'aprocher troppes marchant devant ceux qui seront plus qualifiés et se mettront avec les autres gentilshommes de Sa Majesté et si l'on marche en cérémonie aincy qu'il leur sera ordonné.'

61 Ibid., 81 :'ne faudront d'accompagner ladite Dame toutes les fois qu'elle ira dehors soit à pied ou à cheval et pour etre plus a pareillés aud. service pour l'accompagner si elle va dehors auront pour le moins chacun deux chevaux et outre ce qu'ils en pourront avoir pour leur bagage et lesquels deux chevaux seront tenus les montrer a l'entrée de leur quartier au chevalier d'honneur.'
62 Ibid., 77.
63 The règlement of Henry III does not mention the *honneurs du Louvre* for the *princes étrangers* that also allows them to take their carriages into the courtyard, but this right was stipulated in the regulations of Charles IX of 1572, *Règlement de la maison du Roi*, 114.
64 Caroline zum Kolk, 'The Household of the Queen of France in the Sixteenth Century', *The Court Historian* 14, no. 1 (2009): 3–22.
65 Marisa Gazzotti, 'L'espace symbolique: La cour d'Henri III de Paris à Mirandole', *Études de lettres*, no. 1–2 (2013): 68.
66 *Traité des droits, fonctions, franchises, exemptions, prerogatives et privileges annexés en France à chaque dignité et à chaque office,* vol. I, ed. Joseph-Nicolas Guyot (Paris: Visse, 1786), 401.
67 *Règlement de la maison du Roi*, 122r.
68 Zum Kolk, 'The Household of the Queen of France in the Sixteenth Century'.
69 Knecht, *The French Renaissance Court*, 71.
70 *Règlement de la maison du Roi*, 122r.
71 Ibid., 11v.
72 Ibid., 122r.: 'Le Roy soupera les dimanches, lundis, mardis, mecredis et jeudis avec les reines, et vendredis et samedis soupera seul en public ou en son cabinet ainsi qu'il commandera de le matin desd. jours si autrement il ne commandoit de sa propre bouche'.
73 Marguerite de Valois, *Mémoires et autres écrits*, 187.
74 *Règlement de la maison du Roi*, 47r.: 'Le maître d'Hôtel servant baillera la serviette à Monsieur le Grand Maître [de France] s'il y est lequel la baillera à la Reine si elle est présente et si elle n'y est point lesd. Grand Maître la baillera lui meme'.
75 Potter, 'La cour de France sous Henri III vue par un Anglais', 328.
76 Marguerite de Valois, *Mémoires et autres écrits*, 117–18.
77 Marguerite de Navarre, *Heptaméron,* ed. Renja Salminen (Geneva: Droz, 1999), chapter 21.
78 Archives nationales, Paris, KK 544 fols. 1r°-7r°, *Letter of Catherine de Medici to her son,* transcript available at: https://www.chateauversailles-recherche.fr/IMG/pdf/1._lettre_de_catherine_de_medicis.pdf (accessed: 3 October 2016). 'Et après disner, pour le moins deux fois la semaine, donnez audience qui est chose qui contente infiniement vos subjetz. Et après, vous retirer et venir chez moy ou chez la reyne afin que l'on cognoisse une façon de cour qui est chose qui plaist infiniement aux François pour l'avoir accoustumé.'
79 Potter, 'La cour de France sous Henri III vue par un Anglais', 328.
80 *Règlement de la maison du Roi*, 121v.
81 Ibid., 'Tous les dimanches et jeudis si ce n'est quelque grande annuelle, ou en Carême ou qu'il soit autrement commandé de par le Roy seront allumés des flambeaux à la salle du bal, et mandés tous les joueurs d'instruments pour le bal, et apporteés les chaires de leur Majestés et un vingtaine d'autres sièges tant tabourets que scabeaux pour ceux et celles qui devront asseoir et ce avant que le fruit soit de servy de devant Sa Majesté, et commandera lesd. maître d'Hôtel au valet de fourrière d'en avoir le soin

et pour les joueurs d'instruments le maître d'Hôtel qui sera en service en avertira l'ecuyer.'
82 Chatenet, *La cour de France au XVIe siècle*, 244.
83 Musée du Louvre, Anonymous painter, École française, 1581, oil on canvas, inv. 8731; discussed in Le Roux, *La faveur du roi*, 488–9.
84 Potter, 'La cour de France sous Henri III vue par un Anglais', 329.
85 Ibid.
86 Gazzotti, *L'espace symbolique: la cour d'Henri III de Paris à Mirandole*, 8.

5

Courtly and ceremonial spaces in Spanish royal sites: An evolution from the renaissance to the baroque

José Eloy Hortal Muñoz

The last twenty years have witnessed an unprecedented increase in research within the field of Court Studies focusing on the late medieval and early modern periods.[1] These studies reveal that the Court constituted a political system defined by a rationale that was based on the reception of classical ethics and politics, where moral virtues such as prudence, fidelity, and liberality were requisites for the exercise of political power.[2] For this reason, the Court must be framed as contemporaries did; that is to say, as a moral and political community whose philosophical basis was formed from the joining together of the disciplines of ethics, *oeconomica* (from Greek *oikos* or 'house') and politics. In this sense, early modern monarchs, rather than relying entirely upon rationally organized institutions, governed as a *pater familias* via patronage and personal relationships by conferring favours and rewards. By doing this they expanded their networks of loyal supporters and strengthened their power bases. Royal Courts and associated Royal Sites played a crucial and active role in this process, providing the space in which these relationships could coalesce and evolve.

It should be noted that 'courtly space' was not always a fixed concept, and to better understand it, we must consider how the definition of the term 'Court' evolved through different moments in history. In the case of the Spanish monarchy, the primary definition that Alfonso X 'the Wise' gave in his *Segunda Partida* can be used as a starting point:

> Court is the name given to the place occupied by the king and his vassals and officials, who serve and advise him, and others from the kingdom who are there because of the King's honour, because they have obtained the right, or because they

---

* This chapter has been funded as part of the projects 'Protection, Production and Environmental Change: The Roots of Modern Environmentalism in the Iberian Peninsula (XVI-XVIIIth centuries)' (AZ 60/V/19); 'Las raíces materiales e inmateriales del conservacionismo ambiental de la Península Ibérica (SIGLOS XV-XIX)' (V-790); 'Madrid, Sociedad y Patrimonio: pasado y turismo cultural' (H2019/HUM-5898); and 'Corte y Sitios Reales: espacios de poder, representación y producción (siglos XVII-XVIII)' (COSREPR/V947).

have served him in some other aspect, and the name derives from the Latin term *cohors*, which refers to a council as well as a company, as all those who are to serve the king and guard the kingdom form part of it. The other Latin term, *curia*, refers to the place where the *cura* is located, for all of the acts of the land, because it is there where it is decided what corresponds to each person according to their right or their status.[3]

This definition provides a basis for an understanding of the Court throughout Spanish history, as it established a duality between the physical space where the Court was located and the entirety of the individuals that composed it and held positions of power. This dichotomy was derived from the classical Greek and Roman world, where different words existed for the two concepts (*curia* and *cohors*), and it exposes the relevance that physical space had in the definition and evolution of the Court.

In this sense, recent studies have attempted to clarify our understanding of court spaces based on the so-called 'spatial turn' in scholarship that has taken place across disciplines,[4] including history,[5] following a trend that was established by the historian Henri Lefebvre in the 1980s.[6] As a result of these studies, historians have begun to pay closer attention to the uses and definitions of space, understood here as the placement, distribution and connection of entities, actions, and ideas; and to place space at the core of theoretical conceptions. No doubt, space, understood as well as a human construction, could help us to better understand social structures and the roles they played in historical processes and conflicts.[7]

There is no doubt that space played a key role in shaping the Court, although until just a few years ago it was only studied in relation to palaces and cities where rulers, dynasties and courts lived and worked, notably the impact that courts had on those places.[8] However, the so-called 'spatial turn' has changed the way that political interactions, cultural symbols and institutional structures within the Court should now be studied.[9] New fields have emerged as a result, for example, the politics of access to rulers,[10] and, of course, ceremonial practices, which will be examined in this chapter. As a result, the Court cannot merely be defined as the physical space where the ruler and his or her entourage and family lived; rather, we should also consider the symbolic and ceremonial spaces where the presence of rulers and dynasties was established through symbols, and where their actual presence was rarely expected, except on special occasions.

The institutional development of different monarchies throughout the sixteenth and seventeenth centuries provides a key example of this, especially the Spanish monarchy. These institutions revealed the personal relationships that monarchs chose to invest in – as a monarch could not personally attend to all of the requests he received. The pace at which this process developed depended on each monarchy, but changes in the administration or management of the Court appear in all of them. As a result, the Court began to be regarded not just as an *ad hoc* organization for a prince's household and administrative needs, but as an institution separate from the individual needs of its principal inhabitants all across Europe.

This chapter therefore will analyse how court spaces evolved at the Spanish monarchy during the Early Modern period, taking into account especially the Royal Sites and the customs of Etiquette and Ceremonial that were developed and took place there. It becomes clear that the definition and codification of court space in the Spanish monarchy was much more clear by the seventeenth century that it had been previously, due to the changes that took place at the various Royal Sites related to the evolving needs of the Court, an emergence of a new style of monarchy, from Renaissance to Baroque.

Court space in the Spanish Monarchy during the Early Modern period

In the Spanish monarchy, the changes related to the institutionalization of its Court took effect in just a few years. If Sebastián de Covarrubias in his *Tesoro de la lengua castellana o española*, written in 1611, still defined the Court as Alfonso X did, Gil González Dávila in his *Teatro de las Grandezas de la villa de Madrid*, published in 1623, already incorporated significant innovations that can be observed in the structure of his work. It was composed of four books: the first two focus on the history of the city of Madrid, while the third examines the royal households specifically, and the fourth the royal councils and their officials.

These changes taking place in the Monarchy, shifting the emphasis of the Court as merely a royal residence to an institution of state governance, increasingly gained importance, notably in Alonso Núñez de Castro's *Solo Madrid es Corte y el cortesano en Madrid*, published in 1658. This book further developed the idea of the representation of the Court from an institutional point of view. While the last three volumes are dedicated to offering advice to all who visit Madrid, the first volume consists of an etymological study of the word 'court', with an analysis of its different components: councils, the *Junta de Obras y Bosques* (Board of Works and Woodlands), the *alcaldes de Casa y Corte*,[11] the *Junta de Aposento* (Board of Lodging), representative assemblies across the kingdoms (*cortes*), royal households, grandees, and revenues of the Crown. All these components were universally accepted as the most significant ones for the Court, with some differences depending on each monarchy. This definition would last until the breakdown of the court system in the nineteenth century.

The date of this publication is no mere coincidence, considering the re-configuration of the Spanish monarchy that began under the reign of Charles V (1516–56), and then questioned during the crisis years of the reign of Philip IV (1621–65), culminating in the 1640s. Consequently, Philip's reign of more than forty-four years turned into a desperate quest to re-shape the monarchy socially and politically, as well as spacially.[12] The main cause of the decline of the system was that many of the monarchy's subjects could no longer be integrated into the Royal Household, and therefore were excluded from the safety offered by the protective umbrella that the monarch, as *pater familias*, had provided up until then, because the constitution of the Monarchy itself prevented it from successfully absorbing the various social groups of the different kingdoms, as the household had done in the past.[13] This integration finally ended when Philip IV adopted a series of measures, carried out for economic reasons, that deconstructed the model of political organization that had underpinned the Spanish monarchy since the time of his great-grandfather Charles V. In the face of long-standing traditions, Philip's first minister, the Count-Duke of Olivares, began cutting costs in the Royal Households,[14] monitoring the efficiency of the Ordinances of the Household of Burgundy of 1624.[15] These measures damaged the political foundations of the union of the Monarchy by tarnishing the monarch's reputation as *pater familias*, because he no longer provided compensation to his subjects for their services.

As a result of these changes, access to most middle and low level posts in the Royal Households became more and more restricted, limited mostly to those belonging to families with a long tradition of service to the monarchy and its court. This made it impossible for new officers to join the royal entourage, despite their service to the monarch. The so-called 'patrimonialization' of key court posts was supported by the monarchs, and some servants received privileges such as the ability to pass their posts on to their sons or *para con quién casare* (children's spouses) over one or even two generations.[16]

An example of this was constituted by the *porteros de cámara* (keepers of the chamber) of the Household of Castile.[17] Their main task was to control the access of courtiers to the monarch in his diverse places of residence, not only at the royal palaces, but also in the many peripheral manifestations of the Court, where the king was hardly present, such as the *chancillerías* (chanceries) located in Valladolid, Ciudad Real (1494–1500) and Granada (1500-onwards), as well as the Royal Sites surrounding these chanceries. The great significance of the *porteros* in these locations made this office the most patrimonialized of the Royal Household, and there are numerous cases to be seen where the post passed from generation to generation.[18] We find that in some cases the offices were even sold, an example of venality that was not typical in the Spanish royal household as it had become in France and other monarchies.[19] This office was more than just an object of dynastic patrimony; it was a key component in the process of controlling and configuring courtly territory and courtly space.

Another example of court space undergoing reconfiguration is seen in the Royal Sites. In order to better understand the term 'Royal Sites' we must first develop a definition. In the early modern period, the term referred to properties that belonged to the ruling dynasty where the ruler and other members of the dynasty lived, had lived or where the expectation existed that they could stay for short or long periods. These sites included not only palaces, but forests, gardens, agricultural spaces, manufacturing spaces and urban centres. They also included royal monasteries and convents founded and/or financed by the royal family, therefore linked to the dynasty, to which a royal apartment or funeral pantheon was often attached or where some members of the ruler's family could commit themselves to a life in the church, usually female members; as was the case of the monasteries of San Lorenzo de El Escorial in Castile, or in other monarchies, Westminster, Val-de-Grâce or Mafra. These spaces set new trends in art, fashion and education, and constituted a diverse, global network that made royal power more visible and effective. At the same time, however, and perhaps more importantly, Royal Sites served as centres of power that helped shape early modern European monarchies, especially in the seventeenth century, when different monarchs used them to address challenges to their authority.

According to the classical definition, the Court was composed of three parts: the royal or princely households, the councils, and the courtiers.[20] Royal Sites must be included as a fourth element within the court system, especially during the seventeenth century, as has been studied for the Spanish case.[21] Thanks to these studies, we can conclude that Royal Sites therefore must be considered as a type of royal geography. The term 'geography' is used here as the physicality of spaces and landscapes acted upon and produced through political, social and cultural practices. This interlacing of physical and human agency is naturally wide-ranging and encompasses image-making, as well as architectural, agricultural and administrative processes.

In the case of the Spanish monarchy, the importance of Royal Sites in relation to court spaces increased with the application of a strategy that had the aim of reversing negative trends within the Monarchy, like the already outlined breakdown of the system of integration. This consisted of selecting members of the Royal Household to govern and manage Royal Sites, connecting them more closely to the Court by establishing a kind of 'extension of the Court', and thereby merging Court, Household and territory. The relationship between the Royal Hunt and Royal Guards and the Royal Sites, for example, was especially important.[22]

It is worth noting that during the sixteenth and early seventeenth centuries, in the monarch's absence, these Royal Sites were looked after and guarded by a minimal number of servants who were often related to one another. Just a few sites had 'life' all year long during this period, such as Aranjuez, San Lorenzo de El Escorial and Valladolid (when the Court settled there from 1601–6). This changed radically from the reign of Philip IV onwards, when these places were revitalized. The main reason for this development was the increase in the number of staff serving at practically all of the Royal Sites, a phenomenon linked to the already mentioned over-staffing of the collapsed central Royal Households (see Figures 5.1 and 5.2).

Figure 5.1 *Map of the Royal Sites around Madrid ca. 1600.* © María Luisa Walliser Martín.

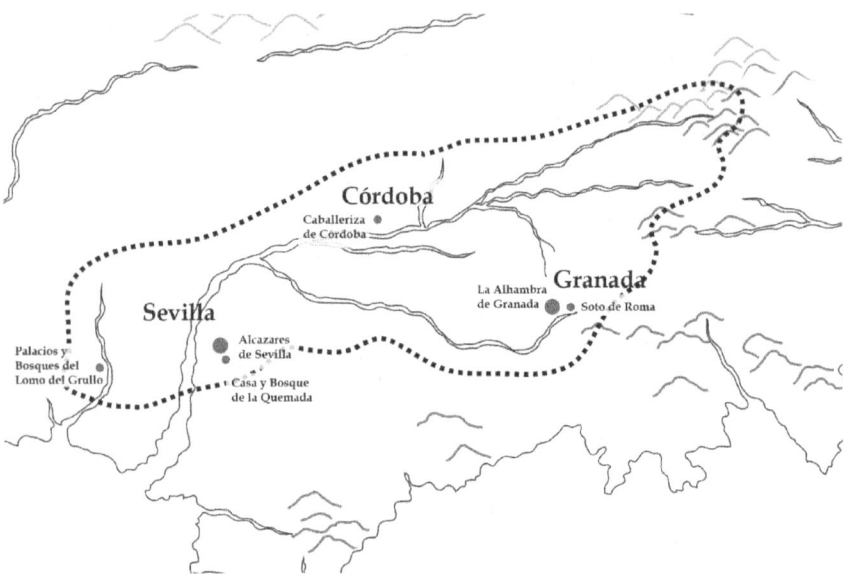

Figure 5.2 *Map of the Royal Sites in the south of the Iberian Peninsula ca. 1600.* © María Luisa Walliser Martín.

The Count-Duke of Olivares was the first to sense the potential of Royal Sites, and aimed to secure the *alcaidías* (governorships) of several of them himself. The previous occupants of these posts had been courtiers of lower ranks, rather than the king's favourites, apart from exceptional cases when the affairs of the site involved family matters or proximity to their own estates, as was the case with the Duke of Lerma. Olivares, however, changed this pattern when he was appointed as governor of the Royal Apartment of the monastery of San Jerónimo – which later became part of the Palace of Buen Retiro – in 1630 as well as of the palaces of Zarzuela and Vaciamadrid, combining these with the governorship of the Royal *Alcázares* of Seville, which he had inherited. He also extended his control over other Royal Sites by appointing his 'creatures' to governorships and to the *Junta de Obras y Bosques*, which was the institution in charge of managing all the royal domains of the Castilian kingdom.[23] Future favourites like Luis de Haro applied the same policy; he accumulated even more titles than his predecessor. As a result of this trend, we can say that the link between the Royal Sites and the Court was much closer from the time of Philip IV.

These two examples (keepers of the chamber and governors of Royal Sites), demonstrate clearly that the Court was not just the place where the ruler and his/her entourage and family lived, but that it included all the locations where the king was present, physically as well as metaphorically. This circumstance was crucial in relation to the ceremonial development of the Court in particular, and acquired special relevance in the Spanish monarchy during the seventeenth century.

Ceremonial customs and etiquette in the Spanish Monarchy: from Renaissance to Baroque

In the 1726 edition of the Spanish *Diccionario de Autoridades*, the word *Etiqueta* (Etiquette) is defined as: 'Ceremonial styles, uses and customs, which must be observed and kept in royal households'.[24] These so-called 'etiquettes' were sets of rules, codes and regulations that ensured the dignity and security of the royal figure, in which obligations, privileges and courtier hierarchies were noted, and also ensuring that the service provided to the monarch and his family members was undertaken with the required decorum and dignity.[25] Palace etiquettes sought, therefore, to maintain a well-regulated service for the Royal Households, creating both physical and emotional distance, thus protecting the monarch from any intruder who might attack his person, and producing an almost divine aura around the king.[26] In addition, they drew up guidelines for conduct and codes of behaviour that should be respected by all courtiers; good breeding and knowledge of these guidelines allowed observers to distinguish the noble from the plebeian.

Many administrative arrangements, in turn, affected the uniformity of ruling elite customs and were manifested in a multitude of details concerned with taste, language or formal behaviour. Etiquette, thus, came close to formulating an abstract rule underpinning its own specific role in determining social and political structures, as well as court space.[27] In this sense, the ordinances, etiquettes and ceremonies imposed a hierarchical articulation of order emanating from the person of the king through a mythical conception of the monarchy and conceiving society as a coherent 'body'. They governed the life of the prince and the functioning of all aspects of the Royal Household,[28] although this did not prevent some issues from remaining subject to customary practices and others from being changed in accordance with the wishes of the prince or the current political environment.

Based on this, court rituals tended to enforce political harmony,[29] although power relationships evolved and conflicts inevitably arose.[30] Indeed, these rituals were part of the factional struggle that arose as a result of individuals continuously seeking the king's favour, given that an appearance in a specific moment of a different spatial position could be used as a precedent for future occasions. Moreover, struggles emerged to maintain and improve the ceremonial space that each courtier or power group possessed, resulting in intense conflicts that were magnified further by their public manifestations. At the same time, the ruler acted as the final judge of such conflicts, as well as mediator in the constant negotiations that took place between rivals. The ruler could also intervene in the ritual order to impose his particular interests through the designation of favoured courtiers for important offices.[31]

The configuration of the complex network that defined the public image of the monarch inside and outside the sphere of the Court was particularly important for court rituals and ceremonies.[32] When the monarch ventured outside the palace, this provided an opportunity for him to be seen in all his majesty, and projected an image of him that demonstrated his wealth, the sacralization of his figure, and the distance that separated him from his subjects. This *mise en scène* in different ceremonies, such as the public presentation of royal heirs, processions, receptions and so on, revealed the splendour of the Court and, above all, the power of the prince by means of a semiotic series that penetrated the viewers' awareness directly and influenced their thinking. These appearances played an essential role in embodying the royal image, given that most of the etiquettes and ceremonies in which the king took part were invisible to his lesser subjects, for example, the public meals at the royal palace. The Royal Stables, as organizers of much of the monarch's public appearances, were thus the most important household department in this respect,[33] although the Royal Guard[34] also occupied a privileged place in public appearances.

For the Spanish monarchy, the development of the Royal Stables was of unique importance,[35] helping to construct a more remote and sacralized figure of the king. Carefully crafted vehicles such as carts and carriages transformed the appearances of the king in public, revealing a process of distancing and exalting the monarch. The most significant example of this change was the royal entry by coach, a practice that broke with or rejected the traditional chivalric entry, on horseback and under a canopy. In these entries, the use of the coach highlighted both the distance and the sacred quality of the king.

Although previously introduced in the Royal Stables starting with Charles V, it was in the 1580s when the use of state vehicles proved decisive in emphasizing the remoteness of the figure of the king, as a result of the process of institutionalizing the Spanish monarchy under Philip II.[36] From that time onwards, and in close alignment with changes in palace etiquette and the publication of the *Pragmática de las cortesías* in 1586,[37] the figure of the sovereign was glorified, and access to the king became more and more restricted. After this, very few people had close access to Philip II, and under his successors, court spaces became even more tightly regulated. Philip, the 'Prudent King', completed this process with an exhaustive control over the entrance of carriages and horses into the courtyards of royal palaces, and through his retirement to more remote locations, such as the Monastery of San Lorenzo de El Escorial. This royal concealment even influenced the fine arts and was reflected particularly in portraits.[38]

But it was not until the reign of Philip IV that the most important regulating effort of the courtier space in the whole history of the Spanish monarchy took place, especially in matters related to palace spaces, in the preparation and publication of the *Etiquetas Generales de Palacio*.[39]

We must frame this compilation of etiquettes and court regulations in a European context, as most contemporary princely courts were adapting the inherited medieval organizational models into more modern systems, more suited to a Baroque political culture. During the first half of the sixteenth century, the Renaissance style was extended throughout Europe. It was a period in which public festivals were the means by which rulers expressed and reflected their wealth and magnificence; such rulers were presented as noble representatives of their dynasties and inherited virtues by means of erudite representations.[40] The philosophical and artistic evolution that European courts went through at the end of the sixteenth century changed this tradition of iconographical representation, shifting towards visual representations of desired ideas with more clarity, with less need for interpretation. Moreover, and more importantly for us, the themes of the Renaissance court festival went from being the contemplation of cosmic harmony and its reflection in society to those of the Baroque, with the monarch as the genesis of such harmonious representation himself, in a different sphere from his subjects and completely out of their reach.

In this sense, it became important to provide a clear set of rules that any level of society could interpret. Most European courts therefore developed a process of codification etiquette systems for court spaces. In 1619 in France, for example, Théodore Godefroy assembled a collection of ceremonial texts, which were published in an extended version by his son Denis II in 1649 as *Le ceremonial françois*.[41] In Florence, until 1589, there was no such thing as an etiquette code, but by the seventeenth century we find thirty-three.[42]

The Spanish monarchy did the same, and Philip IV ordered some of his most knowledgeable courtiers to compile the diverse ceremonial and jurisdictional uses of his Royal Households, to clearly fix rules of access to his person and to ceremonial spaces. This process took place between 1647 and 1651, when the *Etiquetas Generales de Palacio* were published.[43] The document was complemented by a series of explanatory plans designed by the royal architect Juan Gómez de Mora, in which the ceremonial spaces devoted to every royal household section, as well as to representatives from every part of the different realms that composed the Spanish monarchy, were clearly fixed.[44] Since its publication, it has been considered one of the best defined and most important of its kind in Europe. The same was done for other courts of the Spanish monarchy in the second half of the seventeenth century, especially Brussels[45] and Naples.[46]

The aforementioned evolution led to a shift, at least within the Spanish monarchy, as festivities were gradually transferred to the interior of the royal palaces, where they took place in full view of the courtiers but beyond the reach of the general population. As a result, the relevance of Royal Sites beyond the palace increased.

Ceremonies and the transformation of court space in Spanish Royal Sites

Royal Sites had to adapt to the changes and new needs of the Court. The first step in this process was finishing the codification of rules and laws related to them.[47] Although much of this had been fixed during Philip II's reign, Philip IV decided to establish and compile new rules establishing the tasks assigned to different officers and their jurisdictions.[48] In this way, the boundaries of these Royal Sites became more well defined.

This newly delineated space, reserved only for courtiers, firstly needed an increasing number of personnel to demarcate its boundaries. For example, royal guards units were specifically assigned to protect the Royal Sites where ceremonies and other royal functions would take place, clearly marking the detachment of these spaces from the rest of society. In this sense, a paradigmatic example was set by France, a realm that had enormously increased its number and quality of guards units due to the unstable political situation following the death of King Henry II in 1559 and the beginning of the Wars of Religion. While the number of guards and units increased, a division appeared between the guards *du dedans* and *du dehors* – inside and outside – of the Louvre.[49] In the aftermath, we find that the entirety of the French royal guards around 1625 encompassed about 6,000–7,000 soldiers, whose different units occupied the physical and ceremonial space around the king. Amongst the *gardes du dedans du Louvre*, the *Archiers de corps* were always positioned around the monarch, while the *Cent Suisses* and the *Gardes de la Porte* guarded the entrance to the palace and the *Cent-gentilshommes* appeared at the great celebrations of the court. In contrast, the *gardes du dehors du Louvre*, the *Gardes Françaises*, *Suisses* and *Écossaises*, watched over the exteriors of royal palaces, and the *Chevaux-légers*, *Gendarmes* and *Mousquetaires* escorted the king at public functions outside the palace walls.

This division, which became the model for numerous European kingdoms, could not be fully adapted for the royal guards of the Spanish monarchy, who were more like a parade and ceremonial body than a real military force prepared to guard the Royal Sites.[50] Indeed, specific and effective units in charge of these tasks were not created until the eighteenth century.[51] Meanwhile, we find mounted and dismounted guards and wardens in Royal Sites as El Pardo, Aranjuez, La Casa de Campo, El Escorial or El Soto de Roma,[52] which indicates that they were already clearly differentiated spaces from their surroundings.

The next stage in this process was the creation of new infrastructures in the Royal Sites specifically designed for court celebrations, such as illuminated stages, which encouraged indoor performances and the construction of permanent theatres,[53] as happened in other monarchies in this period, for example the Banqueting House in London, or the court theatres at the royal palaces like the Palais-Royal in Paris. Philip III had already intended to build a theatre at the *Casas del Tesoro* (Houses of the Treasure) in Madrid, but the project was not completed. Philip IV tried two other times, close to the *Juego de pelota* (ball game playing field) near the Alcázar of Madrid (1622 and 1655),[54] but he also was unable to finish the project due to the opposition of the city council of Madrid. After that, all the efforts went into building the Coliseum of the Buen Retiro, which was inaugurated on 4 February 1640.[55] The palace of La Zarzuela is another important example,[56] as it greatly influenced court festivities – in fact, the very name Zarzuela was incorporated into the Spanish language as a musical genre, after the style of lyric drama performed in its gardens on numerous occasions. The first of these was the *Golfo de las Sirenas* by Calderón de la Barca in 1657, in which some of the most relevant actors and actresses of the moment were characterized as Royal Sites (as La Zarzuela, Aranjuez, La Casa de Campo, El Pardo, Valsaín or Buen Retiro), paying homage to the monarch.[57]

Even though court theatre is a phenomenon that has been widely studied by specialists of the history of theatre, I should like to draw attention in this context to an anonymous play, *Loa de la Etiqueta y oficios de las Casas Reales*, which was presented to the royal family at Aranjuez during a celebration on 2 May 1681, in honour of the Duke of Orléans, father of the Queen, Maria Luisa.[58] Although it is not a work of great quality, it reveals valuable information about etiquette and about how offices of the Royal Household served as a reflection of society of the time.[59] It was specifically designed to be performed in the setting of a Royal Site like Aranjuez. There were no permanent theatres there until the eighteenth century, so these performances would have been staged inside the palace or in its gardens, as was the case of the temporary theatre that Cesare Fontana had set up in the *Jardín de la Isla* (Island Garden) on 15 May 1622 to perform *La Gloria de Niquea* by the Count of Villamediana.[60]

Throughout this process of defining the boundaries and usages of Royal Sites, there is no doubt that the favourites of the Spanish kings, or *validos*, men fully aware of the importance of the various palace spaces and Royal Sites of the Spanish monarchy, played a fundamental role in the modifications that these Sites underwent during the seventeenth century.

Accordingly, we must bear in mind that both the Duke of Lerma and the Count-Duke of Olivares ensured their influence over courtly spaces by holding personally the office of *Sumiller de Corps*, the head of the royal Chamber in the Burgundian household, with the means to control the most private spaces of the royal residences. It should be added that Olivares also occupied the post of *Camarero mayor* (Great Chamberlain) from 1636 onwards, after a thorough reform of the Chamber, leading to a new set of court regulations, the *Instrucción y orden que se ha de observar de aquí adelante en el servicio del aposento de su Majestad* (Instruction and order which has to be observed from this moment onwards in the service of the Chamber of His Majesty) of 1637.[61]

In their daily practice of government, the *validos* or minister-favourites like Lerma and Olivares confirmed that the royal palaces were political spaces, and they strove to submit these spaces to their control. In this sense, the Instruction of 1637 focused on restricting the access in the royal apartments, with the Chamber at their heart. The closer one got to the centre, the more restrictions. The regulations introduced by this document would be further refined two decades later in the *Etiquetas Generales de Palacio*.[62] Such codification shaped the principal palatial buildings of the court of Madrid and became particularly relevant in a moment in which those buildings were necessarily adapted to the new outlined usages of the Baroque court.

In addition, the *validos* Lerma and Olivares decided to control the Royal Sites directly with the provision of the *alcaidías* (governorships) of the most relevant Royal Sites directly in their hands or in those of their family or noble clients, as described above. Consequently, the *validos* had the opportunity to organize every monarch's living spaces, not only at the main palace, the *Alcázar* of Madrid, but also during time spent at Royal Sites such as Aranjuez, El Pardo, Buen Retiro, etc.

These aspects are illustrated by the evolution of the principal palaces of the realm during the seventeenth century and by the control that the favourites exercised in remodelling them. The residences reached a height of splendour as a result of the construction projects to bring them up to date with current artistic trends. As I have written elsewhere,[63] Lerma exerted great influence in the refurbishment of places such as the royal residences of Valladolid, the Casa de Campo or El Pardo, while Olivares had a similar role in the reshaping of sites such as the Buen Retiro, Zarzuela and Vaciamadrid. At the same time, both of them influenced enormously the different works carried out at the *Alcázar* of Madrid and Aranjuez.

All these changes led, by the end of the seventeenth century, to a better defined court space in the Spanish monarchy, and the increased importance of Royal Sites.

Conclusion

Court space was crucial in shaping the ceremonies of European early modern monarchies. Depending on their purposes, different festivals and ceremonies were celebrated in one specific location or another. The shift that took place from the last decades of the sixteenth century in the Spanish monarchy – which led to the gradual transfer of festivities into the interiors of royal palaces, so that they were in full view of the courtiers but beyond the reach of the general population – ultimately increased the importance of Royal Sites.

Admittedly, there were still some ceremonies where ordinary people could see and join the feast, as in the case of the processions of Corpus Christi, *Autos de Fé* or bull fights in the Plaza Mayor of Madrid; especially under Philip IV, who wanted to convey an image of piety for his dynasty and for himself, and had ceremonial intentions for reforms of the city of Madrid.[64] Nevertheless, the extension of court space beyond the capital in the seventeenth century imprinted the royal image more strongly on other locations, leading the court system to reach its peak during this period. No doubt, the role that Royal Sites played in this process, as we have seen, was crucial.

Notes

1 For an up-to-date state-of-the-art survey on the Court and Court Studies, see Jeroen Duindam, 'Rulers and Courts', in *The Oxford Handbook of Early Modern European History, 1350–1750*, vol. 2, *Cultures and Power*, ed. Hamish Scott (Oxford: Oxford University Press, 2015), 440–77.

2 As explained, with full bibliography, in José Eloy Hortal Muñoz and Gijs Versteegen, *Las ideas políticas y sociales en la Edad Moderna* (Madrid: Síntesis, 2016).

3 'Corte es llamado el lugar donde está el rey y sus vasallos y sus oficiales con él, que le han comunicado de aconsejar y servir, y los otros del reino que se llegan allá o por honra de él, por alcanzar derecho, o por hacer recaudar las otras cosas que han de ver con él, y tomó este nombre de una palabra del latín que dicen cohors, que muestra tanto como ayuntamiento de compañías, pues allí se allegan todos aquellos que han de honrar y aguardar al rey y al reino. Y otrosí tiene nombre en latín, curia, que quiere tanto decir como lugar donde está la cura, de todos los hechos de la tierra, pues allí se ha de considerar lo que cada uno ha de haber según su derecho o su estado', *Las siete partidas del Rey Don Alfonso el Sabio: cotejadas con varios códices antiguos por la Real Academia de la Historia* (Alicante: Biblioteca Virtual Miguel de Cervantes, 2008), Title 9 – *Cuál debe ser el rey con sus oficiales, y con los de su casa y de su corte, y ellos con él*, Law 27, 82.

4 As explained in *The Spatial Turn: Interdisciplinary Perspectives*, ed. Barney Warf and Santa Arias (London: Routledge, 2009), especially the introduction.

5 We find numerous bibliographies, such as those included in Mike Crang, 'Spaces in Theory, Spaces in History and Spatial Historiographies', in *Political Space in Pre-industrial Europe*, ed. Beat Kümin (Farnham: Ashgate, 2009), 249–65; or Ralph Kingston, 'Mind Over Matter? History and the Spatial Turn', *Cultural and Social History* 7 (2010): 111–21.

6 Although some authors go back to earlier times, as the study of the past has long been saturated with spatialized concepts, as treated by Paul Stock, in the introduction to his

edited volume, *The Uses of Space in Early Modern History* (New York: Palgrave Macmillan, 2015), 2-5.
7   As sketched in *Territoires, lieux et espaces de la révolte, XIVᵉ-XVIIIᵉ siècles*, ed. Paloma Bravo and Juan Carlos d'Amico (Dijon: Editions Universitaires de Dijon, 2017). Bibliography for the 'Spatial Turn' see page 23, note 2. An up-to-date state-of-the-art bibliography concerning social and cultural history until 2014 can be found in the review article, Fiona Williamson, 'The Spatial Turn of Social and Cultural History: A Review of the Current Field', *European History Quarterly* 44, no. 4 (2014): 703-17.
8   The impact of the Court upon the city is currently being intensively studied, as evidenced by the special issue of *Studies in European Urban History (1100-1800)* 35 (2015), edited by Léonard Courbon and Denis Menjot, entitled *La cour et la ville dans l'Europe du Moyen âge et des Temps Modernes*. John P. Spielman pioneered this field with *The City and the Crown: Vienna and the Imperial Court 1600-1740* (West Lafayette, IN: Purdue University Press, 1993).
9   An early aplication of the 'Spatial Turn' approach to court space can be seen in *The Politics of Space: European Courts ca. 1500-1750*, ed. Marcello Fantoni, George Gorse and Malcolm Smuts (Rome: Bulzoni Editore, 2009), where its parameters are given in the introduction, on page 13, as 'The juxtaposition of human bodies and physical objects in space provided courts with a supple language, through which hierarchical distinctions of rank and honor were defined and contested, and complex political messages conveyed. Focusing on spatial issues provides a way of decoding the mysteries of early modern court societies, by reconstructing the largely unwritten rules that shaped them from within'. Some points were sketched in previous studies such as Fernando Bouza Álvarez, 'El Espacio en las Fiestas y en las Ceremonias de Corte: Lo Cortesano como dimensión', in *La fiesta en la Europa de Carlos V*, ed. Fernando Villaverde (Seville: Sociedad Estatal para la Conmemoración de los Centenarios de Felipe II y Carlos V, Exhibition Catalogue, 2000), 155-73.
10 See *The Key to Power? The Culture of Access in Princely Courts, 1400-1750*, ed. Dries Raeymaekers and Sebastiaan Derks (Leiden-Boston: Brill, 2016).
11 Royal officers in charge of enforce justice at Court.
12 As studied in *La Corte de Felipe IV (1621-65): Reconfiguración de la Monarquía Católica*, ed. José Martínez Millán and José Eloy Hortal Muñoz (Madrid: Polifemo, 2015).
13 For a study of this integration, see *La Corte de Carlos V*, ed. José Martínez Millán (Madrid: Sociedad Estatal para la Conmemoración de los Centenarios de Felipe II y Carlos V, 2000); *La monarquía de Felipe II: La Casa del Rey*, ed. José Martínez Millán and Santiago Fernández Conti (Madrid: Fundación Mapfre Tavera, 2005); *La monarquía de Felipe III: La Casa del Rey*, ed. José Martínez Millán and Maria Antonietta Visceglia (Madrid: Fundación Mapfre, 2008); *La Corte de Felipe IV*; and *La Casa de Borgoña: La Casa del rey de España*, ed. José Eloy Hortal Muñoz and Félix Labrador Arroyo (Leuven: Leuven University Press, 2014).
14 Households is plural, even under the rule of one monarch, since the Spanish monarchy of the sixteenth and seventeenth centuries consisted of several territorial units, which, prior to their integration into the Habsburg dominions, had each enjoyed their own political systems, their own rulers, and hence their own princely courts and royal households. So, although the Spanish monarchy was a single political entity, its kings had several complete, fully functioning royal households (Castile, Aragon, Naples, Sicily, Portugal, Navarre and Burgundy) under the overall umbrella of the Burgundian one (See *La Casa de Borgoña, passim*).

15 Transcribed and studied in detail at *La monarquía de Felipe III*, vol. 1, 324–48.
16 This happened in other monarchies in this period, like France, as can be seen in Jonathan Spangler, 'Holders of the Keys: The Grand Chamberlain, the Grand Equerry and Monopolies of Access at the Early Modern French Court', in *The Key to Power?*, 153–77.
17 Ignacio Javier Ezquerra Revilla, 'El valor espacial agregativo de la cámara real de Castilla en el plano jurisdiccional: los porteros de cámara del Consejo Real y las chancillerías', in *La Corte de Felipe IV*, vol. 1/2, 405–40.
18 See for example the Cruzate family, who were *porteros de cámara* in the chancery of Valladolid for three generations: Jerónimo Cruzate (1614–38), Jerónimo Cruzate Barrientos (1638–94) and Leonor Cruzate (1694–onwards), although, as she was underage, the office was filled in the first years by Felipe de Volasechitano. Archivo General de Palacio, Madrid (hereafter: AGP), Personal, box 16817/22.
19 See José Eloy Hortal Muñoz, 'Reservados y pensionistas: Una nueva vía de integración de los reinos en la Casa Real', in *La Corte de Felipe IV*, vol. 1/3, 2322–27.
20 See Hortal Muñoz and Versteegen, *Las ideas*, 20–59.
21 All processes and related historiography are covered in José Eloy Hortal Muñoz, 'La integración de los Sitios Reales en el sistema de Corte durante el reinado de Felipe IV', *Libros de la Corte* 8 (2014): 27–47. For the evolution of the type of personages who lived at the Royal Sites during the sixteenth and seventeenth centuries, see José Eloy Hortal Muñoz, 'El personal de los Sitios Reales desde los últimos Habsburgos hasta los primeros Borbones: de la vida en la periferia a la integración en la Corte', in *Siti Reali in Europa: Una storia del territorio tra Madrid e Napoli*, ed. Lucio D'Alessandro, Félix Labrador Arroyo and Pasquale Rossi (Naples: Università suor Orsola Benincasa, 2014), 75–95. See, as well, the dedicated chapters at *La Corte de Felipe IV*, or some of the works compiled in *La extensión de la Corte: Los Sitios Reales*, ed. Concepción Camarero Bullón and Félix Labrador Arroyo (Madrid: Universidad Autónoma de Madrid, 2017).
22 See José Eloy Hortal Muñoz, 'La unión de la Corte, la Casa y el Territorio en la Monarquía Hispana de los siglos XVI y XVII: Las Guardas Reales y los Sitios Reales', *Revista Escuela de Historia* 16, no. 1 (2017). Available online at http://portalderevistas.unsa.edu.ar/ojs/index.php/reh/article/view/1468 (accessed 7 April 2021).
23 See María Victoria García Morales, 'Los artistas que trabajan para el rey: La Junta de Obras y Bosques', *Espacio, Tiempo y Forma: Historia del Arte* 3 (1990): 123–36 and especially Francisco Javier Díaz González, *La Real Junta de Obras y Bosques en la época de los Austrias* (Madrid: Dykinson, 2002). More recently, José Martínez Millán, 'La descomposición del sistema cortesano: La supresión de la Junta de Obras y Bosques', in *Europa e America allo specchio: Studi per Francesca Cantù*, ed. Paolo Broggio, Luigi Guarnieri Calò Carducci and Manfredi Merluzzi (Rome: Viella, 2017): 159–86.
24 'Ceremonial de los estilos, usos y costumbres, que se deben observar y guardar en las Casas Reales, donde habitan los Reyes', *Diccionario de Autoridades* (Madrid: Real Academia Española, 1726) http://web.frl.es/DA.html (accessed 28 February 2013).
25 For the role of ceremonial rites and etiquette in royal european courts, see Hortal Muñoz and Versteegen, *Las ideas*, 48–59.
26 See Yves Bottineau, 'Aspects de la cour d'Espagne au XVIIè siècle: l'etiquette de la chambre du roi', *Bulletin Hispanique* 74, no. 1–2 (1972): 138–57; *Rituale, cerimoniale, etichetta*, ed. Sergio Bertelli and Giuliano Crifò (Rome: Bompiani, 1985); David Cannadine, 'Introduction: Divine Rites of Kings', in *Rituals of Royalty: Power and Ceremonial in Traditional Societies*, ed. David Cannadine and Simon Price

(Cambridge: Cambridge University Press, 1987), 1–19; Alain Boureau, 'Ritualité politique et modernité monarchique', in *L'État ou le Roi: Les fondations de la modernité monarchique en France (XIVᵉ–XVIIᵉ siècle)*, ed. Neithard Bulst, Robert Descimon and Alain Guerreau (Paris: Maison des sciences de l'homme, 1996), 9–25; Maria Antonietta Visceglia, 'Cérémonial et politique pendant la période moderne', in *Cérémonial et ritual à Rome (XVIᵉ–XIXe siècle)*, ed. Maria Antonietta Visceglia and Catherine Brice, (Rome: Ecole française de Rome, 1997), 1–19; and Maria Antonietta Visceglia, *Guerra, Diplomacia y Etiqueta en la Corte de los Papas (Siglos XVI y XVII)* (Madrid: Polifemo, 2010). See also the project carried out in recent years by the *Centre de recherche du Château de Versailles*: 'Court Etiquette: Normative Texts and Customs': http://chateauversailles-recherche.fr/english/research/research-programmes/archives/court-etiquette-normative-texts (accessed 24 September 2019).
27 *La corte e il cortegiano*, vol. 2, *Un modello europeo*, ed. Adriano Prosperi (Rome: Bulzoni, 1980); Antonio Álvarez-Ossorio Alvariño, 'Corte y cortesanos en la monarquía de España', in *Educare il corpo, educare la parola nella trattatistica del Rinascimento*, ed. Giorgio Patrizi and Amedeo Quondam (Rome: Bulzoni, 1998), 297–365.
28 Maria José del Río Barredo, 'El ritual en la corte de los Austrias', in *La fiesta cortesana en la época de los Austrias*, ed. María Luisa Lobato López and Bernardo J. García García (Salamanca: Junta de Castilla y León, 2003), 17–34.
29 Well studied by anthropologists, beginning with Marc Bloch, founder of the *Annales* School, in his *Les rois thaumaturges: Étude sur le caractère surnaturel attribué à la puissance royale particulièrement en France et en Angleterre* published in 1924.
30 Edward Muir, *Ritual in Early Modern Europe* (Cambridge: Cambridge University Press, 1997).
31 Bouza Álvarez, 'El Espacio', 157–60.
32 Scholarly interest in the ceremonial rites of the Spanish monarchy is growing, as we can see with works such as Alejandro López Álvarez, 'Some Reflections on the Ceremonial and Image of the Kings and Queens of the House of Habsburg in the Sixteenth and Seventeenth Centuries' in *A Constellation of Courts: The Courts and Households of Habsburg Europe, 1555–1665*, ed. René Vermeir, Dries Raeymaekers and José Eloy Hortal Muñoz (Leuven: Leuven University Press, 2014), 267–322; *Festival Culture in the World of the Spanish Habsburgs*, ed. Fernando Checa Cremades and Laura Fernández-González (Farnham: Ashgate, 2015); or *La fiesta barroca: La corte del rey (1555–1808)*, ed. Víctor Mínguez et al. (Castelló de la Plana: Universitat Jaume I, 2016).
33 The importance of studies of Royal Stables in the early modern period is increasing in recent years, with several publications, such as *The Culture of the Horse: Status, Discipline, and Identity in the Early Modern World*, ed. Karen Raber and Treva J. Tucker (New York: Palgrave Macmillan, 2005), or *Las caballerizas reales y el mundo del caballo*, ed. Juan Aranda Doncel and José Martínez Millán (Córdoba: Reales Caballerizas, 2016); as well as conferences such as *Horses and Courts: An International Symposium*, held at The Wallace Collection, London, 21–23 March 2018, and a special issue of *The Court Historian* published in December 2019, *The Court Historian* 24, no. 3 (2019): 197–297, especially Donna Landry and Philip Mansel's *Introduction: Horses and Courts: The Reins of Power*, 197–204.
34 For a study on Royal Guards of the Spanish monarchy, see José Eloy Hortal Muñoz, *Las Guardas Reales de los Austrias hispanos* (Madrid: Polifemo, 2013). For the role of Etiquette specifically, see 381–409, and idem, 'Les gardes royales des monarques

Habsbourg hispaniques et l'étiquette: La lutte pour la proximité avec le souverain', *Bulletin du Centre de recherche du château de Versailles: Sociétés de cour en Europe, XVIe–XIXe siècle – European Court Societies, 16th to 19th Centuries*, 2017, https://doi.org/10.4000/crcv.14628

35 For a study on Royal Stables at the Spanish monarchy, Alejandro López Álvarez, *Poder, lujo y conflicto en la Corte de los Austrias: Coches, carrozas y sillas de mano, 1550-1700* (Madrid: Polifemo, 2007).

36 See the relevant chapters in *Felipe II (1527-1598): La configuración de la monarquía hispánica*, ed. José Martínez Millán and Carlos Javier de Carlos Morales (Valladolid: Junta de Castilla y León, 1998).

37 This was a regulation in which the way of addressing each and every courtier was specified, both orally and written. See José Martínez Millán, 'El control de las normas cortesanas y la elaboración de la pragmática de las cortesías (1586)', *Edad de Oro* 18 (1999): 103–33.

38 Fernando Checa Cremades, 'Monarchic Liturgies and the "Hidden King": The Function and Meaning of Spanish Royal Portraiture in the Sixteenth and Seventeenth Centuries' in *Iconography, Propaganda and Legitimation*, ed. Allan Ellenius (Oxford: Oxford University Press, 1998), 89–104.

39 See Félix Labrador Arroyo, 'La formación de las Etiquetas Generales de Palacio en tiempos de Felipe IV: la Junta de Etiquetas, reformas y cambios en la Casa Real', in *La Casa de Borgoña*, 99–128.

40 Roy Strong, *Art and Power: Renaissance Festivals, 1450-1650* (Berkeley: University of California Press, 1973).

41 Théodore Godefroy, *Le Ceremonial François: Contenant Les Ceremonies Observées en France aux Sacres & Couronnemens de Roys, & Reynes, & de quelques anciens Ducs de Normandie, d'Aquitaine, & de Bretagne* . . . vol. I (Paris: Sébastien Cramoisy and Gabriel Cramoisy, 1649).

42 Mariana Fubini Leuzzi, 'Un'Asburgo a Firenze fra etichetta e impegno político: Giovanna d'Austria', in *Le donne Medici nel sistema europeo delle corti: XVI–XVII secolo*, ed. Giulia Calvi and Riccardo Spinelli (Florence: Polistampa, 2008), 233–56.

43 The text is fully published at *La monarquía de Felipe II*, vol. II, 835–999.

44 The original plans are currently kept in AGP, Plans, numbers from 4096 to 4108 (previously in Sección Histórica, box 51). There are copies, for example those referred to by John E. Varey in 'Processional Ceremonial of the Spanish Court in the Seventeenth Century', in *Studia Iberica: Festschrift für Hans Flasche*, ed. Karl-Hermann Körner and Klaus Rühl (Bern-München: Francke Verlag, 1973), 643–52, in the British Library, Additional Ms 28459. There, we find instructions for twelve ceremonies such as princes' oaths at San Jerónimo, holy mass in the Royal Chapel, royal entrances (by coach) of the king and the queen, and Corpus Christi processions, amongst others.

45 *El ceremonial en la Corte de Bruselas del siglo XVII: Los manuscritos de Francisco Alonso Lozano*, ed. José Eloy Hortal Muñoz, Africa Espíldora García and Pierre-François Pirlet (Brussels: Commission Royale d'Histoire/Koninklijke Commisie voor Geschiedenis, 2018).

46 See the website of the *Progetto Cerimoniali di Napoli* and its several publications: https://www.progettocerimoniali.org/ (accessed 25 November 2019).

47 All the ordinances and instructions of Philip IV's reign, included those ones related to Royal Sites, are compiled in vol. 2 of *La Corte de Felipe IV*.

48 This process ended with the final compilation produced by two brothers, both of them holding the title of *alcalde de casa y corte*, Pedro and Miguel Ángel Cervantes,

Recopilación de las Reales Ordenanzas y Cédulas de los Bosques Reales del Pardo, Aranjuez, Escorial, Balsaín y otros (Madrid: Oficina de Melchor Álvarez, 1687).

49 For a study on French royal guards and a bibliographical compilation concerning them, Hortal Muñoz, *Las Guardas Reales*, 63–80.
50 As treated in José Eloy Hortal Muñoz, 'Las guardias de los Austrias, ¿cuerpo militar o de parada?', in *Perspectivas jurídicas e institucionales sobre guerra y ejército en la Monarquía Hispánica*, ed. Sara Granda Lorenzo, Leandro Martínez Peñas and Manuela Fernández Rodríguez (Madrid: Dykinson, 2011), 119–51.
51 Enrique Martínez Ruíz and Magdalena de Pazzis Pi Corrales, *Protección y seguridad en los Sitios Reales desde la Ilustración al Liberalismo* (Alicante: Universidad de Alicante, 2010).
52 See *La Corte de Felipe IV*, CD at tom. II.
53 For a study on this theatre–court relationship in the Spanish monarchy, see the classic work *Teatro y fiesta en el Barroco: España e Iberoamérica*, ed. José María Díez Borque (Barcelona: Serbal, 1986).
54 Teresa Ferrer Valls, 'Teatros cortesanos anteriores a la construcción del Coliseo del Buen Retiro', *Quaderns de filologia. Estudis literaris* 1, no. 1 (1995): 355–72.
55 María Asunción Flórez Asensio, 'El Coliseo del Buen Retiro en el siglo XVII: teatro público y cortesano', *Anales de Historia del Arte* 8 (1998): 171–95.
56 A convincing, definitive study of this Royal Site still does not exist and the bibliography is meagre. The latest study is by María Ángeles Toajas Roger, 'La heredad de la Zarzuela: Nuevos documentos de su historia', *Anales de Historia del Arte* 17 (2007): 85–116.
57 María Luisa Lobato López, 'Fiestas teatrales al infante Felipe Próspero (1657–1661) edición del baile "Los Juan Ranas" (XI-1658)', *Scriptura* 17 (2002): 233.
58 The whole title is *Loa de la Etiqueta y oficios de las Casas Reales, que se representó a sus Magestades en el Real Sitio de Aranjuez en la fiesta que los criados de ambas Casas Reales hizieron el día de San Phelipe a dos de mayo de este año de 1681 a la celebridad del nombre del Serenísimo Señor Duque de Orleans, Dignísimo Padre de la Reyna nuestra señora Doña María Luisa de Borbón, que Dios guarda* (A Short Play [Spanish *loa*] in praise of Etiquette and Offices of the Royal Households, which was performed for their Majesties at the Royal Site of Aranjuez at the festival that the servants of both Royal Households organized on St. Philip's day on the second of May of this year of 1681 in celebration of the name of the Most Serene Lord Duke of Orleans, Most Worthy Father of the Queen Our Lady Doña María Luisa de Borbón, may God keep her). There are copies of this work in the Biblioteca Nacional de España and in the Hispanic Society of America.
59 'Etiquette' was one of the characters of the play, and she introduced herself by saying that 'I treat the courtiers as children for what I have as school, as do I teach, they come to me as the teacher' – 'A tales (a los cortesanos) trato de niños por lo que tengo de escuela, que como enseño, se vienen a mí como la maestra'. Then, the different offices of the Royal Household were introduced, as well as characters of the play.
60 María Teresa Chaves Montoya, *La gloria de Niquea: Una invención en la Corte de Felipe IV* (Aranjuez: Doce Calles, 1991).
61 AGP, Administración General, bundle 939/15, s. f. There is another copy at Biblioteca Universitaria de Salamanca, Manuscript 1712, fols. 138r–153r.
62 For a study of this process, see José Eloy Hortal Muñoz, 'A Reign Characterized by Regulations: Etiquettes and Ordinances of the Royal Chamber of Philip IV of Spain (1621–65)', in *Making Room for Order: Court Ordinances as a Source for Understanding*

Space at Early Modern Princely Residences, ed. Fabian Persson and Charlotte Merton (Leiden–Boston: Brill, 2022, forthcoming).

63 José Eloy Hortal Muñoz, 'Reality or myth? The "Domestication" of the Nobility through the Codification of Space and Ceremonial: Royal Sites and Palaces during the Reigns of Philip III and Philip IV of Spain (1598–1665)', in *Court Residences as Places of Exchange in Late Mediaeval and Early Modern Europe 1400–1700*, ed. Krista De Jonge and Stephan Hoppe (Turnhout: Brepols, 2021, forthcoming).

64 The festive itinerary followed in Madrid is described in Alicia Cámara Muñoz, 'El poder de la imagen y la imagen del poder: La fiesta en Madrid en el Renacimiento', in *Madrid en el Renacimiento* de VVAA [Exhibition Catalogue] (Alcalá de Henares: Comunidad de Madrid, 1986), 68–9.

6

Royal baptism in the Spanish court: Art and ritual from the sixteenth to the eighteenth century

Inmaculada Rodríguez Moya

In the complex universe of rituals and ceremonies of the Spanish monarchy, the celebration of the baptism of a member of the royal family was one of the more private ritualistic events. However, a royal baptism was at the same time one of the most significant, highlighting the importance of certain members of the court to the rest of its members as well as to the general public. This was likely because the ceremony had few political implications and allowed the monarchy to demonstrate instead the importance of court bonds. The act of selecting participants for the baptism underlined the importance of family networks for the Habsburgs, the pre-eminence of the favourite, and the consideration of the rank of 'Grandee of Spain' as virtual (if not actual) relatives of the king. In addition, baptismal ceremonies were also a reflection of the special features of certain royal spaces and of the special regard given to the luxury objects needed to carry out court protocols and the ecclesiastical liturgy. For example, the baptism ceremony was one of the moments in which Spanish monarchs could show off their luxurious collection of tapestries. The ritual itself had been designed on an *ad hoc* basis by the peripatetic House of Trastámara, and later codified and settled during the reign of the House of Habsburg (1516–1700), with very precise etiquette for each baptism.[1] The first Bourbon king in Spain, Philip V, worked to rejuvenate Spanish etiquette, particularly by making it more intimate with regard to royal birth and baptism ceremonies. Nevertheless, the role of the noble participants in the ritual continued to reflect the wider court hierarchy and the importance of the royal relationship to its leading court families.[2]

The establishment of an etiquette for royal baptism

The baptismal ceremonies performed during the reign of the House of Trastámara (1369–1516) did not have a set ritual, as they were not yet deemed an event for the political legitimation of royal heirs. With the advent of the rule of the House of Habsburg in the early sixteenth century, the ritual started to define itself, based mainly on the ceremonies they had inherited from the court of Valois Burgundy, notably for the baptisms of the children of Juana of Castile and Philip the Handsome, for example, that of Charles V in Ghent, in which the triumphal arch decorations and rich tapestries, noble retinues and the role of the godparents were given a central role.[3] From Ghent, the ceremony relocated to Valladolid. The baptism of Charles's son, Philip II, was very similarly organized and decorated as his father's had been.[4] Philip II would, in some way, standardize this baptism etiquette, and made it dependent on the queen's household.

The National Library of Spain conserves a manuscript from 1701 that includes the regulations for court etiquette first delineated in 1562, then amended by Philip III in 1617.[5] Regarding the 'Baptism of Princes and Infantes' in particular, these 'Etiquetas Generales' compiled aspects that are also seen in the documentation from the Palacio Real of Madrid dating from the end of the sixteenth century.[6] For example, they state that, ordinarily, the baptism would be celebrated within the parish of the Palace, which at that time was a nearby church. It also mandates the creation of a passage from the Palace to the parish church and of a stage in its main chapel. The latter would hold a bed and the font in which Saint Dominic had been baptized in the twelfth century. This font would be moved there from the nearby Monastery of Santo Domingo de la Caleruela. The church would be decorated with rich tapestries. A procession would be organized, starting from one of the halls of the Palace – above the entrance hall – which would take the newborn and the baptismal implements – or *emblemas* – to the chapel.[7] Moreover, two canopies were placed: one in the hall of the Palace and the other at the entrance of the church. On that day, streets were decorated and luminaries were organized at night. If the baptism took place in the Royal Chapel within the Palace – because of the weakness of the newborn, for instance – the procession would be through the Palace's corridors in public. If the Court was in mourning, the procession would only process from the hall to the Royal Chapel through the galleries in which the king listened to mass.

Royal baptisms in the sixteenth century took place in different churches, as the consideration of what constituted the royal parish changed during this period. San Gil was the focus until 1609, when its parishioners and functions were absorbed by the nearby Church of San Juan Bautista.[8] Sometimes baptism took place in the Royal Chapel in the Palace, but also in other parishes or chapels depending on where the monarchs were residing at the time. Thus, for example, it was celebrated in the Church of San Pablo in Valladolid when the court resided in that city; or in the convent of Las Descalzas Reales in Madrid, in San Lorenzo el Real in Burgos, and even at the hunting lodge of Valsaín, near Segovia.

Starting in September 1622, shortly after ascending the throne, Philip IV decided to formally establish a king's household, separate from the former queen's household in use since the adoption of the Burgundian system in the early sixteenth century. In the following years, he systematically approved a series of regulations that affected this household and that of the queen culminating in 1647 with the creation of a 'general etiquette' for the king's household. After several years of study and debate, the Etiquette Commission delivered to the King in February 1651 the *Etiquetas Generales de Palacio*, in which the ceremonies and public events involving the king or his family were specified, as well as the roles to be performed by household officers. This new set of protocols standardized the new ritual for the 'Baptism of the prince and infantas, with the order of procession and the plan of the Church of San Juan in Madrid for the baptisms'.[9] The layout of the rooms of the different ceremonies was planned by architect Juan Gómez de Mora.

In essence, the text from the *Etiquetas Generales de Palacio* gathered together the norms set in the previous century regarding decoration and organization of the procession, but it also established more detailed protocols and the different roles to be performed by members of the court. The High Steward was in charge of organization, ordering other stewards to notify the Grandees that they had been appointed to carry the implements and of their position in the convoy; and to notify and later receive the members of the Spanish Royal Councils and place them in their assigned locations. The General Etiquettes also established regulations for decoration, as well as illumination of the passages and stairways of the palace, terraces and chapel. It detailed the placement of two canopies and the decoration of the church or chapel with tapestries. In front of the elevated platform, the *emblemas bautismales* and silver trays should be placed on three tables covered by tapestries. In addition to the canopy in the main chapel under which the font was placed, a second closed canopy was located on the Epistle side (the right-hand side facing the altar) under which the prince or infante would be undressed on a bed.[10]

The implements and offerings were placed before the start of the ceremony on three tables in the king's antechamber in the Royal Palace. These were composed of a baby's bonnet, a candle, a wash basin, some marzipan, a salt shaker and a towel. The convoy was to meet in this chamber and in the room above the entrance hall previously mentioned. The Etiquettes set the order: marshals of the court with their batons, the king's pages, the child's tutor, the household gentlemen, the infante's stewards, four *maceros* (mace bearers), the queen's stewards, Grandees, kings of arms (heralds), the Grandees bearing the *emblemas* and, finally, the prince or infante. As the centrepiece of the convoy, the ceremonial arrangements for the newborn were more elaborate. Sometimes the king would designate a great lord or a person from the royal family to carry the newborn. If not, the child was carried by his or her governess on a chair carried by the *reposteros de cámara* (grooms of the chamber). On both sides, the newborn was normally accompanied by more people: another infante and a cardinal, or the papal nuncio and the emperor's ambassador. After this child, there were two rows of ambassadors, then the godparents, who were accompanied by the child's high stewards and tutors. Following this were the ladies of honour, the *guardia mayor* (the princely guard), the dames in pairs holding hands, and at the end the ladies in waiting. The king was not part of this procession and attended the baptism in seclusion, observing from a stall or balcony of the church.

Once all the people had arrived at their assigned place in the church or chapel, the musicians began to perform, to receive the prelate officiating over the ceremony, with his assistants, all in pontifical dress. The royal child's governess was in charge of undressing the newborn on the bed, while the King's Chapel choir sang motets.[11] Then, the Grandees delivered the implements used during the ritual. After the baptism, the procession returned to the Palace, where the queen would receive the prince or infante.

The Royal Archive of the Palace preserves some drawings of baptisms of royal children, where we can see the placement of all these elements and of the protagonists. For example, from 1601 there is a simplified drawing of the main Chapel of San Pablo of Valladolid for the baptism of Infanta Ana, future queen of France and daughter of Philip III.[12] From the late eighteenth century, we have two drawings by Teodoro Ardemans, copied from those made by Gómez de Mora, which establish, first, the location of all the elements in the Royal Chapel of the Palace and, second, the order of the convoy (see Figures 6.1 and 6.2). Both allow us to verify that the chapel's set-up changed very little from the seventeenth to the eighteenth century, with regard to royal baptisms.

The centuries of Grandee pre-eminence: The participation of the nobles in the sixteenth and seventeenth centuries

After noting the codification of the ceremony and the order of the procession, we must reference who its main actors were in the sixteenth and seventeenth centuries. In general, in the sixteenth century, the godparents were the relatives of the king and of the newborn boy or girl. They were in charge of carrying the baby to the font after it was undressed and covered by a small sheet. However, during the convoy, the baby was normally carried by a Grandee of Spain, while six other representatives of the highest nobility – waiving their privilege of wearing their hat in the presence of the monarch (here represented by the child) – carried the baptismal tools. The royal parents themselves did not attend the baptism, as already noted.

Visits by family members to the court of Philip II, notably those of his nephews, the Archdukes Wenceslaus and Albert of Austria, and their sister Archduchess Joanna, were opportunities for them to act as godparents of several of the King's children. For example, in 1571, the baptism of the heir, Prince Fernando, born on 4 December, was celebrated only a few days later, on 16 December, in San Gil.[13] The godparents were Wenceslaus and Joanna, with the latter being in charge of undressing the Prince. The honour of carrying the child during the procession was bestowed on the 4th Duke of Béjar, Francisco de Zúñiga y Sotomayor. Béjar, a Grandee of Spain, had a relevant role in the dynastic celebrations of Philip II's court: he had been part of the reception committee for Archduchess Anna of Austria when she had arrived in Spain, and participated prominently in the subsequent marriage festivities. The next child of Philip II, Prince Diego, was born on 12 July 1575, and baptized at San Gil on the 25th that month. On this occasion, the godparents were again family members: Archduke Albert of Austria and Infanta Isabella Clara Eugenia, the child's older sister. Infanta Catalina Micaela and Archduke Wenceslaus were also present in the retinue. The Duke of Alba, Fernando Álvarez de Toledo, who was the *Mayordomo mayor* of the King at the time and thus in charge of the protection of the King's children, carried the child in his arms. Prince Felipe, the future Philip III, was also baptized at San Gil, on 1 May 1578, with the godparents being the same as those for his older brother, Albert and Isabella. Due to the presence of Prince Pietro de' Medici at the Spanish court, he was given the honour of carrying the child, with archdukes Albert and Wenceslaus at his sides. Pietro

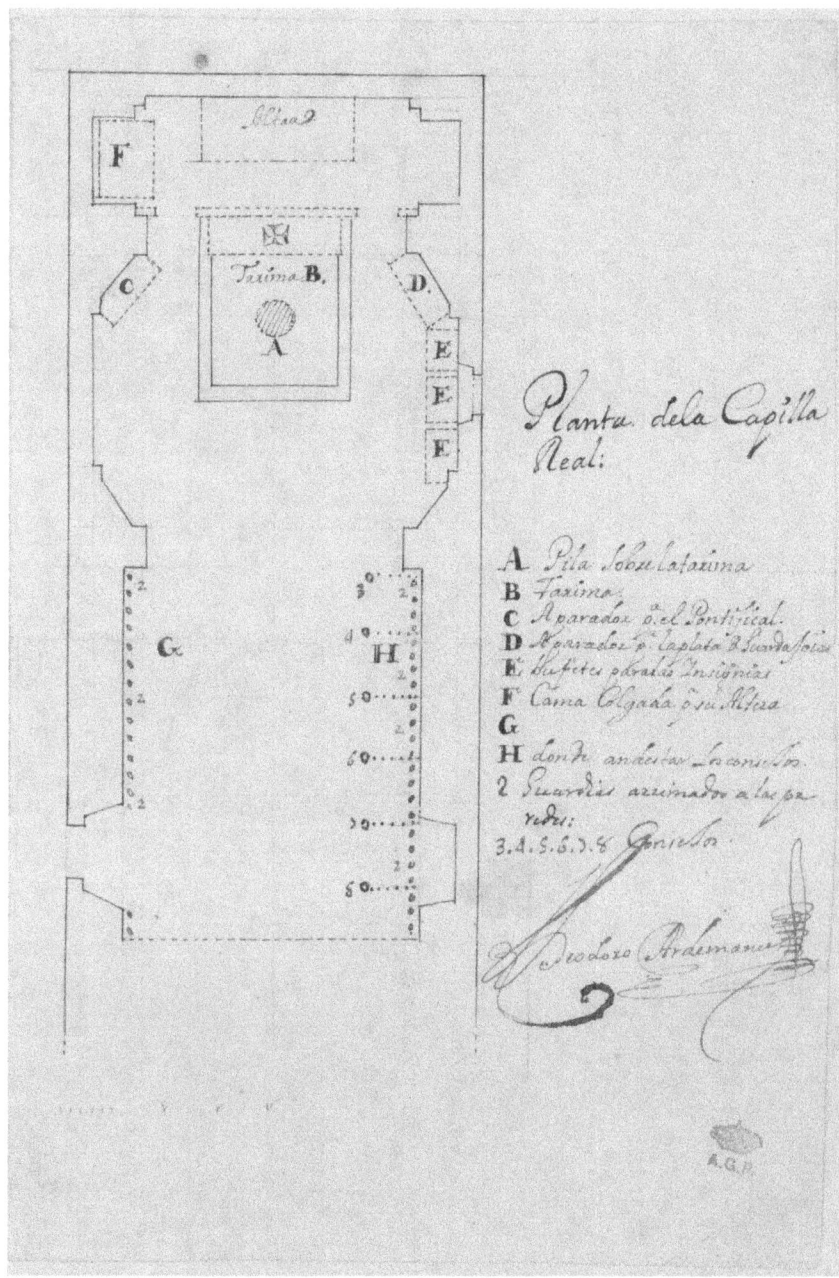

Figure 6.1 Teodoro Ardemans, *Plan of the Royal Chapel*, eighteenth-century drawing (Madrid, General Archive of Royal Palace). © Patrimonio Nacional.

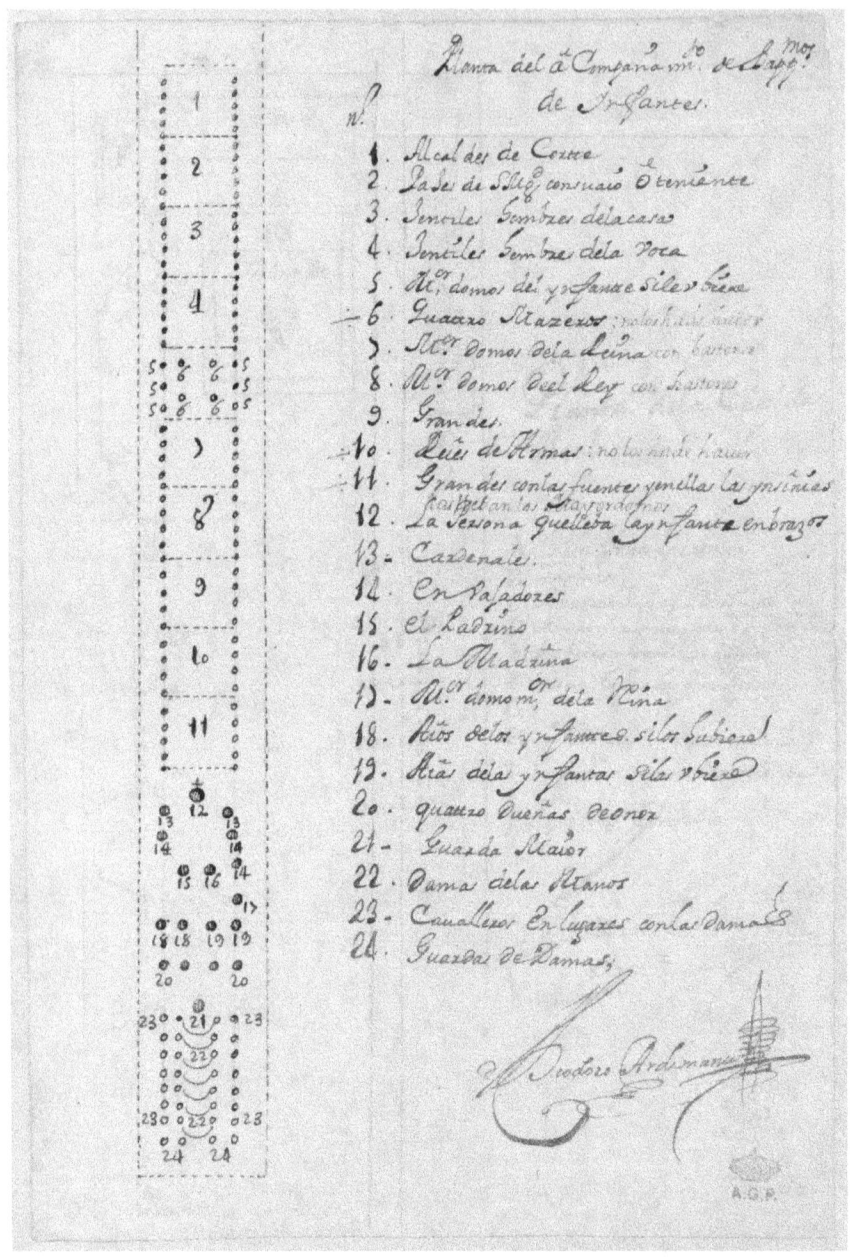

Figure 6.2 Teodoro Ardemans, *Plan of the convoy for the prince's baptism*, eighteenth-century drawing (Madrid, General Archive of Royal Palace). © Patrimonio Nacional.

was the son of Cosimo I de' Medici and Eleonora di Toledo (herself a daughter of the Spanish viceroy of Naples), and brother of the Grand Duke of Tuscany, Francesco I de' Medici, who had appointed him as his ambassador to the Spanish king, in part to keep him away from Florence following the controversial death of his wife.[14]

The children of Philip III were baptized in Valladolid and at San Lorenzo de El Escorial, due to the court being in those cities at the time, with the exception of Infante Carlos who was baptized in the Royal Chapel of the Real Alcázar in Madrid due to his poor health. It became common for Philip III's children to have their own siblings as godparents. Infanta Ana – the future queen of France – was, for example, the godmother of all her younger brothers, and after Prince Felipe was born, he was often a godfather too. The Duke and Duchess of Lerma had a prominent role in these ceremonies too, as favourites of the King. They participated in all of the baptisms as godparents or as bearers of the newborn. Thus, for example, Infanta Ana and Prince Felipe were baptized in San Pablo in Valladolid in October 1602 and May 1605, respectively. The Duchess of Lerma was Ana's godmother, together with the Duke of Parma as godfather, who carried the girl in a white band of cloth hanging from his neck during the procession. Prince Felipe's godparents were Prince Victor Amadeus, eldest son of the Duke of Savoy and of Infanta Catalina Micaela, and his sister Infanta Ana. In this instance, the Duke of Lerma carried the child. In 1610, Infanta Margarita was baptized in the Collegiate Church of Lerma; her godfather was the Duke of Lerma and her godmother, again, her sister Ana.[15]

There is much less information for the baptisms that took place at San Lorenzo de El Escorial, as they must have been very intimate occasions given the low numbers of courtiers present. We only know that the children were baptized at the main altar. Infanta Maria Anna was baptized in September 1606, with Infanta Ana and the Duke of Lerma as godparents. Infante Fernando was baptized in June 1609. His godparents were his older siblings Ana and Felipe, and he was carried by the Duke. In October 1611, Infante Alfonso Mauricio was baptized with his older siblings as godparents and carried on this occasion by Prince Emanuel Philibert of Savoy (also a son of Catalina Micaela), in the presence of the dukes of Lerma and Alba. It was a sad rather than festive occasion, due to the court's state of mourning for the death of the Queen, Margaret of Austria.[16]

With Philip IV, the location of the court parish changed. It was decided that the court of Madrid would attend the Church of San Juan. The first daughter to be baptized there was Infanta Margarita Maria Catalina, on 8 December 1623, who died two weeks later. The godparents were Infante Carlos and Infanta Maria Ana, her uncle and aunt. The bearer of the Infanta was the Count-Duke of Olivares, Master of the Horse and the King's minister-favourite, who used the traditional strip of white cloth to carry the child. In this case, the King had set specific instructions for the ceremony, which he provided to the Duke of the Infantado, his High Steward, to be followed precisely. For example, he introduced the presence of the members of the Royal Councils into the retinue. The instructions included the placement of the silver objects on three tables beside the altar, as well as the presence of a canopy with silver pillars covering the font. The Grandees carried their *emblemas bautismales* as usual, but their order in the retinue was determined, in this instance, by the implement they chose to carry, instead of their personal noble rank and seniority at court. This was probably because the child was a girl and there was still hope for a son, and in the case of a male heir, the monarch would select the order himself. As stated above, the monarchs did not attend the baptism publicly; they concealed themselves and observed it from a closed gallery, without been seen by the courtiers. The Queen was provided with a cot due to her state of recovery. Margarita Maria Catalina was the only infanta baptized in San Juan; the infantas Maria Eugenia in 1626, Maria Antonia Dominica in 1635, and Maria Teresa in 1638, were all christened at the Chapel of the Real Alcázar. The godparents were also different: the Papal Legate and the Infanta Maria Ana (the newly betrothed Queen of Hungary) in the first case; and the Duke of Modena and Marie of Bourbon-Soissons, princess of Carignan, in the third case.[17]

Prince Baltasar Carlos was baptized in the Church of San Juan in 1629. On that occasion, a chair made from (or enclosed by) crystal, in which the Prince was carried, is mentioned for the first time in the sources. The Countess-Duchess of Olivares sat on the chair carrying the Prince on her lap. As it is the first reference to this extraordinary chair, it had possibly been created to specially designate the heir to the throne; however, information about its features is very brief.[18] The godparents were his uncle and aunt, the infantes Carlos and Maria Ana.

In 1657, the new heir, Prince Felipe Próspero, was baptized in the Chapel of the Real Alcázar.[19] The godmother was Infanta Maria Teresa and he was carried by the Countess of Salvatierra, on the crystal and gold chair, decorated in coral. His brother Carlos (the future Charles II) was baptized in 1661 in the same place. However, only his sister, Infanta Margarita (the future empress), was his godmother, maybe because he was born sickly. He was carried in the crystal chair by the Marquesa of Los Vélez, who was in charge of displaying him to the large audience standing in the corridors.[20] On that occasion, the Duke of Alba had the honour of lifting the child from the chair and handing him to his godmother. The following people were in charge of carrying the implements: the Duke of Alburquerque, the wash basin; the Admiral of Castile, the candle; the Duke of Medina de las Torres, the bonnet; the Constable of Castile, a scent bottle; the Duke of Terranova, the salt shaker; and the Duke of Pastrana, the marzipan.

A change towards royal intimacy: Bourbon baptism ceremonies

The House of Bourbon in Spain was a very prolific dynasty that did not face the succession problems the Habsburgs had in the previous century. Therefore, there are many documentary sources for their baptisms; nevertheless, the information is relatively brief because the ceremony was simplified by the new dynasty. Philip V modified the complex baptism ritual for the princes and infantes, making it much faster and simpler for the children who were not destined directly to become kings or queens. The new king introduced a new custom whereby the Grandees of Spain, the members of the governing councils, foreign ambassadors, other nobles, the court clergy and the Patriarch of the Indies would attend the labour of the queen. Thus, after washing the newborn, the baptism was carried out in the same room in which the labour had taken place, with all these people present, or in the nearby Royal Chapel.[21] In this case, a small procession was organized and the Grandees carried the ritual baptismal tools, as usual. In addition, there were two new ritual objects added during the eighteenth century: the insignia of the Order of the Golden Fleece and the Grand Cross of the Order of Charles III (established in 1771), which were given to the newborn princes.[22]

The first ceremony to make the change was the baptism of Prince Luis in December 1707,[23] which did not vary in splendour and rich decoration from previous Habsburg ceremonies, as he was the heir apparent, but it did introduce significant novelties. The ceremony took place in the Chapel of the Royal Palace of Madrid. The godfather was the King of France, represented by the Duke of Orléans, and the godmother was the Duchess of Burgundy (wife of the King's eldest grandson), represented by the *Camarera Mayor*, the first lady of the Queen's Chamber. As novelties, a new window was opened in the corridor for the monarchs to watch the convoy, and a lattice constructed on the Epistle side of the Chapel, for them to attend the baptism secretly. Nevertheless, it was during the baptism of the Prince where the protocol of the sixteenth and seventeenth centuries was broken, when the monarchs 'could not contain themselves' and they came to the font at the key moment. Additionally, Philip V had ordered that the traditional canopies (one for the font, one for the bed) would not be placed, therefore the governess had to be assisted by a lady of the bedchamber, the mistress of the household and the godmother to undress the child before pouring the holy water over its head.

Another important change was that the godparents were the child's grandparents, uncles and aunts, or absent family members who were represented by nobles. For instance, for the baptism of the Infante Felipe in 1720, the godfather was the Elector of Bavaria (represented by the Marquis of Santa Cruz), and the godmother was the Duchess of Parma (represented by the Marquesa of Mirandola). The godfather of the future Ferdinand VII was his grandfather, King Charles III. If the royal children were born in the Palacio de Aranjuez or the Escorial, the same reduced protocol was followed. Many of the Bourbon baptisms did in fact take place at these two locations, as the court resided there frequently. For example, Infante Carlos Maria Isidro in 1788 was baptized at the Aranjuez Palace, and the future Ferdinand VII at the Escorial.[24] In Aranjuez, the ceremony took place in the parish church of Santa Maria, with a maximum of around forty courtiers. The procession was done inside the palace, through several richly decorated rooms. At the Escorial, the baptism took place in the Royal Chapel, also with the presence of the Grandees with their baptismal objects.

Although Philip V endeavoured to make the baptismal ritual simpler and faster, he was only successful regarding the ceremonies for the infantes. For the heir as already mentioned, the ceremony remained very similar to those conducted by the Habsburgs: though courtier participation was less, there was also less ornamentation (notably eliminating the canopies), the baptismal implements changed and the ritual now always took place in a royal palace. Nevertheless, in both types of baptism, the ritual became more domestic and familiar, with the clear engagement of the monarchs themselves and the participation of close relatives as godparents.

The magnificence of a royal baptism: The display of silver and opulent cloth from the royal collections

As we have seen, the preparation of two types of artistic decoration stood out at the baptisms of princes and infantes in early modern Spain. Combined with the ceremonial music and the rich outfits of the participants, it would result in the use of what Jeroen Duindam has called 'special effects': colours, outfits, sounds and symbolic objects.[25] On the one hand, these included the baptismal tools and the silver items that were part of the ritual. On the other, it refers to the decoration of the spaces used for the ritual. Both revealed to observers the wealth surrounding life at the palace and the rituals of the Habsburg and Bourbon dynasties. Because their use and preservation were strictly regulated by Spanish etiquette, there is therefore a wealth of documentation regulating the activities for organizing these ceremonies.

The baptismal font of Santo Domingo was the cornerstone, and it was present at all of the baptisms of Spanish royal princes and infantes. It was a stone font with a white silver stand. In the eighteenth century, for the baptism of Prince Luis, documentation shows that it was embedded within another gold-plated font in the shape of a boat, with white silver ornaments and mounted precious gems. The silver vessel – i.e. trays and cups – and especially the baptismal tools were fundamental. Regarding the implements, the salt shaker was a spectacular piece, made out of agate stone, completely engraved, varnished in colours and decorated in gold, gems and pearls. The wash basin, in contrast, was a fairly ordinary piece. There is documentation for two different basins used: one in the shape of a jug with the body made of agate, and a stand and lid made of silver and another made in gold-plated silver, with Italian style engravings. The towel and the bonnet were elegant fabric pieces, sometimes with gold or silver thread. The candle was generally ornamented with the prince's or the infante's coat of arms supported by angels. In the case of the infantas, the coats of arms were prepared to house the shield of a future husband, thus one half of the shield was left blank.[26] The marzipan was normally a sweet dish prepared by the king's confectioner and could be of great size. As for its shape, there are very interesting stories of the baked forms it took. For example, for the infantes Fernando, Diego and Maria (children of Philip II) and for Infanta Margarita Maria (daughter of Philip IV) the marzipan was a confection in the shape of a royal crown.[27] The baptismal marzipan in Valladolid for the future Philip IV had a very elaborate shape, in the form of a city, on whose walls there were figures bearing the coats-of-arms of the kingdoms of Philip III. The lower part of the city had a great shield with royal eagles and a crown that covered the whole cake.[28]

The crystal chair had special prominence. It was a sedan chair which the *reposteros* (grooms) carried. It was made out of eight large quartz plates that made up the four sides, with a crimson velvet cover trimmed with gold braid. Sometimes it is mentioned that it was adorned with coral.[29] There is not much more information about it, although documentary references suggest that it was made for the baptism of Baltasar Carlos of Habsburg and was used, at least, until that of Prince Luis of Bourbon.

The two canopies used for the ritual were very important decorative elements. The Habsburg dynasty used a canopy composed of four silver pillars covered by a crimson and gold fabric, similar to the famous curtain used by Habsburg monarchs to conceal themselves during worship services. The same material was used as a coverlet for the bed on which the newborn was undressed. Sometimes the cloth was made of green or white brocade. The royal inventories include many references to different canopies and beds, all quite similar, that could have been used. Two rich canopies were also prepared: one for the door of the hall from which the convoy departed, and one for the entrance of the chapel or church. The inventories of Joanna of Castile and of her grandson Philip II reference these types of canopies many times, as they were highly valued, for example, the one for Charles V.[30]

The corridors, passages, platforms, columns and chapel were embellished with the monarchy's most valuable materials: lavish rugs and fabrics. It is especially interesting to see the opulent tapestries the Habsburgs used to decorate the corridors and rooms visited by the baptismal procession. According to Fernando Checa, the tapestries, the sumptuous fabrics and the silver objects were essential vehicles to represent the classical virtue of magnificence.[31] In particular, the Spanish monarchy preserved the high status of tapestries in the royal collection and they were used for baptisms with a commemorative value until well into the eighteenth century.[32] At the baptism of Philip II at San Pablo in Valladolid, for example, the *Golden Cloth* and *The Honours* series were hung;[33] for Infanta Maria, his daughter, the Chapel of the Alcázar Real was decorated with the *Apocalypse* tapestry; while the tapestries of *The Conquest of Tunis* hung in the Church of San Pablo in Valladolid for the baptisms of Infanta Ana, daughter of Philip III, in 1601, and Philip IV in 1605.[34] For the baptism of Infanta Margarita, daughter of Philip IV, the Church of San Juan was decorated with the tapestries of *The Story of Noah*, among others.[35]

Despite the fact that in the eighteenth century tapestries no longer predominantly decorated the walls of the royal palaces, having been replaced by paint, these luxurious fabrics were still used on special occasions such as royal baptisms. During the baptism of Prince Luis of Bourbon (the future King Louis I), at the Chapel of the Royal Palace, the *Apocalypse* series was hung once more and, in the queen's corridor, different tapestry series were shown representing Biblical stories, Roman battles and the victories of the Caesars. For the baptism of Infanta Isabella Maria in 1741, daughter of Infante Felipe, the rooms and corridors of the Aranjuez Palace were ornamented with the tapestries *Vertumnus & Pomona*, *Psyche & Cupid*, *The Life of Man* and *The Spheres*, as well as the canopy called *Of Herminda* and the sumptuous tapestries of *Our Lady* by Bosch, among other rich tapestries, luxurious textiles from China, and high quality draperies.[36]

Conclusion

Fernando Checa has previously revealed the dangers of granting the presence of luxury items like these cloths any ideological content related to the event, or indeed to some of the people present in the ceremonies.[37] Nevertheless, the value as an element of ostentation and as a sign of the importance that these tapestries carried for the Habsburgs and Bourbons is evident. As this survey of a changing ritual has demonstrated, all of these ritual objects (silver items, baptismal tools, canopies, rich textiles, tapestries), all of the people involved (monarchs, Grandees, other nobles, courtiers, court clergy, domestic staff), and all these ceremonies (processions, baptism, mass) configured a very fixed ritual of recognition of a new member of the royal family as a sanctified Christian within the Roman Church. For the Spanish Monarchy this ritual was so important that it was included in the book of *Etiquetas*, and all the baptismal implements were preserved by the Royal Jeweller throughout the early modern period, until finally they were looted by invading French troops in 1808.

Notes

1. For the rituals employed by the House of Trastámara, see José Manuel Nieto Soria, *Ceremonias de la realeza: Propaganda y legitimación en la Castilla Trastámara* (Madrid: Nerea, 1993), 47–51; for those of the House of Habsburg, José Jaime García Bernal, *El fasto público en la España de los Austrias* (Seville: Universidad de Sevilla, 2006), 251; and *La Casa de Borgoña: La Casa del rey de España*, ed. José Eloy Hortal Muñoz and Félix Labrador Arroyo (Leuven: Leuven University Press, 2014), 100.
2. A first approach to the topic, but more focused on ritual and nobility in the sixteenth- and seventeenth-century Spanish Monarchy, was published as: Inmaculada Rodríguez Moya, 'El bautismo regio en la corte hispánica: Arte y ritual del siglo XVI al XVII', *Archivo Español de Arte* 91, no. 364 (2018): 349–66.
3. See, for example, for the baptism of Charles V: Fray Prudencio de Sandoval, *Historia de la vida y hechos del emperador Carlos V: Máximo, fortissimo, Rey Católico de España y de las Indias, Islas y Tierra firme del mar Océano* (Antwerp: Geronymo Verdussen, 1681), 2–3.
4. Jesús F. Pascual Molina, *Fiesta y poder: La corte de Valladolid (1502–1559)* (Valladolid: Universidad de Valladolid, 2013), 149–64, narrates and analyses this baptism in detail. Valladolid would also host the birth and baptism of Infante Carlos of Spain in August 1545. Due to the death of the Queen, the ceremony was simple and officiated in the palace chapel. The godparents were the Bishop of León and the High Steward of the deceased queen, and the First Lady of the Bedchamber. Pascual, *Fiesta y poder*, 249.
5. National Library of Spain, Ms 1041, *Etiquetas generales que han de observar los criados de la Casa de Su Majestad en el uso y ejercicio de sus oficios*.
6. Archivo General de Palacio, Madrid (hereafter: AGP), Historical Section, Births and Baptisms, Box 94, Folder 173, Relacion de los papeles que se remiten a el Sr. Condestable Mayor pertenenciente a las prevenciones de partos de Principes Infantas con las funciones de sus Bauptismo que ha sido todo lo que se ha podido descubrir en estos oficios de contratos y grefier en cumplimiento de la orden de 16 de mayo de este presente año de 1707; ibid., Folder 175, Bautizo del príncipe Fernando y boda de Felipe II y Ana de Austria.
7. Although the Spanish word 'emblema' usually refers to an image, for these rituals the sources use this term for baptismal implements or tools. This indicates the sacred signification of these objects. See later in the chapter for their full description.
8. See Miguel Ángel Fuertes García, *Las primitivas iglesias de Madrid* (Madrid: Ediciones La Libreria, 2004). San Juan Bautista was a small church erected in the twelfth century, with three aisles, and was demolished during the urban reforms ordered by Joseph I Bonaparte.

9 *La Casa de Borgoña*, 123; *La Corte de Felipe IV (1621–1665): Reconfiguración de la Monarquía católica*, ed. José Martínez Millán and José Eloy Hortal Muñoz (Madrid: Polifemo, 2015). For the manuscript, see AGP, Historical Section, Box 51, Case file 1, Etiquetas Generales de Palacio, 1651. For the plan of San Juan see AGP, Plans 4098, Planta de la iglesia de San Juan para los Bautismos. For the plan of the convoy: ibid., Plans 4099, Plan del acompañamiento para los bautismos. The Etiquettes inform us that the church was so small that the chapel grid was removed in order to make space for the bed on which the baby would be undressed.
10 When we use the term 'prince', we refer to the heir or the eldest son of the monarch. In the Spanish Monarchy the other sons and the daughters were called 'infantes' for boys or 'infantas' for girls (or 'infantes' collectively).
11 The Palace Archive preserves also a detailed document with the religious ritual and the music for that ceremony. See AGP, Royal Chapel, Box 1, Folder 3, Doc. 1, Expedientes sobre ceremonial y protocolo en actos religiosos a celebrar en la real capilla.
12 Chantal Grell, *Ana de Austria: Infanta de España y reina de Francia* (Madrid: Centro de Estudios Europa Hispánica, 2009), 12–13. The account of the baptism is in: *Relación de la orden que se tuvo en el bautismo de la señora Infanta, hija primogénita del Invictísimo Rey Don Felipe III, nuestro Señor, en Valladolid a siete de octubre de mil y seiscientos y un años* (Valladolid: Herederos de Bernardino de Santo Domingo, 1602).
13 AGP, Births and Baptisms, Box 94, Folder 173, Extracto de lo que se ha executado en funciones de Baptismos, 1707.
14 Pietro de' Medici had been accused of murdering his wife, Eleonora di Garzia di Toledo (his first cousin) in 1576. During this visit of Pietro de' Medici to the Spanish court, he was granted the Order of the Golden Fleece, 29 November 1593, for which a ceremony of the Order was organized. Miguel Ángel Zalama Rodríguez, 'The Ceremonial Decoration of the Alcázar in Madrid: The Use of Tapestries and Paintings in Habsburg Festivities', in *Festival Culture in the World of the Spanish Habsburgs*, ed. Fernando Checa Cremades and Laura Fernández-González (Farnham: Ashgate, 2015), 46–54.
15 Bernardo José García García, 'Las fiestas de corte en los espacios del valido: La privanza del Duque de Lerma', in *La fiesta cortesana en la época de los Austrias*, ed. María Luisa Lobato López and Bernardo José García García (Valladolid: Junta de Castilla y León, 2003), 63–4.
16 AGP, Births and Baptisms, Box 94, Folder 173, Extracto de lo que se ha executado en funciones de Baptismos, 1707.
17 Ibid. The Princess of Carignan was the wife of Prince Thomas of Savoy, yet another son of Infanta Catalina Micaela. The Duke of Modena, Francesco d'Este, was the same Infanta's grandson.
18 *Segunda y mas verdadera relación del bautismo del Principe de España nuestro señor, Baltasar Carlos Domingo, con todos los nombres de los Caualleros, y títulos que yuan en el acompañamiento* (Madrid: Bernardino de Guzmán imp., 1629).
19 Regarding the birth, baptism and celebrations on the occasion of the birth of Felipe Próspero, there is a wide bibliography. See Lucian Clare, 'Un nacimiento principesco en el Madrid de los Austrias (1657): Esbozo de una bibliografía', in *El libro antiguo español: Actas del primer Coloquio Internacional (Madrid, 18 al 20 de diciembre de 1986)*, ed. María Luisa López-Vidriero Abello and Pedro Manuel Cátedra García (Madrid: Ediciones de la Universidad de Salamanca-BNM-SEHL, 1988), 119–37;

and Lucian Clare, 'Une fête dynastique à Grenade en 1658', in *La fiesta, la ceremonia, el rito*, ed. Jean-Pierre Etienvre and Pierre Córdoba (Granada: Universidad de Granada–Casa de Velázquez, 1990), 21–42. See also the relevant sections of Jenaro Alenda y Mira, *Relaciones de solemnidades y fiestas públicas de España* (Madrid: [n.p.], 1903), 331–44, who lists thirty printed narrations, though certainly more were published. For a wider study of the festivities surrounding the birth of this child in the Spanish monarchy, see: Inmaculada Rodríguez Moya, 'La esperanza de la monarquía: Fiestas en el imperio hispánico por el nacimiento de Felipe Próspero', in *Visiones de un Imperio en Fiesta*, ed. Inmaculada Rodríguez Moya and Víctor Mínguez Cornelles (Madrid: Fundación Carlos de Amberes, 2016), 93–119.

20 AGP, Births and Baptisms, Box 94, Folder 190, Births and Baptisms, Bautismo del Príncipe Carlos.
21 Ibid., Box 95, Folder 1, Bautismo de Luis I y misa de purificación de Luisa Gabriela de Saboya en 1707; ibid., Folder 2, Bautismo del infante Felipe y su entierro en 1709.
22 'Ceremonial del bautizo del Serenísimo Señor Infante D. Fernando', in *Memorial literario instructivo y curioso de la Corte de Madrid*, vol. 3 (Madrid: Imprenta Real, 1784), 85.
23 *Pompa magnífica con que se celebró el bautismo de el Serenissimo Señor Príncipe de las Asturias, executada en la Real Capilla, con todas las circunstancias muy por extenso de este dia, y los demás que se siguieron al cumplimiento de esta celebridad, el dia ocho de Diciembre de 1707* (Madrid: [n.p.], 1707).
24 'Ceremonial del bautizo del Serenísimo Señor Infante D. Fernando', 85.
25 Duindam refers to these 'special effects' as part of the ceremonial elements, according to Théodore Godefroy in *Cérémonial François*, cited in Jeroen Duindam, *Vienna and Versailles: The Courts of Europe's Dynastic Rivals, 1550–1780* (Cambridge: Cambridge University Press, 2003), 183.
26 For instance, for the baptism of the Infanta Maria of Austria in 1580. AGP, Births and Baptisms, Box 94, Folder 178, Baptismo de la Infanta Maria en 1580.
27 Ibid., Folders 175, 176, 178 and 182.
28 Ibid., Folder 80, Bautizo del príncipe Felipe IV.
29 For instance, in the baptismal record for Prince Felipe Próspero in 1657. Ibid., Folder 189, Fiestas que se celebraron en la corte por el nacimiento de D. Phelipe Prospero, Príncipe de Asturias.
30 Fernando Checa Cremades, *Los inventarios de Carlos V y la familia imperial* (Madrid: Fernando Villaverde Ediciones, 2010), 76. Dolores María del Mar Mármol Marín, *Joyas en las Colecciones Reales de Isabel la Católica a Felipe II* (Madrid: Fundación Universitaria Española, 2001), 301.
31 Fernando Checa Cremades, *Tesoros de la Corona de España: Tapices flamencos en el Siglo de Oro* (Brussels: Fons Mercator, 2010), 56.
32 Zalama Rodríguez, 'The ceremonial decoration', 41–66.
33 Fray Prudencio de Sandoval, *Historia de la vida y hechos del Emperador Carlos V* (Pamplona: Bartholome Paris, 1614), 3; and Checa Cremades, *Tesoros de la corona de España*, 112, no. 34.
34 AGP, Royal Chapel, Box 1, Case file 3, Expedientes sobre ceremonial y protocolo en actos religiosos a celebrar en la real capilla. Also mentioned in *Relación de lo sucedido en la ciudad de Valladolid, desde el punto del felicissimo nacimiento del Príncipe Felipe Dominico Víctor nuestro señor* (Valladolid, 1605).

35 All of them are preserved as part of the Patrimonio Nacional [National Heritage] of Spain. See: Paulina Junquera de Vega, Carmen Díaz Gallegos and Concha Herrera Carretero, *Catálogo de tapices de Patrimonio Nacional*, 3 vols. (Madrid: Editorial Patrimonio Nacional, 1986–2000).
36 AGP, Births and Baptisms, Box 95, Case file 11, Bautismo de la infanta María Isabel, hija del infante Felipe y de Luisa Isabel de Francia (1741–1748).
37 Checa Cremades, *Tesoros de la Corona de España*, 56.

7

From marshal to monarch: State ceremonies and Jean-Baptiste Bernadotte in post-napoleonic Sweden

Mikael Alm

On 20 October 1810, as the raging autumn storms temporarily eased on Öresund, Jean-Baptiste Bernadotte was finally able to cross the strait and for the very first time set foot on Swedish soil in Helsingborg. Salutes were fired from the beaches and the fortress. With him were parts of his Swedish entourage of chamberlains and aides-de-camp, alongside the archbishop of Uppsala, who on the previous day had conducted the Catholic Frenchman's conversion to the Lutheran faith in the Danish port town Helsingør. As he disembarked, he was received by a number of dignitaries of State, including the Marshall of the Realm, a field marshall and several excellencies of the Realm.[1] These events opened the Scandinavian part of post-absolutist monarchic Europe. The Napoleonic wars were still raging on the Continent, but the political turmoil started by the French Revolution, and continued through decades of war, fundamentally changed the political map of Europe, shifting the prerequisites of legitimate rule and authority. A decisively new kind of monarchy was to rise from the ashes of the old regime.[2]

Swedish events were particularly complex. In 1807, Sweden, following years of neutrality, was drawn into the wars, and was subsequently crushed by the allied forces of Russia, Denmark and France. In the midst of war, King Gustav IV Adolf was arrested, deposed in March 1809, and sent into exile along with his queen, the crown prince, and his three daughters. Gustavian absolutism was toppled, and a new constitution, reasserting the power of the Assembly of the four estates (the diet), was adopted in summer 1809. The deposed king's ageing (and childless) uncle was elected to the throne as Charles XIII. In the following peace treaty with Russia, Finland was lost. The old Baltic realm was cut in half, depriving Sweden of half its area and a third of its population.

The story takes an unusual twist with the arrival of Bernadotte. The son of a common prosecutor in Pau, he had risen through the military ranks during the Revolutionary wars, fighting against the kings of Europe, and had reached the very highest echelons in the service of Napoleon, named one of eighteen Marshals of the Empire, and later Prince of Ponte Corvo (a principality near Naples), and in 1810 he was invited by the estates of the realm to take on the mantle of kingship in Sweden, as heir to the childless Charles XIII. This was the stuff of post-absolutist kingship, and he was not the only one of his kind: Napoleon famously manned conquered parts of Europe with relatives and confidants.[3] However, they would all (Napoleon included) be gone within five years, erased by the Congress of Vienna. But not Bernadotte. He was successfully established on the Swedish throne, on which his descendants still sit today.

Following the usual formal greetings and the jubilant speeches on that windy quay in 1810, the company set off in procession in the dark autumn afternoon into the illuminated town, where a ceremonial programme of receptions, dinners, presentations and humble deputations followed suit.[4] Bernadotte was immediately enveloped by ceremonial arrangements: salutes, processions, illuminations, courtly receptions – the first in a row of state ceremonies to be acted out around him on his way to and during his reign on the Swedish throne. This chapter will examine the ritual surrounding the elevation of a new monarch and the formation and legitimacy of a new dynasty. The blending of old traditions and new practices demonstrates the challenges faced by the post-absolutist monarchies. The ritual transformation of the French marshal into a royal prince and dynastic founder will be pursued through three key ceremonies: the entry and acclamation in 1810, the coronation in 1818, and the funeral in 1844. The persistence of royal traditions, and an effort to claim continuity from the past, will stand out. But there is also a new Bernadotte 'dialect' of martial accomplishments and democratic ideals pointing to the wider participation of the ceremonial aspects of power in this post-revolutionary world.

A prince

On the morning of 2 November 1810, there was a bustle around Stockholm Palace. Hundreds of horses neighed, dozens of carriages creaked, while squadrons of guardsmen and cuirassiers, along with numerous courtiers, state servants and officers – dressed in dazzling uniforms, brilliantly coloured liveries and rustling court robes – made their way to their assigned posts and places. About nine o'clock, the procession was set in motion, from the inner courtyard, down towards the waterside, and across the bridge. It opened with the clatter of hooves as a squadron of mounted Life Guardsmen rode by. Next came the rhythmic beats of a mounted kettledrummer and the blasts of eight mounted trumpeters. Then came the carriages. On each side, rows of court lackeys marched, never less than two per carriage. First rode the carriage of the Marshal of the Court, followed by several carriages with courtiers, followed by the carriage of the Lord Chamberlain. Next came the Marshal of the Realm, whose carriage was drawn by six horses and escorted by footmen in livery. Then came the crescendo of the procession: the – still – empty carriage of the Crown Prince Elect, drawn by eight horses with eight grooms. Two pages stood on the back of the carriage and two walked on foot behind it. A mounted Lieutenant of the Life Guard and four footmen walked on each side, and another six men with their officer from the King's Bodyguard marched behind. Next came a carriage with the king's *cavaliers*. The procession closed with the renewed clatter of hooves as a squadron of mounted cuirassiers in shining helmets and breastplates rode onto the bridge.[5]

The grand procession with the empty carriage proceeded through the city of Stockholm, westwards towards Drottningholm Palace. This was the launch of Bernadotte's ritual transformation into a Swedish crown prince.

The entry

The magnificent scenes on the bridge on the morning of 2 November were quite different from the quiet scenes that had played out there on the evening of 30 October. That evening, incognito, with a small entourage, in a 'simple court-carriage, drawn by six horses', Bernadotte had entered Stockholm from Drottningholm, crossed the bridge and pulled into the inner courtyard of the palace, where he was greeted by Charles XIII, the queen and the king's sister.[6]

This first visit that evening was illustrative of the larger meaning of the ceremonial entry that would take place on 2 November. His arrival at the Royal Palace enacted his physical induction into the dynasty. He entered as the elected heir to the throne, but through the personal union with the king, his metamorphosis was confirmed and he was ritually acknowledged as a member of the royal family. But the official spectacle of his elevation had been preceded by an unofficial meeting, where Bernadotte, secretly and without ceremonial fuss, was introduced to his new family.

On that evening, Bernadotte was escorted up through the palace, to a smaller room adjacent to the King's Apartment. The whole thing was over in less than an hour. He was introduced to the king, and then escorted on to the queen, where the procedure was repeated. 'Shortly after 8 in the evening', the Master of Ceremonies noted in his journal, 'the journey back to Drottningholm commenced'.[7] The royal mystique had begun to work on the French *maréchal*.

This was the procedure that was repeated with full pomp and circumstance on 2 November, as Bernadotte entered the capital, this time formally. At the city gates, the Lord Governor, the magistrates and the City Elders received him, and joined the procession towards the palace. At the given sign, a massive thunder of salutes from artillery and man-of-war-ships began.[8] Reaching Gustav Adolph Square, the procession turned right and crossed the bridge, passed the palace, and began the encirclement of the main island: along the quay to the floodgates to the south, turning north up the street to the House of Nobles, and then eastwards, up the gentle slope to the Cathedral, and then on to the western palace gates and into the courtyard. This journey followed the traditional route of royal entries. The first elected (but shortly after deceased) crown prince, Prince Charles August of Augustenburg, had entered along the same bridges, squares, streets and gates in January that same year, as had Queen Frederica in 1797, and Queen Sophia Madeleine in 1766.[9]

Leaving his carriage, Bernadotte was escorted into the palace by the Marshal of the Realm. At the foot of the King's Stairs, he was received by the Marshal of the Court and courtiers, who escorted him up three flights of stairs – all lined by double rows of Life Guardsmen – and into the King's Apartment, heading for the King's Bedroom. In the

Dining Hall, the Marshal of the Court and the courtiers came to a halt, and stayed with the additional courtiers assembled there, while Bernadotte, still escorted by the Marshal of the Realm, continued through the Audience Chamber, and on to the double-door of the King's Bedchamber.[10]

Those modest presentations from the other evening were now repeated with full ceremony. One by one, according to rank, Bernadotte called on the existing members of the royal family. Royal presentations had an inaugurating function. A courtier was only fully inaugurated into his or her charge once they had been formally introduced to the royal persons they were set to serve, and foreign ambassadors were only fully recognized in their ambassadorial function once they – following strict protocol – had called on and been introduced to the king and the royal family. For Bernadotte, of course, this inauguration was of a particularly pregnant kind: he was inaugurated as a fully royal member of the ruling dynasty.[11]

The first presentation was with the king, Charles XIII, who received him surrounded by some twenty men who – by virtue of the high government offices they held – represented the machinery of State.[12] The king walked halfway through the room to receive Bernadotte. This was a favour that princes paid only to other princes. A foreign ambassador would have had to walk all the way up to the king, pausing three times for the prescribed reverences. The embrace in the middle of the room created a scene of familiar intimacy, which was later strikingly rendered in a letter by the Queen, Hedvig Elisabeth Charlotte, as the king's meeting with his 'fully-grown born son'. The intimacy was enhanced as the king led Bernadotte into an adjacent room, where they spent time together in ritualized privacy. The assembled dignitaries were then called into the room, one by one, where the king himself introduced them to Bernadotte.[13]

Introductions completed, the king escorted Bernadotte on through the palace halls, to the Queen's Bed Chamber, where the procedure was repeated. The Queen's Household met him halfway into the chamber, while the queen waited for him by the door to an adjacent room, where she – again in ritualized privacy – received him and the king. The king introduced them, whereupon the royal party proceeded to the final station of the introductions: the king's sister, Princess Sophia Albertina.[14]

Bernadotte's completed integration into the royal family was effectively staged in the ensuing reception and public dinner. Having been escorted from royalty to royalty in order to *become* royal, now showed himself to *be* a royal among royalty. In the Grand Gallery, he assumed his place in the royal family, as courtiers and foreign emissaries marched past. At the royal table, he took to his seat, next in rank to the sovereigns, on the king's right side. The pinnacle of the day's ceremonies was reached. The spatial aspects of Bernadotte's integration unfolded, as he – along with the other members of the royal family – withdrew, and he formally took possession of his princely apartment at Stockholm's Royal Palace.[15]

Nevertheless, beyond the staged harmony that pervaded the ceremonial spectacle, the strains of the past upheavals remained present. As everyone returned to their apartments, a final item remained on the programme. There was another member of the royal family to deal with – present in the palace, but not visible at the spectacle: the Queen Dowager Sophia Madeleine, the mother of the deposed King Gustav IV Adolf. The printed programme was silent on the events that took place later that evening, but they were carefully described in the hand-written journal of the Master of Ceremonies. At seven in the evening, the Marshal of the Realm called on Bernadotte in his apartment, and escorted him to the Queen Dowager's apartment. The introduction procedure was repeated yet again. But the timing and forms of this final introduction were poignant. While Bernadotte had been made circumstantially and tangibly a part of the royal family, the Queen Dowager, by her absence, had been effectively detached from the events. Her introduction was a mere formality – a courtesy – decidedly separated from the ceremonial displays.[16]

The ceremonial entry had thus defined the royal family, and by extension, the kind of monarchy that Bernadotte became part of. Sharp dividing lines were drawn around the new political order of 1809. Charles XIII, his queen, and his sister were parts of that order. In this context, Sophia Madeleine represented the face of the overthrown absolutism, and a jarring echo of the old regime and its deposed and exiled royal family. There was no room for her in the royal launch.[17]

The Oaths of Allegiance

On 5 November, following a two day's break, the ceremonial machinery got back to work for the second act of Bernadotte's transformation: the Oaths of Allegiance. Bernadotte's dynastic integration in the royal family was followed up by his legal and constitutional installation as the heir to the Swedish throne. He was sworn in to his elevated office, and invested with the right to one day be king and to rule.[18]

The procession set off from the King's Apartment at around twelve noon. It was headed by the King's Bodyguard with kettledrums and trumpets, followed by no less than seventeen segments consisting of the very highest representatives of the royal court and government. Charles XIII himself, under a canopy, formed the final, majestic, section, while Bernadotte walked immediately in front of him as the sixteenth section.[19] Down the stairs, the procession headed for the monumental Hall of the Realm (*Rikssalen*). There, members of the noble estate had taken their customary seats to the right of the raised podium with the silver throne. The other three estates (Sweden had four) sat according to rank on the left side – the clergy closest to the throne, then the burghers, and the peasants at the very back.

This was the moment when, for the first time, Bernadotte appeared in front of the four estates who had elected him to be heir to the throne, and who on that day were going confirm that election and complete his elevation by the oaths they were set to take. For most of them, he was just a name representing the grand virtues and illustrious achievements that had been presented to them ahead of the election earlier that year.

The visual representation of Bernadotte in the minds of the estates probably bore the stamp of the so called 'Örebro Portrait' – Pierre Michel Alix's etching – which had been exhibited to them during the Diet: the general in uniform, leading his attacking forces on a battlefield shrouded in gunpowder smoke. As the procession proceeded up the aisles of the Hall of the Realm, a rather different vision modified this impression. Bernadotte now wore the princely ceremonial gown of silver which Gustav III had introduced in the 1770s. With it, he wore the insignia of his dignity: the open crown of the hereditary prince on his head, and the blue princely mantle trimmed with ermine on his shoulders. The sartorial message was clear: the French general was no more; here was the Swedish heir to the throne.[20]

As the king took to his throne at the top of the platform, Bernadotte was given a seat a couple of steps down, on the right side of the throne. He literally installed himself at the steps of the throne.[21] The stage was set and manned. The Chancellery and court officers were seated on benches by the sides of the podium. The four estates were seated in rows in front of it. The queen, the princess and additional courtiers were seated in a balcony to the right, while foreign emissaries were seated in a matching one to the left. The thirteen heralds, with capes and batons, had taken their stations at the entrance to the throne area. Along the aisle, the Royal Guard were posted, standing with their plumed helmets and swords drawn in attention, and the halberdiers were posted by the doors leading out of the Hall.[22]

The spectacle began. The Marshal of the Realm called for silence. What followed, can be described as a ritual dialogue with reciprocal oaths between the three main acts on stage: the king, the elected heir to the throne, and the four estates.

The first to speak was the king. Sitting on his throne, he recited the Act of Adoption, instituted by the Assembly of the Estates. The wording narrated Bernadotte's metamorphosis. Initially, he was addressed as the 'Prince of Ponte Corvo' (the title given to him by Napoleon in 1805) and called by the crude Swedish version of his name: 'Johan Baptist Julius'. Once the Act had been proclaimed, he was immediately elevated to 'Our Son and Successor', and was given his new name: 'Charles' (*Karl*) from the king, and 'John' (*Johan*) as the only remainder of his former self (Jean).[23]

Prince Charles John now took his turn. Hand on the Bible, he knelt on a *prie-dieu*, and swore his oath of allegiance to the king. The union between monarch and heir was sealed in a majestic fashion: Bernadotte rose, climbed the podium to the throne, and kissed the king's hand; the king rose and – in front of everyone assembled – embraced him. Bernadotte had thus responded to the king, and he returned to his seat as the son and embraced heir of Charles XIII. He then began the third part of the ceremony with a speech in French, one to each of the four estates. Among his courtly phrases, conventional politeness and solemn pledges, were several key phrases: regarding his dynastic induction, the king had adopted him 'as his son' and the king was now his 'high father'; regarding the constitutional integration, the four estates had elected him as the heir by their 'free and unanimous vote', and at today's ceremony, the 'bonds' that connected him with them had been forged into 'an indissoluble knot'.[24]

Then, concluding the ritual dialogue, the estates took their turn. The Marshal of the Realm called for silence, then the members of the four estates all rose from their benches, and – in one voice – pledged their oath to Bernadotte as their elected crown prince.[25]

The whole act was completed in less than an hour and a half, and Bernadotte returned to his apartments in procession.[26] His ceremonial entry and inauguration ceremonies had observed the strict order of things that had been established and repeated through the history of the Swedish monarchy. The ceremony was identical to the one that had been observed for Charles August six months earlier, which – in turn – had closely mirrored the one observed at the arrival of Adolf Frederick of Holstein-

Gottorp in 1743.[27] These ceremonial continuities are to be expected. The power of ceremonies to a high degree drew on repetition of allegedly ancient traditions. Their function was to manage decisive changes in political life and anchor them in a framework that could lend them meaning and rationality.[28] Bernadotte processed along the same routes as the heirs before him had; he was escorted by equivalent processions; he dressed like they did; he wore the same regalia as they had; passed through the same rituals they did. In short, he was cast in the same royal mould as they had been, and thus became a Swedish prince like them.

However, within the traditional and familiar framework, that unmistakable 'dialect' that would accompany Bernadotte throughout his reign, made its distinct marks. For, in reality, he was nothing like those other princes. Charles August had, as had Adolf Fredrick, descended from one of the revered dynasties of Europe, tracing their royal ancestry back into the Middle Ages. Bernadotte lacked a royal pedigree; he was not even of noble birth.

While the ceremonial spectacle ran its familiar course, it was in the words spoken in the Hall that the 'dialect' found its first expressions. As the Act of Adoption was read out loud, that image of the warrior on the Örebro Portrait literally swept through the aisles. He was, it said, 'a Prince, whose brilliant fate proves that real merit demands its reward, not only by posterity, but by its own age'. He was, the reading continued, 'a Prince, whose manly feats recall the victorious memories of Sweden's late kings'. These are references to medieval kingship, from a time before hereditary monarchies, and a time when the lords among themselves elected the most competent commander to be their king. The references in the Act of Adoption were vividly enhanced by Bernadotte himself, as he turned to the estates and described himself as 'raised in an army camp'. His lack of royal birth was countered by military merit.[29]

This notion of kingship was more elaborately staged later that evening, as the festivities were rounded off with a gala performance at the Royal Opera. On stage, the opera 'Gustaf Wasa' by Johann Gottlieb Naumann was performed. The opera had premiered in 1786, and had served as a frequent propaganda piece for Gustavian absolutism. The last time it had been performed was in 1797, at the wedding festivities of Gustav IV Adolf.[30] The Gustavian Vasa cult, with its invocations of the blood lines between the Vasa and the Holstein-Gottorp dynasties,[31] was in part applicable to Bernadotte as well. By the adoption of Charles XIII, Bernadotte – however indirectly – had also become related to the Vasa dynasty. But the performance staged another, much more potent parallelism, beyond blood lines. Bernadotte was just like Gustav Vasa. The narrative of the sixteenth-century nobleman whose martial feats saved the realm from Danish tyranny, who was then elected king by the Swedish people and crowned the first king of a new royal dynasty, fit well with Bernadotte's claims. He, too, had proven his worth and earned his place on the throne through valour on the battlefield; he, too, was elected by the Swedish people; and he, too, was the founder of a new royal dynasty.

That was the kind of prince he was, according to the ceremonial displays of 1810. What royal dignity he lacked from birth, he had proven through action. He was the warrior who had made himself worthy of the Swedish people's election, and worthy – in time – to take his seat on the throne as their king.

A king

Eight years later, on 7 February 1818, Bernadotte once again made his way through the Hall of the Realm – though this time, he climbed all the way up to the throne. As before, the Marshal of the Realm called for silence, then the Chancellor of the Court read out the royal oath that Bernadotte had already sworn. Then the new king's son Oscar, now Crown Prince, stepped up. On his knees he swore the oath of allegiance to his father. As he took his seat by the side of the throne, the representatives of the four estates of Sweden rose from their benches, and – in unison – swore the oath of allegiance to their king.[32] Oaths accomplished, Bernadotte rose, and left the Hall in procession, accompanied by the repeated exclamations 'Long live the king!'.

With that, it was done: the succession was completed in accordance with the decision of the Diet in 1810. Bernadotte – Charles XIV John – was king.[33] However, the brief ceremony was but the prelude to what was to follow. Two days earlier, on the evening of 5 February, Charles XIII, following years of illness, had passed away at Stockholm Palace, and thus his funeral was next on the ceremonial agenda. In May, the mourning of the dead king would change into the celebrations for the new king. The most royal of all ceremonies was just around the corner: the coronation.[34]

The coronation

In 1810, Bernadotte had appeared in most of the ceremonial spaces that had crystallized around the Swedish monarchy across the centuries. A Swedish coronation had its traditional spaces, too. On the morning of 11 May 1818, to the loud chimes from all the church bells in town, as the royal guards took to their designated spots, in double rows, shoulder to shoulder with presented arms, they marked out the traditional route of coronation processions. From the royal apartment, their rows led out to the inner courtyard, out onto the Palace Hill, down to the quay, circling the palace, down to the House of Nobles, then back up the hill, to the Cathedral gates.[35]

The procession was grand, with fifty-five segments in all from the royal guards marching in front, including Bernadotte himself under a canopy as the twenty-sixth section, to the members of the state colleges, the consistories and the Stockholm magistracy at the rear. It took nearly an hour and a half for everyone to get out of the palace and into the Cathedral.[36]

A Swedish coronation – as ritually set at the coronation of Erik XIV in 1561 – largely followed the same medieval ritual which, with minor national variations, was observed in most early modern European monarchies. Over time, the ritual's tangibly king-making qualities had been weakened. While a medieval king could hardly title himself as such until he was crowned, most European coronations were now more of a confirming ceremony. Nonetheless, those almost mystical rites that since medieval times had surrounded and articulated that monumental metamorphosis – becoming a king – were still observed around Europe, Sweden included.[37] Thus, as Bernadotte entered the Cathedral that May morning, he was still, in the ceremonial sense, a prince, although he had ruled as a king for three months. He wore the open princely crown on his head and the princely blue mantle on his shoulders. The royal insignia were carried in front of him, but they were not yet his to wear. As he left the Cathedral hour later, the metamorphosis was complete. He was now King Charles XIV John: he wore the royal crown on his head, the purple mantle on his shoulders, the sceptre in his right hand, the orb in his left, while the ceremonial key and unsheathed sword were both carried raised and in full view behind him.[38]

Bernadotte's appearance as he marched, sat and stood was particularly royal. His coronation robes, with a long coat in silver cloth and high boots in velvet embroidered with coronets, followed the patterns set at Gustav III's coronation in 1772, and which, with lesser adaptations according to changing fashions, had been observed at the coronations of Gustav IV Adolf in 1800 and Charles XIII in 1809. That was the way Swedish kings had dressed for their coronations for decades. But in Bernadotte's dress, the royal crowns that the predecessors had woven into their silver cloth were replaced by military symbols: borders with oak leaves and laurel branches, with an outer edge of leaves from the badge of a general's rank alongside the front and back, on the cuffs, the high collar and on the belt. A traditionally royal symbol of sartorial expression was thus fused with traditionally military sartorial expressions. The result was a striking reminder of the foundations of his claim on royal dignity.[39]

These foundations echoed in the coronation music and the words sung by choirs and soloists. They sang about his 'Name, used by Great Heroes', but also about how 'the lustre of Purple honour/gives way to the lustre of His virtues'; they sang about him as 'a Son of Charles' and 'a Sapling sprung from the high Vasa Tree', but also about his 'thousand conquered banners' and 'Patriotic lineage', and they sang about 'the Throne of Gustavs and Charleses' that he has 'inherited', but also that he has done so with 'the right of virtues, and the honour of merit'. A traditional language of thrones and bloodlines was woven in with that Bernadotte 'dialect' of virtues and merits.[40]

The Cathedral space, too, reminded those present about the martial background and feats of Bernadotte. The account books show that the traditionally royal symbols shared the space with a formidable arsenal of martial symbols. The walls and pillars were adorned with sixty flagpoles topped with pikes or spears, twenty-six trophy staffs, sixty rifles, seventy-two sabres, eight shields, eighteen fasces, and twenty axes.[41]

In this spatial setting, the ritual metamorphosis progressed through three customary steps. The first step – the royal oath – commenced after the divine service. Bernadotte rose from the royal armchair, the music played and the choirs incanted the words 'Receive this revered, ancient Crown'. He walked over to the silver throne, raised on a podium, under a canopy, by the altar. There, he remained standing, and his metamorphosis began: Bernadotte shed his skin. Courtiers approached and removed the princely crown and mantle. His old self undressed, Bernadotte sat down on the throne. An Excellency of the Realm (*En av Rikets Herrar*, the highest honorary title and rank given in Sweden) and the archbishop of Uppsala stepped forward and dressed him as his new self with the purple mantle. The music fell silent. Bernadotte placed three fingers on the Bible, and renewed his royal oath.[42]

Then followed the most religiously charged part of the ceremony: the ointment. Bernadotte fell to his knees and opened his shirt. The Archbishop anointed him on the forehead, the chest, the temples and the wrists, all the while chanting the words 'God

Almighty and Eternal infuses his Holy Spirit into Your Soul, Mind, Intentions and Doings.' Even though the theocratic notions of divine kingship had become weaker by this time, here in this rite their power was performed: he was now the Lord's Anointed and representative on Earth. To love him was to love God; to defy him was to defy God.[43]

Bernadotte took his seat again, and the third ritual step commenced: the investiture. He was literally invested with the signs of his royal authority. The First Minister and the Archbishop placed the crown on his head, followed by the sceptre, the orb, the key and the sword. Each part of the regalia symbolized real things, and their symbolic meanings were explained by the Archbishop in the prayers he read during the act. The crown represented his royal dignity, the sceptre his worldly power, the orb his being the Lord's Anointed, the key his power to shut out evil and relieve suffering, and the sword his right and duty by law to protect the good and punish the evil.[44]

A few items still remained on the programme. The Archbishop was to give his blessings, Crown Prince Oscar was to swear his oath, and the ministers theirs. But with the investiture the royal metamorphosis was completed. The Herald of the Realm climbed to the top of the podium and exclaimed: 'Now, Charles XIV John is crowned King of the Lands of Swedes and Goths and subjected Provinces, He and no one else'. He raised his herald's staff, the drums and trumpets struck up the music, and a unison 'Long Live Charles XIV John' was raised.[45]

The homage

In the midst of this pomp and splendour, the coronation day was markedly short. As the procession returned to the palace, the first major change in the ceremonial protocol was announced. The new king, as announced by the noticeably surprised Master of Ceremonies, had decided to cancel the coronation banquet in the Hall of the Realm.[46] Instead, and in line with his martial image, Bernadotte had taken off his regalia and donned a 'black hat à la Henri IV, adorned with white ostrich plumes and jewels', mounted a horse, and gone off to the Royal Garden, to inspect the troops that had gathered in the capital to serve at the coronation.[47]

This was no light matter. An age-old tradition was broken. Ceremonially, these changes meant that all focus was shifted towards the third and final act of the coronation: the homage on 19 May, when Bernadotte received the oaths of allegiance from the four estates.

The chosen location was in line with tradition. Swedish homages were usually staged outdoors, and since the completion of Stockholm Royal Palace in the 1750s, they (apart from Gustav IV Adolf's homage, which took place in the town of Norrköping) had been arranged in the area around the palace building. Gustav III's homage in 1772 was staged on the raised terrace on the east side of the palace, while that of Charles XIII in 1809 took place on a raised stage around the statue of Gustav III on the south-eastern corner of the palace. Now Bernadotte's homage would be staged on the ramps leading up to the northern entrance, with the façade of the palace as a mighty backdrop. The royal throne was placed in front of the palace gate, at the high point of the ramp. Along the sides, two amphitheatre-shaped stands for the four estates stretched the full length of the palace (close to 120 metres). The bridge in front of the palace (the very one Bernadotte had crossed back in 1810) provided space for spectators.[48]

The throne presented a particularly striking view. The arrangements resembled a military tent, raised on lances and fasces, and with martial trophies on each side of a crown ornament. The intended message was explained in contemporary press reports. 'This building', one report ran, 'recalled to memory the original reason for such celebrations: the Commander, who in a tent raised by lances and fasces, would receive the oaths of allegiance by the army and a redeemed People'.[49] That former Bernadotte dialect still resounded. He was like the old – the original – kings: he was the great warrior whose feats had made him worthy to be hailed as king by his people.

As the royal procession entered the site of the homage ceremony, a second breach in coronation traditions appeared. Late in the planning process, the decision had been made that the four estates should walk in the procession. The printed instruction says that the estates – in line with set tradition – were to take their seats ahead of the procession, but in the preserved copy of the Marshal of the Realm, that paragraph has been changed by hand: 'The Instruction was changed, and the Estates of the Realm formed part of the procession', where they marched as an inserted section '5½', between the 'Court Staff' and 'Two Heralds of the Chancellery'.[50]

This was without precedent. The ceremonial display with the estates in their seats and a king marching in and taking his seat on the throne delineated the strict boundaries between those in power and those subordinated: the king embodied power that entered and took centre stage, while the estates were reduced to passive spectators. Now these boundaries were abolished: the estates marched in with the king, as an integrated part of authority. The importance of the estates – and through them, the Swedish people – in the royal metamorphosis of Bernadotte was thus emphasized: it was by their election that he had become king, and they literally accompanied him to the throne.[51]

Before the only item on the day's programme commenced, Bernadotte saluted the four estates individually. The non-Swedish speaking king then left the floor to his son, the Swedish-speaking Crown Prince Oscar, who delivered his father's speech to the estates. A cogent identification with the past was enlisted. There, at the north side of the palace, with the statue of Gustav III comfortably obscured, the speech called attention to the square on the other side of the bridge, and the equestrian statue of Gustav II Adolf, the greatest of Swedish warrior kings. Here, ran the royal command, 'in view of the Monument that the nation's gratitude erected in memory of the Great King, who fell fighting for the freedom of belief, I call upon you, Swedish men, to swear the Oath to Your Lawfully Crowned King, as Our Laws prescribe'.[52]

At the king's command, the ceremonial procedures which – as phrased in the speech – would 'for each and all' manifest the 'indissoluble bonds' that united him with the Swedish people, began. The Marshal of the Realm called for silence. The Herald of the Realm ascended onto the throne podium and called the members of each estate in turn to rise from their benches, raise two fingers, and swear the oath.[53]

When the oaths were sworn, rolling salutes from artillery on land and man-of-wars anchored by the quay erupted. Accompanied by their thunderous roar, the homage was completed in its traditional manner, as – one by one, during the next hour – the nearly 1,000 members of the four estates climbed to the throne and kissed the king's hand.[54]

A dynasty

Despite their bombastic forms, ceremonies had their limitations as means of communication. They were limited to their immediate audiences, and not even those who were present were able to take in a ceremony in its entirety. Those who were seated in the Cathedral in 1818 did not see the procession, and at the same time the public that lined the procession route did not see the events inside the Cathedral. For the great majority of people, a coronation amounted to what they managed to see between the guards. Therefore, the printing presses became a vital tool to mediate and explain ceremonies to larger audiences.[55]

This was made evident as Bernadotte's royal career came to an end. He died at Stockholm Palace on 8 March 1844, and when his coffin was finally placed in its chapel in the Riddarholm Church on 26 April, it was the climax of the ceremonial course of a traditional royal funeral. The reading public were soon able to follow the course of all the ceremonial events in the rather lavish publication, *From the Deathbed to the Chapel. A complete account of the solemnities at the Late Royal Majesty King Charles XIV John's funeral in the Riddarholm church*. A narrating text of fifteen pages guided the reader through the events, and on a foldout panorama – close to one meter in length – the events were illustrated by a chronological series of engravings.[56]

The first engraving depicted the royal deathbed. The dying king is seen surrounded by a grieving family, providing a powerful illustration of the new dynasty's continuation. There are no less than three future Bernadotte kings present: Oscar (I) leans over his father in a mourning pose, while Oscar's firstborn son Charles (XV) stands crying at the head of the bed, and his second son Oscar (II) stands with his head lowered next to the mourning Queen Desideria.

The second engraving depicts the first stage of the actual funeral proceedings: the *lit de parade*. The public display of dead kings (and queens) had a long history. It was an integral part of the ritualized mourning of the funeral ceremony. Here, the dead king, embalmed and dressed, appeared one last time as mourning dignitaries and subjects filed past the open coffin. Bernadotte's body was, in accordance with tradition, dressed in the ceremonial robes of the Royal Order of the Seraphim, and placed in the Hall of the Seraphim in the western wing of Stockholm Palace. The purple-lined coffin was placed on an ermine-trimmed catafalque, on a podium clad in black. This is the scene depicted on the engraving. Four large candelabras stood behind the coffin, an additional eight smaller ones shone from the pillars, and an excess of 600 candles ran along the cornice. The royal regalia lay on tables, while on the equally black-clad walls, there were additional symbols of Bernadotte's royal regiment. At the back wall, there were two large trophies with Swedish and Norwegian flags, and in all the wall panels there were Swedish and Norwegian coats of arms. Between them, in rows of two, ran the escutcheons of the twenty-three Swedish and four Norwegian provinces.[57]

In addition to the royal family, dignitaries of state and foreign diplomats, as many as 30,000 members of the general public was said to have filed by the coffin. In line with the mysteries of kingship, the dead king's royal status was staged as something tangibly real. The regalia in front of the coffin still belonged to him, and he was at all times surrounded by his usual royal suite: the colonels of his personal guard stationed around the coffin, the excellencies of the realm seated on tabourets around it, and heralds posted in front of it. The highest ranking servants of state and the court were on parade inside the railing, and its entrance was guarded by six guards with mourning crepe in their spears.[58]

The funeral

In the morning hours of 26 April, the final royal ceremony to be enacted around Bernadotte got started. Members of the public began to assemble along the designated route of the procession, and at the Royal Palace, the royal insignia and the royal coffin were made ready, and black-clad dignitaries and servants took up their positions in the palace halls, stairwells and courtyards.[59]

The procession connected the two main acts of the funeral: the *lit de parade* at the palace and the actual burial at the Riddarholm Church. Again, the route, marked out by double rows of guards, followed the pathways of history: down the palace stairs and out into the outer courtyard, down to the House of Nobles, across the bridge to island of the church, and on to its gates.[60] Along this route marched the grandest procession ever formed around Bernadotte. The printed instruction lists no less than sixty-four sections, from the singing orphanage boys at the head, 'the Royal Body' in the middle, to the mounted Life Guards at the rear.[61] The procession was the object of the showpiece of a great printed panorama. Unfolded, it depicted three stops along the route: the charity boys and guards at the church gates to the far left; the royal coffin under its canopy in front of the House of Nobles, escorted by a riderless horse, heralds, courtiers and the royal orders of chivalry; and – at the back of the procession – the royal family (with the new Dowager Queen under a canopy), additional courtiers and the state dignitaries outside the palace.[62]

The proceedings followed the adjusted order that had been introduced at the funeral of Charles XIII in 1818. According to the older order, introduced at the funeral of queen consort Ulrika Eleonora the Elder in 1693 and observed until the funeral of Gustav III in 1792, the proceedings had been divided into two parts. First, the coffin was brought to the church in procession and placed on its catafalque, then second, the funeral procession marched into the church for the actual burial. In 1818, this two-part procession was merged into one.[63]

The decorated interior of the church is the object of the final engraving of the panorama. Its walls were dressed in black. By the altar, in front of a monumental and heavily lit group depicting Bernadotte surrounded by female characters, the catafalque was placed under a black canopy. This is where the coffin was brought upon entering the church, at a slow pace, to the sound of church bells outside and funereal music inside. The majestic appearance was enhanced by the lighting arrangements. No less than 1,600 candles lit the church interior, in chandeliers, candelabra and in rows along the cornices.[64]

In the sculpture group behind the catafalque, that familiar image of Bernadotte appeared in a concentrated expression. With its white lustre and colossal size – the figure of the king was almost three meters tall – it presented a majestic sight in itself. His martial career proceeding to the royal throne was symbolized by two tall female representations of Victory that flanked the monarch/central figure, but it was even more explicit in the grouping itself. Bernadotte was depicted standing on a shield, raised by four female figures, each representing one of the cardinal virtues: Justice with her scales, Bravery with her lance, Clemency with her olive wreath, and Prudence with her lamp. Already, the message stands out: this was a king elevated by his virtues, not his birth. Yet the composition had more to tell. It alluded to the obscure history of the very first kings, and to the historic claim that Sweden was in fact the original home of the Goths. Raising kings on shields was a Gothic practice (today perhaps best known from the comic series *Asterix*), and was the symbolic act that confirmed the election of a king. In this way, the Visigoths had hailed Thorismund at the Catalaunian plains in Gaul, following the death of King Theodoric at the victorious battle against Attila and the Huns in the year 451. In this way, closely following the Gothic past, the Iberian Visigothic kings had been proclaimed well into the eleventh century. And this was how Bernadotte was hailed in 1844: as with the Gothic kings on ancient battlefields, he had made himself worthy of his crown.[65]

When then coffin was in place and everyone had taken their seats, the second part of the ceremony began: the funeral service. Following hymns and a sermon, Erik Gustaf Geijer, professor in history at Uppsala University, rose and recited the commemorative speech on the life and deeds of the late king. It must have taken its time; the later printed speech was, in all, thirty-two closely written pages. Again, it was the glorious history of the warrior king that resounded in the church. 'A life so great', Geijer humbly started off, 'cannot be rightly described by the open grave', and that 'no one should even dare to attempt it'. The king's life was too great, too glorious, to be summarized. But this was a rhetorical move, and Geijer's task was to do just that. 'The King', he declared, 'who was now mourned by two peoples [Sweden and Norway] (…) was the son of his own exploits, and was not distinguished by the lustre of lineage'. Then followed a thorough exposition of Bernadotte's bellicose feats; of the thirty-two pages, twenty-four treated his military career in Napoleonic Europe – the campaigns, the battles, the victories, the courage – before he came to Sweden as the elected heir to the throne.[66]

As Geijer returned to his seat, the third and final component of the ritual commenced: the burial. The funeral music played, the Marshal of the Realm took his place at the head of the coffin, and the excellencies of the Realm and knights of the Order of the Seraphim raised the coffin onto their shoulders. The final procession began, headed by the heralds, and culminating with the new king, the new crown prince, the royal dukes, and the king's first minister. Down in the crypt, the Archbishop and two bishops waited. Here, the First Minister performed the deeply symbolic act which, in accordance with the mystique of the royal office, released the royal authority from the dead king, in preparation for its transition to the new king, Oscar I, at the upcoming coronation. He bent down and removed the full-scale funeral crown from the lid of the coffin. Slowly and in pace with the music, he proceeded up from the crypt, out into the church, and up to the altar, where he placed the crown on a table by the catafalque.[67]

At that very moment, the Archbishop released a first handful of dust on to the coffin down below in the crypt chapel. Cannons started their roaring salutes from bridges and squares around the city. Now, Bernadotte was dead in a ceremonial sense. He had been separated from the royal office; its regalia were no longer his. The dynastic cycle was ready to start anew.[68]

The king is dead, long live the king!

The opening paragraph in the narrative that accompanied the funeral panorma declared:

> The 8 March 1844 is a remarkable day in the history of the Swedish People, yes, even in Europe's. The ageing patriarch of Sweden's new royal house; the illustrious victor of so many battles; the man whose innermost wish and determined ambition it was to win 'the love of the people' as the 'reward' for his labour;[69] the veteran among the princes of Europe, the only plebeian that, still remaining after the greatest of upheavals, sat on a throne, as secure as had any purple-born King – on this day, Charles XIV John breathed his last.[70]

It makes for a striking panegyric. Bernadotte's death became the remarkable end of a remarkable life. Born 'plebeian' – a strong word, denoting the lowest social echelons – he, 'the illustrious victor', had advanced through the turmoil of revolution and war ('the greatest of upheavals'), taken his seat on a throne, and founded a new dynasty. He died as 'the veteran among the princes of Europe'.

In this manner, he was hailed as a king among kings. His simple origins and his rise to the pinnacles of glory was ever present. But rather than a shortcoming, as it had been back in 1810, it had become a strength and a mark of quality. He sat 'as secure as had any purple-born King'. Here is the essence of the narrative that the state ceremonies had staged and performed around him since his very first steps on Swedish soil. His standing and that of the new dynasty rested on the election by the Swedish people, which in turn had been based on his remarkable virtues and accomplishments. None of this made him or his dynasty weaker or less royal than time-honoured kings and dynasties with age-old ancestries. It made him better, grander, stronger – almost *more* royal.

Notes

1 Carl Axel Löwenhielm, *Min lefvernes beskrifning* (Stockholm: Lars Hökbergs bokförlag, 1923), 125–7; Torvald T:son Höjer, *Carl XIV Johan: Kronprinstiden* (Stockholm: Norstedts, 1943), 39–40.

2   A more comprehensive version of this chapter was published in Swedish: Mikael Alm, 'Riter och ceremonier kring Karl XIV Johan', in *En dynasti blir till: Medier, myter och makt kring Karl XIV Johan och familjen Bernadotte*, ed. Nils Ekedahl (Stockholm: Norstedts, 2010), 37–77. Also on this subject by the Author: 'The Making of a King: State Ceremonies and Royal Imagery in Post-Napoleonic Sweden', in *Mächtepolitik und Friedenssicherung. Zur politischen Kultur Europas im Zeichen des Wiener Kongresses*, ed. Reihard Stauber, Florian Kerschbaumer and Marion Koschier (Münster: LIT Verlag, 2014), 153–67; and 'Dynasty in the Making: A New King and His "Old" Men in Royal Ceremonies 1810-1844', in *Scripts of Kingship: Essays on Bernadotte and Dynastic Formation in an Age of Revolution*, ed. Mikael Alm and Britt-Inger Johansson (Uppsala: Opuscula Historica Upsaliensia, 2008), 23–48.
3   Philip Mansel, *The Eagle in Splendour: Napoleon I and His Court* (London: George Philip, 1987), chapter X.
4   Magnus Martin af Pontin, *Samlade skrifter*, vol. 1 (Stockholm: Hörberg, 1850), 88.
5   *Ordning, Då Hans Kongl. Höghet Swerges Utkorade Kron-Prins Prins JOHAN BAPTIST JULIUS Håller Sit Intåg I Recidencet, Den 2 November 1810* (Stockholm: Kongl. Tryckeriet, 1810), § 3. See also the Master of Ceremonies' copy of this print, attached in his Journal, and with several inserted notes on the hours, numbers, and so forth, in Swedish National Archives (hereafter: SNA), Ceremonimästarens arkiv, Journaler, vol. 22.
6   SNA, Ceremonimästarens arkiv, Journaler, vol. 22, 174.
7   Ibid., 174–6.
8   *Ordning, Då Hans Kongl. Höghet Swerges Utkorade Kron-Prins Prins JOHAN BAPTIST JULIUS Håller Sit Intåg I Recidencet, Den 2 November 1810*, § 4.
9   Ibid., On Charles August, se *Ordning Wid Hans Kongl. Höghets Thronföljarens Emottagande och Intåg I Recidencet, 1810* (Stockholm: Kongl. Tryckeriet, 1810), § 4. On Frederica, see *Ceremonial Wid Hans Kongl. Maj:ts Konung GUSTAF IV ADOLPHS Tillkommande Gemåls Hennes Kongl. Höghets Prinsessan FREDERICA DOROTHEA WILHELMINAS Af Baden Emottagande och Intåg til Residencet, Samt den påföljande Förmälningen* (Stockholm: Kongl. Tryckeriet, 1797). On Sophia Madeleine, see Henning Stålhane, *Gustaf III:s bosättning, brudfärd och biläger: Kulturhistorisk skildring* (Stockholm: Nordisk rotogravyr, 1946).
10 *Ordning, Då Hans Kongl. Höghet Swerges Utkorade Kron-Prins Prins JOHAN BAPTIST JULIUS Håller Sit Intåg I Recidencet, Den 2 November 1810*, § 5.
11 See for example Lena Rangström, 'Cour och levé – hovpresentation på Gustav III:s tid', in *Hovets dräkter*, ed. Tony Lewenhaupt, Lena Rangström and Angela Rundquist (Stockholm: Livrustkammaren, 1994).
12 SNA, Ceremonimästarens arkiv, Journaler, vol. 22, 178–9.
13 Ibid., 178–9. See also *Ordning, Då Hans Kongl. Höghet Swerges Utkorade Kron-Prins Prins JOHAN BAPTIST JULIUS Håller Sit Intåg I Recidencet, Den 2 November 1810*, § 5. The Queen's description, see *Hedvig Elisabeth Charlottas dagbok:1807–1811*, vol. 8, ed. Cecilia af Lewenhaupt Klercker (Stockholm: P. A. Norstedts & Söners Förlag, 1939), 608, footnote **).
14 SNA, Ceremonimästarens arkiv, Journaler, vol. 22, 179–82. *Ordning, Då Hans Kongl. Höghet Swerges Utkorade Kron-Prins Prins JOHAN BAPTIST JULIUS Håller Sit Intåg I Recidencet, Den 2 November 1810*, § 6.
15 SNA, Ceremonimästarens arkiv, Journaler, vol. 22, 182–4.
16 Ibid., 184–6.
17 Ibid., 184–5.

18 *Svenska Akademiens Ordbok*, H 1363.
19 *Ordning, Då Hans Kongl. Höghet Thronföljaren Aflägger Tro- och Huldhets-Eden Den 5 November 1810* (Stockholm: Kongl. Tryckeriet, 1810), § 6.
20 Ibid., § 6: 16–17. On the coronation robes, see Gudrun Ekstrand, *Kröningsdräkter i Sverige* (Stockholm: Carlssons, 1991); Lena Rangström, *Kläder för tid och evighet: Gustaf III sedd genom sina dräkter* (Stockholm: Livrustkammaren, 1997), 189–97.
21 *Ordning, Då Hans Kongl. Höghet Thronföljaren Aflägger Tro- och Huldhets-Eden Den 5 November 1810*, § 8.
22 Ibid., § 7–8. See also SNA, Ceremonimästarens arkiv, Journaler, vol. 22, 197–8.
23 *Ordning, Då Hans Kongl. Höghet Thronföljaren Aflägger Tro- och Huldhets-Eden Den 5 November 1810*, § 8; SNA, Ceremonimästarens arkiv, Journaler, vol. 22, 198–9.
24 *Ordning, Då Hans Kongl. Höghet Thronföljaren Aflägger Tro- och Huldhets-Eden Den 5 November 1810*, § 8; SNA, Ceremonimästarens arkiv, Journaler, vol. 22, 199. *Hedvig Elisabeth Charlottas dagbok: 1807–1811*, vol. 8, 610–11. *Formulaire, til Hans Kongl. Höghets Kron-Prinsens Tro- och Huldhets-ed åt Hans Kongl. Maj:t.* (Stockholm: Kongl. Tryckeriet, 1810); *Discours Prononcé par S. A. R. Le Prince Royal, à La Salle des Etats Le 5 Novembre 1810* (Stockholm: Kongl. Tryckeriet, 1810).
25 *Ordning, Då Hans Kongl. Höghet Thronföljaren Aflägger Tro- och Huldhets-Eden Den 5 November 1810*, § 9; Nationalmuseum in Stockholm, NMH: 82/1885.
26 *Ordning, Då Hans Kongl. Höghet Thronföljaren Aflägger Tro- och Huldhets-Eden Den 5 November 1810*, § 10. The Master of Ceremonies noted that the procession arrived at the Hall of the Realm at 'shortly after 12', and that the ceremony was concluded 'around 1/2 to 2 pm'. SNA, Ceremonimästarens arkiv, Journaler, vol. 22, 197, 199.
27 With the childless marriage of Ulrika Eleonora (sister of Charles XII) and King Frederick I (of Hesse), the Swedish estates, in a manner similar to the election of Bernadotte in 1810, elected Adolph Frederick (r. 1751–1771), Prince-Bishop of Lübeck, as a crown prince and heir to the throne in 1743. He later married Louisa Ulrica, the sister of Prussian King Frederick II (the Great), and was the father of King Charles XIII.
28 Edward Muir, *Ritual in Early Modern Europe* (Cambridge: Cambridge University Press, 1997), 2–3; Mårten Snickare, *Enväldets riter: Kungliga fester och ceremonier i gestaltning av Nicodemus Tessin den yngre* (Stockholm; Raster förlag, 1999), 80–1; Sebastian Olden-Jørgensen, 'Ceremonial Interaction across the Baltic around 1700: The "Coronations" of Charles XII (1697), Frederick IV (1700), and Frederick III/I (1701)', *Scandinavian Journal of History* 28 (2003): 244.
29 *Hedvig Elisabeth Charlottas dagbok:1807–1811*, vol. 8, 607; *Discours Prononcé par S. A. R. Le Prince Royal, à La Salle des Etats Le 5 Novembre 1810*.
30 *Hedvig Elisabeth Charlottas dagbok:1807–1811, vol. 8*, 614; Birgitta Schyberg, '"Gustaf Wasa" as Theatre Propaganda', in *Gustavian Opera: an interdisciplinary reader in Swedish Opera, Dance and Theatre 1771–1809*, ed. Inger Mattsson (Stockholm: Royal Swedish Academy of Music, 1991); Karin Hallberg, 'Opera's Role in Royal Image Making: Repertoire and Performances 1810–1826', in *Scripts of Kingship: Essays on Bernadotte and Dynastic Formation*, 100–4.
31 The consanguinity between the Vasa and the Holstein-Gottorp dynasties ran by way of the daughter of Charles IX of Vasa (r. 1599–1611), who married the Count Palatinate John Casimir, whose daughter in turn married the Margrave of Baden-Durlach, and whose son married a princess of Holstein-Gottorp and became the ancestor of Adolph Frederick.
32 *Post och Inrikes Tidningar* no.17, 9 February 1818.

33 *Protocoll, hållet inför Konungen, I närwaro af Swea Rikes Ständer, på Riks-Salen i Stockholm den 7 Februarii 1818* (Stockholm: Kongl. Tryckeriet, 1818).
34 On the funeral of Charles XIII, see *Ordning Wid Högstsalig Hans Kongl. Maj:ts Konung CARL XIII:s Begrafning i Riddarholms Kyrkan den 20 Martii 1818* (Stockholm: Kongl. Tryckeriet, 1818).
35 *Ordning Wid Hans Kongl. Maj:ts, Konung CARL XIV. JOHANS Kröning och Hyllning wid Riksdagen i Stockholm år 1818* (Stockholm: Kongl. Tryckeriet, 1818), §§ 10–11; Juliusz A. Chrościcki, 'Ceremonial Space', in *Iconography, Propaganda, and Legitimation*, ed. Allan Ellenius (Oxford: Clarendon Press, 1998), 207–11.
36 *Ordning Wid Hans Kongl. Maj:ts, Konung CARL XIV. JOHANS Kröning och Hyllning wid Riksdagen i Stockholm år 1818*, § 18. The hours appear in the marginal notes by the Marshal of the Realm. See Royal Palace Archives, Stokholm (hereafter: RPA), Ceremonieller, Riksmarskalksämbetets arkiv, F:2:5.
37 On the Swedish coronation ceremony, see Malin Grundberg, *Ceremoniernas makt. Maktöverföring och genus i Vasatidens kungliga ceremonier* (Lund: Nordic Academic Press, 2005), 69–70, 75–90. On coronation ceremonies, see also Richard A. Jackson, *Vive le Roi! A History of the French Coronation from Charles V to Charles X* (Chapel Hill: University of North Carolina Press, 1984); Snickare *Enväldets riter*, 140–2; Roy Strong, *Coronation: A History of Kingship and the British Monarchy* (London: Harper Collins, 2005).
38 *Ordning Wid Hans Kongl. Maj:ts, Konung CARL XIV. JOHANS Kröning och Hyllning wid Riksdagen i Stockholm år 1818*, § 18:26, 40.
39 Ekstrand, *Kröningsdräkter*, 90–4; Mikael Alm, 'Dynasty in the Making: A New King and His "Old" Men in Royal Ceremonies 1810–1844', in *Scripts of Kingship: Essays on Bernadotte and Dynastic Formation*, 34.
40 *Ord till Musiken i Kyrkan vid Konung CARL XIV. JOHANS Kröning* (Stockholm: Kongl. Tryckeriet, 1818).
41 RPA, Husgerådskammarens materialräkning 1818, Kröningsräkenskaper, G:13:2.
42 *Ordning Wid Hans Kongl. Maj:ts, Konung CARL XIV. JOHANS Kröning och Hyllning wid Riksdagen i Stockholm år 1818*, §§ 24–7.
43 Ibid., § 28; Snickare, *Enväldets riter*, 67.
44 *Ordning Wid Hans Kongl. Maj:ts, Konung CARL XIV. JOHANS Kröning och Hyllning wid Riksdagen i Stockholm år 1818*, §§ 29–34; Rudolf Cederström, *De svenska riksregalierna och kungliga värdighetstecknen*, (Stockholm: Livrustkammaren, 1942).
45 *Ordning Wid Hans Kongl. Maj:ts, Konung CARL XIV. JOHANS Kröning och Hyllning wid Riksdagen i Stockholm år 1818*, §§ 34–5. In 1814, Sweden conquered Norway from Denmark, and a monarchic union was forged (until it was dissolved in 1905). Thus, Bernadotte was also king of Norway (as Charles III John). A Norwegian coronation followed later the same year, in Trondheim.
46 SNA, Ceremonimästarens arkiv, Journaler, vol. 30, 102.
47 Ibid., 101–2.
48 *Ordning Wid Hans Kongl. Maj:ts, Konung CARL XIV. JOHANS Kröning och Hyllning wid Riksdagen i Stockholm år 1818*, § 20. See also SNA, Ceremonimästarens arkiv, Journaler, vol. 30, 120–4.
49 *Konst och Nyhets Magasin för Medborgare af alla Klasser*, vol. 1 (Stockholm 1818), 5.
50 *Ordning Wid Hans Kongl. Maj:ts, Konung CARL XIV. JOHANS Kröning och Hyllning wid Riksdagen i Stockholm år 1818*, § 44; RPA, Ceremonieller, Riksmarskalksämbetet, F:2:5.
51 Snickare, *Enväldets riter*, 131–6.

52 *Ordning Wid Hans Kongl. Maj:ts, Konung CARL XIV. JOHANS Kröning och Hyllning wid Riksdagen i Stockholm år 1818*, § 49; *Kongl. Maj:ts TAL Till Rikets Ständer, wid Hyllningen den 19 Maji 1818* (Stockholm: Kongl. Tryckeriet, 1818); SNA, Ceremonimästarens arkiv, Journaler, vol. 30, 125.
53 *Ordning Wid Hans Kongl. Maj:ts, Konung CARL XIV. JOHANS Kröning och Hyllning wid Riksdagen i Stockholm år 1818*, § 50.
54 Ibid., § 51. See also SNA, Ceremonimästarens arkiv, Journaler, vol. 30, 125.
55 Laura Lunger Knoppers, *Constructing Cromwell: Ceremony, Portrait, and Print, 1645–1661* (Cambridge: Cambridge University Press, 2000), 21, 69–76, 132. See also Snickare, *Enväldets riter*, 75–7.
56 *Från dödsbädden till grafchoret: Fullständig historik öfver högtidligheterna vid Högstsalig H. M. konung Carl XIV Johans begrafning i Riddarholmskyrkan den 26 april 1844* (Stockholm: Albert Bonnier, 1844).
57 *Ordning vid Högstsalig Hans Kongl. Maj:t Konung Carl XIV Johans Begrafning i Riddarholms kyrkan den 26 april 1844* (Stockholm: Kongl. Tryckeriet, 1844), § 1; *Från dödsbädden till grafchoret*, 3–4; *Sveriges Stats-Tidning* no. 87, 16 April 1844.
58 *Från dödsbädden till grafchoret*, 6–7; *Sveriges Stats-Tidning* no. 96, 26 April 1844.
59 *Ordning vid Högstsalig Hans Kongl. Maj:t Konung Carl XIV Johans Begrafning i Riddarholms kyrkan den 26 april 1844*, §§ 6–7; *Sveriges Stats-Tidning* no. 97, 27 April 1844.
60 *Från dödsbädden till grafchoret*, 4.
61 *Ordning vid Högstsalig Hans Kongl. Maj:t Konung Carl XIV Johans Begrafning i Riddarholms kyrkan den 26 april 1844*, § 10.
62 *Från dödsbädden till grafchoret. Ordning vid Högstsalig Hans Kongl. Maj:t Konung Carl XIV Johans Begrafning i Riddarholms kyrkan den 26 april 1844* (Stockholm 1844, § 10.
63 *Ordning Wid Högstsalige Hans Kongl. Maj:ts Konung GUSTAF III:s Bisättning J Riddarholms Kyrkan Den 13 April 1792* (Stockholm: Kongl. Tryckeriet, 1792); *Ordning Wid Högstsalig Hans Kongl. Maj:ts Konung GUSTAF III:s Begrafning J Riddarholms Kyrkan Den 14 Maji 1792* (Stockholm: Kongl. Tryckeriet, 1792); *Ordning Wid Högstsalig Hans Kongl. Maj:ts Konung CARL XIII:s Begrafning i Riddarholms Kyrkan den 20 Mars 1818* (Stockholm: Kongl. Tryckeriet, 1818). For the older ceremony, see also Snickare *Enväldets riter*, 106–7.
64 *Sveriges Stats-Tidning* no. 97, 27 April 1844. See also Snickare, *Enväldets riter*, 90–1.
65 *Magasin för konst, nyheter och moder* no. 21 (1844); *Sveriges Stats-Tidning* no. 97, 27 April (1844). On the Spanish customs, see Teofilo F. Ruiz, 'Unsacred Monarchy: The Kings of Castile in the Late Middle Ages', in *Rites of Power: Symbolism, Ritual, and Politics Since the Middle Ages*, ed. Sean Wilentz (Philadelphia: University of Pennsylvania Press, 1985).
66 *Ordning vid Högstsalig Hans Kongl. Maj:t Konung Carl XIV Johans Begrafning i Riddarholms kyrkan den 26 april 1844*, § 11; *Personalier uppläste wid Högstsalig Hans Majestät Konung Carl XIV Johans Begrafning i Riddarholms Kyrkan den 26 April 1844* (Stockholm: Kongl. Tryckeriet, 1844).
67 *Ordning vid Högstsalig Hans Kongl. Maj:t Konung Carl XIV Johans Begrafning i Riddarholms kyrkan den 26 april 1844*, § 11.
68 Ibid., §§ 11–13.
69 This alludes to Bernadotte's royal motto: 'The love of the people, my reward' (*Folkets kärlek, min belöning*).
70 *Från dödsbädden till grafchoret*, 3.

Part Three

Ceremonial of Institutions and Representative Bodies

8

Not the ruler, but the land: Estates and ceremonial order at the diet of besztercebánya, 1620

Gábor Kármán

In the summer of 1620 a diet of the Kingdom of Hungary was organized in Besztercebánya (German Neusohl, today's Banská Bystrica in Slovakia), with the attendance of a variety of foreign ambassadors. As was usual, many of them were sent by rulers, such as the Holy Roman Emperor, the Ottoman sultan or the king of Poland. There were, however, also others who represented the estates of nearby lands, such as Bohemia, Moravia and Silesia, as well as Upper and Lower Austria. Before their audience with the ruler of Hungary, a longer discussion took place, where the Austrians insisted on having precedence before the Moravians; the latter were not inclined to cede this, and found support among the Silesian envoys. The question came up several times during the two and a half months the envoys spent at Besztercebánya, and although the Austrians decided *in situ* to accept compromise solutions, in the background they did everything they could to come out as winners from the conflict.

Similar quarrels are certainly not unknown from the history of seventeenth-century Europe, the most familiar being the struggle for pre-eminence between the kings of France and Spain that raged through the entire century. Controversies or at least preliminary discussions concerning which participant would take which place were part of organizing most major events in early modern Europe.[1] Even among the provinces of the Habsburg Empire there was a venerable tradition of questioning each other's rights for specific ceremonial places on the occasions of coronations or royal burials. In the collections of the Provincial Archives for Upper Austria there is a 600-folio-strong volume that contains the documentation of the precedence struggle that took place between Upper Austria, Styria, Carinthia and Carniola between 1614 and 1618. Producing this massive argumentative material – including myriads of sections on legal precedence, relevant references from chronicles, numismatic and other visual sources, as well as extracts from the dynasty's account books that show

---

* This chapter is the result of funding for archival research made possible through the generous support of the Hungarian Reformation Memorial Fund.

which province contributed more to the common expenses – must have provided work for a number of lawyers for years.² How is it possible then that not much later, at the diet in Besztercebánya such questions had to be once more renegotiated? And how is it possible that the Moravians could force the Austrians to cede concessions, when it was supposedly established that any margrave of the Holy Roman Empire (which was the ruler's official title in Moravia) had to cede pre-eminence to an archduke – the rank used by the ruler of Austria? Addressing these two specific questions and outlining the argumentations of both sides highlights a phenomenon that can be studied only relatively rarely. Collective political bodies regularly participated in the early modern contest of diplomatic self-representation, as a recent study has shown using the example of the imperial cities.³ Even so, peculiar and extraordinary situations, such as the political context around the Diet of Besztercebánya, were necessary for situations to occur, where we can see what happened when it was not the rulers but the lands who struggled for the acknowledgement of their rights and reputation at an event of international diplomatic relevance.

The conflict

Abraham von Dohna and Caspar Dornau (Dornavius), the two envoys of the Silesian estates at the Diet of Besztercebánya, noted in their report (which is the main source for this ceremonial conflict) that they arrived on 13 June at Körmöcbánya (German Kremnitz, today's Kremnica, Slovakia), where they were supposed to prepare the common entry of the various provinces' representatives at the neighbouring Besztercebánya. They had just missed the Bohemian envoys, who could not wait for them, since they had been summoned by Gábor Bethlen, prince of Transylvania, the head of the Hungarian estates' revolt that was then being waged against King Ferdinand II.⁴ Nevertheless, they managed to meet the Moravian envoys, Rudolph von Schleinitz, Paul Wolfram and Friedrich Meinrath, and they were also visited by the representatives of Upper Austria, Erasmus von Landau and Wolf Christian von und zu Schallenberg, as well as those of Lower Austria, Ludwig von Starhemberg and Zacharias Starzer. It was thus even before entering the town, which on this occasion housed the Hungarian diet, that the protagonists of the forthcoming ceremonial conflict met.

The first problem happened straightaway on the day of the Silesians' and Moravians' entry into Besztercebánya. At a certain moment the Austrian envoy left his place and rode forward to the Hungarian noblemen leading the train, thus depriving the Moravian and Silesian envoys of their precedence of entering the town. The rather confusing report of Dohna and Dornavius states that after the joint protest of the discriminated envoys the ceremonial order was re-established according to their wishes; nevertheless, this incident already cast a shadow upon the ceremonial occasions to come. The Silesian envoys do not specify which Austrian envoy used this trick to initiate the ceremonial conflict, but it is clear that in the months to follow the Lower Austrians proved to be much more active in steering the debate than their Upper Austrian colleagues.

Strangely enough, the participants of the ceremonial conflict did not initiate negotiations among themselves: the person with whom the Moravian and Silesian envoys had the occasion to debate the question of pre-eminence was a Bohemian representative, Jan Jessenius. The first round of discussions took place directly after the entry to Besztercebánya, the second one on 17 June, and the Silesian envoys were happy to record that the head of the Bohemian delegation, Baron Smil Hodějovský z Hodějova, stood up for their cause against his colleague.[5] There is no trace of a personal consultation concerning the question of pre-eminence between the Moravian, Silesian and Austrian envoys at Besztercebánya, but the latter decided to go directly to a higher authority. They wrote a short and rather indignant letter to the Moravian estates, in which they pointed out that raising the question of pre-eminence endangered the collective audience of the provinces' delegates with Gábor Bethlen – thus they requested the magistrates to order their representatives not to put public order in peril. The diet of the Moravian estates quickly assured them, as well as the Lower Austrian estates that this must have been a misunderstanding and promised to order their envoys at Besztercebánya to change their attitude.[6] The Moravian envoys indeed received orders from the estates in early July to avoid any discussions concerning pre-eminence with the Austrians in the future – a decision which caused quite an uproar among the Silesian diplomats, who were appalled that the Moravian diet had passed such a decision upon hearing only the claims of the Austrians.[7]

The debate was renewed more than a month later, when it was already clear that the Hungarian estates would make the radical step many had expected for months, and, using their right to freely choose their monarch, and following upon their previously expressed concerns related to the election of Ferdinand II, would elect Gábor Bethlen as king of Hungary. The ceremonial act was going to be another public event, where the various delegations had to be present together and thus their ceremonial order was again going to be visible. The Austrians sent a stern note to the Bohemian, Moravian and Silesian representatives, also attaching their correspondence with the Moravian estates, and requested them to give up their futile ceremonial struggle. This, however, only motivated the other party to write a quite tense memorial, a long and elaborate discussion to prove their point – or, in the case of the Moravians, for whom further discussion was prohibited by their superiors in the estates, to state their arguments without further purpose, as they specifically noted in the text. It is thanks to this exchange of documents that we have a deeper insight into the arguments used by both parties.[8]

In their report, Dohna and Dornavius were keen to note that they did not suffer any ceremonial defeat from the Austrians. Their enthusiastic tone is somewhat discredited by the fact that the formulas we find in their account are quite vague concerning the actual solutions used at ceremonial occasions when they had to be present together with the two Austrian delegations. On 25 June they attended a common public audience with Gábor Bethlen, and the Silesian envoys mention that the representatives of each province were taken to the princely lodgings in separate coaches, but fail to mention their order. They also give a rather confusing description of the order of the seating, claiming that the Austrian envoys were seated 'after and among us', on a separate bench.[9] They also noted that on the occasion of Gábor Bethlen's election as king of Hungary, on 25 August, the Austrian envoys pushed the issue of their pre-eminence in a very aggressive manner, a challenge which neither they, nor the Moravians wanted to respond to – and they nevertheless found a (not specified) solution, which gave them the precedence, but at the same time did not hurt Austrian interests.[10] The recurrence of such enigmatic formulations in the report of Dohna and Dornavius could easily motivate the reader to suspect that the Moravian and Silesian envoys were actually forced to cede the pre-eminence to the Austrians, and only attempted in this text to preserve their reputations and calm their audience, which would have been impossible had they started to share the particularities of the specific events. However, a reference in a report written by the Upper Austrian envoys indeed confirms that at the common audience of 25 June they yielded their places after the Bohemian delegation to the Moravians and Silesians. At least on this occasion, Dohna and his colleagues managed to win a ceremonial victory.[11]

The context

The main reason why the question of pre-eminence between the provinces had to be renegotiated was that since the Bohemian uprising of 1618, an entirely new situation emerged among the lands that had earlier all been ruled by the Habsburg dynasty. The first attempts for the estates of these provinces to communicate with each other by circumventing their lords date back to 1604, the start of István Bocskai's uprising in Hungary. In the same decade, the first alliance (under the name *confoederatio*) was formed by the Austrian, Hungarian and Moravian estates in order to replace Emperor Rudolph II with Archduke Matthias as their ruler as part of the famous *Bruderzwist*, the 'quarrel of brothers' between the members of the Habsburg dynasty.[12] As the movement was successful and managed to achieve the abdication of Rudolph, it is not much of a surprise that the plans for the estates to cooperate behind the back of their rulers resurfaced repeatedly in the next few years. When in 1614 – motivated by Gábor Bethlen's accession as prince of Transylvania with Ottoman support – Matthias summoned a general meeting of the estates of all of his lands to Linz, he had to face the fact that they closed their ranks and sabotaged his plans (and those of his most important councillor, Melchior Khlesl) for a war against the sultan, Ahmed I.[13] The years after 1618, however, established a framework for an even closer cooperation.

After having started their uprising in 1618, the Bohemian estates managed step by step to secure the support of the so-called incorporated lands of the Bohemian kingdom, that is, the Moravians, the Silesians and the Upper and Lower Lusatians for their endeavour – a cooperation that was sealed with the so-called *Confoederatio Bohemica* on 31 July 1619. This document created practically a new form of government, in which the position of the Bohemian king was subordinated to the power of the estates: it was not only that every hint of a hereditary monarchy was rooted out from the form of government, but the royal prerogatives were also heavily circumscribed, especially in the questions where the estates saw the need to defend the rights of Protestantism.[14] The treaties signed two weeks later, on 16 August 1619 in Prague with the representatives of Upper and Lower Austria, although also called *confoederatio*, prescribed cooperation on a much lower scale. In spite of introducing a new institution borrowed from Bohemia to the Austrian political framework (that of the *defensores*, a collective body that was going to take care of the country's administration), the treaties actually prescribed only military cooperation, as well as the defence of the estates' rights, more specifically the Protestant estates' rights.[15] The *confoederatio* that was concluded with the rebellious estates of Hungary, led by Gábor Bethlen on 19 January 1620 at the Diet of Pozsony (German Pressburg, today's Bratislava in Slovakia), created an even weaker bond, being little more than a military alliance. The same can be said about the inclusion of the Transylvanian estates on 25 August 1620 at the Diet of Besztercebánya.[16]

The constitutional developments in the region were also mirrored by the provinces' attitude towards the Habsburg Monarchy. Emperor Matthias, who after Rudolph's death in 1612 took control over Bohemia and Silesia as well, died childless in March 1619. The succession of the dynasty had been secured in the previous year by having Ferdinand II, an offspring of the younger Styrian branch of the House of Austria, elected as king of Bohemia and Hungary. However, the young archduke was treated with suspicion due to his reputation as a proponent of forceful Counter-Reformation, and upon his first actions vehement protests followed from the estates of both territories. Ten days after having established the *Confoederatio Bohemica*, the Bohemian estates also elected a new, Calvinist king, Frederick V, elector of the Palatinate;[17] and the assembly of the Hungarian estates in Pozsony at the turn of 1620 also offered the royal title to Gábor Bethlen. The prince of Transylvania had to proceed cautiously: he did not find his position stable enough, and, being a tributary of the Ottoman Empire, also had to wait for the consent of the sultan (now Osman II). Nevertheless, he accepted the offer to exercise royal prerogatives and assumed the title *princeps* of Hungary.[18] The rule of the Habsburgs over the two Austrias (Upper and Lower) was more secure; however, a large part of the estates in both of these territories refused to accept Archduke Ferdinand as their ruler, rather trying instead to invite Archduke Albrecht, the last surviving brother of Matthias, who had been active in the Netherlands for several decades. As long as the debates had been going on, the estates (at least the Protestant nobility) refused to perform the customary act of swearing homage to Ferdinand, which would have made the Styrian archduke the uncontested ruler of the land, and aimed at keeping local administration in their own hands.[19]

All in all, even if we acknowledge all possible subtleties and the various levels of dedication to the common cause, by the time of the Diet of Besztercebánya, a new state formation seemed to be emerging in the East Central European region, with very strong participatory regimes among its constituent members. And as this new state formation was a conglomerate of nine territories, a conflict was bound to happen, as everyone desired, predictably, to secure the best possible position for themselves.

The arguments

Even if the political circumstances do explain why the Moravian and Silesian diplomats thought that the occasion had arrived in 1620 when they could change their position in the ceremonial order, it still does not automatically justify their claim. The status of the provinces did not change after 1618: Moravia was still a margraviate, Silesia a duchy and both Austrias were archduchies – the hierarchy is clear. A closer look at the arguments provided by them, however, reveals not only the quite skilful rhetorical abilities of the diplomats who conceived them, but also some of the structural problems of the state-in-formation, as well as the political legitimacy of their joint endeavour.

This latter aspect played the most prominent role in the refutation of the most obvious argument, referring to Upper and Lower Austria's status as archduchies. The Moravians and Silesians pointed out that an archduchy consists of two elements: the archduke and the land – out of which only the second was represented in Besztercebánya, and that only in part. They touched upon a sensitive point: as noted before, neither of the Austrias had an uncontested ruler at the moment and the estates of Lower Austria were divided among themselves. Since 1608, the Protestant and the Catholic estates had been acting separately and thus neither party was actually the representative of the entire country. The situation in Lower Austria was further complicated during the Diet of Besztercebánya, as some members of the Protestant estates there ultimately decided to pay homage to Ferdinand – thus, Starhemberg and Starzer eventually only represented the most radical (although numerically still not much inferior) group, who for obvious reasons could not convene in Vienna and found refuge at Retz, a small town close to the Moravian border.[20] As Dohna and Dornavius pointed out, they did not have credentials from a single town from their country and only represented a section of the noble estate. Since the Austrian provinces at the moment did not have an archduke, they could not claim pre-eminence based on the status of their country, especially not towards Silesia: the Lower Austrian estates consisted currently only of noblemen, and although their ranks may have included some magnates, some of the Silesian dukes and counts were offspring of kings and electors.[21]

The Austrian argument is, remarkably, not known from their own letter from August, which refrains from arguing and only presents the Moravian and Silesian claims as an act of incomprehensible arrogance that should be stopped immediately. The only source concerning their reasoning is Dohna's and Dornavius's summary of Jessenius's argumentation presented to them in favour of the Austrians in June. Apart from the reference to the status of the Austrian provinces as archduchies, their most important points are allusions to the old traditions (*altes Herkommen*) of their pre-eminence – theoretically a very strong argument in the political culture of the estates, where any novelty was regarded with a deep suspicion.[22] Jessenius presented two specific examples for Austrian pre-eminence: the order of the emperors' titles and the texts of old treaties. The Silesians found arguments to refute both. They claimed that it was at the emperor's discretion to choose the order of his titles, whereas he could not be a judge here; and old treaties, such as the treaty of Vienna from 1276 between Rudolph of Habsburg and King Ottokar II were irrelevant in this case, since they mirrored a situation before the establishment of the conglomerate labelled as 'Bohemia and its incorporated lands'.[23]

With this, they introduced their main point, which skilfully turned the argument of the *altes Herkommen* upon its head. Dohna and Dornavius called attention to the fact that giving pre-eminence to the Austrians would disrupt a long-standing tradition, that of Bohemia and its incorporated lands. Treaties concerning the lands belonging to this state formation had for 280 years followed a clear order: Bohemia, Moravia, Silesia,

Upper and Lower Lusatia. The necessity to find a place for the Austrians in this sequence came only in the previous year, with the establishment of the *confoederatio*; and thus if they gave the Austrians the pre-eminence, they would disrupt this tradition and break the coherence and unity of the incorporated lands – and thus commit exactly the sin they were blamed for by the Austrians.[24]

Thus, against the Austrian perspective, which can be labelled as universalist (since it regarded only the general status of the land), the Moravians and Silesians contrasted a particularist point of view, which was interested of the status of the specific lands in the *confoederatio*. This standing point also allowed them to bring forward another argument, built upon the principle *prior tempore, potior jure* (first in time, greater in right): they claimed that as the *confoederatio* in its current form had been built upon the previously existing unit of 'Bohemia and its incorporated lands', the latecomers in the alliance could not challenge the status of those, who had been there earlier. They pointed to the example of Uri, Schwyz and Unterwalden, which, although being relatively small and insignificant (as they put it, 'bad villages') were by right given pre-eminence, as original members of the Swiss Confederation, by much more powerful cantons such as Basel, Solothurn, Freiburg or Schaffhausen.[25]

The notion of treating the incorporated lands as one unit, the inner hierarchy of which had to be respected by everyone, was also supported by written sources as well as precedents. The documents of the *confoederatio* with the Hungarians from January 1620 indeed listed first the kingdom of Bohemia and its incorporated lands and only afterwards the Austrians as signing partners of the treaty.[26] Both sides tried to bring up examples of earlier ceremonial occasions, such as public events at the Hungarian diet at Pozsony in January 1620, or during the publication of the Hungarian *confoederatio* in St. Vitus Cathedral in Prague in March the same year. However, these precedents showed a contradictory pattern, and both sides could explain them with the statement that the concessions on those occasions were made out of courtesy and did not establish a custom.[27]

The stakes

Both sides pointed out repeatedly that this was the worst occasion to bring up these questions, and if we look at the events taking place in the region we can only agree with them. The *confoederatio* was losing ground. As mentioned before, the weakest link was Lower Austria, where only a relatively small radical group continued to resist Ferdinand's pressure. Upper Austria stood its ground, but the province had already been pawned by Ferdinand II to Maximilian, duke of Bavaria, in exchange for his military support and Bavarian troops were on the march towards Linz. Habsburg armies were stationed in southern Bohemia, and Silesian territories had been attacked by a Polish army.[28] We should not forget that the events took place only a few months before the battle of the White Mountain, which would decide the fate of the Bohemian uprising as well as the country's king, Frederick of the Palatinate. As for Hungary, Gábor Bethlen, who had signed an armistice with Ferdinand for a few months, was under pressure to start peace negotiations, and tried repeatedly, though in vain, to convince the Emperor to open discussion not only with him, but also with his allies. At the same time he had to keep an eye on the reaction of the Ottomans, which was far from unambiguous. Moreover, the assistance expected from England or the Protestant Union in the Empire was not forthcoming, while, on the contrary, the Emperor had managed to secure support from the Pope and the King of Spain.[29] One would have the impression that in these quite pressing conditions, ceremonial issues should have been the last things to hinder cooperation.

In truth, they did not. Although the Austrians blamed the Moravian and Silesian envoys both in their personal communication as well as in the correspondence with the Moravian estates, claiming they were risking the success of the joint venture by coming up with novel claims, the other party was careful not to bring the conflict to a level that would have hindered cooperation.[30] As noted before, for each representative event a specific compromise solution was found, and although for the common meeting of all the provinces, the Upper and Lower Austrian envoys had to make concessions, the Moravians and Silesians also must have at least turned a blind eye towards some specificities of the actual solutions at public events. There was only one occasion when questions of pre-eminence hindered joint action: on 30 July, upon hearing the news about the preparations for a Bavarian invasion of Upper Austria, Landau and Schallenberg requested an audience with Gábor Bethlen and invited the representatives of all other provinces as well to support their requests. The Moravians and Silesians showed themselves ready, only expecting the Austrians to cede to them their place after the Bohemians – they even had a recent reference point for their claim in the common audience in June. This time the Austrians decided not to make concessions and went to see the prince of Hungary only in the company of Hodějovský, whose pre-eminence as representative of the Kingdom of Bohemia was to them beyond doubt.[31]

This episode may seem to suggest that cooperation inside the *confoederatio* was indeed seriously hindered by this ceremonial strife; in fact, the reason why the Austrians could so light-heartedly forgo their request for the Moravians' and Silesians' assistance, was that it was not really necessary. The presence of the other provinces' delegates might have given more weight to their requests, but the situation was grave enough for Gábor Bethlen, also a member of the *confoederatio*, to realize that failing to react would be detrimental to the common cause. It was logical that the Moravians and Silesians had to insist on receiving the same concessions they had received on the previous occasion – and also that the Austrians did not give it to them, since they risked very little with this decision in the sphere of political action. The Silesians, Dohna and Dornavius do not mention this episode in their report, which may hint at their unease for not having assisted the common cause, but also at their attributing little significance to their own absence at the Austrians' audience.

Another ceremonial dispute related to the Besztercebánya diet can highlight how the attitude of those involved changed when one of the parties had actual power to press his own agenda and thus that the decisions taken on ceremonial questions had real stakes. In late July, a new ambassador, Johannes von Cöln, came to town, accredited by King Frederick and the confederated Bohemian lands to travel to the Sultan together with an ambassador from the Hungarian estates.[32] Having witnessed the ceremonial problems among the confederates, the leaders of the Hungarian estates decided that the questions of precedence concerning this mission should be decided before the departure of the envoys, and insisted that the Hungarian representative should have pre-eminence. This was in fact not an obvious conclusion: although the kingdom of Hungary traditionally did have precedence over Bohemia, the latter had at that moment a crowned king, whereas Gábor Bethlen presently only held the title *princeps* (and although later on his election did take place, during the diet – even afterwards – he was never crowned).[33]

In any case, Count Imre Thurzó, the speaker of the Hungarian estates, presented eleven arguments for the pre-eminence of the would-be Hungarian ambassador in regards to Cöln, including references to the *altes Herkommen*, creative interpretations of the *confoederatio*'s text, and even the customs of the Sublime Porte, and the titulature used by Ottoman sultans in their correspondence with Gábor Bethlen. As Dohna and Dornavius put it, they found some of these rather weak and could have refuted most without any problem, but they had to consider the one argument that proved to be decisive: Thurzó also called to his partners' attention that if they were not ready to cede pre-eminence, Gábor Bethlen was inclined to postpone this mission altogether for a later occasion. And contrary to the Austrians, who were in dire need of the confederates' assistance, the prince of Transylvania was actually in the position of making such a step as he had been offered separate peace negotiations by Ferdinand II: his allies at least had the impression that they depended much more on his good will than vice versa. The envoys from the provinces thus would have accepted the conditions without much discussion – Cöln, however, had concerns, pointing out that the king of Hungary had always had pre-eminence over the king of Bohemia, but to give the same honour to the currently 'kingless' estates of Hungary would be too far-fetched. The envoys of the provinces had to mobilize their legal skills to convince him – against their own conviction, as we have seen earlier – that even if Bethlen's title did not make him a king, he did have royal prerogatives; and as the situation was similar to an interregnum, giving the Hungarians precedence did not endanger King Frederick's honour. There was thus no obstacle to sending the joint embassy, which seemed to be of crucial importance at that point, to the Ottoman court.[34]

There was no similar pressure in the relationship between the Austrians and Bohemia and its incorporated lands, thus both parties were content with making and accepting temporary concessions and never a decisive one. In spite of the worrying military situation, they had to consider the possibility that they might also win against the Habsburg emperor and the *confoederatio* might survive. In this case their concessions at the Diet of Besztercebánya could have served as precedents in later discussions: as they regularly had made use of earlier – sometimes even thirteenth-century – cases, as reference points, they had to be aware that what they did could also have achieved a similar relevance at a later date. Such representative occasions served as the only sphere in which early modern political units could measure their relevance – and in an international system that did not yet follow the principle of equality between its members, this had enormous significance.[35] No wonder that the players of this game made all possible steps to ensure that they did not create a precedent that would have harmed the future interests of their side: when Gábor

Bethlen named the Austrians before the Moravians in the credentials of his envoy to the Sublime Porte, the Silesian envoys found it important to have a special certificate issued by him, which stated that the Prince was aware of the problems of pre-eminence and that his letter by no means decided the debate.[36]

No escape?

What was the way out of this situation? No one was in a position to judge between the two provinces – without defeating the military power of the estates and disregarding the constitutional developments of the previous years, as Ferdinand II indeed later on did – and the Silesians made it clear that Gábor Bethlen, who on the occasion of the Besztercebánya diet could have been an obvious choice, was not familiar enough with the old customs of the lands involved to make a judgement.[37] But then, if both sides defended their own position and tried to make sure not to give up anything, does this mean that they were bound to go on with these debates for all eternity? If this *confoederatio* had survived, would such discussions have started all over again at each occasion when envoys from the lands came together? The answer is probably no, as the Austrian envoys seemed to be ready to give up their universalist attitude and presented a quite inventive solution to the main problem. They suggested that the members of the *confoederatio* should be delegated into three 'classes'. The establishment of a Hungarian, a Bohemian and an Austrian class would have solved the problem, rendering Austria behind the kingdom of Bohemia and its incorporated lands as a group, where it also stood in the traditional hierarchy, without harming its reputation as pertained to the individual provinces.[38]

In fact, there was no time for such an arrangement to take place, as in a few months the *confoederatio* collapsed under the pressure of Imperial and Bavarian forces and even its memory was damned as that of an act of treason.[39] The conglomerate of the former Habsburg-ruled provinces, politically dominated by their estates, remained merely a dream that never came true. Nevertheless, the ceremonial debates between its members in the extraordinary circumstances at the Diet of Besztercebánya still serve as an excellent illustration showing that in the early modern society of princes it was not only dynasties that paid keen attention to their honour and attributed enormous importance to defending it at each public occasion. As also illustrated by the case of the imperial cities, corporate political units accepted the same set of values and followed the same rules of communication when they participated in public acts as individual persons did.[40] Although having different places in the hierarchy, the rulers and the lands they governed were seeking their places in the same public sphere.

Notes

1   William J. Roosen, 'Early Modern Diplomatic Ceremonial: A Systems Approach', *The Journal of Modern History* 52, no. 3 (1980): 452–76; Barbara Stollberg-Rilinger, 'Zeremoniell als politisches Verfahren: Rangordnung und Rangstreit als

Strukturmerkmale des frühneuzeitlichen Reichstags', in *Neue Studien zur frühneuzeitlichen Reichsgeschichte*, ed. Johannes Kunisch (Berlin: Duncker & Humblot, 1997), 91–132; Jan Hennings, *Russia and Courtly Europe: Ritual and the Culture of Diplomacy, 1648–1725* (Cambridge: Cambridge University Press, 2016), 1–24; André Krischer, 'Souveränität als sozialer Status: Zur Funktion des diplomatischen Zeremoniells in der Frühen Neuzeit', in *Diplomatisches Zeremoniell in Europa und im Mittleren Osten in der Frühen Neuzeit*, ed. Ralph Kauz, Giorgio Rota and Jan-Paul Niederkorn (Vienna: Verlag der Österreichischen Akademie der Wissenschaften, 2009), 1–32; Barbara Stollberg-Rilinger, 'Die Wissenschaft der feinen Unterschiede: Das Präzedenzrecht und die europäische Monarchien vom 16. bis zum 18. Jh.', *Majestas* 10 (2002): 1–26.

2 Oberösterreichisches Landesarchiv Linz (hereafter: OÖLA), Ständisches Archiv, Handschriften Hs 111.

3 André Krischer, *Reichsstädte in der Fürstengesellschaft: Zum politischen Zeichengebrauch in der Frühen Neuzeit* (Darmstadt: Wissenschaftliche Buchgesellschaft, 2006).

4 The report of Dohna and Dornavius survived in two seventeenth-century copies: Geheimes Staatsarchiv Preußischer Kulturbesitz (Berlin) VI. Hauptabteilung, Hausarchiv Dohna-Schlobitten Kt. 7b; and Biblioteka Uniwersytecka we Wrocławiu, Oddział Rękopisów, Akc. 1948/790. I used an early twentieth-century copy made for the Hungarian Historical Association: Magyar Tudományos Akadémia Könyvtár Kézirattár (hereafter: MTAKK), Ms 4942/a. On the meeting at Körmöcbánya, and the entry, see pages 9 and 10 of this manuscript. On Bethlen's position in Hungary during the summer of 1620, see Katalin Péter, 'The Golden Age of the Principality (1606–1660)', in *History of Transylvania*, vol. 2, *From 1606 to 1830*, ed. László Makkai, András Mócsy and Zoltán Szász (Boulder, CO: Social Science Monographs, 2002), 71–7; Dénes Harai, *Gabriel Bethlen, prince de Transylvanie et roi élu de Hongrie, (1580-1629)* (Paris: L'Harmattan, 2013), 109–25.

5 MTAKK, Ms 4942/a, 10–5, 18–20.

6 MTAKK, Ms 4942/a, 266–70 (appendices LXXXV/A–C), the Austrian representatives to the Moravian estates (n. d.), and their response, Olomouc, 30 June 1620, as well as extract from the Lower Austrian estates' letter to their representatives, Retz, 6 July 1620. See also their copies in Národní archív in Prague (hereafter: NA), Stará Manipulace (hereafter: SM), Kart. I. 1074. K 1/137.

7 NA, SM, Kart. I. 1074. K 1/137: the Moravian envoys to the Silesians [Besztercebánya, 7 July 1620] and their response, Besztercebánya, 8 July 1620.

8 MTAKK ,Ms 4942/a., 262–6, 271–82 (appendices LXXXV, LXXXVI).

9 MTAKK, Ms 4942/a.,40: '... die Österreichischen Gensandten nach undt unter uns Schlesischen undt Lausitzschen abgefertigten auff einer absonderlichen Banck gesetzt worden'. Dohna and Dornavius represented not only the Silesian estates, but also those of Upper and Lower Lusatia. See their credentials from the Upper Lusatian estates (Bautzen, 16 June 1620) Archiwum Państwowe w Wrocławiu, Archiwum Stanów Krajowych Górnych Łużyc, 2272, f. 92–5.

10 MTAKK, Ms 4942/a., 156–7: 'Bey diesem Actu Publico haben sich die Österreichischen Abgesandten der praeeminenz so fern angemasst, das sie sich mitt grosser begierde undt ehrgeitz selbst herfürgedrungen, die ersten nach den Böhmen undt die vorgehenden haben sein wollen. Welche zwar weder von unss noch den Mährischen Abgesandten mitt gewallt oder übelstande zurückgehalten, Ist aber gleichwohl eine solche moderation von uns getroffen worden, das Mähren undt

Schlesien inn Comitio, dann auch inn beglaitung inn und auss der Kirche den vorzug gehabt und erhalten, die Österreicher aber auss diesem actu kein praejudicium vor sich anziehen können'.

11 Anton Gindely, *Geschichte des Böhmischen Aufstandes*, vol. 3 (Prague: F. Tempsky, 1878) 490, Erasmus von Landau and Wolf Christian von und zu Schallenberg to unknown, Besztercebánya, 3 August 1620.
12 Kálmán Benda, 'Absolutismus und ständischer Widerstand in Ungarn am Anfang des 17. Jahrhunderts', *Südostforschungen* 33 (1974): 85–124; idem, 'A Habsburg-abszolutizmus és a magyar nemesség a 16. és 17. század fordulóján', *Történelmi Szemle* 27, no. 3 (1984): 445–479; Joachim Bahlcke, 'Durch "starke Konföderation wohl stabiliert": Ständische Defension und politisches Denken in der habsburgischen Ländergruppe am Anfang des 17. Jahrhunderts', in *Kontakte und Konflikte: Böhmen, Mähren und Österreich: Aspekte eines Jahrtausends gemeinsamer Geschichte*, ed. Thomas Winkelbauer (Horn-Waidhofen an der Thaya: Waldviertler Heimatbund, 1993), 173–86; idem, *Religionalismus und Staatsintegration im Widerstreit: Die Länder der Böhmischen Krone im ersten Jahrhundert der Habsburgerherrschaft, 1526–1619* (Munich: Oldenbourg, 1994), 309–60; Arno Strohmeyer, *Konfessionskonflikt und Herrschaftsordnung: Widerstandsrecht bei den österreichischen Ständen (1550–1650)* (Mainz: Philipp von Zabern, 2006), 130–77. See also *Religion und Politik im frühneuzeitlichen Böhmen: Der Majestätsbrief Kaiser Rudolfs II. von 1609*, ed. Jaroslava Hausenblasová, Jiří Mikulec and Martina Thomsen (Stuttgart: Franz Steiner, 2014).
13 Strohmeyer, *Konfessionskonflikt*, 203; Bálint Ila, 'Az 1614-iki linzi egyetemes gyűlés', *A Gróf Klebelsberg Kuno Magyar Történetkutató Intézet Évkönyve* 4 (1934): 231–53; Teréz Oborni, 'Gábor Bethlen and the Treaty of Nagyszombat (1615)', *Hungarian Historical Review* 2, no. 4 (2013): 771–5; Zsuzsanna Cziráki, 'Das Siebenbürgen-Konzept der Kriegspartei in Wien von 1611 bis 1616 anhand der schriftlichen Gutachten von Melchior Khlesl', *Ungarn-Jahrbuch* 31 (2011–2013): 139–79; eadem, 'Szemelvények Melchior Khlesl és a bécsi Titkos Tanács 1611 és 1613 között keletkezett, erdélyi vonatkozású írásos véleményeiből', *Levéltári Közlemények* 83 (2012): 319–69.
14 Bahlcke, *Regionalismus*, 400–45; Hans Sturmberger, *Aufstand in Böhmen: Der Beginn des Dreißigjährigen Krieges* (Munich–Vienna: Oldenbourg, 1959), 46–51; Karel Malý, 'Die Böhmische Konföderationsakte und die Verneuerte Landesordnung: Zwei böhmische Verfassungsgestaltungen zu Beginn des 17. Jahrhunderts', *Zeitschrift der Savigny-Stiftung für Rechtsgeschichte: Germanistische Abteilung* 122 (2005): 285–300.
15 Hans Sturmberger, *Georg Erasmus Tschernembl: Religion, Libertät und Widerstand: Ein Beitrag zur Geschichte der Gegenreformation und des Landes ob der Enns* (Graz-Köln: H. Böhlau, 1953), 298–315; Strohmeyer, *Konfessionskonflikt*, 240–54.
16 Dávid Angyal, *Magyarország története II. Mátyástól III. Ferdinánd haláláig* (Budapest: Athenaeum, 1898), 248, 263–4; Kálmán Demkó, 'A magyar-cseh confoederatio és a besztercebányai országgyűlés 1620-ban', *Századok* 20 (1886): 105–21, 209–28, 291–308. The joining of Transylvania to the *confoederatio* (which eventually passed without any effect) has received very little attention in the historiography: see Bahlcke, *Regionalismus*, 444; Thomas Winkelbauer, *Ständefreiheit und Fürstenmacht: Länder und Untertanen des Hauses Habsburg im Konfessionellen Zeitalter*, vol. 1 (Vienna: Carl Ueberreuter, 2003), 64. For the text of the *confoederatio*: *Documenta Bohemica Bellum Tricennale Illustrantia*, vol. 2, *Der Beginn des Dreißigjährigen Krieges: Der Kampf um Böhmen: Quellen zur Geschichte des Böhmischen Krieges (1618–1621)*, ed. Miroslav Troegel (Prague: Akademia, 1972), 237–43 (no. 672). See also MTAKK, Ms 4942/a., 160–1.

17 Peter H. Wilson, *Europe's Tragedy: A History of the Thirty Years War* (London: Allen Lane, 2009), 281-93.
18 On Bethlen's concerns, see Péter, 'The Golden Age', 73-5; Sándor Papp, 'Bethlen Gábor, a magyar királyság és a Porta (1619-1629)', *Századok* 145 (2011): 915-73.
19 Sturmberger, *Georg Erasmus Tschernembl*, 275-335; Strohmeyer, *Konfessionskonflikt*, 208-90; Luc Duerloo, *Dynasty and Piety: Archduke Albert (1598-1621) and Habsburg Political Culture in the Age of Religious Wars* (Farnham-Burlington: Ashgate, 2012), 469-70.
20 Sturmberger, *Georg Erasmus Tschernembl*, 275-335; Strohmeyer, *Konfessionskonflikt*, 208-90. Since the Lower Austrian Protestant estates sent a memorial with their grievances (*gravamina*) to the Hungarian diet, the Catholic estates also sent a letter to the Hungarian estates trying to discredit them, Landesarchiv Niederösterreich (St. Pölten), Ständische Akten, A-4-14. fols. 68-71, Vienna, 14 August 1620. On 1620 as a turning point in the history of the Lower Austrian estates, see William D. Godsey, *The Sinews of Habsburg Power: Lower Austria in a Fiscal-Military State 1650-1820* (Oxford: Oxford University Press, 2018), 48-50.
21 MTAKK, Ms 4942/a., 13, 279-80. Cf. Matthias Weber, *Das Verhältnis Schlesiens zum Alten Reich in der Frühen Neuzeit* (Köln-Weimar-Wien: Böhlau, 1992); Joachim Bahlcke, 'Deutsche Kultur mit polnischen Traditionen: Die Piastenherzöge Schlesiens in der Frühen Neuzeit', in *Deutschlands Osten - Polens Westen: Vergleichende Studien zur geschichtlichen Landeskunde*, ed. Matthias Weber (Frankfurt am Main: Peter Lang, 2001), 83-112.
22 Strohmeyer, *Konfessionskonflikt*, 99-103, 184-7, 302-17, 402-14.
23 MTAKK, Ms 4942/a., 11-4. See also the reference on *altes Herkommen* in the report of Landau and Schallenberg, Besztercebánya, 3 August 1620, in Gindely, *Geschichte des böhmischen Aufstandes*, 490.
24 MTAKK, Ms 4942/a., 278; NA SM Kart. I. 1074. K 1/137, Dohna and Dornavius to the Moravian envoys, Besztercebánya, 8 July 1620.
25 MTAKK, Ms 4942/a., 13, 279; NA SM Kart. I. 1074. K 1/137, Dohna and Dornavius to the Moravian envoys, Besztercebánya, 8 July 1620.
26 Ibid., 276-7. For the editions of the act of the *confoederatio*, see *Documenta Bohemica*, vol. 2, 195 (no. 518).
27 Ibid., 12-15; see also in the letter of the Lower Austrian estates to the Moravian estates (n.d.), ibid. 268-269.
28 Sturmberger, *Georg Erasmus Tschernembl*, 325-35; Wilson, *Europe's Tragedy*, 285-99.
29 Peter Brightwell, 'Spain and Bohemia: The Decision to Intervene', *European Studies Review* 12, no. 2 (1982): 117-41 and idem, 'Spain, Bohemia and Europe, 1619-1621', *European Studies Review* 12, no. 4 (1982): 371-99; Josef Polišenský, *Tragic Triangle: The Netherlands, Spain and Bohemia 1617-1621* (Prague: Charles University, 1991), 157-90; Wilson, *Europe's Tragedy*, 294-9.
30 See the debate concerning this in the Austrian memorial and the response of the envoys of Bohemia and its incorporated provinces, as well as the Austrian envoys' letter to the Moravian estates: MTAKK, Ms 4942/a., 262-6, 271-5, 267-9. Cf. Bahlcke, *Regionalismus*, 444.
31 Landau and Schallenberg to unknown (Besztercebánya, 3 August 1620), in Gindely, *Geschichte des böhmischen Aufstandes*, 490.
32 His presence at Besztercebánya caused in itself a ceremonial problem, since he demanded the premier place among the envoys coming from the confederated lands, with the argument that contrary to the most prominent member so far, Baron Smil

Hodějovský z Hodějova, he was not only accredited by King Frederick, but also by each province. He was contradicted with the claim that his accreditation was valid for the Sultan's court, but not for Besztercebánya, where Hodějovský still was the head of the royal delegation from Bohemia; thus, Cöln had to be content with the second place. Obviously, the banquet organized for his welcome was also a public event where the conflict between the Austrians and the Silesians was bound to resurface. Again, a compromise was found: the names of the Austrians were announced immediately after the Bohemians, but in the seating order the Moravians and Silesians had partly higher, partly equal positions to them – at least according to the account of Dohna and Donavius, see MTAKK, Ms 4942/a., 94–6.

33 On the traditional pre-eminence of Hungary to Bohemia, see Géza Pálffy, 'Kaiserbegräbnisse in der Habsburgermonarchie – Königskrönungen in Ungarn: Ungarische Herrschaftssymbole in der Herrschaftsrepräsentation der Habsburger im 16. Jahrhundert', *Frühneuzeit-Info* 19, no. 1 (2008): 41–66.

34 MTAKK, Ms 4942/a., 100–3, 145–6. On Cöln's embassy, see the rather strongly pro-Habsburg account of Reinhard-Rudolf Heinisch, 'Habsburg, die Pforte und der Böhmische Aufstand (1618–1620)', *Südost-Forschungen* 34 (1975): 110–14.

35 See the recent discussions of Stollberg-Rilinger, 'Die Wissenschaft der feinen Unterschiede'; Krischer, 'Souverenität als sozialer Status'; Hennings, *Russia and Courtly Europe*, 15–19.

36 MTAKK, Ms 4942/a., 164–5 and 329–30 (appendix CL).

37 Ibid., 15.

38 Ibid., 280 for the memorial of the envoys from Bohemia and its incorporated lands to the Austrians, as well as NA, SM; Kart. I. 1074. K 1/137, Dohna's and Dornavius's letter to the Moravian envoys, Besztercebánya, 8 July 1620.

39 Even the archived documents of the *confoederatio* were cut, sliced with a blade, in order to invalidate them, see OÖLA, Ständische Urkunden, no. 128–30; OÖLA, Landschaftsakten Sch. 30. fols. 233–7, 282–4, 398–9. Also Sturmberger, *Georg Erasmus Tschernembl*, 304 (illustration on the opposite page).

40 Cf. Krischer, *Reichsstädte*.

9

Oath-taking and Hand-Kissing: Ceremonies of sovereignty in a 'Monarchia composita', the states of the house of savoy from the sixteenth to nineteenth centuries

Andrea Merlotti

When thinking of court ceremonies, it is generally the coronation that comes to mind: it was traditionally the most sumptuous, and rich in fascinating symbolism. Not all dynasties, however, could indulge in such rituals. A coronation in its ideology was connected not to the dynasty but rather to the state, and in many states, due to different historical developments, no such ceremony had been developed at all. This was the case with the Kingdom of Spain, the Kingdom of Sardinia, and several smaller Italian and German states, both within and outside the Holy Roman Empire.[1] Moreover, even in states where the coronation was part of the historical tradition, there could still be notable differences. Symphorien Champier in his treatise *De monarchia gallorum*, dated 1537, recalled that in fact only four monarchies had a tradition of holy unction: 'Sunt inter christianos quatuor tantum reges qui unguntur more Davidis et Salomonis, scilicet Ierosolymitanus, Francorum, Anglorum et Siculorum.'[2]

This text will focus on the provisions that regulated the coronation in a state that was unified, at least in its early history, by the dynasty alone, not by any concept of 'nation': the *Stati sabaudi*, or States of Savoy, that is to say the domains ruled by the House of Savoy, a composite monarchy within the Holy Roman Empire.[3] The legal, judicial and cultural position of the States of Savoy within the Empire affected therefore whether or not its princes were considered 'royal' and thus needed a coronation ceremony, and the nature of a 'Monarchia composita' likewise affected this consideration: if there was to be a tradition, whose would it be? This chapter will look at the evolution of some of these ideas connected to sovereignty, ritual, and in particular, ceremonies marking a prince's accession to the throne. Without a tradition of coronation, what other rituals were used? The chapter will examine shifts in focus of Savoyard court ceremonial during the transition from one princely rule to another, from funeral to acclamation, in particular, oath-taking and hand-kissing. It will conclude by looking at how these traditions were transmitted into the nineteenth century and foundational for the creation of the Kingdom of Italy by the House of Savoy in 1861.

The Duchy of Savoy (*Ducato di Savoia*) was the most prominent of these States of Savoy and for this reason all the territories under the rule of its dynasty were known almost invariably by this term. In fact, however, the Savoy rulers officially referred to their possessions as *Gli Stati del duca di Savoia* (the States of the duke of Savoy), and later, as kings of Sardinia from 1720 to 1861, as *Gli Stati del re di Sardegna* (the States of the king of Sardinia). The States of Savoy were characterized by a complex array of political entities, with different backgrounds, institutions, languages and cultures, that had been brought together under the rule of one dynasty. According to the French historian Laurent Ripart, the States of Savoy corresponded to a state entity which '(...) importe ... ne pas juger ... au paradigme du modèle anglo-française d'État-nation, mais de constater qu'il offrait un modèle d'organisation étatique suffisamment solide pour qu'il pût se maintenir jusqu'à l'époque contemporaine'.[4] Guido Castelnuovo defined this alternative type of state as 'supra-regional', showing that it was a frequent occurrence in the Middle Ages, particularly in the Alpine area, where there was a need to ensure the peaceful cohabitation under the same princely dominion of a number of heterogeneous entities.[5]

From the tenth century until 1848 the States of Savoy were never an 'État-nation', but a community of territories that were turned into states (in the plural) by virtue of a shared princely sovereignty that governed them all legally, administratively, militarily. From the standpoint of imperial law – which served as a main reference point for the House of Savoy, and from which stemmed their power and political legitimacy until the early nineteenth century – '... non esisteva (giuridicamente!) un unico Stato sabaudo: c'erano vari distretti dell'Impero sui quali era infeudata ai Savoia la superiorità territoriale'.[6] The Savoy Dynasty regarded themselves – and were regarded – as a German ruling house, descending from Saxon kings and emperors; as such, they acted as vicars, or place-holders, on behalf of the emperor in Italy, and jurisdictionally they were considered to be part of the Empire. These were crucial aspects of dynastic identity that the Savoy rulers would build on for at least four centuries – from the fifteenth century to the first half of the nineteenth century – to underscore their distance from the princes of the Italian peninsula. Time and again they would impose their precedence over the Medici, the Gonzaga and other Italian dynasties by virtue of their German ancestry.[7] But it also impacted their decisions with regard to how they marked princely accessions and succession ceremonies.

Every manifestation of Savoy princely rule until 1848 – when King Charles Albert issued the *Statuto*, the constitution that would later be adopted by the Kingdom of Italy in 1861 under its first king, Victor Emmanuel II, and would remain in force until 1946[8] – presented the Savoy monarchy as a group of territories and not a unitary state. It was only following their decision to lead the movement for Italy's national unification, in 1848, that this would change. It is therefore not surprising that the ritual that accompanied the accession to the throne of the ruler of the States of Savoy reflected this composite landscape.

As noted already, no accession to the throne by a member of the House of Savoy was marked by a coronation, with one notable exception: the coronation of Victor Amadeus II of Savoy as king of Sicily in 1713. This was the only occurrence when a Savoy ruler was the protagonist in a coronation ceremony, held in the Cathedral of Palermo.[9] It should be noted that this ceremony was, however, related to the specific title of king of Sicily, which applied to the House of Savoy only from 1713 to 1720, when they were forced to exchange Sicily for Sardinia, a kingdom for which no such ceremony had ever been part of its tradition.[10]

In fact, it was other rituals that marked this transition of rule. Until the mid-fifteenth century the accession to the throne by a Savoy ruler was signified by the funeral ceremony of the previous ruler. The ritual for the burial of Savoy rulers had developed traditionally into two distinct phases: a few days after the sovereign died, the body would be buried, but the sumptuous funeral ceremony would be held later, even a few months after the actual death had occurred. During that time the duke's vassals were able to travel to the capital from across the Savoy territories to pledge their loyalty to the new sovereign. In the mid-fifteenth century, however, the public funeral was replaced by the acclamation of the new prince before the 'assemblea dei ceti' (assembly of the social orders), which was celebrated soon after the passing of the previous ruler, a development that clearly issued from the decline in princely authority relative to the States of Savoy that followed the death of Amedeo VIII.[11]

At the same time, another practice had gained momentum: the princely *entrée*, a ritual utilized by many other ruling houses. In the States of Savoy it allowed the sovereign to receive, as he travelled from town to town, the oaths of allegiance of all the *Pays* and *Patriae* that made up the Savoy possessions. In 1553, Emanuele Filiberto became duke while he was in Flanders at the head of the Spanish troops, fighting to have his territories restored after two decades of French occupation: he thus entrusted a delegate to visit the towns and communities under Savoy rule to receive their oath of allegiance. In 1559, after being restored to his estates following the Peace of Cateau-Cambrésis, he entrusted a similar mission to his lieutenant general, particularly for the purpose of ensuring the loyalty of the nobility. Upon entering his dominions with his spouse Marguerite of France, he took the opportunity for a number of *entrées* during which he was recognized and legitimized by his subjects.[12]

These ceremonies changed progressively under Duke Carlo Emanuele I (1580–1630), when practices and rituals were set up that would last, at least in part, until the early nineteenth century.[13] Carlo Emanuele I initially maintained the tradition of the *entrées*, but progressively concentrated this ceremony, among others, in Turin, the capital of the States since 1563. It was around that time that the States of Savoy embraced a new tradition, whereby the duke would no longer travel to the capitals of his *Pays* for the oath-taking (and to confirm privileges), but instead the representatives of the *Pays* would congregate in Turin to participate in a solemn – and single – ceremony to take their oath in the Cathedral of Turin.[14]

This evolution is evident when comparing the ceremonies for the oath of loyalty to the prince of Piedmont (the title traditionally bestowed upon the heir to the throne) in 1575, 1602 and 1607. In the first of these, upon the death of Duchess Marguerite de France, Emanuele Filiberto arranged a ceremony for the oath of loyalty to be given to his son Carlo Emanuele. The Duke followed the example set by Charles V for the oath to his own son, Philip II, that had consisted of a number of *entradas* in the domains of the Spanish Crown.[15] Thus the twelve-year-old Carlo Emanuele, after having witnessed the oath-taking from his subjects who were in Turin, then travelled to the capitals of the main *Pays* of the States in Piedmont and in Savoy. Thirty years later, the now Duke Carlo Emanuele I arranged a similar ceremony first in 1602, with oaths to his son Filippo Emanuele, and, upon the latter's death, to the new heir to the throne, Vittorio Amedeo, in 1607. In this case, however, he discontinued the traditional *entradas*, and instead summoned to Turin the representatives of the nobility and the communities of the provinces, according to a formula that would remain largely unchanged thereafter.

The transformation of the oath-taking ceremony was a clear sign of the new balance of power between the Crown and the community: the duke would no longer travel to the towns of his domains to be recognized by and to meet his aristocratic subjects, but the representatives of the towns and the aristocracy would come to the capital – by then the sole *urbs ducalis* – to take their oath. In the early seventeenth century the solemn ceremony of the oath of loyalty in the Cathedral of Turin thus became the main ceremony that marked the accession to the throne for the House of Savoy, and would remain so throughout the early modern period. Scant documentation remains of the solemn oath-taking ceremonies prior to 1637, and only five are still documented, from the ceremony for the accession to the throne of the young Francesco Giacinto (1638), who died prematurely at the age of six, to Charles Emmanuel III (1730–1773): the oaths taken in 1637, 1638, 1646, 1675, and 1730.[16]

In looking more closely at the oath-taking ritual, the first aspect to consider is the sacred character of the ceremony. The oath was taken under divine authority and therefore the ceremony took place in the Cathedral before the archbishop of Turin. Next to him stood the highest political representatives of the state, whose oath-taking had been organized separately from that of the representatives of the provinces and the nobility, and had already taken place as a court ceremony prior to the public event in the Cathedral.[17]

During the ceremony the duke and his family would sit under a canopy, next to the altar. Between them was a table, covered in black cloth, where a missal and a cross would be found. Sitting behind the table was the archbishop, with the grand chancellor of Savoy at his side, along with the president of the auditors of the *Camera dei Conti* (Chamber of Accounts) and the first secretary of state. Their presence attested to the weight given to the ceremony. After the herald had spoken,[18] the secretary of state read out the text of the oath. The first to take the oath were the princes of the blood, followed by the legitimized 'natural' princes (that is, princely bastards, sons of the dukes born outside of marriage). There followed the oath of the Knights of the Annunziata (the most exclusive chivalric order of the House of Savoy) and then the representatives of the nobility and the communities. These followed an order based on a principle that had earlier been applied to the domains *di là de' monti* (those 'across the mountains', or Savoy proper, the cradle of the dynasty, which also included the Aosta Valley), who would take the oath before those *al di qua de' monti* (those who were 'this side of the mountains'). The order would be set according to the feudal title that the territory possessed within the Savoy domains (for example, the marquisate of Saluzzo preceded the county of Asti). It is important to notice that the oath did not precede, but followed the accession of the prince to the throne and it took place after the funeral of the deceased sovereign.

As noted above, the raising in rank from duke to king in 1713 was marked by a coronation in Palermo, but the subsequent transfer of regal status to kings of Sardinia in 1720 does not seem to have affected the rituals surrounding accession in the core lands of Savoy and Piedmont. There were, however, some significant changes recorded in the oath-taking of 1730, organized for the accession to the throne of Charles Emmanuel III, including a new order for the presentation of noblemen and communities. For the first time it was decided to arrange them not according to the ancient feudal territories (for which the House of Savoy had been invested with Imperial power), but by provinces, the juridical and administrative units created by Emanuele Filiberto in 1559. But there were other changes: the representatives of the provinces would now be called in alphabetical order, without taking into account other claims of precedence. The appearance of modern provinces in the ancient oath-taking ceremony was a clear sign of the developments in the rationalization of the State between the sixteenth and the eighteenth centuries. The oath-taking ceremony of 1730 also turned out to be the last one of the *ancien régime*. For in 1773, Victor Amadeus III decided to abandon the oath-taking tradition, thus fulfilling the wish of at least part of the aristocracy, who perceived it as a sign that their loyalty to the Crown was being questioned. Almost all noblemen, after all, served in the military or held public office and were therefore required to take their oath of loyalty to the sovereign anyway.

The oath-taking ceremony was revived by Charles Felix, the fifth son of Victor Amadeus III, who unexpectedly ascended the throne in 1821, after the abdication of his brother Victor Emmanuel I following the *Carbonari* revolts in March. This had followed the even more turbulent period of the French Revolution, when the monarchy of Sardinia had been forced to abandon its core territories, in 1798. Unlike his brother-in-law, King Charles X of France (who in 1824 reinstated the medieval ceremony of the *sacre* as the primary French coronation ritual), Charles Felix was well aware that the times had changed and that no ceremony could ever turn back the clock. The ceremony was, however, an efficient and symbolic way to reaffirm his power.[19] In fact, this was the only time that the king desired the production of an iconographic representation of the ceremony (Figure 9.1). Yet the reaction of the nobility to the need for the oath was, unsurprisingly, one of ill-concealed annoyance: the ministers who hoped that the oath would reinforce the bond between the Crown and the aristocracy had clearly miscalculated.

Another ceremony that rose to prominence in the eighteenth century, was the hand-kissing ceremony marking the New Year, a ritual that traditionally took place in the week between 25 December and 1 January. Like the oath-taking, the hand-kissing brought to court representatives of the main state institutions (magistrates) and the nobility.[20] This ritual harkened back to very ancient practices. Within the culture of seventeenth-century Europe, the practice was considered a legacy of Imperial Rome, which later spread across feudal society.[21] Hand-kissing rituals can be found at most European courts, particularly those that took the Imperial court as their model, and the Italian courts of the eighteenth century were no exception. As a clear expression of the bond of loyalty between the nobility and the Crown, even the supposedly revolutionary Napoleonic courts resorted to it extensively: in Naples, Joachim Murat reintroduced

Figure 9.1 F. Festa, *The Oath of Allegiance to Charles Felix of Savoy, king of Sardinia, in the Cathedral of Turin 14 March 1822* (Turin, Biblioteca Reale, U.IV.57). Su concessione del Ministero per i Beni e le Attività Culturali e per il Turismo, Musei Reali-Biblioteca Reale, Torino. © Biblioteca Reale, Torino.

the ceremony in an attempt to win the support of the aristocracy;[22] as did Joseph Bonaparte when he became king of Spain.[23]

As regards the States of Savoy, it is notable that at the time of the *Restaurazione*, upon returning to Turin after the French occupation (1798–1814), King Victor Emmanuel I celebrated his first contact with the nobility not with an oath-taking ceremony, but through a hand-kissing ceremony. It was staged according to the pattern adopted in the previous centuries: on 31 December the ritual focused on the magistrates, while members of the court followed on 1 January. When Carlo Alberto of Savoy-Carignano succeeded his cousin Charles Felix on to the Sardinian throne in 1831, the hand-kissing ceremony was once again revived with great splendour, while the oath-taking was abandoned altogether. The last hand-kissing ceremony at the court of Turin was held on 1 January 1848, but by then it appeared grossly anachronistic: the state was entering the era of the *Statuto albertino*, the first Italian constitution, and the court itself was preparing for major reforms.[24] This was not the case, however, at the opposite end of the Italian Peninsula, in the Kingdom of the Two Sicilies, where the House of

Bourbon would continue to stage the hand-kissing as the major court ceremony, for the very same reasons that it had been abolished in Piedmont.[25] Significantly, even after national unification under Victor Emmanuel II and the adoption of Savoy rituals across the country, the 'hand-kissing' habit has persisted to this day in the southern regions of Italy, at least idiomatically and in private.

Before reaching the conclusion, there is one more question that is important to address: how much of those ancient rituals of the House of Savoy would pass from the Kingdom of Sardinia over to the Kingdom of Italy? First, it is important to note that in 1861 – when the Kingdom of Italy was born – the House of Savoy was at the zenith of its thousand-year history. After 1848, it was the oldest dynasty in Europe to be still on the throne, with a continuity uninterrupted from the eleventh century. Contemporaries sensed the significance and potential of the dynasty – the American historian Adolphus Louis Koeppen wrote in 1854:

> The history of the House of Savoy is one of the most interesting among the royal dynasties in Europe. By the eminent talents of the chiefs and the unclouded success which attended their arms they formed in the course of centuries that magnificent kingdom on both sides of the Alps and the shores of the Mediterranean from which we in future hope and expect the deliverance and regeneration of Italy.[26]

In 1862 Maria Pia, daughter of the King, became queen of Portugal. In 1870, Victor Emmanuel II entered Rome, which thus became the new capital of the Kingdom. The same year his second son, Amedeo, duke of Aosta, ascended the throne of Spain. It seemed for a while that the House of Savoy was destined to play a hegemonic role in Mediterranean Europe. For this goal to succeed, an alliance with the British monarchy was essential. This bond was confirmed at the royal level by the membership of the kings and princes of the House of Savoy in the British Order of the Garter. In 1878, King Umberto I was appointed a Knight of the Garter in the Quirinal Palace, a location that only a few years before had been the seat of the 'Pope-King' – a potent symbolic setting. What was, then, the relationship between this reinvigorated House of Savoy and its ancient traditions? In particular, those that marked the accession to the throne: would the monarchy of Italy adopt a formal coronation ceremony?

King Charles Albert of Sardinia, the first member of the House of Savoy to become a constitutional monarch, in 1848/9 had ended the history of the States of the House of Savoy as a 'composite monarchy'. At the same time, he undertook a comprehensive reform of the court, looking at the models of the courts of the king of Belgium and of Louis-Philippe in France. *Gentiluomini*, *scudieri*, *paggi* and all the noble courtiers who had served the dukes of Savoy, and then the kings of Sardinia, for at least five centuries gave way to a 'Casa militare', made up of officers who were also *aiutanti di campo* (aides-de-camp) of the king. Only the queen's household maintained its *gentiluomini* and *dame*.[27] When in 1861 Victor Emmanuel II became king of Italy, the Savoy court was thus significantly different – and much more modern – than it had been in the long centuries of the *ancien régime*.[28]

One of the most significant differences was that the House of Savoy had incorporated territories with a tradition of crowns and a coronation ritual. Foremost amongst these was the *corona ferrea* (Iron Crown), the crown of the Kingdom of Italy, conserved in the Cathedral of Monza, near Milan. The Iron Crown first was used by the Langobard rulers between the sixth and eighth centuries, and then by Charlemagne and his descendants. From 963, the title of king of Italy was assumed by the emperors of the Holy Roman Empire, as *Rex romanorum* ('king of the Romans'): centuries later, in 1530, Charles V was crowned in Bologna by Pope Clement VII, first as king of Italy, with the Iron Crown, and then as emperor. It was used again by Napoleon, when he proclaimed himself 'king of Italy' in 1805. From 1814 to 1859, the Habsburgs had used the Iron Crown for their ephemeral *Regno Lombardo-Veneto*, and in 1859, after the loss of Lombardy, Emperor Franz Joseph removed the crown from Monza to Vienna. In 1866, at the end of the Third War of Independence, Victor Emmanuel II secured the return of the Iron Crown from the Emperor. He then attempted to put in place a coronation ceremony, but that was not to be the case.[29]

Two years later, in 1868, on the occasion of the wedding of Prince Umberto, the King established the Ordine della corona ferrea d'Italia (Order of the Iron Crown of Italy), thus renewing what had been done by Napoleon in 1805, and extended by Emperor Francis II in 1815, in setting up the Order of the Iron Crown with the aim of creating new honours systems in his role as king of Italy (the Emperor, however, did not close the Austrian order, which continued to exist until World War I).[30]

The Kingdom of Italy was established at the price of a dramatic rift with the Church, a rift that led in 1870 to the physical conquest of Rome by military force. The resulting anger of the Pope prevented any inclusion of the sacred dimension in the ceremonies of the new Savoy monarchy.[31] Historically, most European rulers had used divine sanction as one of their most powerful tools for the legitimization of their rule.[32] Even Napoleon had seen the need to be crowned by the Pope. But this was not possible for Victor Emmanuel II, as an excommunicated sovereign in a Catholic country.

In Victor Emmanuel II's designs, the ancient Iron Crown – which the Church regarded (and still regards) as a holy relic because it is said to include a nail from the Holy Cross – would be used for the coronation of his son and heir.[33] But his expectations would remain unfulfilled, and when the King died in 1878, the persisting tensions between the Italian state and the Catholic Church still made it impossible to organize a coronation ceremony with the necessary sacral elements. The government decided instead to place great emphasis on the funeral of the 'Padre della patria' (Father of the Homeland). As it had been in the Middle Ages, the accession to the throne of Umberto I was legitimized through the funeral ceremonies for his father. Nevertheless, it is important to note that the Iron Crown was brought to Rome for the funeral, and a bronze copy of it was placed on the tomb of the sovereign.

Conclusion

The coronation ceremony, which during the *ancien régime* had eluded the House of Savoy because of the composite nature of the States under their rule, was in the end prevented by a lack of validation on the part of the holy authority – the Pope – who had become a sworn enemy. The only genuine Savoy ceremonies that survived the establishment of the

Kingdom of Italy in 1861 were thus funereal ones.[34] The transformation of the Pantheon in Rome into the tomb of the kings of Italy, in 1878, was a monumental symbol of the role that funeral ceremonies would take on in the short history of the new monarchy.[35]

And yet, for the kings of Italy, as for the dukes of Savoy, accession to the throne would once again be marked by an oath-taking ceremony, this time in a different form. After 1848, when a new king ascended the throne, his first act was to swear allegiance to the *Statuto*. While previous oath-takers had been the representatives of the nobility, towns and provinces, swearing allegiance to the king on the Bible, inside a church (the Cathedral of Turin), now it was the king who swore, on the Constitution, in front of all the deputies and senators gathered in the Senate of the Kingdom.[36] The rituals had been turned on their heads.[37]

Notes

1 For a useful overview of the court rituals in the early modern period, see Maria Antonietta Visceglia, *Riti di corte e simboli della regalità: I regni d'Europa e del Mediterraneo dal Medioevo all'età moderna* (Rome: Salerno Editrice, 2009).

2 'Among Christians, there are only four kings who are anointed according to the custom of David and Solomon, that is, the king of Jerusalem, the Franks, the English and Sicily'; Symphorien Champier, *De monarchia Gallorum campi aurei: Ac triplici imperio, videlicet Romano, Gallico, Germanico* (Lyons: officina Melchioris et Gasparis Trechsel, 1537), 17 ff.

3 For an up-to-date overview of the history of the States of Savoy, see Paola Bianchi and Andrea Merlotti, *Storia degli Stati sabaudi (1416–1848)* (Brescia: Morcelliana, 2017). See also the essays in *Sabaudian Studies: Political Culture, Dynasty, and Territory, 1400–1700*, ed. Matthew Vester (Kirksville, MO: Truman State University Press, 2013). A useful historiographical approach to Sabaudian history are the essays collected in *Gli spazi sabaudi: Percorsi e prospettive della storiografia*, ed. Blythe Alice Raviola, Claudio Rosso and Franca Varallo (Rome: Carocci, 2018). For the definition of the *Stato composito* (composite state), that was applied in particular to the Spanish monarchy and the Holy Roman Empire, see Helmut G. Koenigsberger, *Estates and Revolutions: Essays in Early Modern European History* (Ithaca, NY: Cornell University Press, 1971) and more specifically John H. Elliott, 'A Europe of Composite Monarchies', *Past and Present* 137 (1992), 48–71.

4 '(…) should not … be judged … according to the paradigm of the Anglo-French model of the nation-state, but instead noted that it offered a model of state organization sufficiently durable that it could maintain itself all the way into the contemporary era', Laurent Ripart, 'Nice et l'État savoyard: Aux sources d'une puissante identité régionale (fin XIVe–milieu XVIe siècle)', in *Le Comté de Nice: De la Savoie à l'Europe: Identité, mémoire et devenir*, ed. Jean–Marc Giaume and Jérôme Magail (Nice: Serre Editéur, 2006), 16.

5 Guido Castelnuovo, 'Principati regionali e organizzazione del territorio nelle Alpi occidentali: l'esempio sabaudo (inizio XIII–inizio XV secolo)', in *L'organizzazione del territorio in Italia e Germania: secoli XIII–XIV*, ed. Giorgio Chittolini and Dietmar Willoweit (Bologna: il Mulino, 1994), 81–92.

6 '(…) there was not, legally, a single Savoyard state: there were various districts of the Empire on which territorial superiority was given to the House of Savoy', Giovanni

Tabacco, *Lo Stato sabaudo nel Sacro Romano Impero* (Turin: G.B. Paravia & C, 1939), 185. On the imperial character of the Savoyard monarchy see the essays collected in *Stato sabaudo e Sacro Romano Impero*, ed. Marco Bellabarba and Andrea Merlotti (Bologna: il Mulino, 2014), especially: Saniye Al-Baghdadi, 'Da Vitichindo a Beroldo: Sulle origini dei Savoia nella storiografia, nell'araldica e nell'arte', 49–68, and Clara Goria, '"Saxonicae gloriae" dipinte: Spazi e figure per le origini dinastiche sabaude', 93–112. See also Saniye Al-Baghdadi, 'La dynastie de Savoie et le traitement royal au XVIIe siècle: Mythes, symbols dynastiques et une pratique religieuse impériale', in *De Paris à Turin: Christine de France duchesse de Savoie*, ed. Giuliano Ferretti (Paris: L'Harmattan, 2014), 229–46; eadem, 'Die Erfindung der Sabaudia und die Historisierung des Alpenraums im Spiegel savoyischer Hofpublikationen', in *Transferprozesse zwischen dem Alten Reich und Italien im 17. Jahrhundert*, ed. Sabina Brevaglieri and Matthias Schnettger (Bielefeld: transcript Verlag, 2018), 287–322.

7   Andrea Merlotti, 'I Savoia: una dinastia europea in Italia', in *I Savoia: I secoli d'oro d'una dinastia europea*, ed. Walter Barberis (Turin: Einaudi, 2007), 87–133.

8   This periodization choice is documented in Bianchi and Merlotti, *Storia degli Stati sabaudi*, 5–13.

9   Elisabeth Wünsche-Werdehausen, '"La felicità in trono": l'entrata di Vittorio Amedeo II a Palermo nel 1713', *Artes* 13 (2005-7): 361–88; Tomaso Ricardi di Netro, 'Il duca diventa re: Cerimonie di corte per l'assunzione del titolo regio (1713–1714)', in *Le strategie dell'apparenza: Cerimoniali, politica e società alla corte dei Savoia in età moderna*, ed. Paola Bianchi and Andrea Merlotti (Turin: Silvio Zamorani, 2010), 133–46; Paolo Cozzo, 'Le couronnement de Victor Amédée II roi de Sicile (1713): langages religieux et politiques après le traité d'Utrecht', in *Sacres et couronnements dans l'Occident chrétien: rite, État et société, du Moyen Age à nos jours* (forthcoming, Presses Universitaires de Rennes).

10 On the peculiarities of the Kingdom of Sardinia, another 'composite kingdom' born from four sub-principalities known in the Middle Ages as the 'giudicati', which passed under Aragonese then Spanish rule, before a short Austrian decade (1708–1717), Spanish recovery (1718–1720), and finally a handover to the House of Savoy, see Bruno Anatra, John Day and Lucetta Scaraffia, *La Sardegna medievale e moderna* (Turin: UTET, 1984); Bianchi and Merlotti, *Storia degli Stati sabaudi*, 84–96.

11 In 1440 Amedeo VIII abdicated to become anti-pope under the name of Felix V. When he died (1451), his son was already duke so the immediate succession was secure, but during the latter fifteenth and early sixteenth centuries, the importance of the House declined due to a series of weak rulers, culminating in a French occupation of Savoy (1536–59). See *Amédée VIII-Félix V, premier duc de Savoie et pape (1383-1451): Colloque international, Ripaille-Lausanne, 23–26 octobre 1990*, ed. Bernard Andenmatten and Agostino Paravicini Bagliani (Lausanne: Fondation Humbert II et Marie José de Savoie, 1992); Luisa Clotilde Gentile, *Riti ed emblemi: Processi di rappresentazione del potere principesco in area subalpina (XIII–XVI secc.)* (Turin: Silvio Zamorani, 2008).

12 On Emanuele Filiberto, see Pierpaolo Merlin, *Emanuele Filiberto: Un principe tra il Piemonte e l'Europa* (Turin: SEI, 1995).

13 On Carlo Emanuele I, see Pierpaolo Merlin, *Tra guerre e tornei: La corte sabauda nell'età di Carlo Emanuele I* (Turin: SEI, 1991); *Politica e cultura nell'età di Carlo Emanuele I: Torino, Parigi, Madrid*, ed. Mariarosa Masoero, Sergio Mamino and Claudio Rosso (Florence: L.S. Olschki, 1999); Stéphane Gal, *Charles-Emmanuel de Savoie: La politique du précipice* (Paris: Payot, 2012).

14 Merlotti, 'I Savoia: una dinastia europea in Italia', 121-4.
15 Valeriano Castiglione, *Della vita del duca di Savoia Carlo Emanuele I*, Turin State Archives (hereafter: ASUT), Corte, Storia della Real Casa, categoria III, mazzo 14.
16 For 1637 and 1638, *Registro del cerimoniale del conte Francesco Canalis di Cumiana, mastro di cerimonie (1632-1643)*, Royal Library of Turin, Storia patria, 726/1. For subsequent oaths, *Regolamento da osservarsi nel solenne giuramento di fedeltà* (1675), ASUT, Corte, Cerimoniale, Avvenimenti alla corona, mazzo 2, fol. 7.
17 Merlotti, 'I Savoia: una dinastia europea in Italia', 122.
18 For the herald, or 're d'armi', see Luisa Clotilde Gentile, 'Du héraut au blasonatore: Les "techniciens de l'héraldique" et l'évolution de leur fonction dans les États de Savoie, du Moyen Âge au XIXe siècle', in *Généalogie et héraldique: Actes du 24e congrès international des sciences généalogique et héraldique, Besançon (France), 2-7 mai 2000*, vol. 2, *Héraldique*, ed. Jean Morichon (Paris: Fédération Française de Généalogie, 2002), 97-110.
19 Andrea Merlotti, *L'enigma delle nobiltà: Stato e ceti dirigenti nel Piemonte del Settecento*, (Florence: L. S. Olschki, 2000), 274-87.
20 Andrea Merlotti, 'Una muta fedeltà: Le cerimonie di baciamano fra Sei e Ottocento', in *Le strategie dell'apparenza*, 91-131.
21 See Henri Morin, 'Des baisemain', in *Histoire de l'Académie Royale des Inscriptions et Belles Lettres avec Les Mémoires de Littérature tirés des Registres de cette Académie, depuis l'année MDCCXI jusques et compris l'année MDCCXVII*, vol. 3 (Paris: Imprimerie Royale, 1723), 74-7.
22 See Nicoletta D'Arbitrio, *La Tavola del Re: Cronache dei Reali Offici di Bocca: Feste Pubbliche e Private alla Corte dei Borboni* (Naples: Edizioni Scientifiche Italiane, 1997), 77; Elena Papagna, '"Conservare con tanta esattezza le consuetudini e l'etichette spagnuole": Note sul regno di Carlo di Borbone a Napoli', in *Corte e cerimoniale di Carlo di Borbone a Napoli*, ed. Anna Maria Rao (Naples: Federico II University Press, 2020), 53.
23 [Jean-Baptiste-Honore-Raymond] M. Capefigue, *L'Europe pendant le consulat et l'empire de Napoléon*, vol. 8 (Brussels: Wouters, Raspoet et Ce, 1842), 240.
24 Paolo Colombo, *Storia costituzionale della monarchia italiana* (Rome-Bari: Laterza, 2001); idem, *Con lealtà di Re e con affetto di padre: Torino, 4 marzo 1848: La concessione dello Statuto albertino* (Bologna: il Mulino, 2003); Pierangelo Gentile, *Alla corte di re Carlo Alberto: Personaggi, cariche e vita a palazzo nel Piemonte risorgimentale* (Turin: Centro Studi Piemontesi, 2013).
25 See Raffaele de Cesare, *La fine di un regno (Napoli e Sicilia)* (Città di Castello: S. Lapi, 1900), 548-54.
26 Adolphus Louis Koeppen, *The World in the Middle Ages*, vol. II (New York: D. Appleton and Company, 1854), 496.
27 Paolo Colombo, *Il re d'Italia: Prerogative costituzionali e potere politico della Corona (1848-1922)* (Milano: Franco Angeli, 1999); Andrea Merlotti, '"La corte sabauda dal Regno di Sardegna al Regno d'Italia", in *Diademi e Gioielli Reali: Capolavori dell'arte orafa italiana per la Corte Sabauda*, ed. Stefano Papi and Tomaso Ricardi di Netro (Turin: Daniela Piazza, 2009). See also the essays collected in a catalogue of an exhibition presented in Reggia di Venaria, 25 March-2 July 2017, *Dalle regge d'Italia: Tesori e simboli della regalità sabauda*, ed. Silvia Ghisotti and Andrea Merlotti (Genoa: Sagep, 2017).
28 See Carlo M. Fiorentino, *La corte dei Savoia (1849-1900)* (Bologna: il Mulino, 2008); and Pierangelo Gentile, *L'ombra del re: Vittorio Emanuele II e le politiche di corte* (Turin: Comitato di Torino per la Storia del Risorgimento Italiano, 2011).

29 Andrea Merlotti, 'La regalità sabauda', in *Dalle regge d'Italia*, 82–5; Luisa Clotilde Gentile, 'Tante corone, nessuna corona', ibid., 111–15; and Pierangelo Gentile, 'Il Re d'Italia: Un titolo tra storia e leggenda', ibid., 130–3.
30 The Austrian order continued to exist until 1918 and the Italian order until 1946.
31 Andrea Merlotti, 'Il "sacro" alla corte sabauda di Vittorio Emanuele II da Torino a Roma (1849–1878)', in *Casa Savoia e Curia romana dal Cinquecento al Risorgimento*, ed. Jean-François Chauvard, Andrea Merlotti and Maria Antonietta Visceglia (Rome: Ecole française de Rome, 2015), 155–74.
32 *Dynastic Change: Legitimacy and Gender in Medieval and Early Modern Monarchy*, ed. Ana Maria S.A. Rodrigues, Manuela Santos Silva, Jonathan W. Spangler (London: Routledge, 2019).
33 Too many years had passed since his proclamation as king of Italy, in 1861, for a coronation of Victor Emmanuel II to be possible.
34 Umberto Levra, *Fare gli italiani: Memoria e celebrazioni del Risorgimento* (Turin: Comitato di Torino dell'Istituto per la storia del Risorgimento italiano, 1992).
35 Bruno Tobia, *Una patria per gli italiani: Spazi, itinerari, monumenti nell'Italia unita (1870–1900)* (Rome–Bari, Laterza, 1991); Carla Nardi, 'Il pellegrinaggio al Pantheon nel XXV anniversario del Risorgimento', *Clio* 41, no. 2 (2005): 305–15.
36 Luigi Lacché, 'Salendo il trono: Il giuramento costituzionale dei Savoia', in *Dalle regge d'Italia*, 144–5.
37 After the signing of the Concordat, in 1929, relations between church and state in Italy returned to normality. Victor Emmanuel III, however, did not want to innovate royal ceremonies. Thus there were no coronations when, following Mussolini's expansionist policy, he became Emperor of Ethiopia and King of Albania. On relations between Victor Emmanuel III and Mussolini see Paolo Colombo, *La monarchia fascista: 1922–1940* (Bologna: il Mulino, 2010).

Part Four

Tangible and Intangible Elements in Staging Ceremonies

10

Jagiellonians and habsburgs: Heraldic dynastic representation in Central Europe from the fifteenth to the seventeenth century

Géza Pálffy

Research into symbolic communication, representations of power and the role of ceremonies and rituals has been in the vanguard of historical investigation for the last few decades across Europe. This fact is underlined by numerous international research projects, conferences organized in various countries, and numerous monographs and edited volumes on the subject.[1] The present essay will examine a thus far neglected aspect of the field of dynastic representation, namely the heraldic representation of Central European dynasties (especially Habsburg and Jagiellonian) in late medieval and early modern royal funerals and coronations. There are several reasons why these royal events are worth studying. According to Richard Bonney's famous classification, the fifteenth to seventeenth centuries in Europe constituted the age of dynastic states,[2] while on the other hand, John Elliot spoke of European composite monarchies when considering the same period.[3]

In the context of these two visions of key European structures, this chapter seeks to answer the following questions: What role did coats of arms and heraldic flags play in late medieval and early modern dynastic representation in Central Europe? On which monuments and in which ceremonies did they appear? What function did they fulfil at coronations and royal funerals? To what extent did they represent dynastic composite monarchies or particular kingdoms? Did the heraldic representation of different dynasties influence each other? Which monuments or events had long-lasting significance? Furthermore, can detailed research uncover examples of heraldic mistakes in these representations of power?

Habsburg and Jagiellonian heraldic representation in late medieval Central Europe

From the fourteenth century, coats of arms and later heraldic flags (banners, or in German, *Wappenfahnen*) gained an emphatic role in the power and artistic representation

* The study was prepared with the support of the 'Lendület' Holy Crown of Hungary Research Project of the Institute of History, Research Centre for the Humanities, Budapest.

of ruling dynasties. Through the usage of these, dynasties primarily wanted to emphasize the importance of lands and provinces in their possession, or, using Elliot's terminology, the 'composite states' that they ruled. This applied to every competing dynasty of the region from the fourteenth century to the sixteenth: the Luxembourgs and Jagiellonians as well as the Habsburgs and individual rulers such as Matthias Corvinus, King of Hungary (r. 1458–1490). Moreover, they influenced and competed with each other in the fields of dynastic representation and identity establishment. Due to these processes, there was an increase in the number of territorial coats of arms on representative memorials, during court celebrations, funerals and coronations, and on seals and books.[4]

This process can be illustrated with a few examples. For the Luxembourg rulers in Bohemia, excellent examples include the series of renowned fourteenth-century coats of arms on the tower of Charles Bridge in Prague and on the castle gate at Točník. In Hungary, the heraldic tower of King Sigismund of Luxembourg (r. 1387–1437) in Buda might have fulfilled a similar role (sadly, it was later destroyed). As for the Habsburgs, outstanding instances are the still extant *Wappenwand* of Emperor Frederick III (r. 1440–1493) in Wiener Neustadt, and the *Wappenturm* of Emperor Maximilian I (r. 1493–1519) in Innsbruck, which was completed in 1499, as well as the heraldic murals in the house of the municipal judge Walter Zeller, dating from 1495.[5] The manuscript of the famous *Triumphzug* (1512–15) of Emperor Maximilian can also be considered an equally monumental memorial of dynastic representation, as is the printed *Ehrenpforte* by Albrecht Dürer (1526).[6]

The aspirations of Emperor Maximilian were carried on by Emperor Charles V (r. 1519–1556) in the West and his brother, Ferdinand I (King of Hungary and Bohemia 1526–1564; German Emperor 1556–1564) in the East. Around 1565, after the death of Ferdinand, the founder of the Central European Habsburg Monarchy,[7] his *Reichsherold*, Hans Francolin (1522–after 1580) compiled a *Wappenbuch* in which he listed all the coats of arms of the lands possessed and claimed by the Emperor.[8] Before that, an autodidact city historian and herald of Augsburg, Clemens Jäger (ca 1500–1561), compiled a grandiose genealogy of the Habsburg family in 1550,[9] which might have been the basis of the famous *Habsburger Pfau* painting in Ambras Castle in Innsbruck.[10] It is worth noting that the earliest detailed, coloured depiction of the Holy Crown of Hungary, the main symbol of the Hungarian state and nation, is attributed to this heraldist of Augsburg.[11]

Coats of arms were also present in the dynastic representation of Matthias Corvinus and his Jagiellonian successors in Hungary and Bohemia between 1490 and 1526. Although few of these remain on buildings today, the heraldic monument of Matthias (1486) in Bautzen (the capital of Upper Lusatia, part of the Bohemian Crown) belongs in this scarce category.[12] The Hungarian king preferred also to use heraldic representation for the volumes of his famous library, the *Bibliotheca Corviniana*.[13] The same effort is very nicely demonstrated by Johannes Thuróczy's *Chronica Hungarorum*, published in 1488 (Figure 10.1).[14] Moreover, the coats of arms of the Hungarian and Bohemian lands ruled by King Matthias were present on numerous seals as well.[15]

The Jagiellonians were keen on maintaining the aspirations of the Habsburgs and Matthias Corvinus. They placed the Hungarian and Bohemian coats of arms on their seals and coins, too. As an example, the Hungarian royal double seal (*sigillum duplex*) of Władysław II (1490–1516) from the autumn of 1493 features the whole collection:

Jagiellonians and Habsburgs: Heraldry 173

Figure 10.1 Coats of Arms of the Central European Lands and Provinces ruled by the Hungarian King Matthias Corvinus from *Chronica Hungarorum of Johannes Thuróczy*, 1488 (Budapest, Országos Széchényi Könyvtár). © Országos Széchényi Könyvtár.

the Lands of the Bohemian Crown (Bohemia, Moravia, Silesia, Lusatia), plus the Lion of Luxembourg on the heraldically least prominent left side, and the Lands of the Hungarian Crown (Hungary, Dalmatia, Bosnia, Slavonia, but not Croatia) on the right (see Figure 10.2).[16]

Nevertheless the Hungarian and Bohemian coats of arms scarcely appeared together on buildings in the Late Middle Ages. Yet, an outstanding rare example is a feature of one of the most notable late Gothic relics in Central Europe: the famous Royal Oratory in the Saint Vitus Cathedral in Prague (Figure 10.3).[17] The ten coats of arms featured— Dalmatia, Croatia, Bosnia, the Polish eagle, Hungary, Bohemia, Moravia, the Lion of Luxembourg (used also by the Jagiellonians), Silesia and Lusatia—illustrate very well the conglomerate of Hungarian and Bohemian lands ruled by the Jagiellonians in Central Europe between 1490 and 1526. But I think that this series has so far been mistakenly dated. In view of the Bosnian coat of arms (an armour-plated arm with sword) depicted on it we can state that the series of coats of arms was *not* made in the beginning of the 1490s but in the 1510-20s, presumably around the time of the coronation of Mary of Habsburg, Queen of Hungary (1505–1558) in the Cathedral of Prague on June 6, 1522. In fact, this Bosnian coat of arms made it to the Oratory, not as a Jagiellonian symbol, but under the influence of the heraldic dynastic representations

Figure 10.2 Hungarian Royal Double Seal of King Władysław II Jagiellon, 1493 (Budapest, Magyar Nemzeti Levéltár Országos Levéltára, Diplomatikai Levéltár, no 19968). © Magyar Nemzeti Levéltár.

Figure 10.3 Royal Oratory in the Saint Vitus Cathedral in Prague. © Géza Pálffy.

Figure 10.4 Silver Schaumünze of Bernhard Beheim with Coats of Arms of the Hungarian and Bohemian Lands, 1525, Kremnica (Budapest, Magyar Nemzeti Múzeum). © Magyar Nemzeti Múzeum.

of the Habsburg Emperor Maximilian I, as seen in the previously mentioned *Wappenturm*, the *Triumphzug* and the *Ehrenpforte*.[18]

This conglomerate was also symbolized by the different coins of Louis II, King of Hungary and Bohemia (1516–1526), for example, the silver *Schaumünze* or *Halbtaler* in 1525 (Figure 10.4),[19] and the set of Bohemian–Hungarian coats of arms on Bohemia's earliest map, published in 1518 in Nuremberg and designed by Mikuláš Klaudyán.[20] From this time on, coats of arms became regular adornments for printed maps, which could thus act as a form of dynastic representation. This is effectively demonstrated by the coats of arms on Hans (Johann) Siebmacher's map of the Danube from 1596/97,[21] which provided the basis for many maps and heraldic works that followed, and presented the colourful composite monarchy ruled by the Habsburgs in Central Europe after the collapse of the Jagiellonian Hungarian–Bohemian conglomerate, following the Battle of Mohács in 1526.[22] In sum, in contrast to the earlier medieval rulers of Central Europe, from the fifteenth century, coats of arms played an increasingly important and prominent role in dynastic representation in the region. Naturally, the traditional ceremonies making use of heraldry had antecedents in Italy and also western European ruling dynasties, notably in Burgundy, before the advent of the Habsburgs in those provinces at the end of the fifteenth century.

Heraldic representation in the funerals of Habsburg emperors

It is no surprise that coats of arms had special roles during various court ceremonies. In great numbers, they could primarily be observed during funerals where they presented the lands and provinces of a ruler as a form of dynastic representation, symbolizing the power of the deceased and the greatness of his empire. An early, pictorial example (as an engraving) is the *Weißkunig*, the well-known 'autobiography' of Emperor Maximilian I, which presents the coats of arms of countries ruled or claimed by his father, Emperor Frederick III, during the latter's funeral in December 1493 in the Saint Stephen Cathedral in Vienna.[23] Some of the wooden coats of arms from this ceremony still remain, now in the Vienna City Museum.[24]

Such funerary practices already had solid antecedents earlier in the fifteenth century for many Central European rulers, regardless of their dynasty of origin. Heraldic dynastic representation can be documented from the funeral ceremony of Albert II of Habsburg, king of Germany (1438–1439), and king of Hungary and Bohemia (1437–1439), held in October 1439, in Székesfehérvár.[25] In both the funeral of Emperor Frederick in Vienna, noted above, and that of Albert in the autumn of 1439, coats of arms were carried during the ceremonial processions (see Table 10.1). This clearly indicates that in the second half of the 1430s, the notion of a Habsburg composite monarchy already existed in Central Europe. The residence city was Buda, but the necropolis – in line with Hungarian traditions since the eleventh century – was the coronation and funeral site, Székesfehérvár.

However, with the accession of Władysław I Jagiellon (1440), and later Matthias Corvinus to the Hungarian throne (1458), the Habsburg residence city was transferred first to Wiener Neustadt (Frederick III), then to Innsbruck (Maximilian I), and the Lands of the Hungarian and Bohemian Crowns left the framework of the Habsburg composite state. These were governed by Matthias Corvinus (partly), then by the Jagiellonians after 1490 (in their entirety).[26] Although very little is known about funerals of the Jagiellonian dynasty held in Székesfehérvár in 1490 (Władysław II) and

Table 10.1 Coats of arms of lands and provinces paraded in the funeral processions of German King Albert II and Emperor Frederick III of Habsburg (in the order in which they processed)

Albert II (1439, Székesfehérvár)	Frederick III (1493, Vienna)
Upper Austria	Upper Austria
Burgau	Wendish Mark
Kiburg (in Swabia)	Pfirt
Portenau (Pordenone in northeast Italy)	Portenau
Pfirt (today's Ferette in Alsace)	Kiburg
Habsburg	Burgau
Alsace	Alsace
Wendish Mark	Tyrol
Tyrol	Habsburg
Moravia	—
Carniola (today's Slovenia)	Carniola
Carinthia	Carinthia
Styria	Styria
Lower Austria	Lower Austria
Bohemia	—
Hungary	Hungary
Holy Roman Empire	Holy Roman Empire

Sources: 1439: Hauser, 'Der Trauerzug'; 1493: Zelfel, 'Wappenschilde und Helme'.

1526 (Louis II), the funeral of King Matthias in April 1490 featured coats of arms in abundance because they made up an organic part of his royal representation, as shown above. A variety of sources mention twelve heraldic flags from the funeral, though there are no specific details.[27] Based on the above investigation, it can be stated with certainty that they symbolized the new composite state of the Hungarian king in Central Europe in the hierarchic order, as indicated by the new reconstruction shown in Table 10.2. So, even though Matthias Corvinus was not from one of the pre-eminent multi-national late medieval dynasties, he acted like he was.

Naturally, heraldic dynastic representation did not disappear with the Jagiellonian dynasty in Central Europe after 1526. On the contrary, it continued more emphatically, facilitated by several factors. On the one hand, the successor of Maximilian I, Emperor Charles V, created a global empire after 1519, 'on which the Sun never set'. Thus, during the symbolic funerary ceremony in December 1558 in Brussels, organized by his son the Spanish King Philip II (1556–1598), heraldic flags from across his enormous empire were lined up in long processions. This was documented in several languages by a series of ornamented, printed publications.[28] However, it is less well known that the tradition was also carried on by the Austrian branch of the dynasty. Thus, while the heraldic dynastic representations of Emperor Frederick III and Emperor Maximilian I might have first strengthened the ceremonial practices of Charles V in Spain and the Low Countries, these, in turn, significantly influenced Central European ceremonies.

The funeral ceremony in Brussels at the end of 1558 for Charles V served in terms of its heraldic and other important elements as a model for a subsequent monumental and symbolic funeral organized by Ferdinand I for his brother in the imperial city of Augsburg at the end of February 1559.[29] One chief organizer of this ceremony was Johann Ulrich Zasius (1521–1570), the future *Reichsvizekanzler* (1566–1570), who subsequently

Table 10.2 Reconstruction of the twelve flags on the funeral of Matthias Corvinus in 1490

1. Hungary: old coat of arms*
2. Hungary: new coat of arms**
3. Bohemia
4. Dalmatia
5. Bosnia
6. Austria
7. Moravia
8. Silesia
9. Lusatia
10. Luxembourg (lion)
11. Hunyadi Family (raven = *corvus*)
12. County of Beszterce (lion)

Notes: * Hungary: old coat of arms = four Argent (silver) and four Gules (red) stripes;
** Hungary: new coat of arms = an Argent (silver) double cross on Gules (red) base, on the central of three Vert (green) hills.

became one of the principal directors of the funeral processions for Emperor Ferdinand I in the summer of 1565 in both Vienna and Prague.[30] Later on, these funerary ceremonies for Ferdinand were the main models for those of Emperor Maximilian II (r. 1564–1576) in 1577, and Rudolph II (r. 1576–1612) in 1612, both in Prague.[31] Thus, the fifteenth-century heraldic dynastic representational traditions of Székesfehérvár and Vienna were renewed in sixteenth-century Innsbruck, Brussels and Augsburg, and then transmitted back to Vienna and even to early seventeenth-century Prague.

During the funerary ceremonies of Emperor Ferdinand I and his successors, the heraldic flags of some twenty countries and provinces demonstrated emphatically that after the Battle of Mohács in 1526, the Hungarian–Bohemian state of the Jagiellonians had been firmly replaced by a new composite monarchy led by the Austrian branch of the Habsburg dynasty. As is shown in Table 10.3, besides the leadership of the Holy Roman Empire, this composite monarchy consisted of several kingdoms, archduchies, duchies, margraviates and counties. At these funerals, the Lands of the Hungarian Crown were represented by five flags (Hungary, Dalmatia, Croatia, Slavonia and the common flag of Bosnia, Serbia, Cumania and Bulgaria), and the Lands of the Bohemian Crown by four (Bohemia, Moravia, Silesia, and the common flag of Upper and Lower Lusatia) (See Figure 10.5 for the Silesian flag).[32]

During the funeral of Emperor Ferdinand I in the summer of 1565, the composite flag of Castile, Aragon, Leon and Sicily was also present because, unlike his successors, Ferdinand was a Spanish *infante* (Latin *infans Hispaniarum*) as well. During funerals, catafalques (Latin *castrum doloris*, German *Trauergerüst*) of the deceased rulers bore the coats of arms of the most significant countries they had ruled (or at least claimed) as well as copies of the regalia.[33] The catafalque of Ferdinand I in 1565 clearly bore the arms of the Castilian and Aragonese crowns; thus the Iberian and south Italian coats of arms made it to Central Europe in the mid-sixteenth century.

However, sometimes the reverse was true, and the coats of arms of the lands of the Hungarian and Bohemian Crowns appeared in lands governed by the Spanish branch of the Habsburgs, like the Low Countries. During the funeral of Archduke Albert of Austria (1559–1621), the governor of the Spanish Netherlands (from 1598), which took place in the spring of 1622 in Brussels, both the lands of the Hungarian and Bohemian Crowns were meticulously represented by their coats of arms and banners – at least, pictorial sources of the funeral by the Flemish court architect and copper plate engraver Jacob Franquart (1582/83–1657) (*Pompa Funebris Alberti*, Brussels, 1623) clearly show them, notably on the Triumphal Chariot of *Liberalitas* (the virtue of Liberality), which had been constructed for the funeral procession (Figure 10.6).[34] The reason for this was that the Archduke, as the youngest brother of Emperors Rudolph II and Matthias (reigned as Emperor, 1612–1619), was from the Austrian branch of the dynasty and could even be presented as a symbolic successor to Emperor Charles V, an inheritor of both western and eastern Habsburg composite states, projecting a collective identity for the dynasty as a whole. Later on, in 1633, some of these coats of arms of the lands of the Hungarian and Bohemian Crowns were also present on the catafalque of his widow and co-governor, the Infanta Isabella Clara Eugenia (1566–1633) in Brussels, as seen in a French-language depiction found recently in the Viennese archives of the Order of the Golden Fleece.[35]

Table 10.3 Flags of lands and provinces paraded in the funeral processions of Albert II, Frederick III, Ferdinand I, and Maximilian II of Habsburg (in the order in which they processed)

Albert II (1439, Székesfehérvár)	Frederick III (1493, Vienna)	Ferdinand I (1565, Vienna)	Maximilian II (1577, Prague)
—	—	Gorizia	Gorizia
Upper Austria	Upper Austria		
Burgau	Wendish Mark	Common flag of Pfirt, Swabia, Alsace, Tyrol, and Habsburg	Common flag of Pfirt, Swabia, Alsace, Tyrol, and Habsburg
Kiburg	Pfirt		
Portenau	Portenau		
Pfirt	Kiburg		
Habsburg	Burgau		
Alsace	Alsace		
Wendish Mark	Tyrol		
Tyrol	Habsburg		
—	—	Upper and Lower Lusatia	Upper and Lower Lusatia
		Carniola	Carniola
		Carinthia	Carinthia
		Styria	Styria
—	—	Silesia	Silesia
Moravia	—	Moravia	Moravia
—	—	Burgundy	Burgundy
		Upper Austria	Upper Austria
Carniola	Carniola		
Carinthia	Carinthia		
Styria	Styria		
Lower Austria	Lower Austria	Lower Austria	Lower Austria
—	—	Common flag of Bosnia, Serbia, Cumania, and Bulgaria	Common flag of Bosnia, Serbia, Cumania, and Bulgaria
—	—	Slavonia	Slavonia
—	—	Croatia	Croatia
—	—	Dalmatia	Dalmatia
—	—	'Spain' = Castile, Aragon, Leon and Sicily	—
Bohemia	—	Bohemia	Bohemia
Hungary	Hungary	Hungary	Hungary
Holy Roman Empire	Holy Roman Empire	Holy Roman Empire	Holy Roman Empire

Sources: 1439: Hauser, 'Der Trauerzug'; 1493: Zelfel, 'Wappenschilde und Helme'; 1565: Österreichisches Staarsarchiv, Vienna [hereafter ÖStA Vienna], Haus-, Hof- und Staatsarchiv [HHStA] Familienakten Kart. 60, Konv. 5, Tod Kaisers Ferdinand I, 5.8.1565, fols 1–8; ibid., sine dato 'Khay. exequien 1565', fols. 1–3; 1577; ibid., Familienakten Kart. 61, Konv. 1, Tod des Kaisers Maximilians, fols. 425–7, fols 438–41; and ÖStA Vienna, Hofkammerarchiv, Reichsakten Fasz. 202/A fols. 270–1.

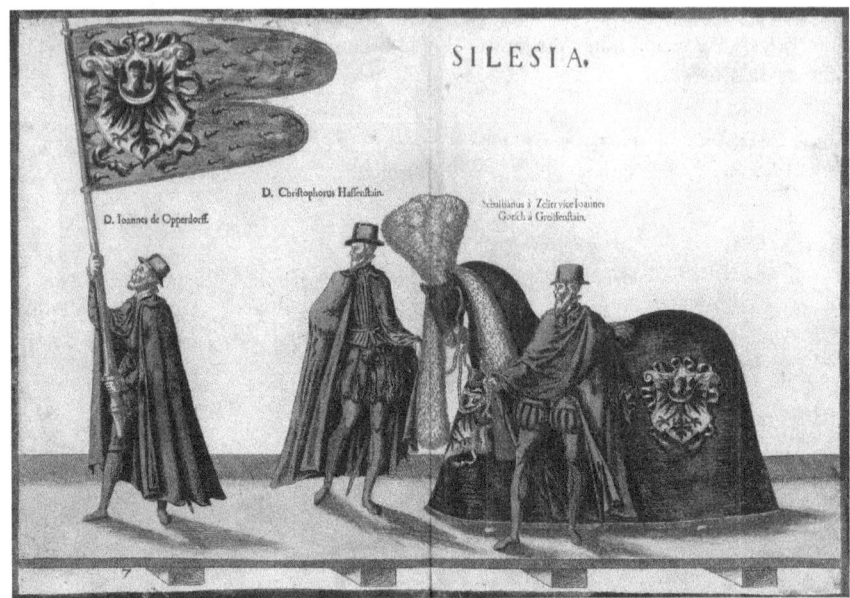

Figure 10.5 Flag of Silesia in funeral procession of Ferdinand I, 1565 (Wien, Wien Museum, no 116845/8). © Wien Museum.

Figure 10.6 Triumphal Chariot of Liberalitas in funeral procession of Archduke Albert of Austria from Jacob Franquart, *Pompa Funebris Alberti*, Brussels, 1623. © Géza Pálffy.

Finally, it is worth noting that during both funerals and court ceremonies, perfectly understandably, heralds also played an important role in dynastic representation. Five heralds served in the seventeenth-century Imperial court in Vienna. Each represented one of the main groups of territories within the monarchy: the Holy Roman Empire was represented and symbolized by the heralds of the Emperor and the Empire, the Hungarian Crown by the Hungarian herald, the Bohemian Crown by the Bohemian herald and the Austrian Provinces by the Austrian herald. These heralds had important roles especially in funerals where they participated in the procession, standing guard around the catafalque, as is shown by an engraving of the catafalque of Emperor Ferdinand III (r. 1637–1657) from 1657.[36]

Territorial flags during Hungarian coronations in the sixteenth and seventeenth centuries

Besides funerals, heralds were also present during coronations. Dynastic representation played a role in these ceremonies, too. The portrayal of heralds on the engraving depicting the Hungarian coronation of Leopold I as king (later reigning as emperor, 1659–1705) that took place in the summer of 1655 in Pozsony (the capital of Hungary, today's Bratislava), also provided an opportunity to define Hungary's place within the composite Habsburg monarchy in Central Europe (Figure 10.7).[37] In every Hungarian

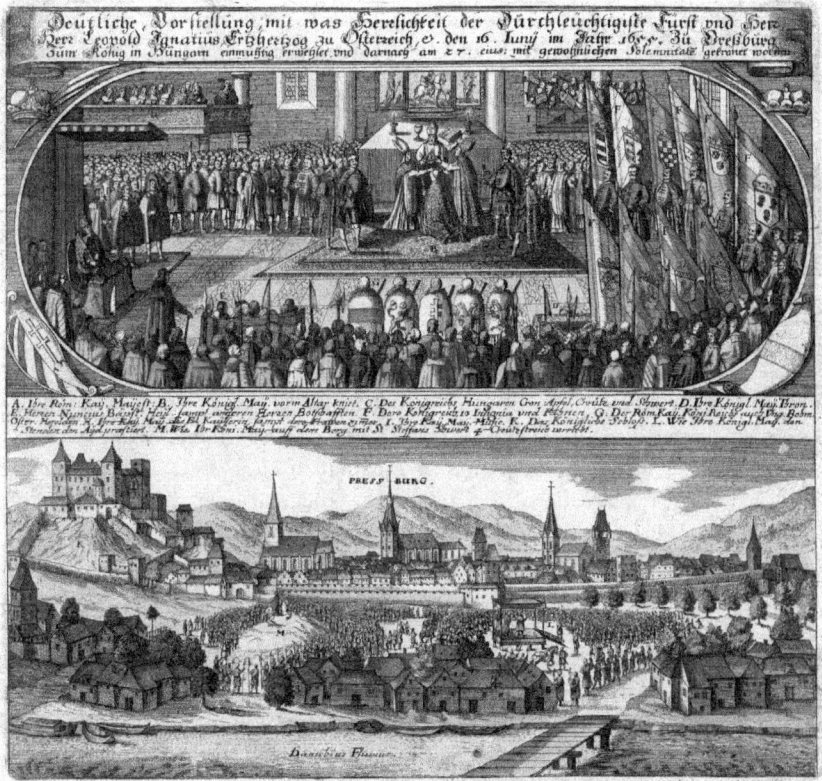

Figure 10.7 Coronation of Leopold I as Hungarian King in Pozsony, 27 June 1655 (Budapest, Magyar Nemzeti Múzeum). © Magyar Nemzeti Múzeum.

coronation from 1563 (that of Maximilian II, also in Pozsony), each grouping of territories in the monarchy was represented in a specific hierarchy by heralds who wore cloaks ornamented with that territory's coat of arms. The five figures on the engraving from 1655, in the centre, with their backs to the viewer, are the Imperial herald, the Emperor's herald, and the Hungarian, Bohemian and Austrian heralds. The prominent position of the Hungarian herald indicates that Hungary followed the Holy Roman Empire in terms of rank within the Habsburg composite state, preceding the Kingdom of Bohemia not only in terms of royal titles and diplomatic protocol but also in ceremonial practices.[38]

Dynastic representation was present at both coronations and funerals in the composite state, but it was in the coronation ceremonies for each individual territory that they were of lesser importance. In accordance with the interests of the Hungarian estates, Hungarian coronations primarily emphasized political significance, ancient traditions and the sovereignty of the Kingdom of Hungary throughout its history.[39] However, there could be a partial overlap in the interests of the estates and that of the dynasty. The authority of the Habsburg Monarchy in Central Europe was considerably increased by the fact that after 1526, not merely a territory, but the Sovereign Realm of Saint Stephen[40] (though in a much diminished form) was attached to it. This state had been the bulwark of the Faith, and a beef larder for Central Europe as well, for a long time,[41] and following the expulsion of the Ottomans in the late seventeenth century, it formed an core part of the more grandiose Habsburg Danubian Monarchy, with great military and economic significance.

All this is exquisitely demonstrated in a visual manner by the heraldic flags of territories presented during coronations,[42] for example, on the previously mentioned coronation engraving for Leopold I in 1655. These flags represented ten countries that *de facto* belonged to the Lands of the Hungarian Crown, or those claimed countries (German *Anspruchsländer*) that once, nominally or partially, belonged to it in the Middle Ages: Hungary, Dalmatia, Croatia, Slavonia, Bosnia, Serbia, Galicia, Lodomeria (Volhynia), Cumania (Wallachia) and Bulgaria (Figure 10.8). Almost all of these place names had been listed in the full royal titles of Hungarian kings from the end of the thirteenth century[43] – in a similar manner to the multiple titles used by other rulers of conglomerate states, such as Spanish kings, Russian tsars or Ottoman sultans.

During the Hungarian coronation of Maximilian II in 1563, only seven flags (Hungary, Dalmatia, Croatia, Slavonia, Bosnia, Serbia and Bulgaria) were presented, out of the usual ten countries in the royal titles, while at the next coronation in Pozsony, that of Rudolph II in 1572, all the countries of the Hungarian Crown had their separate flags. Although in reality, the Realm of Saint Stephen was significantly diminished due to the Ottoman conquest between 1521 and 1566 (i.e. the fall of Belgrade and Szigetvár),[44] the Hungarian political elite did everything to maintain its one-time glory and distinguished role via political representation and symbolic communication. This sixteenth-century invention of tradition turned out to be quite successful: the ten flags were presented at every ceremony up until the coronation of the last Hungarian King, Charles IV (r. 1916–1918) at the end of 1916 in Budapest.[45]

Besides the representation of the Hungarian state, coronation flags also played a prominent role in showing the power of the secular elite. New flags were sewn for every

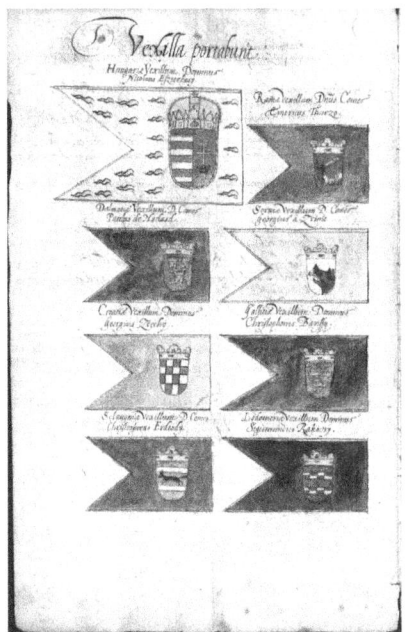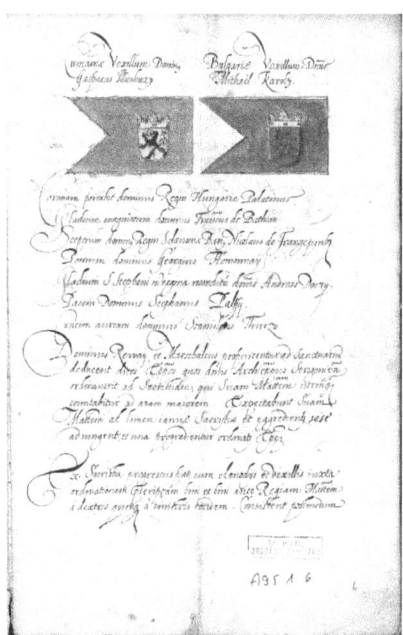

Figure 10.8 Flags of the ten Lands of the Hungarian Crown in the Coronation Ordinance of Ferdinand II in Pozsony, 1618 (Budapest, Magyar Nemzeti Levéltár Országos Levéltára, A 95, Acta diaetalia, 1618, fol. 5v–6r). © Magyar Nemzeti Levéltár.

occasion, though only Hungarian aristocrats had the right to bear them, and they could take them home as souvenirs. They were representatives of the most prominent and most influential families of the Hungarian aristocracy (Andrássy, Barkóczy, Batthyány, Bánffy, Csáky, Erdődy, Esterházy, Forgách, Károlyi, Keglevics, Nádasdy, Orczy, Pálffy, Rákóczi, Szapáry, Széchényi, Széchy, Sztáray, Thurzó, Zichy, Zrínyi). These banners were displayed in coronations from 1563 in Pozsony to 1916 in Buda. The full listing of the surnames of flag bearers across this entire period speaks for itself.[46]

Evolution and errors in heraldic dynastic representation

As the early modern period progressed, these heraldic dynastic representations continued to evolve, usually with the additions of new territories (for example, the addition of Milan in 1713 and Venetia in 1815). But sometimes these representations were incorrect. For example, regarding the already discussed engraving of the catafalque of Emperor Ferdinand III in 1657, it is clear that it makes use of the Habsburg coats of arms that had been present on the Danube map of Hans Siebmacher (1596/97), which had been re-issued in multiple editions of his *Wappenbuch*.[47] But the catafalque of the Emperor in 1657 is accompanied by the herald of Transylvania bearing the Báthory family's coat of arms with its distinctive 'teeth' pattern. Due to the multiple alliances (1595, 1597, 1599) between Emperor Rudolph II and Sigismund Báthory, Prince of Transylvania (r. 1588–1602),⁴⁸ the principalities of Transylvania, Wallachia and Moldavia entered the heraldic representation of the Habsburg dynasty at the end of the sixteenth century; indeed their coats of arms also appeared on Rudolph's Hungarian royal double seal (Figure 10.9).⁴⁹ Although this alliance was no longer a reality in the mid-seventeenth century, for readers unacquainted with the world of heraldry or those watching the funerary ceremonies, accuracy was not the most important concern.

In fact, there are earlier instances to be found of 'errors' in dynastic and territorial representation. For example, as unbelievable it may seem, there is a grave heraldic 'error' on the sarcophagus of Emperor Rudolph II in Prague.⁵⁰ Here the coat of arms of the late

Figure 10.9 Hungarian Royal Double Seal of Emperor Rudolph II, 1607 (Budapest, Magyar Nemzeti Levéltár Országos Levéltára, E 148, Neo-regestrata acta Fasz. 828, no 17). © Magyar Nemzeti Levéltár.

Jagiellonians and Habsburgs: Heraldry 185

Figure 10.10 Hungarian Coronation Medal of King Ferdinand II with Coats of Arms of the ten Lands of the Hungarian Crown, 1618 (Budapest, Magyar Nemzeti Múzeum). © Magyar Nemzeti Múzeum.

medieval territory of Slavonia, which had been granted to its estates by King Władysław II in 1496,[51] were labelled as Bulgaria (a claimed kingdom from the thirteenth century, see above). But this mistake can also answer an important question: from what source did the makers of the sarcophagus take the Emperor's coats of arms of the Lands of the Hungarian Crown? To our knowledge, this 'swap' of coats of arms at first originated with the German heraldist and mayor of Constance, Conrad Grünenberg (1442–1494) in his famous manuscript *Wappenbuch* (1480s), then repeated in the sixteenth century by, among others, the renowned engraver from Nuremberg, Virgil Solis (1514–1562), in his *Wappenbüchlein* published in 1555, and even later replicated by the Imperial herald, Hans Francolin in his *Wappenbuch* of 1565.[52] Thus, we can rightfully consider this work of Francolin as the main source for the series of coats of arms on the Emperor's sarcophagus later in the seventeenth century.

The Slavonian–Bulgarian swap of coat of arms appears in different forms on several heraldic artefacts in connection with the seventeenth-century Viennese court. It appears on the Hungarian coronation medals of Matthias II, Ferdinand II and Ferdinand III (1608, 1618 and 1625),[53] and is also seen in the previously mentioned French sources about the coats of arms on the sarcophagus of the Infanta Isabella in Brussels, 1633 (Figure 10.10). We should not be surprised by this. The by now nearly solidified heraldic swap lived on into the later seventeenth and eighteenth centuries.[54] But not always: in contrast to all these, it is remarkable that depictions of the funeral of Isabella's husband, Archduke Albert of Austria in 1622, show both the Slavonian and Bulgarian coats of arms, in accordance with the hierarchic order in the Hungarian royal titles (see p. 182). Unfortunately, we do not yet know the exact primary source of its maker Jacob Franquart.[55] In the end, what this means, is that the accuracy wasn't that important, just the overall impression and the success of representation and propaganda.

Conclusion

Using some of the above criteria, we can draw some conclusions: as earlier in Italy and Western Europe, from the fifteenth century onwards, the coats of arms and heraldic flags played an increasing role in dynastic representation in Central Europe. This is seen on the physical spaces and court ceremonies in the residences of the Luxembourgs, Jagiellonians and Habsburgs in Prague, Wiener Neustadt, Innsbruck, Vienna and Buda. Moreover, these dynasties influenced and competed with each other in the fields of dynastic representation and identity establishment. So, even though the Hungarian king Matthias Corvinus was not from one of the pre-eminent dynasties of Europe, he acted like one. The numerous (even sometimes erroneous) coats of arms in the Habsburg funerals from the mid-sixteenth century clearly indicated that after the collapse of the Hungarian–Bohemian conglomerate of monarchy of the Jagiellonians at the Battle of Mohács in 1526, the Habsburgs not only possessed an enormous and variegated composite monarchy in the Spanish branch (the Spanish Monarchy), but also had a significant conglomerate of states and lands in Central Europe, including the Holy Roman Empire, the Lands of the Hungarian and Bohemian Crowns, and the Austrian Hereditary Lands. In the early modern period, dynastic representation was not primarily about authenticity of the coats of arms but rather the success of propaganda, that is, making an overall impression. In the end, from the mid-sixteenth century, in funerals of the Habsburg emperors the coats of arms represented especially the structure and power of their dynastic composite monarchy, but in coronations they fulfilled a function to symbolize the sovereignty and the political significance of particular kingdoms within the monarchy.

Notes

1 A few excellent examples from the past decades: *Coronations: Medieval and Early Modern Monarchic Ritual*, ed. János M. Bak (Berkeley: University of California Press, 1990); Regine Jorzick, *Herrschaftssymbolik und Staat: Die Vermittlung königlicher Herrschaft im Spanien der frühen Neuzeit (1556–1598)* (Vienna: Geschichte und Politik, 1998); Gabriel Guarino, *Representing the King's Splendour: Communication and Reception of Symbolic Forms of Power in Viceregal Naples* (Manchester: Manchester University Press, 2010); Barbara Stollberg-Rilinger, *Rituale* (Frankfurt am Main–New York: Campus, 2013); eadem, *The Emperor's Old Clothes: Constitutional History and the Symbolic Language of the Holy Roman Empire* (New York–Oxford: Berghahn Books, 2015); *Alles nur symbolisch? Bilanz und Perspektiven der Erforschung symbolischer Kommunikation*, ed. Barbara Stollberg-Rilinger, Tim Neu and Christina Brauner (Cologne–Weimar–Vienna: Böhlau, 2013); *Les funérailles princières en Europe, XVIe-XVIIIe siècle*, vol. 1–3, ed. Juliusz A. Chrościcki, Mark Hengerer and Gérard Sabatier (Rennes and Versailles: Presses universitaires de Rennes/Centre de recherche du château de Versailles, 2012–2015).
2 Richard Bonney, *The European Dynastic States, 1494–1660* (Oxford: Oxford University Press, 1991; reprint: 2012).
3 John H. Elliott, 'A Europe of Composite Monarchies', *Past and Present* 137 (1992): 48–71.

4   For Hungarian examples, see Szabolcs de Vajay, 'Das "Archiregnum Hungaricum" und seine Wappensymbolik in der Ideenwelt des Mittelalters', in *Überlieferung und Auftrag: Festschrift für Michael de Ferdinandy zum sechzigsten Geburtstag 5. Oktober 1972*, ed. Josef Gerhard Farkas (Wiesbaden: Guido Pressler, 1972), 647–67; and more recently, Géza Pálffy, 'Kaiserbegräbnisse in der Habsburgermonarchie – Königskrönungen in Ungarn: Ungarische Herrschaftssymbole in der Herrschaftsrepräsentation der Habsburger im 16. Jahrhundert', *Frühneuzeit-Info* 19, no. 1 (2008): 41–66.
5   Franz-Heinz von Hye, 'Pluriumque Europae provinciarum rex et princeps potentissimus – Kaiser Maximilians I. genealogisch-heraldische Denkmäler in und um Innsbruck', in *Staaten: Wappen: Dynastien: XVIII. Internationaler Kongress für Genealogie und Heraldik in Innsbruck vom 5. bis 9. September 1988*, ed. Franz-Heinz von Hye (Innsbruck: Stadtmagistrat Innsbruck, 1988), 35–63; idem, 'Der Wappenturm – zur Vorgeschichte einer heraldisch-künstlerischen Idee', *Veröffentlichungen des Tiroler Landesmuseum Ferdinandeum* 70 (1990): 99–109.
6   *Werke für die Ewigkeit: Kaiser Maximilian I. und Erzherzog Ferdinand II. Ausstellungskatalog des Kunsthistorischen Museums, Schloss Ambras 6. Juli bis 31. Oktober 2002*, ed. Wilfried Seipel (Vienna: Kunsthistoriches Museum, 2002), 120–3, no. 52; *Albrecht Dürer: Ausstellungskatalog der Albertina 5. September – 30. November 2003*, ed. Klaus Albrecht Schörder and Maria Luise Sternath (Vienna: Hatje Cantz, 2003), 448–53, no. 154; *Emperor Maximilian I and the age of Dürer*, ed. Eva Michel, Maria Luise Sternath and Manfred Hollegger (Munich–New York–Vienna: Prestel-Albertina, 2012), passim.
7   See Thomas Winkelbauer, '1526 – Die Entstehung der zusammengesetzten Monarchie der österreichischen Linie des Hauses Habsburg', in *Von Lier nach Brüssel: Schlüsseljahre österreichischer Geschichte (1496–1995)*, ed. Martin Scheutz and Arno Strohmeyer (Vienna: Studienverlag, 2010), 59–78.
8   Johann von Francolin, *Weyland Kaysers Ferdinandi säliger vnd hochloblichister gedäctnus vnnd dem ganczen hochberhümbten hauß Österreich angehörig Wappen* (Augsburg: Philipp Ulhart, ca. 1565), Österreichische Nationalbibliothek, Vienna [hereafter ÖNB Vienna] 48.W.7; see also Egon von Berchem, Donald Lindsay Galbreath and Otto Hupp, *Beiträge zur Geschichte der Heraldik* (Berlin: Verlag für Standesamtswesen, 1939), 152–6; and recently, Kees Teszelszky, 'Wirklichkeitsgetreue Darstellungen der ungarischen Krone um 1608', in *Wiener Archivforschungen: Festschrift für den ungarischen Archivdelegierten in Wien*, István Fazekas, ed. Zsuzsanna Cziráki et al. (Vienna: Ungarisches Nationalarchiv–Institut für Ungarische Geschichtsforschung in Wien, 2014), 133–41, here 137–8, and 417–18, fig. 3–4.
9   ÖNB Vienna, Handschriftensammlung Cod. 7390, fols I–II, Brevis Descriptio Genealogicae Austriacae Conscripta a Clemente Jeger, and fols. 1–26 (unedited).
10 Thomas Kuster, '"...den Neidern und Feinden des habsburgischen Namens und Ruhmes zum Trotze und Spotte...": Der Habsburger Pfau – ein kurioser Wappenträger', *Jahrbuch des Kunsthistorischen Museums Wien* 13–14 (2011–2012): 76–103.
11 Enikő Buzási and Géza Pálffy, *Augsburg – Vienna – München – Innsbruck: Die frühesten Darstellungen der Stephanskrone und die Entstehung der Exemplare des Ehrenspiegels des Hauses Österreich: Gelehrten- und Künstlerbeziehungen in Mitteleuropa in der zweiten Hälfte des 16. Jahrhunderts* (Budapest: Institut für Geschichte des Forschungszentrums für Humanwissenschaften der Ungarischen Akademie der Wissenschaften, 2015).
12 Manfred Thiemann, 'Mathias Rex anno 1486: Das Matthias-Corvinus-Denkmal in Bautzen', *Ungarn-Jahrbuch: Zeitschrift für interdisziplinäre Hungarologie* 29 (2008):

1–32; Szilárd Papp, 'Mátyás emlékezete Bautzenben', in *Rex invictissimus: Hadsereg és hadszervezet a Mátyás kori Magyarországon*, ed. László Veszprémy (Budapest: Zrínyi Kiadó, 2008), 213–36.

13 Csaba Csapodi and Klára Csapodi-Gárdonyi, Bibliotheca Corviniana, 1490–1990: International Corvina Exhibition on the 500th Anniversary of the Death of King Matthias: National Széchényi Library, 6 April – 6 October 1990 (Budapest: National Szechenyi Libary, 1990); Árpád Mikó, *The Corvinas of King Matthias in the National Széchényi Library* (Budapest: Országos Széchényi Könyvtár, Kossuth Kiadó, 2008); *Matthias Corvin, les bibliothèques princières et la genèse de l'état moderne*, ed. Jean-François Maillard, István Monok and Donatella Nebbiai (Budapest: Országos Széchényi Könyvtár, 2009).

14 János Thuróczy, *A magyarok krónikája [Chronica Hungarorum]*. Facsimile edition (Budapest: Helikon Kiadó, 1986).

15 Lajos Bernát Kumorovitz, 'Mátyás király pecsétjei', *Turul* [Budapest] 46 (1932): 5–19; Iván Bertényi, 'I. Mátyás király címerváltozatai', *Levéltári Közlemények* [Budapest] 79 (2008): 77–100, here 83–6.

16 Magyar Nemzeti Levéltár Országos Levéltára (Hungarian National Archives, Hungarian State Archives) Budapest [hereafter: MNL OL Budapest]; Diplomatikai Levéltár (Diplomatic Archives), no 19968 (28 October 1493); see Zenon Piech, 'Die Wappen der Jagiellonen als Kommunikationssystem', in *Hofkultur der Jagiellonendynastie und verwandter Fürstenhäuser*, ed. Urszula Borkowska and Markus Hörsch (Ostfildern: Thorbecke, 2010), 13–34, here 25–6.

17 Ivo Hlobil, *Der Prager Veitsdom* (London: Opus, 2006), 34; Jiří Kuthan and Jan Royt, *Katedrála sv. Víta, Václava a Vojtěcha: Svatyně českých patronů a králů* (Prague: Nakladatelství Lidové noviny – Katolicka teologicka fakulta Univerzity Karlovy v Praze, 2011), 385–9.

18 For the new interpretation and dating, see Géza Pálffy, 'Heraldische Repräsentation der Jagiellonen und der Habsburger: Die Wappen des königlichen Oratoriums im Prager Veitsdom im mitteleuropäischen Kontext', *Historie – Otázky – Problémy* 7, no. 2 (2015): 176–90.

19 Lajos Huszár and Béla von Procopius, *Medaillen- und Plakettenkunst in Ungarn* (Budapest: Verlag des Vereins der Medaillenfreunde, 1932), 11, C.II: 302 and 9, C.II: 303.

20 Karel Kuchař, *Early Maps of Bohemia, Moravia and Silesia* (Prague: Ústřední správa geodézie a kartografie, 1961), 11–15; Jaroslav Kolár, 'Takzvaná mapa Čech Mikuláše Klaudiána: Pokus o významovou interpretaci', *Strahovská knihovna: Sborník Památníku národního písemnictví* 14–15 (1980): 49–73; András Végh, 'The Oldest Map of Bohemia', in *Mary of Hungary: The Queen and her Court 1521–1531. Budapest History Museum, 30 September 2005 – 9 January 2006. Slovenská národná galéria, 2 February – 30 April 2006* [Catalogue], ed. Orsolya Réthelyi et al. (Budapest: Budapest History Museum, 2005), 62, 207, no. IV-3.

21 Tibor Szathmáry, *Descriptio Hungariae: Magyarország és Erdély nyomtatott térképei 1477–1600* (Fusignano: Grafiche Morandi, 1987), 215–16, no. 98.

22 R[obert] J[ohn] W[eston] Evans, *The making of the Habsburg Monarchy, 1550–1700: An Interpretation* (Oxford: Oxford University Press, 1979); Thomas Winkelbauer, Österreichische Geschichte 1522–1699, vol. 1, *Ständefreiheit und Fürstenmacht: Länder und Untertanen des Hauses Habsburg im konfessionellen Zeitalter, 1522–1699* (Vienna: Carl Ueberreuter, 2003); Géza Pálffy, *The Kingdom of Hungary and the Habsburg Monarchy in the Sixteenth Century* (New York: Columbia University Press, 2009).

23 *Kaiser Maximilians I: Weisskunig*, vol. 2, *Tafelband*, ed. H[einrich] Th. Musper et al. (Stuttgart: Kohlhammer, 1956), table 211.
24 Hans Peter Zelfel, 'Wappenschilde und Helme vom Begräbnis Kaiser Friedrichs III: Ein Beitrag zum Begräbniszeremoniell', *Unsere Heimat: Zeitschrift des Vereins für Landeskunde von Niederösterreich und Wien* 45 (1974): 201–9; and on the coats of arms of the Habsburg lands more recently: Michael Göbl, *Wappen-Lexikon der habsburgischen Länder*, 2nd enlarged ed. (Schleinbach: Winler-Hermaden, 2017).
25 Wilhelm Hauser, 'Der Trauerzug beim Begräbnis des deutschen Königs Albrechts II. († 1439)', *Adler: Zeitschrift für Genealogie und Heraldik* 85 (1967): 191–5.
26 Recently Antonín Kalous, *Matyáš Korvín (1443–1490): Uherský a český král* (České Budějovice: Veduta, 2009); *The Jagiellonians in Europe: Dynastic, Diplomacy and Foreign Relations*, ed. Attila Bárány and Balázs Antal Bacsa (Debrecen: Hungarian Academy of Sciences – University of Debrecen 'Lendület' Hungary in Medieval Europe Research Group, 2016).
27 *A Magyar Nemzeti Múzeum címeres halotti emlékei*, ed. László Baják (Budapest: Magyar Nemzeti Múzeum, 2007), 10–11; Terézia Kerny, 'Hunyadi Mátyás halála, temetése és székesfehérvári síremléke', in *Mátyás király és a fehérvári reneszánsz*, ed. Terézia Kerny and András Smohay (Székesfehérvár: Székesfehérvári Egyházmegyei Múzeum, 2010), 42–66, here 47–52.
28 Achim Aurnhammer and Friedrich Däuble, 'Die Exequien für Kaiser Karl V. in Augsburg, Brüssel und Bologna', *Archiv für Kulturgeschichte* 62–63 (1980–1981): 101–57, here 116–19; Michael Brix, 'Trauergerüste für die Habsburger in Wien', *Wiener Jahrbuch für Kunstgeschichte* 26 (1973): 208–65, here 209–11; *Kaiser Karl V. (1500–1558): Macht und Ohnmacht Europas: Eine Ausstellung des Kunsthistorischen Museums Wien, 16. Juni bis 10. September 2000*, ed. Wilfried Seipel (Vienna–Milan: Kunsthistorisches Museum – Skira, 2000), 351–2, no. 416.
29 Beatrix Bastl and Mark Hengerer, 'Les funérailles impériales des Habsbourg d'Autriche, XVe–XVIIIe siècle', in *Les funérailles princières en Europe XVIe–XVIIIe siècle*, vol. 1, *Le grand théâtre de la mort*, 91–116, here 94–6; Bruno Thomas, 'Die Augsburger Funeralwaffen Kaiser Karls V: Ein Beitrag zur 400: Wiederkehr des Tages seiner Totenfeier', *Waffen und Kostümkunde* 3, no. 1 (1959): 28–47; *Kaiser Karl V.*, 352, no. 417–20.
30 Bartholomaeus Hannewald, *Parentalia Divo Ferdinando Caesari Avgvsto patri patriae etc. a Maximiliano imperatore etc., Ferdinando et Carolo serenissimis Archiducibus Austriae Fratribus singulari pietate persoluta Viennae, Anno Domini M.D.LXV. VIII. Idus Augusti.* (Augusta Vindelicorum: Meyerpeck et Sorg, 1566), fol. 4^v [a colourful Exemplar: Wien Museum, Vienna Inv. 116.845]: 'pompae totius rectores erant dominus Georgius Proskousky, Baro in Proskaw etc. [Jiří Pruskovský z Proskau (Germ. Georg Proskovsky)], dominus Rudolphus Kuen a Belasi [Rudolf Khuen von Belasy], uterque a cubiculis Caesareae Maiestatis et eiusdem a secretis consiliis, dominus Ioannes Vdalricus Zasius iuris utriusque doctor, cui in exequiis Caroli V. idem onus demandatum fuerat'. Cf. *Kaiser Ferdinand I, 1503–1564: Das Werden der Habsburgermonarchie: Eine Ausstellung des Kunsthistorischen Museums Wien, 15. April bis 31. August 2003*, ed. Wilfried Seipel (Vienna–Milan: Kunsthistorisches Museum – Skira, 2003), 567–9, no. XI. 26.
31 Rosemarie Vocelka, 'Die Begräbnisfeierlichkeiten für Kaiser Maximilian II, 1576/77', *Mitteilungen des Instituts für österreichische Geschichtsforschung* 84 (1976): 105–36; Václav Bůžek, 'Die Begräbnisfeierlichkeiten nach dem Tod Ferdinands I. und seiner

Söhne', *Historie – Otázky – Problémy* 7, no. 2 (2015): 260–75; Václav Bůžek and Pavel Marek, *Smrt Rudolfa II* (Prague: Nakladatelství Lidové noviny, 2015).

32 Géza Pálffy, 'Ungarn in der Habsburgermonarchie: Ungarische Herrschaftszeichen an der Wiener Begräbniszeremonie Ferdinands I. 1565', in *Wien und seine WienerInnen: Ein historischer Streifzug durch Wien über Jahrhunderte: Festschrift Karl Vocelka zum 60. Geburtstag*, ed. Martin Scheutz and Vlasta Valeš (Vienna–Cologne–Weimar: Böhlau, 2008), 29–46; idem, 'Die Repräsentation des Königreichs Ungarn am Begräbnis Kaiser Maximilians II. in Prag 1577', in *Per saecula ad tempora nostra: Sborník prací k šedesátým narozeninám prof. Jaroslava Pánka*, vol. 1, ed. Jiří Mikulec and Miloslav Polívka (Prague: Historický ústav Akademie věd České republiky, 2007), 276–83.

33 Cf. Brix, 'Trauergerüste für die Habsburger'.

34 Tamar Cholcman, '"Moritorum Monumentum Non Morituris Cineribus": Jacob Franquart's Funeral Procession for Albert of Austria, 1622', *Explorations in Renaissance Culture* 33, no. 1 (2007): 109–32, here 120, Fig. 6, 124–5; Luc Duerloo, *Dynasty and Piety: Archduke Albert (1598–1621) and Habsburg Political Culture in the Age of Religious Wars* (Farnham–Burlington: Ashgate, 2012), 511–20, Fig. 13.

35 ÖStA Vienna, HHStA, Archiv des Ordens vom Goldenen Vliess Cod 43, unfoliert: Funeral Isabella Clara Eugenia y el Cardenal Infante; cf. *Albert & Isabella, 1598–1621: Essays*, ed. Werner Thomas and Luc Duerloo (Turnhout: Brepols, 1998), passim.

36 John Roger Paas, *The German Political Broadsheet 1600–1700*, vol. 8, *1649–1661* (Wiesbaden: Harrassowitz, 2005), 184, P-2376 (1657).

37 See Friedrich Polleroß, 'Austriacus Hungariae Rex: Zur Darstellung der Habsburger als ungarische Könige in der frühneuzeitlichen Graphik', in *'Ez világ, mint egy kert...' Tanulmányok Galavics Géza tiszteletére*, ed. Orsolya Bubryák (Budapest: MTA Művészettörténeti Kutatóintézet–Gondolat Kiadó, 2010), 63–78, here 71–2; Géza Pálffy, 'Ponaučenia z korunovačnej rytiny z polovice 17. storočia: nový pohľad na bratislavské korunovácie v ranom novoveku', in *Korunovácie a pohreby: Mocenské rituály a ceremónie v ranom novoveku*, ed. Tünde Lengyelová and Géza Pálffy (Budapest–Békéscsaba: Historický ústav Filozofického výskumného centra Maďarskej akadémie vied – Výskumný ústav Slovakov v Maďarsku, 2016), 9–46, here 9–11.

38 Pálffy, *The Kingdom of Hungary*, 193–208.

39 Géza Pálffy and Ferenc Tóth, 'Les couronnements en Hongrie à l'époque moderne (1526–1792): Représentations et outils politico-diplomatiques', *Revue d'histoire diplomatique* 131, no. 3 (2017): 253–75.

40 Pál Engel, *The Realm of St. Stephen: A History of Medieval Hungary, 895–1526* (London–New York: I.B. Tauris, 2001).

41 Géza Pálffy, 'The Bulwark and Larder of Central Europe (1526–1711)', in *On the Stage of Europe: The Millennial Contribution of Hungary to the Idea of European Community*, ed. Ernő Marosi (Budapest: Research Institute for Art History of the Hungarian Academy of Sciences–Balassi Kiadó, 2009), 100–24.

42 Idem, *Die Krönungsfahnen in der Esterházy Schatzkammer auf Burg Forchtenstein: Die Geschichte der Krönungsfahnen der Länder der Stephanskrone vom Spätmittelalter bis Anfang des 20. Jahrhunderts* (Eisenstadt: Esterházy Privatstiftung, 2018); idem, 'Korunovačné zástavy krajín Uhorskej koruny od neskorého stredoveku do začiatku 20. Storočia', in *Galéria: Ročenka Slovenskej národnej galérie v Bratislave*, ed. Katarína Kučerová Bodnárová (Bratislava: Slovenská národná galéria, 2011 [2013]), 7–30.

43 Lajos Bernát Kumorovitz, 'Die Entwicklung des ungarischen Mittel- und Großwappens', in *Nouvelles études historiques publiées à l'occasion du XIIe Congrès*

International des Sciences Historiques par la Commission Nationale des Historiens Hongrois, vol. 2, ed. Dániel Csatári, László Katus and Ágnes Rozsnyói (Budapest: Akadémiai Kiadó, 1965), 319–56, here 319–20; Pálffy, *The Kingdom of Hungary*, 365, Fig. 2.

44 Recently, *The Battle for Central Europe: The Siege of Szigetvár and the Death of Süleyman the Magnificent and Nicholas Zrínyi (1566)*, ed. Pál Fodor (Leiden–Boston–Budapest: Brill–Research Centre for the Humanities, Hungarian Academy of Sciences, 2019).

45 Ferenc Maczó, *Az utolsó magyar királykoronázás: IV. Károly király és Zita királyné koronázási ünnepsége Budapesten 1916. december Végén*, 2nd revised edn (Budapest: MTA Bölcsészettudományi Kutatóközpont Történettudomány Intézet, 2018), 91–3.

46 All flag bearers from 1563 until 1916: Pálffy, *Die Krönungsfahnen*, 183–97: Appendix.

47 Paas, *The German Political Broadsheet*, 184, P–2376 (1657); Szathmáry, *Descriptio Hungariae*, 215–16, no. 98.

48 Roderich Gooss, *Österreichische Staatsverträge: Fürstentum Siebenbürgen (1526–1690)* (Vienna–Leipzig: Adolf Holzhausan – Wilhelm Engelman, 1911), 218–64, no. 34–6.

49 MNL OL Budapest, E 148, Neo-regestrata acta Fasz. 828, no. 17, 16. June 1607, Prague, cf., *Die Siegel der deutschen Kaiser und Könige von 751 bis 1806*, vol. 3, *1493–1711*, ed. Otto Posse (Dresden: Wilhelm und Bertha von Baensch Stiftung, 1912), 25, Tafel 39/3–4.

50 Eliška Fučíková, Beket Bukovinská and Ivan Muchka, *Die Kunst am Hofe Rudolfs II.* (Hanau: Dausien, 1990), 26, Fig. 20; Beket Bukovinská, 'Sarg Rudolfs II', in *Prag um 1600: Kunst und Kultur am Hofe Kaiser Rudolfs II.*, vol. 1, *Ausstellungskatalog*, ed. Jürgen Schultze and Jürgen Fillitz (Freren: Luca Verlag, 1988), 572, no. 457.

51 Dénes Radocsay, 'Renaissance Letters Patent Granting Armorial Bearings in Hungary. Part II', *Acta Historiae Artium* [Budapest] 12 (1966): 72; Mario Jareb, *Hrvatski nacionalni simboli* (Zagreb: Alfa d.d. – Hrvatski institut za povijest, 2010), 26; Dubravka Peić Čaldarović and Nikša Stančić, *Povijest hrvatskoga grba: Hrvatski grb u mijenama hrvatske povijesti od 14. do početka 21. stoljeća* (Zagreb: Školska knjiga, 2011), 74–83. In this period Slavonia included the counties of Zagreb, Križevci and Varaždin, today central Croatia; the modern region of Slavonia (not to be confused with the sovereign country of Slovenia) comprises eastern Croatia.

52 Peić Čaldarović and Stančić, *Povijest hrvatskoga grba*, 77–83; Virgil Solis, *Wappenbüchlein* (Nuremberg: Solis, 1555; Facsimile: Neustadt an der Aisch: Degener, 1974), *sine pagina*; Francolin, *Weyland Kaysers Ferdinandi*, *sine pagina*.

53 Ferenc Gábor Soltész, Csaba Tóth and Géza Pálffy, *Coronatio Hungarica in Nummis: Medals and Jetons from Hungarian Royal Coronations (1508–1916)* (Budapest: Hungarian Academy of Sciences, Research Centre for the Humanities, Institute of History –Hungarian National Museum, 2019), 86–7, no. 38 (1608), 97, no. 51 (1618), 109, no. 72–3 (1625).

54 Pálffy, *Die Krönungsfahnen*, 90–110.

55 Cf. Cholcman, '"Moritorum Monumentum Non Morturis"', 124–5.

11

Operas and masquerades: Court rituals and entertainments under Ernest Augustus and George I of Brunswick-Lüneburg (1660–1727) in the electorate of Hanover and Great Britain

Barbara Arciszewska

At the end of the seventeenth century, the once modest court in Hanover became one of the most lively centres of sophisticated culture in the Holy Roman Empire.[1] The dramatic transformation of Hanoverian court life around 1700, which paralleled the social rise of the House of Brunswick-Lüneburg (elevated to the electoral title in 1692 and selected in 1701 to inherit the thrones of England, Scotland and Ireland – joined as the Kingdom of Great Britain in 1707), was a reflection of the political aspirations and cultural tastes of Hanover's ambitious rulers: Ernest Augustus (1629–1698), Sophia (1630–1714) and their son, George Louis (1660–1727). This chapter explores court culture and ritual under the electors Ernest Augustus and George Louis, who from 1714 became king of Great Britain, focusing on ways in which they exploited the family's glorious past, especially its medieval connections to the Veneto through a distant kinship with the Este family.[2] The lasting impact of Venetian culture on Hanoverian patronage affected all forms of artistic expression (most notably architecture), but in this chapter my attention will be on opera and masquerades and their place in rituals of Hanoverian rule. The title consciously refers to the famous 1724 print by William Hogarth, which aimed to highlight the controversial role of this new style of court culture in contemporary society (Figure 11.1).[3] The main contention to put forward is that (rather paradoxically) some aspects of these court entertainments propelled the processes of modernization and social mobility in contemporary Britain, while at the same time the growing popularity of these court-supported entertainments became a lightning rod for a wider debate questioning the cultural prerogatives of the court and (ultimately) the limits of royal power.

A few words about dynastic history are required at the outset. The Guelph family (*die Welfen*), of which the dukes of Brunswick-Lüneburg ruling in Hanover were one of the junior branches, belonged to one of the oldest princely houses of the Holy Roman Empire.[4] At the end of the Carolingian era this clan of Frankish descent established its power base near Lake Constance, from where it succeeded in extending

Figure 11.1 William Hogarth, *The Bad Taste of the Town* (also known as *Masquerades and Operas*), 1724. © Getty Images.

its patrimony to Swabia, Bavaria and northern Italy by the tenth century. The political position of the dynasty was secured in the middle of the eleventh century by the marriage of the Guelph princess Cuniza to Margrave Azzo II d'Este.[5] Simultaneous expansion north of the Alps added the Duchy of Saxony to the Guelph lands, which was subsequently to become the core of their domain, focused on the town of Brunswick from which the dynasty subsequently took its name.[6] The dynasty reached its early apogee under the reign of Henry the Lion (1129–1195), the most influential prince of the Empire in the twelfth century. The cornerstone of Guelph policy at the time was an alliance with the English king, sealed by the marriage of Henry the Lion with the daughter of Henry II, Mathilda, in 1168.[7] This dangerously swift rise of the House of Brunswick was halted by Emperor Frederick Barbarossa and subsequent emperors.[8] Following these interventions, the family's fortunes changed dramatically. Guelph land in the Duchy of Saxony was divided up repeatedly to provide for the increasing number of family members, and the dynasty declined in political importance.

The figure behind the seventeenth-century revival of the House of Brunswick-Lüneburg (with its bases in Lüneburg, Hanover and Celle; the senior branch ruling from Brunswick itself and nearby Wolfenbüttel), was Duke Ernest Augustus, who succeeded his brother Johann Friedrich in 1679. By a cunning policy of intermarriages, legal negotiations, and by establishing primogeniture within his domain, Ernest Augustus consolidated territories previously scattered between members of his family.[9] The final goal of these political manoeuvres was to restore the House of Brunswick to its previous prominence by securing for the family the coveted electoral title. From a historical perspective, however, it is clear that in spite of achieving the electorate in 1692 (bringing the total number of imperial electors to nine), the most momentous decision of Ernest August's life was to wed Sophia of the Palatinate (1630–1714), a granddaughter of King James I of England (James VI of Scotland).[10] This marriage ultimately brought the dynasty its greatest honour, the royal crown of Great Britain, offered to the Hanoverians in the Act of Settlement in 1701, in order to secure the Protestant succession.

To justify the political ascent of the House around 1700, the Hanoverian dynasty embraced the cardinal political tenets of early Guelph history, including the cultivation of close ties to northern Italy (Venice and the Veneto) and to England.[11] Of the two cultural spheres, the former was the more significant in re-asserting themselves as a European ruling house. The cultivation of family ties to the Este and the Veneto was important for the Guelphs as a sign of status, but the Venetians had a more pragmatic attitude towards the Germans, who were renowned in contemporary Europe for offering their troops for hire. This mercenary tradition attracted the attention of the Venetian Senate, who thus hoped to employ the Guelphs in their conquest of the Morea in southern Greece.[12] In the 1680s the government of Venice practically courted Ernest Augustus and his entourage in the hope of securing his assistance in this effort against the Turks.[13] The Hanoverians, who were received and entertained by the highest echelons of the Venetian aristocracy, acquired a strong taste for local culture, including opera and carnival masquerades. Ernest August deemed it necessary even to establish a permanent residence in Venice. The venerable Palazzo Foscari on the Grand Canal was chosen as the Hanoverian seat in Venice, providing an appropriately imposing stage for the German court.[14] Based in this respectably grand residence, the Hanoverians observed the life of the Venetian aristocracy and participated in the innumerable festivities, balls and regattas prepared by the city's noble families eager to entertain the German princes on whose military aid depended the survival of the Republic.[15] Fancy dressing and music, both instrumental and vocal, provided defining elements of these celebrations, as described in contemporary sources.[16] The climax of the festivities was the great regatta, organized on June 25th 1686, with a splendid floating chariot of Neptune as its centrepiece (Figure 11.2).[17] Equally impressive was a barge of Venus, with oarsmen dressed as Moors, as well as a boat of Mars, decorated with panoplies (suits of armour) and rowed by Roman warriors.[18] A float of Glaucus was covered in seaweed and was propelled by oarsmen dressed as mermen,[19] while Diana's barge featured the scene of a hunt. A float of Pallas-Athena, at last, proudly displayed the Lion of Venice. The opulence of these pageants, affecting all the senses, not just sight alone, must have greatly impressed Duke Ernest Augustus and his court.[20] Not to be outdone, the Hanoverians reciprocated by mounting spectacular displays intended to astonish Venetian society, such as the great manoeuvres of the Hanoverian troops on the Lido in 1685.[21]

The impact of Venetian culture on ritual and patronage in Hanover proved (not surprisingly) very significant. Like their Venetian counterparts the Hanoverian elite enjoyed in their homeland a life divided between the city and the country. The change from the winter to the summer season was marked by the move of the court from the town palace, the Leineschloß, to the suburban place of retreat at Herrenhausen, where

Figure 11.2 Chariot of Neptune, a float in grand regatta, from Giovanni Matteo Alberti, *Giuochi festiui, e militari, danze, serenate, machine, boscareccia artificiosa, regatta solenne, et altri sontuosi apprestamenti di allegrezza esposti alla sodisfattione uniuersale dalla generosità dell'A. S. d'Ernesto Augusto duca di Brunsuich* ... (Venice: Andrea Poletti: 1686). © Barbara Arciszewska.

the court usually remained from May to October.[22] This main suburban residence served as the focus of both physical leisure and intellectual diversions, in the tradition of the villas of the Veneto. To underscore this connection, designs were prepared (most likely by Ernest Augustus himself) to turn this country seat into a perfect rendition of the Rotonda, the most iconic of Palladio's villas (Figure 11.3). The concerts, balls, and gondola rides (there was a court-appointed gondolier) along the illuminated canals of the garden were also a clear effort to recreate in Hanover the refined diversions of the Venetian elite.[23]

The culmination of the winter season in Hanover was the famous 'Venetian Carnival'.[24] This eccentricity at a Protestant court was established as a substitute for actually travelling to the annual festivities in Venice.[25] The programme of celebrations, which usually lasted several weeks in February, included theatre performances, operas, concerts, masques, water shows, and fancy dress balls, in addition to the grand feasts at the princely table.[26] The ceremonial rooms of the Leineschloß served s as the backdrop for these festivities, as well as the spectacular opera house founded in the palatial complex by Ernest Augustus (Figure 11.4).[27] The carnival, an antithesis of the usually strict regulations of social intercourse at the court and thus a necessary outlet of social tension, provided as well an opportunity for the ostentatious entertaining of important guests, and as such was considered an essential part of the new image of the House.[28] The staging of the equivalent of one of Venice's greatest attractions proved to be a costly, yet highly effective means for placing Hanover among the grandest courts of its time, in addition to reminding the European political elite of the dynasty's celebrated roots in the Veneto.

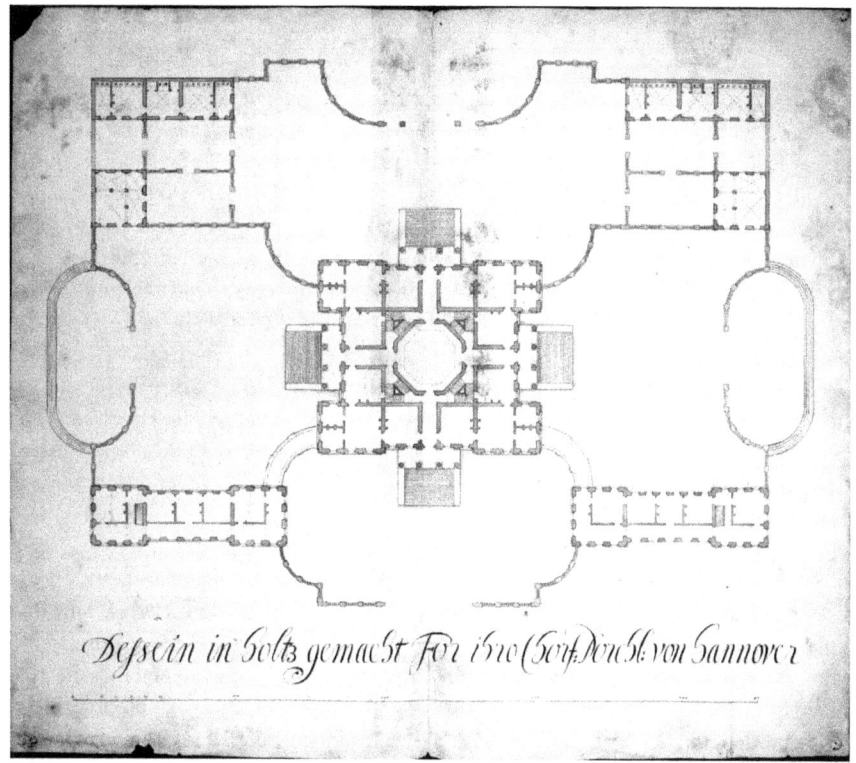

Figure 11.3 Herrenhausen design, attributed to Elector Ernest Augustus of Hanover, c. 1690 (Stadtarchiv Hannover). © Barbara Arciszewska.

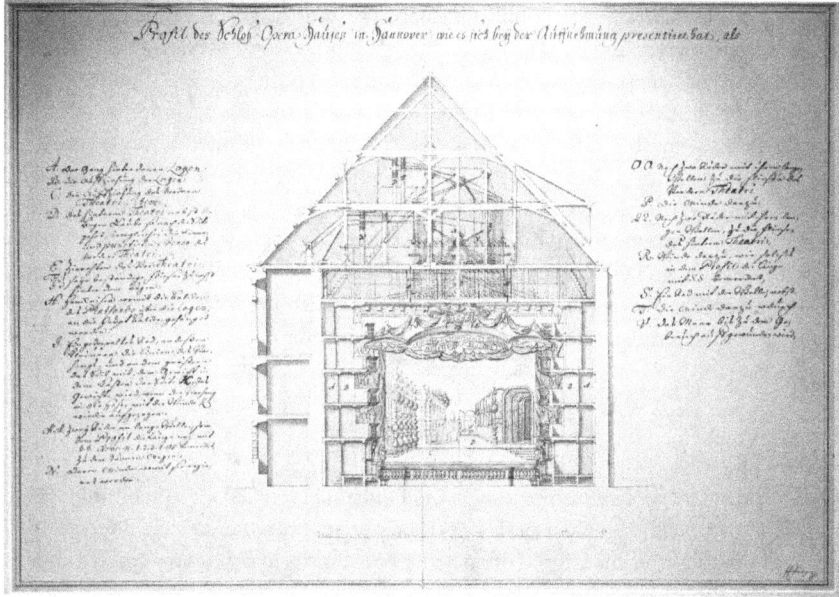

Figure 11.4 Cross-section of the opera house in the Leine Palace, Hanover, 1746. © Alamy Stock Photos.

The Venetian Republic also provided the Hanoverians with artists and craftsmen. Venetian musicians, such as Antonio Sartorio and Vincenzo de Grandis, had been active in Hanover since the 1660s.[29] Even though under Ernest Augustus the court's predilections shifted away from chamber music towards opera, Venice remained the principal source of inspiration in this field.[30] Ernest Augustus was not only an impassioned spectator at all opera performances given in Venice (the family leased loggias – *palchi* – in several Venetian theatres), but he appears to have been a serious patron too, financing several important productions in the city.[31] Between 1654 and 1694 nearly thirty librettos were dedicated to members of the Hanoverian clan.[32] The Duke also employed Agostino Steffani (1654–1728), who hailed from the Veneto, as his court composer in charge of the majority of operas staged in Hanover.[33] The Hanoverian fondness for the opera was clearly genuine, but its role in the contemporary political struggle cannot be overestimated. Opera, like other art forms sponsored by the Hanoverian court, acted primarily as a means of persuasion: through the employment of history and mythology in the skilfully produced libretti, contemporary political objectives were addressed. The ascendancy of the house was given special emphasis. Just like the chronicles of the family's past prepared at the time by Gottfried Leibniz, the opera produced under the auspices of the Hanoverian family served to legitimize the family's supremacy and support its future claims.[34] It was not coincidental that the new opera house in the Leineschloß opened in 1689 with the production of a programmatic work entitled *Enrico Leone*, a story based on the life of the greatest hero from the family's past, Henry the Lion, intended to extol the dynasty's glorious history.[35] Opera was the Baroque art form *par excellence*, unifying word, music and image in one dramatic spectacle, and in its visual aspect calling for the seamless union of architecture, sculpture and painting.[36] Opera had long been a political tool in Venetian diplomacy, and was used as such in Hanover. The political message was thus disguised in the perfect court spectacle, complementing in its artificiality the pompous world of court ceremonial.

The death of Ernest August in 1698 spelled the end of the opera in Hanover. It had fulfilled its political objectives and without this practical justification for its existence George Louis, who found the state finances in deep crisis, deemed it too expensive.[37] The undying interest of the future king in Venetian opera is confirmed, however, by continued lease of the loggias in Venetian theatres, apparently in hope of a future visit.[38] The international reputation of the Hanoverian court for its opera sponsorship, attracted to George Louis's entourage Georg Friedrich Handel (1685–1759), the most celebrated artist ever associated with Hanoverian patronage of music, whose career really took off after his and the court's move to England.[39]

England

The arrival of George I as the new king in England in 1714, called for suitably impressive forms of court culture and ritual. The Hanoverian propaganda machine that had been set up to bolster the King's (often contested) claims to legitimacy could not have overlooked the areas so competently deployed by the Hanoverians back in Germany.[40] Turning to monumental architecture was an obvious tactic, which explains an emphasis on Palladian Classicism, an idiom that the Hanoverians had embraced back on the Continent (as evinced by the Herrenhausen design).[41] King George I's reign thus ushered in new values and new order, which (through discursive practices of Classicism) was to be 'naturalized' as old and venerated. This ambitious, and inherently paradoxical project of protecting the status quo and tradition while normalizing change and modernity through architecture, received a much-needed boost in the form of a new edition of Andrea Palladio's *Four Books* and Inigo Jones's *Designs* both dedicated to the King (Figures 11.5 and 11.6).

Figure 11.5 Frontispiece of *The Architecture of A. Palladio; In Four Books*, ed. Giacomo Leoni (London: John Watts for the Author, 1715). © Barbara Arciszewska.

Figure 11.6 Frontispiece of *The Designs of Inigo Jones, Consisting of Plans and Elevations for Publick and Private Buildings*. (London: William Kent, 1727). © The Metropolitan Museum of Art, New York (public domain).

In addition to promoting Italianate, Classical architecture, the court of George I also continued its sponsorship of Italian opera, which first appeared in London at the beginning of the century. As a cultural import, Italian opera divided contemporary English society, largely according to political lines, with many Tories opposing, and most Whigs supporting this novel form of entertainment.[42] Its popular appeal was driven by spectacular stage productions and by the interest generated by celebrity performers, the star-singers. These admired entertainers (even if they remained socially suspect), enjoyed status and remuneration above that of mere actors or artisans. Francesca Cuzzoni (1698–1770) for instance, a famed soprano, received nearly 2,000 pounds for one season (Figure 11.7).[43] Yet for the Tories, this fondness for evidently 'foreign' and suspiciously 'popish' opera and its effeminate performers signified the corruption of national virtue and a threat to public morality.[44] The Whigs managed to deflect such criticisms, but the main endorsement for this 'suspect' form of entertainment was to come from the new royal dynasty.

For George I, Palladio's architecture and opera were inextricably tied to his memories of Venice and the Veneto. The love of both was fostered by his pleasurable visits in Palladio's villas.[45] Music always played an important part in these occasions. The Hanoverian court paid several visits, for instance, to the Piazzola sul Brenta, the villa then considered to have been designed by Palladio.[46] Marco Contarini, the host to the Electoral court, commemorated a 1685 visit by publishing an illustrated account of the elaborate festivities. Contarini's court poet, Francesco Maria Piccioli (fl. 1679–1710), recorded in pompous verse the course of events, as well as the texts of the poems

Figure 11.7 William Hogarth, *Berenstadt, Cuzzoni, and Senesino*, 1724. © Getty Images.

and libretti of many opera-like musical diversions prepared for the occasion (Figure 11.8).[47] This love of opera continued to define the patronage of the Hanoverian court after its arrival in England. Because of George I's accession, the opera season was opened in 1714 much earlier than usual,[48] and the King enthusiastically attended most performances given in London.[49] He had seen some performances (including some that were not very good) so many times over, that music historians contended that he was either a genuine opera lover or a masochist – more likely the former.[50] We have no detailed information concerning the specifics of the theatre protocol, but the entry and departure of the King from his box were marked by a public show of deference, even though the shy and withdrawn George I did not enjoy this attention. At some point he even abandoned sitting in the centre of the royal box, or left it completely, preferring instead some more secluded spaces and more private contacts, including those with the opera performers. Indeed, most artists involved in the London opera had direct access to the King and sought his patronage. Composer Attilio Ariosti (1666–1729), for instance, felt so encouraged by the King's attention that he decided to seek further preferment and lobbied for a diplomatic post,[51] while in March 1721, George I stood as godfather for the daughter of a celebrated soprano, Margherita Durastante (fl. 1700–1734).[52]

The royal example alone gave opera, an economically sub-marginal entertainment in London at the time, the sufficient impetus to thrive. Most importantly, George I supported the establishment of the Royal Academy of Music (1719, dissolved in 1728)[53] which, remarkably, was a joint stock company (financed through a subscription of £200), operating under a royal charter and with a royal subsidy of £1,000.[54] Its explicit aims had more to do with civic improvement than with profit-making, and the 'Proposall for carrying on Operas by a Company of Joynt Stock' underscored the parallels between the establishment of new standard in music (opera), and promotion of universal values of good taste and ancient virtue.[55] It has been repeatedly suggested that the royal example was critical in attracting the English aristocracy to this institution.[56] Just as Palladianism was to be associated with the Whig faction,[57] Italian opera acquired in eighteenth-century England similar political connotations and, as Leppert has demonstrated, the success of the opera was one of the instruments of promoting the Whig domination of politics for much of the century, and (consequently) a new, more dynamic model of society, allowing greater social mobility.[58] The new cultural societies, such as the Academy, provided an opportunity for social exchange across class boundaries. Incidentally, it was a mechanism essential to the emergence of Freemasonry.[59] What had been an elitist court entertainment thus became in George I's new domain a commercially available popular pastime, supported by subscriptions and by corporations open to all polite members of society.

In this context appears one of the most notorious (and often vilified) court protégés, Johann Jacob Heidegger (1659–1749). This Swiss-born specialist in staging court entertainments (who had started as an opera manager in London back in 1709) was also engaged in the production of opera performances under George I as the Manager of the Royal Opera Company. He was very close to the Hanoverian elites and to the King himself, receiving regular payments from the hands of the celebrated Turkish Groom of the King's Chamber, Mahomet.[60] As the Hanoverian master of ceremonies, Heidegger was polite London's fashion guru, defining what was popular and desirable.[61]

Figure 11.8 Water festivities organized on the canal in Piazzola sul Brenta to mark the visit of Ernest Augustus of Brunswick-Lüneburg in 1685, Francesco Maria Piccioli, *L'orologio del piacere*, part II, *Il Vaticinio della Fortuna*. Piazzola: Nel luoco delle Vergini, 1685. © Wikimedia Commons (public domain).

In addition to promoting opera (which he probably subsidized with the proceeds from more popular entertainments), Heidegger was responsible for commencing in England the craze for Venetian semi-public masquerade balls.[62]

Indeed, masquerade was a novel phenomenon in London around 1700, one of many new cultural offerings available to the English consumer. It has been noted that many contemporary elitist, high art forms (such as Palladian Classicism, satirized in the famous print of the Burlington House; Figure 11.9)[63] were vigorously reworked to meet the demands of an expanding middling-sort audience, favouring the more popular, demotic forms of culture. While exploiting the prestige of the court, and by appealing to 'national' taste, Hanoverian elites unashamedly opened contemporary court entertainments and art forms to consumer-driven appropriation, ultimately reaching beyond the circles of the aristocracy. Thus history painting received its

Figure 11.9 William Hogarth, *Taste: The Gate of Burlington House*, 1731. © Getty Images.

demotic counterpoint in the new moral subjects, the classical epic in the novel, and contemporary opera in the more mundane counterpoint, the masquerade. Its popularity is understandable considering that entertaining before the eighteenth century was restricted to private residences, and there were no public spaces of leisure open to both sexes apart from theatres, with men only traditionally enjoying themselves in taverns and coffee houses.[64] Balls organized by Heidegger in the royal opera house had the aura of court respectability (they were attended by royalty and members of the elite), yet were open to those able to pay the subscription regardless of class, hence were open to cultural subversion. Masquerades soon developed a reputation for unseemly behaviour, unescorted women and assignations, yet beyond this public controversy there was a very serious social phenomenon. Barker Benfield has demonstrated that masquerades were considered by contemporaries as the embodiment of modern consumerism, social mobility and pleasure-seeking that frightened some, but inspired others.[65] Party goers delighted in disguising themselves in fanciful costumes, and moving masked through crowds of strangers, accepting casual encounters with those of different ranks, class or sex.[66] Some of the controversy that surrounded the masquerades was related to the belief that they would encourage female sexual freedom, and possibly even female emancipation.[67] Another problem stemmed from the fact that they were court-endorsed commercial ventures, which posed new questions concerning the dignity of royalty and control of access to the monarch in a dangerously mercantile environment.[68] The illusion of an 'upside-down' world offered by the traditional Venetian masquerade was replaced therefore by a phenomenon that could truly undermine the established social order.

Not surprisingly, the risqué court-sponsored Italianate entertainments did not meet with universal approval. They were rooted in foreign taste and privileged foreign artists, and the commercial dimension of these entertainments was as much admired as it was abhorred. Public opprobrium focused especially on the main purveyors of leisure activities, such as Heidegger, or John Rich (ca. 1692–1761) who specialized in spectacles with opulent stagecraft.[69] Their innovative commercial strategies seemed dangerously close to moral corruption, fed by foreign fashions.[70] If taste signified distinction between the 'vulgar' and the 'barbaric', these negative qualities were most often defined as non-British, a polarity which helped to associate good taste with national, patriotic values.[71] These xenophobic sentiments were strongest among the middle-class – little travelled and little exposed to other cultural models. Combined with religious prejudices, the xenophobia of the middle class found its expression in Hogarth's 1723/24 print (see Figure 11.1), which alludes to the papist inclinations of those harbouring a taste for Italian art. Hogarth contrasts the rage for Italianate court entertainments with the neglect of their British equivalents. We see a wheelbarrow filled with the works of great English dramatists (including Shakespeare), to be sold as 'waste paper', while Londoners flock to watch the pantomime (on the right) and masqueraders pour into the theatre on the left, overlooked by Heidegger.

Now, the final question remains whether the process of transformation of high court entertainments into popular commercial pastimes was consciously championed by George I and his court, or treated as a cultural danger that had to be controlled. Even though Terry Castle has noted repeated government attempts to suppress the masquerade,[72] George I must have realized that controlling British society in an absolutist way (as was done in Hanover) was counter-productive to his cause of legitimizing his rule. He was aware that his British subjects were embracing the Continental mores and tastes of his court. The forces of social and political conformity promoting the dissemination of the new court entertainments were helped by the market, where the demand for this type of leisure was growing, as a result of the progressive atrophy of moralizing sanctions against luxury.[73] The demand for fashionable opera and precarious masquerading began to transcend traditional upper class boundaries, aiding the widespread circulation of cultural patterns associated with the new regime.

Conclusion

The above discussion demonstrates that operas and masquerades, espoused rather unexpectedly by the Protestant court in Hanover as a sign of dynastic ties to Venice and a symbol of political aspirations of the House of Brunswick-Lüneburg, changed their cultural significance in Britain, the new domain of the Guelphs after 1714. Despite widespread contemporary criticism of decadent entertainments associated with the Hanoverian court in England, the subversive dimension of these amusements paradoxically turned them into important mechanisms of modernity and social mobility.

Notes

1 For details, see Barbara Arciszewska, *The Hanoverian Court and the Triumph of Palladio: The Palladian Revival in Hanover and England c. 1700* (Warsaw: DiG, 2002). For a more recent overview, see Martin Wrede, 'The House of Brunswick-Lüneburg and the Holy Roman Empire: The Making of a Patriotic Dynasty, 1648–1714', in *The Hanoverian Succession: Dynastic Politics and Monarchical Culture*, ed. Andreas Gestrich and Michael Schaich (London: Routledge, 2016), 43–72.
2 Arciszewska, *Hanoverian Court*, 35
3 Barbara Arciszewska, 'The Taste of the Town – the Taste of the Nation: Hogarth, Burlington and the Politics of National Taste in Early Georgian Britain', in *Mowa i moc obrazów*, ed. Maria Szewczyk (Warsaw: WUW, 2005), 171–6.
4 For a more extensive discussion of the early Guelph history, see Egon Boshof, 'Die Entstehung des Herzogtums Braunschweig-Lüneburg', in *Heinrich der Löwe*, ed. Wolf D. Mohrmann (Göttingen: Vandenhoeck & Ruprecht, 1980), 249–74; *Schwäbische Chroniken der Stauferzeit*, ed. Erich König, vol. I, (Stuttgart: Kohlhammer, 1938), passim; Karl Jordan, *Henry the Lion: A Biography* (Oxford: Clarendon Press, 1986), 1–3.
5 See Georg Schnath, 'Neue Forschungen zur ältesten Geschichte des Welfenhauses;, *Niedersächsisches Jahrbuch für Landesgeschichte* 31 (1959): 255f.
6 This is today's Lower Saxony, while Upper Saxony was in the upper reaches of the Elbe, centred on Meissen and Dresden. See Ernst Schubert, *Geschichte Niedersachsens. Politik, Verfassung, Wirtschaft vom 9. bis zum ausgehenden 15. Jahrhundert* (Hanover: Hanhnsche Buchhandlung, 1997), 383–90.

7   For details see Jordan, *Henry the Lion*, 143–4.
8   Jordan, *Henry the Lion*, 66–88 and 160–99; and see also Georg Schnath, *Geschichte Hannovers im Zeitalter der neunten Kur und der englischen Sukzession 1674–1714*, vols I–IV, (Hildesheim: August Lax Verlag, 1938–1982), vol. 1, 1–11; and Ragnhild Hatton, *George I: Elector and King* (Cambridge, MA: Harvard University Press, 1978), 22.
9   For an assessment of Ernest August's government, see Hatton, *George I*, 78f.
10 On Sophia and her family background, see Eduard Bodemann, *Herzogin Sophie von Hannover* (Leipzig: S. Hirzel, 1888), Mathilde Knoop, *Kurfürstin Sophie von Hannover* (Hildesheim: August Lax Verlag, 1964); Maria Kroll, *Sophie, Electress of Hanover: A Personal Portrait* (London: Victor Gollancz, 1973); J.N. Duggan, *Sophia of Hanover: From Winter Princess to Heiress of Great Britain, 1630–1714* (London: Peter Owen, 2010).
11 Charlotte Backerra: 'Legitimacy through family traditions? The Hanoverians represented as successors to the throne of Great Britain', in *Dynastic Change: Legitimacy and Gender in Medieval and Early Modern Monarchy*, ed. Ana Maria Rodrigues, Manuela Santos Silva and Jonathan W. Spangler (Abingdon: Routledge, 2020).
12 Schnath, *Geschichte Hannovers*, vol. I, 354 for details. From 1685 to 1688, between two and three thousand Hanoverian troops fought in Greece under the command of the Duke's third son, Maximilian.
13 The Venetian Republic sponsored cultural events (such as opera performances) in order to court the Hanoverians and convince them to provide military support. For details see Lorenzo Bianchoni and Thomas Walker, 'Seventeenth-century opera,' in *Early Music History: Studies in Medieval and Early Modern Music*, ed. Iain Fenlon, (Cambridge: Cambridge University Press, 1984), 269–70; Paolo Camerini, *Piazzola nella sua storia e nell' arte musicale del secolo XVII* (Milan: Ulrico Hoepli, 1929), 268–73; and Carlo Malagola, *Le Lido de Venise à travers l'histoire* (Venice: Marcel Norsa, 1909), 75–6. See also Schnath, *Geschichte Hannovers*, vol. I, 379–81.
14 Even though the visits of the family members in Venice became less frequent after 1686, the residence was maintained with all the necessary paraphernalia, including a small fleet of gondolas. See Schnath, *Geschichte Hannovers*, vol. II, 386–7; and Alvise Zorzi, *Venetian Palaces* (New York: Rizzoli, 1991), 166.
15 See Giovanni Matteo Alberti, *Giuochi festivi e militari, danze serenate, macchine, boscareccia artificiosa, regata solenne et altri sontuosi apprestamenti di allegrezza esposti alla soddisfazione universale dalla generosità dell'Altezza ser. di Ernesto duca di Brunswich e Luneburgo, Principe di Osnabrück ecc. al tempo di sua dimora in Venetia*, (Venice: Andrea Poletti, 1686), for a description of one of the most elaborate festivities enjoyed in Venice by the Hanoverians. See also Clauco Benito Tiozzo, *Le ville del Brenta da Lizza Fusina alla città di Padova* (Venice: Cavallino, 1980), 57; and M. Piccioli, *L'orologio del piacere che mostra l'ore del dilettevole soggiorno havto dall'Altezza serenissima Ernesto Augusto vescovo d'Osnabrug, Duca di Bransuick, Luneburgo etc. nel Luoco di Piazzola de S.E. il Signor Marco Contarini. . .*, Piazzola, 1685, for details of visits to the villas of the mainland.
16 Alberti, *Giochi festivi*, 10. For details of a sumptuous spectacle (a *serenata*), staged to the music by Antonio Gianettinni, see Eleanor Selfridge-Field, *A New Chronology of Venetian Opera and Related Genres, 1660–1760* (Stanford, CA: Stanford University Press, 2007), 603; and Irene Salieri, 'Una festa barocca a Venezia, la giornata di allegrezza del 25 giugno 1686' unpublished MA thesis, Universita Ca' Foscari Venezia,

2016, 67–74, 77–86. The Hanoverians financed these spectacles in hope of securing military contracts, see Salieri, *Una festa barocca*, 97–8.

17 On the grand regattas, see Margherita Azzi Visentini, 'Festivals of State: The Scenography of Power in late Renaissance and Baroque Venice', in *Festival Architecture*, ed. Sarah Bonnemaison, Christine Macy (London: Routledge, 2007), 97–9. Inside the chariot were hidden musicians: 'nelli vacui della stessa Machina, vi erano celebri Sonatori di Trombe, e Piffari [a double-reed musical instrument], che con sinfonia maritime tutto il giorno ricercerono gli Spettatori...'. Alberti, *Giochi festivi*, 15.

18 Ibid., 16.

19 Ibid., 18.

20 The sounds were just as important, with the trumpeters and drummers present on most boats, ibid., 27.

21 For a description, see Malagola, *Le Lido de Venise*, 75–6.

22 See Schnath, *Geschichte Hannovers*, vol. II, 388. See also Carl Ernst von Malortie, *Der Hannoversche Hof unter dem Kurfürsten Ernst August und der Kurfürstin Sophie* (Hanover: Hahn, 1847), 129.

23 See Joachim Lampe, *Aristokratie, Hofadel und Staatspatriziat in Kurhannover: Die Lebenskreise der höheren Beamten an den kurhannoverschen Zentral- und Hofbehörden 1714-1760* (Göttingen: Vandenhoek & Ruprecht, 1963), 121. Herrenhausen was the favourite retreat of Sophia who turned it into a centre of flourishing intellectual life. See for instance Joseph Disponzio, 'Versailles in the Rear View: The "Große Garten" of Herrenhausen and Design of a Ducal Landscape', in *Herrenhausen im internationalen Vergleich: Eine kritische Betrachtung*, ed. Sigrid Thielking and Joachim Wolschke-Bulmahn (Munich: Akademische Verlagsgemeinschaft, 2013), 47–9; see also Günter Scheel, 'Hannovers politisches, gesellschaftliches und geistiges Leben zur Leibnizzeit', in *Leibniz: Sein Leben, sein Wirken, seine Welt*, ed. Wilhelm Totok and Carl Haase (Hanover: Verlag für Literatur und Zeitgeschichte 1966), 83–115.

24 For a contemporary description of the carnival, see Malortie, *Der Hannoversche Hof*, 152–61; Schnath, *Geschichte Hannovers*, vol. II, 5–11, 389–90. The carnival was cancelled only during the period of mourning after the death of Duke Ernest August in 1698. See also Lampe, *Aristokratie, Hofadel*, 116–18; and Urban Lina Padoan, 'Il carnevale veneziano', in *Storia della cultura veneta*, vol. 5, *Della Controriforma alla fine della Repubblica: Il Settecento*, ed. Girolamo Arnaldi and Manlio Pastore Stocchi (Vicenza: Neri Pozza, 1985), 631–46.

25 For a discussion of the traditional Venetian carnival activities, see Edward Muir, *Civic Ritual in Renaissance Venice* (Princeton: Princeton University Press, 1981), 156–81; and more recently, Peter Burke, *The Historical Anthropology of Early Modern Italy* (Cambridge: Cambridge University Press, 1987), chapter 13: 'The Carnival of Venice'.

26 The extant record of the 1693 carnival (which was particularly lavish to mark the newly acquired electoral title) shows that in addition to two operas (by Steffani and Mauro) and several theatre plays, numerous balls and masquerades were held daily in the entire city. See Malortie, *Der Hannoversche Hof*, 152–61; and Schnath, *Geschichte Hannovers*, vol. II, 8–10. See also Lampe, *Aristokratie, Hofadel*, 116–18.

27 Ernest Augustus was rather frugal in his music expenses at the beginning of his reign, but from the late 1680s, his expenditures on this aspect of court life were steadily growing. See Philip Keppler, 'Agostino Steffani's Hannover Opera and a Rediscovered Catalogue', in *Studies in Music History: Essays for Oliver Strunk*, ed. Harold Powers (Princeton: Princeton University Press, 1968), 352–3.

28 For details, see Arciszewska, *Hanoverian Court*, 44–5. Spectacular pageantry accompanied family weddings, such as the 1695 marriage of Charlotte Felicitas to the Duke Rainaldo of Modena, or the 1706 wedding of Sophia Dorothea to Crown Prince Friedrich Wilhelm of Prussia. See Malortie, *Der Hannoversche Hof*, 178–98.
29 Schnath, *Geschichte Hannovers*, vol. I, 31; and Schnath, *Geschichte Hannovers*, vol. II, 393. See also Renato de Grandis, 'Musik in Hannover zur Leibniz-Zeit', in *Leibniz: Sein Leben, sein Wirken, seine Welt*, 117–28.
30 The flowering of Italian opera under Ernest August's aegis is often considered as the most clear indication of his Italianate tastes. See Gerhard Gerkens, *Das fürstliche Lustschloß Salzdahlum und sein Erbauer Herzog Anton Ulrich von Braunschweig -Wolfenbüttel* (Braunschweig: Geschichtsverein, 1974), 32; and Rosemarie E. Wallbrecht, *Das Theater des Barockzeitalters an den welfischen Höfen Hannover und Celle* (Hildesheim: August Lax Verlag, 1974), 177.
31 For Ernest August's patronage of Venetian opera, see Heinrich Sievers, 'Musikgeschichte vom Mittelalter bis ins 18. Jahrhundert', in *Geschichte Niedersachsens*, ed. Hans Patze (Hildesheim: August Lax Verlag, 1983), 785; see also Ellen Rosand, *Opera in Seventeenth-Century Venice: The Creation of a Genre* (Berkeley: University of California Press, 1991) 31–2; Lorenzo Bianconi and Thomas Walker, 'Production, Consumption and Political Function of Seventeenth-Century Opera', *Early Music History* 4 (1984): 269–70.
32 Colin Timms, 'George I's Venetian palace and theatre boxes in 1720s', in *Music and Theatre: Essays in honour of Winton Dean*, ed. Nigel Fortune (Cambridge: Cambridge University Press, 1987), 95–6; Bianconi and Walker, *Seventeenth-century Opera*, 269.
33 Colin Timms, *Polymath of the Baroque: Agostino Steffani and His Music* (Oxford: Oxford University Press, 2003), passim, especially 38–82, 177–80; de Grandis, *Musik in Hannover*, 123–4 for details. Steffani, perhaps the most influential Venetian courtier of Ernest August's reign, was also an important figure in the Hanoverian diplomatic service (hence nearly absent from the court after 1695), see Schnath, *Geschichte Hannovers*, vol. II, 92.
34 See Lampe, *Aristokratie, Hofadel*, 112, Timms, *Polymath*, 52; and see also Schnath, *Geschichte Hannovers*, vol. II, 391. See also Friedrich Beiderbeck, 'Leibniz's Political Vision for Europe', in *The Oxford Handbook of Leibniz*, ed. Maria Rosa Antognazza, (Oxford: Oxford University Press, 2018), 678–81.
35 Lampe, *Aristokratie, Hofadel*, 113–14. The opera was by Steffani and Mauro; Timms, *Polymath*, 52–6.
36 Relatively little is known about the visual aspect of the opera performances, even though they were celebrated for ravishing 'the spirit and the eye', see Timms, *Polymath*, 54; Lampe, *Aristokratie, Hofadel*, 112–14; and Georg Schnath, Helmuth Plath, Rudolf Hillebrecht, *Das Leineschloss: Kloster, Fürstensitz, Landtagsgebäude* (Hanover: Hahn, 1962), 69–75.
37 The revenues from the Osnabrück bishopric were the primary source of money for the upkeep of the opera and, once this source of funds dried out, George Louis decided to close it, see Schnath, *Geschichte Hannovers*, vol. II, 347. See also Ragnhild Hatton, 'In Search of an Elusive Ruler: Source Material for a Biography of George I as Elector and King', in *Fürst, Bürger, Mensch: Untersuchungen zu politischen und soziokulturellen Wandlungsprozessen im vorrevolutionären Europa*, ed. Friedrich Engel-Janosi, Grete Klingenstein and Heinrich Lutz (Vienna: Böhlau Verlag, 1975), 21.

38 See British Library, Ms King's 140, Transcripts related to the House of Hanover, f. 59, for a letter from F. Weyberg, referring to the use of the electoral loggias in Venetian theatres,15 February 1709.
39 Steffani was instrumental in securing the services of Handel, see de Grandis, *Musik in Hannover*, 124–5, who also suggests, that Handel's success in Britain was an indication of a growing interest in Hanoverian court culture in England after the ratification of the Act of Settlement.
40 Timms, 'George I's Venetian palace', 95–130
41 Bernd Adam, 'Barocke Architekturmodelle in Norddeutschland und ihre Stellung im Planungsprozeß', in *Architektur, Struktur, Symbol: Streifzüge durch die Architekturgeschichte von der Antike bis zur Gegenwart: Festschrift für Cord Meckseper zum 65. Geburtstag* (Petersberg: Michael Imhof, 1999), 384–8.
42 'For Tories, Italian opera provided the evidence for a decline in national virtue and an excuse to proclaim a chauvinistic brand of patriotism...'. For Whigs, opera's success 'indicated [their] political ascendancy': Richard Leppert, 'Imagery, musical confrontation and cultural cifference in early 18th-century London', *Early Music* 14, no. 3 (1986): 323–45, here 330.
43 Judith Milhous, 'Opera Finances in London, 1674–1738', *Journal of the American Musicological Society* 37, no. 3 (1984): 567–92.
44 Leppert, *Imagery*, 337 quotes examples of vitriolic critiques of Italian operas and 'squeaking Italians' lampooned in contemporary press.
45 Arciszewska, *Hanoverian Court*, 53–5.
46 Giorgio Fossati, *Delle Fabbriche inedite di Andrea Palladio* (Venice: Dalle Stampe di Giorgio Fossati, 1760), 2.
47 Francesco Maria Piccioli's account published in six unpaginated volumes which, in addition to *L'orologio del piacere*, include *Il merito acclamato. Armonici Tributi d'ossequio consacrati da S.E. il Signor Marco Contarini, Procurator di S.Marco, all' Altezza Serenissima d'Ernesto Augusto..., Il Vaticinio della Fortuna. Musicali Acclamationi consacrati... (etc.), La Schiavitu Fortunata di Nettuno. Voti musicale applauso, consacrati... (etc.), Il Rittrato della Gloria donato all'Eternita. Musicali Applausi consacrati... (etc.), Il Preludio felice. Musicali Acclamationi consacrati... (etc.)*. All volumes were published in Contarini's private press in Piazzola (Nel Luoco delle Vergini) in 1685. The engravings (very large and competently executed) are anonymous.
48 Judith Milhous and Robert D. Hume, 'Opera Salaries in Eighteenth-Century London', *Journal of the American Musicological Society* 46, no. 1 (1993): 31.
49 Donald Burrows and Robert D. Hume, 'George I, the Haymarket Opera Company and Handel's "Water Music"', *Early Music* 19, no. 3 (1991): 323–4.
50 Burrows and Hume, 'George I, the Haymarket Opera', 333.
51 Lowell Lindgren, 'Ariosti's London Years 1716–29', *Music & Letters* 62, no. 3/4 (1981): 331–51, esp. 338–9.
52 Burrows and Hume, 'George I, the Haymarket Opera', 330.
53 John Merrill Knapp, 'Handel, the Royal Academy of Music, and Its First Opera Season in London (1720)', *The Musical Quarterly* 65, no. 2 (1959): 145–7.
54 Milhous and Hume, 'Opera Salaries', 32.
55 Thomas Forrest Kelly, *First Nights: Five Musical Premieres* (New Haven, CT: Yale University Press, 2000), 9.
56 Stanley Boorman, 'Lord Burlington and Music', in *'Apollo of the Arts': Lord Burlington and his circle*, ed. John Wilton-Ely (Nottingham: Nottingham University Art Gallery, 1973), 17.

57 For a recent discussion, see Alexander Echlin and William Kelley, 'A "Shaftesburian Agenda"? Lord Burlington, Lord Shaftesbury and the Intellectual Origins of English Palladianism', *Architectural History* 59 (2016): 221–52.
58 Leppert, *Imagery*, 331.
59 Barbara Arciszewska, 'Edward Oakley, Freemasonry and Popularization of Architectural Knowledge in early Georgian Britain', *Ars Regia* 20 (2012/13): 1–50.
60 Leppert, *Imagery*, 325.
61 G.J. Barker-Benfield, *The Culture of Sensibility: Sex and Society in Eighteenth-Century Britain* (Chicago: University of Chicago Press, 1992), 182–5.
62 Terry Castle, *Masquerade and Civilization: The Carnivalesque in Eighteenth-century English Culture and Fiction* (Stanford: Stanford University Press, 1986), 9–11, 64–5.
63 E. Harris, 'Alexander Pope, Lord Burlington and Palladio's "Fabbriche Antiche"', in *New Light on English Palladianism: Papers given at the Georgian Group symposium, 1988*, ed. Charles Hind (London: Georgian Group, 1990), 12.
64 Anne Wohlcke, *The 'Perpetual Fair': Gender, Disorder and Urban Amusement in Eighteenth-century London* (Manchester: Manchester University Press, 2014), 2–3, 10–11.
65 Barker Benfield, *Culture of Sensibility*, 183–6.
66 Aileen Ribiero, *The Dress Worn at Masquerades in England 1730 to 1790, and Its Relation to Fancy Dress in Portraiture* (New York: Garland, 1984), 32.
67 Mary Anne Schofield, *Masking and Unmasking the Female Mind: Disguising Romance in Feminine Fiction 1713 to 1799* (Newark: University of Delaware Press, 1990), 26, 36; Castle, *Masquerade and Civilization*, 38–41; but cf. Catherine Craft-Fairchild, *Masquerade and Gender: Disguise and Female Identity in Eighteenth-Century Fictions by Women* (University Park: Penn. State University Press, 1993), 53.
68 Castle, *Masquerade and Civilization*, 12–13, 111–13.
69 John Brewer, *The Pleasures of the Imagination: English Culture in the Eighteenth-Century* (New York: Farrar, Straus, Giroux,1997), 291–2; David Dabydeen, *Hogarth, Walpole and Commercial Britain* (London: Hansib Pub., 1987), 42
70 Pat Rogers, *Literature and Popular Culture in Eighteenth-Century England* (Brighton: Harvester, 1985), 11.
71 Regarding the role of the arts in the formation of contemporary national identity, see Brewer, *Pleasures of the Imagination*, 615–61; Ann Bermingham, 'Elegant Females and Gentlemen Connoisseurs: The Commerce in Culture and Self-image in Eighteenth-century England', in *The Consumption of Culture, 1600–1800: Image, Object, Text*, ed. Ann Bermingham and John Brewer (London: Routledge, 1995), 502–4; and see also Keith M. Brown, 'Scottish identity in the seventeenth-century', in *British Consciousness and Identity: The Making of Britain, 1533-1707*, ed. Brendan Bradshaw and Peter Roberts (Cambridge: Cambridge University Press, 1998), 252–7.
72 Castle, *Masquerade and Civilization*, 95.
73 Jules Lubbock, *The Tyranny of Taste: The Politics of Architecture and Design in Britain 1550-1960*, (New Haven, CT: Yale University Press, 1995), 92–137, 179–84.

12

Public staging, visualization and performance of eighteenth-century danish absolutism: Queen Caroline Mathilde's journey across funen as ritual

Michael Bregnsbo

In 1784, the beggar Bodil Sørensdatter in the Danish province of Funen was pretending to be the late Queen Caroline Mathilde. She gained a great following from the rural population and from parts of the urban population as well. She was arrested and placed in the gaol-house in the city of Odense while the authorities were trying to establish her true identity. From prison, the fake Caroline Mathilde even 'held court' and her supporters among the lower layers of society turned up to pay her their respects and bring her gifts. Finally, Bodil Sørensdatter was sentenced for fraud and imprisoned on a minor island in another part of the country. The authorities were hoping that she would thereby be out of sight and out of mind and attract no further attention. But before it came to that, the authorities asked one of her supporters, the peasant Christen Mortensen, why he thought that the woman in gaol was Queen Caroline Mathilde. He replied that he could indeed recognize her as the real Queen Caroline Mathilde as he, back in 1766, had seen her when she as a newlywed was making her journey across Funen on her way from her native country, England, *en route* to Copenhagen.[1] We do not know if Christen Mortensen did genuinely believe that the beggar in prison was the real Queen Caroline Mathilde, but it might very well be true that he had indeed seen her when she was passing across Funen back in 1766. And if so he had certainly not been the only one because the Queen's journey at that time had been used to stage, visualize and publicly perform the Danish system of royal absolutism.

Danish absolutism, which historians normally reckon as lasting from 1660 until 1848, has been characterized as 'literally (...) more absolute than anywhere else in Christendom'.[2] Indeed, it even had such a contradiction in terms as an absolutist constitution, namely the Royal Law (*Lex Regia*) from 1665, according to which the king was in possession of all legislative, executive and judicative powers.[3] Moreover, within the Danish monarchy in this period there were no corporate organs, assemblies of estates or councils of noblemen or clergy to have any say in public affairs. Royal absolutism had been introduced in the wake of two disastrous wars with Sweden (between 1657 and 1658 and between 1658 and 1660), with the first of these causing the kingdom of Denmark to cede one third of its territory to Sweden. Even if the subsequent Swedish attempt to conquer all Denmark during the latter war had not been successful, these two wars nonetheless had left the Danish state in a desperately weakened, impoverished and strategically exposed situation. Absolutism was introduced in direct confrontation to the nobility who up till then had been governing the country jointly with the monarch. In 1660, the aristocratic council of the realm had simply been abolished. So had many of the privileges of the nobility. From then on anyone having enough money could buy landed estates. Certainly, Danish landowners had privileges in relation to their tenant-farmers, however, they had these privileges by virtue of owning landed estates not because they were nobleman. In fact, any landowner – nobleman or commoner – would automatically get such privileges.[4] The last Danish coronation prior to the introduction of absolutism had been in 1648; and following the changes of 1660, the Danish throne was considered to automatically pass from the deceased king to his eldest son, thus no coronation ceremony was considered necessary, only an anointment ceremony. As seen therefore in the first succession under the new regime, in 1671, it is clear that the role and position of the nobility in the accompanying ceremonies and rituals was significantly reduced.[5] Furthermore, the monopoly of the nobility for obtaining officers' commissions and posts as civil servants was abolished; from now on commoners could also obtain such posts, as subsequent kings feared that the nobility might plan to overthrow the absolutist regime and reintroduce their prior privileged position. Thus, people of common or foreign extraction were given preferential treatment regarding royal appointments and promotions. The Danish army officers' corps, for example, had a distinctly non-aristocratic composition in comparison with other European monarchies.[6] Indeed, the absolutist system introduced a new official social status hierarchy, the rank system, which awarded precedence for employees in the service of the Crown rather than those of great wealth and ancient nobility.[7]

At first glance, therefore, one would believe that the Danish system of absolutist government was a 'top-down non-participatory' system of government.[8] And so it was – on paper. In practice, the picture was more nuanced and complicated. The legitimacy of the regime and the acceptance of its constraints seem in many ways to have been dependent on the possibility for the population to participate in it, as participation was not the same as co-determination. But it meant that commoners somehow had the opportunity of interacting and communicating with the regime and in this way demonstrate their loyalty and affection to the king. This might be through petitioning the king for favours (e.g. employment or legal aid), financial or other kinds of assistance, or mitigation of criminal sentences. Usually, such petitions were individual affairs; sometimes, however, a petition might draw the attention of the regime to societal problems of a general nature and thus give an impetus for new legislation or regulations.[9] In other cases, however, the regime contrarily stuck to existing legislation: the Danish penal code included clauses about punishment (especially capital punishment) that were considered barbaric and out of step with contemporary feelings about justice.

However, instead of changing these clauses to refashion them more in accordance with the evolving norms of the age, they were to a large extent retained and criminals continued to be sentenced to these barbaric punishments. Nevertheless, a sentence implying capital punishment and sometimes mutilation and torture would more or less automatically be sent to the king who could then mitigate it according to the prevailing sensibilities. Thereby, the king would appear as both strict but also gracious, and correspondingly, his subjects would feel awe but also gratitude and affection.[10] As the font of all justice, the king would be accessible so that everyone could obtain an audience. In return, the king should also be accessible to the public, so that there could be ample opportunities for the people to praise him and acclaim his rule. In this way, the king and his subjects were playing their respective roles within the absolutist system of government: the king was a powerful, strict and demanding, but also gentle, mild and gracious father to his subjects, whose welfare was always near to his heart. The subjects for their part would play the role of not only obedient, but also loyal, obliging and grateful children. There had to be opportunities for both parts to play their respective roles in order for the system to work.[11]

This face of Danish absolutism was also stressed in public rhetoric by its protagonists (e.g. sermons by the clergy of the Lutheran state church). During the second half of the eighteenth century, the Danish clergy was no longer only depicting the king as a mighty and elevated potentate but also as an affectionate and benevolent father of his subjects. Consequently, subjects ought to obey him willingly and in their own best interest.[12] Thus, it would seem that Danish absolutism was not merely a top-down non-participatory system but was open to input from outside and from below.[13] It was also a system where ritualized interaction and communication between the king and his subjects were playing a major role and where the official rhetoric of the system was primarily to stress that the absolutist regime existed for the general welfare of its subjects.

In this chapter, a royal journey, that of Queen Caroline Mathilde in 1766, will be interpreted in the light of this recent research into the practices and political culture of Danish absolutism. More specifically, this chapter offers an example of the actual functionality of Danish absolutism, with its seemingly contradictory emphasis of public participation. It will be done by focusing attention on a particular royal journey, looking at who was taking part, how the journey was organized and the behaviour of those involved. All of these factors will be interpreted as not simply a means of getting physically from one place to another, but as a ritual and ceremony for the performance of Danish absolutism in that both the members of the royal family and courtiers on the one hand, and the population on the other, were playing their respective roles which thereby confirmed and consolidated the system. This interpretation will be based on applying the details of the specific case to existing research about Danish absolutism and its court culture and political culture in general. Thus, it will be argued that the interpretations can be rendered probable, but not directly proven on the basis of written evidence.

To be more precise, the journey in question was the one taken by Queen Caroline Mathilde across the island of Funen in the Autumn of 1766. The Queen was born a princess of Great Britain, the daughter of Frederick, Prince of Wales and his consort Princess Augusta of Saxe-Gotha. Thus, the new Danish queen was the granddaughter of King George II and the sister of King George III. She was born in July 1751 (a few months after the premature death of her father) and married at Carlton House in London on 1 October 1766 to the young Danish king, Christian VII. The marriage had been arranged for political reasons, and the future spouses had never met before, nor was the bridegroom present at the wedding, but had been represented in a wedding by proxy by one of her brothers (who was also the King's first cousin, since his mother, Louise, was also a British princess). The day after the wedding, Queen Caroline Mathilde and her retinue began the voyage to Denmark. It lasted nearly five weeks from end to end.

In this chapter, however, our focus will be on one segment of this journey, the part that took place across the island of Funen – located between Jutland (the Danish mainland) and the island of Zealand on which the capital, Copenhagen, and most of the royal residences were situated – which lasted from 28 October to 1 November, and where the Queen stayed in the three chartered towns of Middelfart, Odense and Nyborg. By highlighting these days and these towns it will be possible to go into more detail than if the whole journey had been analysed. (Moreover, there is no reason to assume that her visits to other towns during the journey differed substantially from her visits in these three towns). Overall, this close analysis of the Queen's journey across Funen can shed light on the practice and political culture of Danish absolutism by analysing her journey as ritual or ceremony.

A tragic history

Caroline Mathilde's time as queen of Denmark was short, sad and tragic.[14] Her husband, the mentally incapacitated King Christian VII, showed her no interest and she quickly found herself isolated at the Danish court. Things changed, however, when she began a love affair with the German-born physician and the King's chief advisor, Johann Friedrich Struensee. Struensee, whom the King trusted unconditionally, simultaneously acquired power of attorney from the King (who loathed governing and making decisions), which allowed him to issue orders that would have the same validity as if they had been issued by the absolutist king himself.[15] Struensee used his powers to introduce an ambitious but badly prepared reform programme in the spirit of so-called 'enlightened absolutism'. His reforms, however, hit many people within the dominant layers of society financially and his relationship with the Queen outraged many. He was considered an illegitimate usurper and suspected of having locked up the King. He kept his royal patient from appearing in public and thereby prevented the people from performing their role as loyal and grateful subjects, violating the subtle and mostly unwritten rules of the way Danish absolutism functioned. He had, as a foreigner in Denmark and as a commoner at the royal court, no sense for these subtle and unwritten rules – and this would cost him dearly. In January 1772, Struensee was removed by a coup, imprisoned, sentenced to death for lèse-majesté and beheaded. Queen Caroline Mathilde was arrested and her marriage dissolved due to her infidelity. The plan had been to imprison her at a Danish castle, however, due to pressure from her native country Britain, she was allowed to leave Denmark and take up residence at the palace in the city of Celle in the Electorate of Hanover, the old homeland of the

British royal family. Here she passed away in 1775, a few months before her 24th birthday.¹⁶

The retinue in 1766

In 1766, these tragic events were still in the distant and unforeseeable future. The day after her wedding in London, Caroline Mathilde set out on a long journey towards her new country. She first went to the port of Harwich to board a ship; however, due to rough weather the departure had to be postponed by one day. The voyage across the North Sea lasted six days – the sea was rough, not least for a young woman who had never before seen the sea. Finally, the boat arrived at Rotterdam and from there the trip continued in carriages into Germany. Everywhere the retinue arrived, grand receptions and celebrations had been arranged. On 18 October, after more than two weeks *en route*, Caroline Mathilde arrived at the city of Altona in the duchy of Holstein. This duchy was part of the Danish monarchy as the king of Denmark was also duke of Holstein; at the same time Holstein was part of the Holy Roman Empire, and so the king of Denmark was also a German prince.¹⁷ Thus, having arrived at Altona, Caroline Mathilde was for the first time putting her foot on the soil of her new country. She stayed in Altona for three days; here grand festivities in her honour had been arranged with the firing of a salute, splendid decorations, banquets, spectacles and receptions organized by the local elites. Caroline Mathilde's arrival in her new country was also being marked by the fact that all the courtiers and servants that had been on the journey together with her from London were now discharged and returned home to England, and were replaced by household officers and servants from the Danish court who had come all the way to Altona from Copenhagen. The young queen must have felt lonely, as there was from then on absolutely no one in her retinue whom she knew. She had not yet learnt Danish and she was not proficient in German, another language that was spoken within the Danish monarchy. She knew English and French only.¹⁸

On 21 October, the retinue left Altona and continued northwards through the duchy of Holstein into the duchy of Schleswig, which was also part of the Danish monarchy. Caroline Mathilde probably felt very lonely, yet, she was not alone. A huge retinue accompanied her through her new country. It consisted of:¹⁹

1 chief court mistress (*overhofmesterinde*)
1 maid of honour (*kammerfrøken*)
6 ladies in waiting (*hofdamer*)
1 lady of honour (*kammerfrue*)
3 junior maids of honour (*kammerjomfruer*)
5 chamber maids for the lady chamberlain and the ladies in waiting
4 parlour maids for the same
3 maids for the lady of honour and the junior maids of honour (*3 piger hos kammerfruen and kammerjomfruerne*)
2 ladies for the junior maids of honour (*jomfruernes egne*)
1 maid of the apartment

1 laundry maid with an undermaid
1 layer (*borddaekker*) for the chamber table
1 layer for the table of the junior maids of honour (*ved damejomfruerne*)
Privy Councillor (*gehejmeråd*), Baron Dehn with his coachman and 2 footmen
Chamberlain (*kammerherre*) Brockenhuus with his coachman and 2 footmen
Charberlain Gram with two footmen
Chamberlain Ahlefeldt with his coachman and 2 footmen
Chamberlain Kleist with 2 footmen
Groom of the chamber (*kammerjunker*) Moltke with a footman
Groom of the chamber Raben with a footman
Groom of the chamber Rosencrantz with a footman
Groom of the chamber Juel with a footman
Court gentleman (*hofjunker*) Levetzau with a footman
Court gentleman Bertouch with a footman
Court gentleman Høegh with a footman
Court gentleman Count Holck with a footman
6 pages with two footmen
1 lackey to the chamber
8 lackeys
1 courier
2 heyducks (i.e. footmen placed on the back of a coach)
2 footmen
1 wardrobe tailor
1 quartermaster (*kammerfourer*)
1 treasurer
1 physician-in-ordinary
1 inspector of court provisions
1 managing clerk (*fuldmægtig*) of the court scribe (*hofskriveren*)
1 journeyman surgeon
1 male servant in charge of kitchen utensils
3 work hands (*arbejdskarle*)

The kitchen:

> The chef (*mundkokken*)
> 1 deputy chef and 4 journeymen chefs
> 1 maid
> 2 work hands
> 1 plucker

The wine cellar:

> 1 managing clerk
> 1 scribe
> 2 work hands

The office of provisions:

- 1 managing clerk
- 1 scribe
- 2 work hands

The silver chamber:

- 1 managing clerk
- 5 male servants
- 9 work hands and workboys
- 2 maids

The confectionery:

- 3 journeymen
- 2 apprentices

The bakery:

- 1 bread clerk
- 2 baker journeymen

The butchery:

- The court butcher
- 2 journeymen

The stables:

- 1 Her Majesty's coachman
- 10 other coachmen.[20]

Furthermore, the retinue also included some representatives from the Danish court who had gone all the way to London to accompany her to her new country: Chief Court Master (*overhofmester*) Count Bothmar with one coachman and one footman; Lieutenant von Hemmert with one footman; and Groom of the Chamber (*kammerjunker*) Sperling with one footman.[21]

All in all, the retinue of the Queen travelling from Altona towards Copenhagen consisted of around 160 persons: thirty-two women and 128 men. To arrange transportation, feeding and accommodation for so many people was a significant logistical achievement. According to a report by the Lord Chamberlain (who had not been on the journey himself) about the journey everything seems to have gone without a hitch and functioned perfectly. But we should remain sceptical: it seems unlikely that everything really functioned that smoothly and unproblematically during the entire journey. To transport this huge retinue, seventy pairs of horses and 261 peasant's carts were needed. These were requisitioned from the peasants in those areas through which the retinue travelled. Furthermore, seven burgher's carriages, probably meaning carriages with a better spring suspension and upholstery, were needed. Thus, there were more carriages than horses noted in the report: perhaps the court had brought the remaining number of horses itself or they had been placed at the disposal of the court by the local military authorities. To give an impression of the scale of this huge number of wagons it can be noted that the Court Butcher required four wagons whereas twenty-eight wagons were needed to transport all the kitchen supplies. The wine cellar and its staff required twenty-four wagons, the silver chamber thirty-two, the confectionery fourteen and the bakery ten.[22]

Middelfart

On 28 October, the retinue went across the Little Belt (*Lillebælt*, the narrow strait between Jutland and the island of Funen). To this end a number of vessels staffed with officers and sailors from the Danish navy had been provided, thus increasing further the number of those who needed provisioning and accommodation.[23] Around noon the retinue arrived at the town of Middelfart. According to the census of 1769, this town had 736 inhabitants,[24] more or less merely an overgrown village. Nonetheless, it was a chartered town and had importance as a ferry station.[25] Significant measures had been taken on the occasion of such a distinguished visit. The quay of the town was said to be uneven and not easily passable. Therefore, the Lord Chamberlain of the court in Copenhagen had indicated that due to the royal visit the quay should be provided with a path of wooden boards, with a width of four *alen* (an *alen* is approximately sixty-two centimetres). This would be a heavy item of expenditure for a small community like Middelfart, yet the provincial governor (*stiftamtmanden*) had suggested that it would be possible to rent the boards from one of the local merchants. The boards could afterwards be returned to the merchants 'without significant damage'.[26]

The Queen's retinue took lunch in Middelfart. Ten persons were selected for the Queen's Table. Besides this, there were two large rose tables (*roser*), tables where only ladies and gentlemen of the court were allowed. No marshal's table (*marskalstaffel*) was present in Middelfart, that is, a table for those who, due to their lower rank, could not be admitted to the Queen's own table, nor could they attend the rose tables since they were not in the service of the royal court.[27] If there had been such a marshal's table in Middelfart, local residents of lower rank would have had the possibility of participating in the lunch.

Odense

After the luncheon in Middelfart, the retinue continued to Odense. Horses, wagons and carriages had been requisitioned from local peasants as had a number of burgher's carriages. The logistic experts of the court had foreseen that there might not be a sufficient number of burgher's carriages within a town as small as Middelfart and consequently, the local civil servants had been ordered to provide more of that kind of vehicles from landlords, vicars, bailiffs, millers and other persons outside the peasantry in the countryside. The retinue travelled first to the manor-house Rugaard, between Middelfart and Odense, where new horses and carriages were ready,[28] then towards the evening arrived at Odense. Odense was the second largest city of the kingdom of Denmark (but was more than fifteen times smaller than the largest city, Copenhagen), with 5,464 inhabitants according to the 1769 census.[29] Odense was a regional hub for trade, as well as an episcopal residence, a garrison town and a regional administrative, judicial and educational centre.[30]

Caroline Mathilde had by this point been *en route* for nearly a month, and due to the poor and uneven conditions of the highways, her journey could hardly have been an unconditional pleasure. The fact that the journey took place during the autumn hardly made things more pleasant: the highways were not only full of holes but probably soggy from rain as well. The weather had been cold, stormy and maybe foggy, and darkness fell early. It was no wonder that the retinue stayed for two days at Odense before continuing the trip.

During the stay in Odense, receptions and table settings were again in strict accordance with protocol. On the night of 28 October, fourteen persons were admitted to the Queen's dinner table. While two rose tables were set up for twenty-four persons, as before, no marshal's table was established on the first night, so local persons of lower rank who were not in the service of the royal court did not get an opportunity to participate in this element of court ceremony. This was, however, remedied at the luncheon on the following day, 29 October, where a marshal's table for twenty persons was used, together with the Queen's own table and a rose table. This was true for the following day's luncheon as well, giving several local persons of rank the opportunity to participate. On the evening of 30 October, the Queen did not appear at dinner but dined in her chamber – she was not publicly accessible. Yet, the absence of the Queen did not prevent a rose table and a marshal's table from being set up,[31] even if some of the local elites might have been disappointed that the Queen did not show herself.

In Odense, there was also time for some sight-seeing. The Queen visited the cathedral of the city, which had had an extraordinary and thorough clean-up prior to the royal visit.[32] The royal retinue stayed for a final luncheon in Odense on 31 October. The Queen again hosted fourteen persons at her table, and both a rose and a marshal's table were used. The retinue then left Odense and headed for the town of Nyborg.[33]

Nyborg and beyond

In the village of Langeskov halfway between Odense and Nyborg, new horses and carriages awaited the Queen's retinue.[34] Nyborg had 1,637 inhabitants according to the 1769 census,[35] and the town was an important ferry station and garrison town.[36] The retinue arrived in the evening and Caroline Mathilde dined in her chamber. Nonetheless, a public dinner was held, with both a rose and a marshal's table,[37] so that local persons of rank had the possibility of participating in the dinner even if they missed the Queen herself. Just like in Middelfart, improvements to the quay had taken place prior to the visit, and boards had been rented from the local merchants.[38]

On the next morning, Saturday, 1 November 1766, the retinue crossed the Great Belt (*Storebælt*) by boat to the town of Korsør on the island of Zealand. From here, they continued by carriage towards Copenhagen. On 3 November, the retinue arrived at the town of Roskilde and was received by King Christian VII and his entourage. Caroline Mathilde thus for the first time met her husband, to whom she had been married already for around a month. The royal couple then went together in a carriage to the palace of Frederiksberg just outside Copenhagen where they stayed a few days. On 8 November, the royal couple entered the splendidly decorated capital Copenhagen where a second wedding ceremony took place.[39]

The meaning of it all

How should this huge quantity of resources that the court used on this journey be understood in the context of the practices of Danish absolutism? What was the point of observing all the rules of court etiquette even when staying in Danish provincial towns, places that would have seemed small and primitive to the retinue? Many people today would undoubtedly view the journey of the Queen and her retinue first, as a shameless extravagance and a squandering of taxpayers' money; second, as ridiculous snobbishness; and third, as an annoyance for troubling the local population through multiple requests about the acquisition and usage of horses and carriages. Yet, we should look at these things through the social and political customs of the time.

During the eighteenth century, especially but not exclusively, in absolutist states like Denmark, the royal court was an institution central to the exertion of power. The court was not only the home of the royal family, but to a large extent also a public institution. The king and the members of the royal family were public persons. That went, of course, first and foremost for the king himself. At court, the king and other members of the royal family were accessible to visitors, it was possible to get in touch with them, and it was from the court that the king exerted his power. The absolutist king symbolized and embodied the state; it was he who through his person kept the heterogeneous and multi-territorial state – Denmark, Norway, Schleswig-Holstein and so on – together. The queen had a similar function because she was the wife of the absolutist king. Her most important function was to bear an heir to the throne thereby securing the future of the monarchy and the future existence of the state.[40] Seen in this perspective, it was not Caroline Mathilde as a person, nor the Queen of Denmark who was making a journey across Funen under such a display of extravagance, but the physical manifestation of absolutist royal power itself. Thus, all that extravagance was about representation: it was a ritual and a ceremony aiming at making absolutist royal power present and visible for the entire population. It was not only about life at Christiansborg Palace, the main royal residence in Copenhagen, and the other palaces of the royal family, but also when a prominent member of the royal family was making a journey outside (or between) them. The great show of splendour and luxury during a journey through the countryside also aimed at making absolute royal power visible and thereby encouraging the population to be impressed and show respect. Thus, when the inhabitants of Funen were experiencing such a lengthy procession of carriages and wagons and such a strict observation of court protocol, the intention was to make them think that a king who was able to afford that much pomp and splendour must indeed be an elevated and powerful king and therefore one who would command respect. And that was, of course, an impression that the absolutist regime wanted its people to have. Thus, the grandiose pomp and luxury were not goals in themselves but should be seen as a ritual or ceremony playing an important role for the regime's method for consolidating its position and generating an authoritative and respectful image within the population. If the retinue had been smaller and more modest, absolutist royal power would have been correspondingly smaller and modest in the eyes of the population.

Ridiculous observation of etiquette?

The formal order of ranks that was expressed at the official meals during Caroline Mathilde's journey across Funen also had an important function for the exertion of absolutist royal power and for the relationship between the Crown and its subjects. The system of ranks had a great impact on societal life. In church, in the theatre, in public processions (e.g. a royal wedding or if the king was visiting a city) and – as we have seen – at meals at court, people sat, stood or walked according to the order of their rank. Those who did not have any formal rank would therefore only be at the very end after all the people who did, and did not have access at all to the royal tables. If we take a look at which people were included in the official rank system and which were not, we can get an impression of the official, social status hierarchy of the absolutist system. Crucial for being included in the rank system was holding a public office. This meant, for example, a wealthy merchant or a landowner who did not have any public office would not be included and therefore would have to sit, stand, and walk after lowly placed public employees such as a junior secretary or a low-ranking officer. Indeed, apart from the top of the nobility (counts and barons) noblemen were not automatically included in the rank system by virtue of their nobility alone but would have to hold an office as well. Certainly, persons who were not in the rank system because they did not have any public office might apply for a rank title, for payment, if you could get away with it, and many did. A rank title could also be obtained by a special royal favour. Nevertheless, even those persons who were already included in the rank system continued to endeavour to move ever upwards into a higher class of rank and thereby enjoy a more prominent place at public occasions. Instead of grumbling against the absolutist system and working against it, therefore, the official system of rank ensured that the population was actively playing the game of the absolutist system themselves.[41]

A condition for this was, however, that there needed to be opportunities for it to be publicly demonstrated who were included, where in the system they were included, and who were not included at all. Opportunities to demonstrate this came at church services, at the theatre, and in public processions. A visit by a prominent member of the royal family was also an evident opportunity to demonstrate the social order of the absolutist regime. At the meals during the Queen's journey, people sat according to their rank. The most high-ranking people sat at the Queen's table, the most high-ranking gentlemen and ladies of the court sat at the rose table and persons with lower rank had to be content with dining at the marshal's table but were nonetheless included. Certainly, it was not only the members of the court who took part in these meals but also local persons of rank from the towns visited, who, by virtue of their rank, could join in. Often there was not room for all local persons of rank, only those with a sufficiently high place in the rank order to gain a place at the marshal's table. But this inclusion/exclusion also served as a ritual demonstrating the official social order, now at the local level.

The large majority of the population was not included in the rank system at all and had little chance of ever being so. Yet, they were also touched by the system as they – as mentioned – had to yield for even the lowest public employee with rank just as everybody had the opportunity of seeing in public events who was included in the rank system and at which level exactly. But there were other ways in which the ordinary population might feel that a representative of absolutist royal power was passing by. At the popular level, at that time it was common practice during royal journeys that money would be distributed to needy persons seeking out the royal retinue just as money was thrown into the crowds for curious onlookers to scramble for. If this was done during Caroline Mathilde's journey, we do not know for certain. Yet, the account books from her household after her arrival to her new life at the Danish court show that she indeed did this.[42] Even if it was not included in the rank system, the ordinary population did nonetheless get an opportunity to join the festivities as spectators or to lend carriages, wagons and horses to the royal retinue and thus to demonstrate their loyalty and obligation towards royal authority.

Unnecessary troubling of the population?

A royal visit did, of course, lead to extraordinary expenses locally. As we have seen, Caroline Mathilde's journey prompted improvements of the quays in Middelfart and Nyborg and an extraordinary clean-up of the cathedral in Odense. Yet, an expense somewhere is also a source of revenue somewhere else. The money in question remained within the local communities creating sales and employment. The clean-up of the cathedral was – as far as we can see – organized by means of the bell-ringer hiring people to do the job. At the same time, the accommodation and feeding of all those people in the Queen's retinue gave local peasants and tradesmen possibilities of providing the retinue with goods and services, not only food and drink. Thus, the passage of the royal retinue might not only have meant that the local population was troubled, but also helped.

Certainly, many peasants and burghers had to place their horses, wagons and carriages at the disposal of the royal retinue and therefore to do without them for a while. Furthermore there would have been the risk that those horses and carriages had been damaged while on loan. How the peasants and burghers saw things themselves, we do not know. It might be that they felt it as a pleasant interruption from their everyday lives, as an extraordinary experience where even those 'unranked' social groups had the occasion to share in the royal pomp. This itself also served to demonstrate absolutist royal power to the local population of Funen and to contribute to confirming its perceptions about the monarchy and the social order.

Conclusion

In this chapter, the argument has been that the grandiose royal journey across Funen in late October 1766 was not merely about moving Queen Caroline Mathilde from London to Copenhagen. It should also be seen as a ritual or ceremony whereby Danish royal power and the Danish absolutist system of government were being staged and visualized to the Kingdom's subjects and where the local population was being given an opportunity to participate in the absolutist system as spectators, as guests at the royal meals in their capacities as members of the official system of ranks, or as lenders of horses and carriages and wagons and providers of goods and services to the royal retinue as it passed through the country. Thus, the local population was being given an opportunity to perform its role as obedient, but also grateful, loyal and obliging subjects. In this way, the absolutist regime was being confirmed and consolidated. This interpretation has been made in the light of existing research on the practice and political culture of Danish absolutism, stressing its anti-aristocratic tendencies and its openness to people of common extraction; its official hierarchy of ranks giving precedence to state service over wealth and nobility; its tradition of participation (not to be confused with codetermination), interaction and communication of royal subjects through petitioning, audiences and the opportunity to acclaim the king publicly; and all of this woven into an official rhetoric emphasizing the king as benevolent and caring rather than mighty and elevated. In this light, the interpretation of the journey of 1766 seems meaningful: Danish absolutism was not only based on orders from above but also of the active and loyal participation of all layers of the population. Yet, in the nature of the case such an interpretation can only be rendered probable, not provable.

Whether this staging, visualization and performance of absolutism worked successfully is difficult to say. Yet, the story about the peasant Christen Mortensen who was convinced that the beggar in gaol in 1784 was indeed the real Queen Caroline Mathilde because he could recognize her after having witnessed her on the journey across Funen in October 1766, would suggest that the ritual for visualizing and staging power – of which the journey of Caroline Mathilde and her retinue might also be seen as an expression – apparently had not been fully in vain.

Notes

1. Lars Vangen Christensen, 'Den falske Caroline Mathilde', in *Rygternes Magt*, ed. Ulrik Langen and Jakob Sørensen (Copenhagen: Høst & Søn, 2004).
2. Hans Jensen, *Dansk Jordpolitik 1757–1919*, vol. 1 (Copenhagen: Gyldendal, 1936), 13.

3   Ernst Ekman, 'The Danish Royal Law of 1665', *Journal of Modern History* 29, no. 2 (1957): 102–7.
4   Knud J.V. Jespersen, 'Absolute Monarchy in Denmark: Change and Continuity', *Scandinavian Journal of History* 12, no. 4 (1987); idem, 'The Rise and Fall of the Danish Nobility, 1600–1800', in *The European Nobilities in the Seventeenth and Eighteenth Centuries*, vol. 2, *North, East and Central Europe*, ed. Hamish M. Scott (London: Longman, 1995); idem, *A History of Denmark* (Basingstoke–New York: Palgrave Macmillan, 2004), 17–20, 38–52.
5   Sebastian Olden-Jørgensen, 'Statsceremoniel, hofkultur og politisk magt i overgangen fra adelsvælde til enevælde – 1536 til 1746', *Fortid og Nutid* (1996): 3–20.
6   Gunner Lind, 'Military and Absolutism: The Army Officers of Denmark–Norway as a Social Group and Political Factor, 1660–1848', *Scandinavian Journal of History* 12, no. 3 (1987): 221–43.
7   Peter Henningsen, 'Den bestandige maskerade: Standssamfund, rangssamfund og det 18. århundredes honnette kultur', *Historisk Tidsskrift* (Denmark) 101, no. 2 (2001): 313–43.
8   This expression stems from: Thomas Ertman, *The Birth of Leviathan: Building States and Regimes in Medieval and Early Modern Europe* (Cambridge: Cambridge University Press, 1997).
9   Michael Bregnsbo, *Folk skriver til kongen: Supplikkerne og deres funktion i den dansk-norske enevælde i 1700-tallet: En kildestudie i Danske Kancellis supplikprotokoller* (Copenhagen: Selskabet for Udgivelse af Kilder til Dansk Historie, 1997).
10 Ibid.; Michael Bregnsbo, 'Struensee and the Political Culture of Danish Absolutism', in *Scandinavia in the Age of Revolution: Nordic Political Cultures, 1740–1820*, ed. Pasi Ihalainen, Michael Bregnsbo, Karin Sennefelt and Patrik Winton (Abingdon: Routledge, 2011); Knud Waaben, 'Misgerning og straf', in *Dagligliv i Danmark 1720–1790*, ed. Axel Steensberg (Copenhagen: Munksgaard, 1971).
11 Bregnsbo, 'Struensee and the Political Culture', 55–65.
12 Idem, *Samfundsorden og statsmagt set fra prædikestolen: Danske præsters deltagelse i den offentlige opinionsdannelse vedrørende samfundsordenen og statsmagten 1750–1848, belyst ved trykte prædikener: En politisk-idehistorisk undersøgelse* (Copenhagen: Det Kongelige Bibliotek/Museum Tusculanums Forlag, 1997).
13 Harald Gustafsson, *Political Interaction in the Old Regime: Central Power and Local Society in the Eighteenth-Century Nordic States* (Lund: Studentlitteratur, 1994).
14 For the most useful histories of Caroline Mathilde, her short reign and her downfall, see: Asser Amdisen, *Til nytte og fornøjelse: Johann Friedrich Struensee (1737–1772)* (Copenhagen: Akademisk Forlag, 2002); Svend Cedergreen Bech, *Struensee og hans tid* (Copenhagen: Forlaget Cicero, 1972, 2nd edn, 1989); Michael Bregnsbo, 'Danish Absolutism and Queenship: Louisa, Caroline Matilda, and Juliana Maria', in *Queenship in Europe 1660–1815: The Role of the Consort*, ed. Clarissa Campbell Orr (Cambridge: Cambridge University Press, 2004); idem, *Caroline Mathilde: Magt og skæbne: En biografi* (Copenhagen: Aschehoug, 2007); Norman Hall Hansen, *Caroline Mathilde: Dronning af Danmark og Norge 1751–1775* (Copenhagen: Ejnar Munksgaards Forlag, 1947); Ulrik Langen, *Den afmægtige – en biografi om Christian 7* (Copenhagen: Jyllands-Postens Forlag, 2008); and Stella Tillyard, *A Royal Affair: George III and His Troublesome Siblings* (London: Chatto & Windus, 2006).
15 For overviews of Struensee's career see: Amdisen, *Til nytte og fornøjelse*, 14-62; Bech, *Struensee og hans tid*, 25–55; Bregnsbo, 'Danish Absolutism and Queenship', 349–54;

idem, *Caroline Mathilde*, 89–94; Hansen, *Caroline Mathilde*, 9–177; Langen, *Den afmægtige*, 285–391; and Tillyard, *A Royal Affair*, 114–22.

16   Amdisen, *Til nytte og fornøjelse*, 53-160; Bech, *Struensee og hans tid*, 197–393; Bregnsbo, 'Danish Absolutism and Queenship', 349–54; idem, *Caroline Mathilde*, 114–215; Hansen, *Caroline Mathilde*, 94–242; Langen, *Den afmægtige*, 285–392; Tillyard, *A Royal Affair*, 190–261.

17   The Danish state of the eighteenth century was a much larger entity than the present-day state named Denmark. Besides the kingdom of Denmark it also consisted of the kingdom of Norway, the Faroe Islands, Iceland, and Greenland, the duchies of Schleswig and Holstein, and some small oversea colonies in India, Africa and the Caribbean.

18   Hansen, *Caroline Mathilde*, 27 ff.

19   As many of the titles are difficult, not to say, impossible to translate into English, I have in many cases kept the original Danish word in parenthesis, however, the meaning in Danish of many of the words and titles is not constant through time.

20   For records concerning the wedding and coronation see Rigsarkivet (Danish National Archives) Copenhagen (hereafter: DRA Copenhagen), Hoffet (The Royal Court), Overhofmarskallatet (the Lord Chamberlain's Office), Sager vedrørende formælinger og kroninger. 1766: dronning Caroline Mathildes indtog og formæling, pakke 2-I.N.2a. That includes Protokol over Hendes Majestæt Caroline Mathildes indrejse fra Altona til Frederiksberg og indtog til Christiansborg samt Hans Majestæt Kongen Christian VII og Hendes Kongelige Majestæt Dronning Caroline Mathildes høje formæling i året 1766 samt diverse bilag (Queen Caroline Mathilde's journey from Altona to Frederiksberg Palace and her entrance at Christiansborg Palace and His Majesty King Christian VII and Her Royal Majesty Queen Caroline Mathilde's high wedding in the year of 1766 and various enclosures), as well as the list of the retinue.

21   Ibid.

22   Ibid.

23   Rigsarkivet (Danish National Archives) Odense (hereafter: DRA Odense) Middelfart byfoged (town bailiff), Indkomne breve (letters received) 1740–1766, letter of 4 October 1766 from the Lord Chamberlain's Office (*Overhofmarskallatet*) and an enclosed, incompletely preserved list of vessels with officers and crew.

24   *Statistiske Meddelelser*, series 4, vol. 37 (Copenhagen: Statens Statistiske Bureau, 1911).

25   Peter Dragsbo and Harriet Merete Hansen, *Middelfart – Fra færgeby til broby. Middelfarts historie 1200–1940* (Odense: Odense Universitetsforlag, 1996), 88–105. A chartered town (*købstad*) means a town with special privileges of trade and commerce granted by the king and where the administrative and legal structures differed markedly from those in surrounding rural areas.

26   DRA Odense, Middelfart byfoged (town bailiff), Indkomne breve (letters received) 1740–1766: letter dated 4 October 1766 from provincial governor (*stiftamtmand*) Juel.

27   Terms 'marskalstaffel' and 'rose' in *Ordbog over det danske Sprog 1700–1950*:https://www.ordnet.dk/ods

28   DRA Copenhagen, Hoffet, Overhofmarskallatet, package 2-I.N.2a, pro memoria (*memorandum*).

29   *Statistiske Meddelelser*.

30   Hans Chr. Johansen, 'Næring og bystyre: Odense 1700–1789', in *Odense bys historie*, vol. 5, ed. Tage Kaarsted et al. (Odense: Odense Kommune, i kommission hos Odense Universitetsforlag, 1983); and Anne Riising, 'Gudsfrygt og oplysning: Odense 1700–1789', in ibid., vol.4, 11–341.

31 DRA Copenhagen, Hoffet, Overhofmarskallatet, package 2-I.N.2a.
32 DRA Odense, Odense: Skt. Knuds kirkeinspektions arkiv (archives of the church inspection of the cathedral of St. Knud at Odense), Kirkeregnskaber (church accounts) 1766–1767, bilag (voucher) no. 45; and Riising, 'Gudsfrygt og oplysning', 147.
33 DRA Copenhagen, Hoffet, Overhofmarskallatet, package 2-I.N.2a.
34 Ibid.
35 *Statistiske Meddelelser*.
36 Mette Ladegaard Thøgersen, 'Danmarksporten', in *Nyborg – Danmarks riges hjerte*, vol. 2, ed. Mette Ladegaard Thøgersen and Erland Porsmose (Nyborg: Østfyns Museer, 2015).
37 DRA Copenhagen, Hoffet, Overhofmarskallatet, package 2-I.N.2a.
38 DRA Odense, Nyborg magistrat (city corporation), Kopibog over indkomne breve (copy book of letters received) 1752–1770, letter from provincial governor (*stiftamtmand*) Juel, dated 4 October 1766.
39 Amdisen, *Til nytte og fornøjelse*; Bech, *Struensee og hans tid*; Bregnsbo, 'Danish Absolutism and Queenship'; idem, *Caroline Mathilde*; Hansen, *Caroline Mathilde*; Langen, *Den afmægtige*; and Tillyard, *A Royal Affair*.
40 Sebastian Olden-Jørgensen, '"At vi maa frycte dig af idel kjærlighed": Magtudøvelse og magtiscenesættelse under den ældre danske enevælde', *Fortid og Nutid*, no. 4 (1997); idem, 'Statsceremoniel, hofkultur og politisk magt': 239–53.
41 Henningsen, 'Den bestandige maskerade'; Olden-Jørgensen, 'Statsceremoniel, hofkultur og politisk magt'.
42 DRA Copenhagen, Hoffet, Kabinetskassen (one of the cashier's offices at the royal Danish court), Regnskaber (accounts) 1766–1772 and Partikulærkammeret (another cashier's office at the royal Danish court), Caroline Mathildes regnskaber (Caroline Mathilde's accounts) 1766–1772.

Select Bibliography

Al-Baghdadi, Saniye. 'Da Vitichindo a Beroldo: Sulle origini dei Savoia nella storiografia, nell'araldica e nell'arte.' In *Stato sabaudo e Sacro Romano Impero*, ed. Marco Bellabarba and Andra Merlotti, 49–68. Bologna: il Mulino, 2014.

Al-Baghdadi, Saniye. 'Die Erfindung der Sabaudia und die Historisierung des Alpenraums im Spiegel savoyischer Hofpublikationen.' In *Transferprozesse zwischen dem Alten Reich und Italien im 17. Jahrhundert*, ed. Sabina Brevaglieri and Matthias Schnettger, 287–322. Bielefeld: transcript Verlag 2018.

Alberti, Giovanni Matteo. *Giuochi festivi e militari, danze serenate, macchine, boscareccia artificiosa, regata solenne et altri sontuosi apprestamenti di allegrezza esposti alla soddisfazione universale dalla generosità dell'Altezza ser. di Ernesto duca di Brunswich e Luneburgo, Principe di Osnabrück ecc. al tempo di sua dimora in Venetia*. Venice: Andrea Poletti, 1686.

Alm, Mikael. 'Dynasty in the Making: A New King and His "Old" Men in Royal Ceremonies 1810–1844.' In *Scripts of Kingship: Essays on Bernadotte and Dynastic Formation in an Age of Revolution*, ed. Mikael Alm and Britt-Inger Johansson, 23–48. Uppsala: Opuscula Historica Upsaliensia, 2008.

Alm, Mikael, 'Riter och ceremonier kring Karl XIV Johan.' In *En dynasti blir till: Medier, myter och makt kring Karl XIV Johan och familjen Bernadotte*, ed. Nils Ekedahl, 37–77. Stockholm: Norstedts, 2010.

Amdisen, Asser. *Til nytte og fornøjelse: Johann Friedrich Struensee (1737–1772)*. Copenhagen: Akademisk Forlag, 2002.

Anatra, Bruno, John Day, and Lucetta Scaraffia. *La Sardegna medievale e moderna*. Turin: UTET, 1984.

Angyal, Dávid. *Magyarország története II. Mátyástól III. Ferdinánd haláláig*. Budapest: Athenaeum, 1898.

Arciszewska, Barbara. 'Edward Oakley, Freemasonry and Popularization of Architectural Knowledge in Early Georgian Britain.' *Ars Regia* 20 (2012/13): 1–50.

Arciszewska, Barbara. *The Hanoverian Court and the Triumph of Palladio: The Palladian Revival in Hanover and England c. 1700*. Warsaw: DiG, 2002.

Bahlcke, Joachim. *Religionalismus und Staatsintegration im Widerstreit: Die Länder der Böhmischen Krone im ersten Jahrhundert der Habsburgerherrschaft*. Munich: Oldenbourg, 1994.

Barker-Benfield, G. J. *The Culture of Sensibility: Sex and Society in Eighteenth-Century Britain*. Chicago: University of Chicago Press, 1992.

Beaken, Robert. *Cosmo Lang: Archbishop in War and Crisis*. London: I.B. Tauris, 2012.

Bellabarba, Marco and Andrea Merlotti, eds. *Stato sabaudo e Sacro Romano Impero*. Bologna: il Mulino, 2014.

Bertelli, Sergio. *The King's Body*. University Park, PA: Pennsylvania State University, 2001.

Bertelli, Sergio and Giuliano Crifò, eds. *Rituale, cerimoniale, etichetta*. Rome: Bompiani, 1985.

Bianchi, Paola, and Andrea Merlotti, *Storia degli Stati sabaudi (1416–1848)*. Brescia: Morcelliana, 2017.

Bloch, Marc. *Les Rois thaumaturges: Étude sur le caractère surnaturel attribué à la puissance royale particulièrement en France et en Angleterre*. Paris: Gallimard, 1983.

Blomfield, Charles James. *A Sermon Preached at the Coronation of Their Most Excellent Majesties King William IV. and Queen Adelaide in the Abbey Church of Westminster September VIII. MDCCCXXXI*. London: B. Fellowes, 1831.

Bonney, Richard. *The European Dynastic States, 1494–1660*. Oxford: Oxford University Press, 1991. Reprint: 2012.

Bourdeille, Pierre de [Abbé de Brantôm]. *Les Dames galantes*, ed. Pascal Pia. Paris: Gallimard, 1981.

Braddock, Andrew. *The Role of the Book of Common Prayer in the Formation of Modern Anglican Church Identity*. Lewiston, NY: Edwin Mellen Press, 2010.

Bravo, Paloma and Juan Carlos d'Amico, eds. *Territoires, lieux et espaces de la révolte, XIVe–XVIIIe siècles*. Dijon: Editions Universitaires de Dijon, 2017.

Bregnsbo, Michael. *Caroline Mathilde: Magt og skæbne: En biografi*. Copenhagen: Aschehoug, 2007.

Bregnsbo, Michael. 'Danish Absolutism and Queenship: Louisa, Caroline Matilda, and Juliana Maria.' In *Queenship in Europe 1660–1815: The Role of the Consort*, ed. Clarissa Campbell Orr, 344–67. Cambridge: Cambridge University Press, 2004.

Bregnsbo, Michael. 'Struensee and the Political Culture of Danish Absolutism.' In *Scandinavia in the Age of Revolution: Nordic Political Cultures, 1740–1820*, ed. Pasi Ihalainen, Michael Bregnsbo, Karin Sennefelt and Patrik Winton, 55–65. Abingdon: Routledge, 2011.

Burke, Peter. *The Historical Anthropology of Early Modern Italy*. Cambridge: Cambridge University Press, 1987.

Buzási, Enikő, and Géza Pálffy, *Augsburg – Vienna – München – Innsbruck: Die frühesten Darstellungen der Stephanskrone und die Entstehung der Exemplare des Ehrenspiegels des Hauses Österreich: Gelehrten- und Künstlerbeziehungen in Mitteleuropa in der zweiten Hälfte des 16. Jahrhunderts*. Budapest: Institut für Geschichte des Forschungszentrums für Humanwissenschaften der Ungarischen Akademie der Wissenschaften, 2015.

Cannadine, David. 'Introduction: Divine Rites of Kings.' In *Rituals of Royalty: Power and Ceremonial in Traditional Societies*, ed. David Cannadine and Simon Price, 1–19. Cambridge: Cambridge University Press, 1987.

Cannadine, David. 'The Context, Performance and Meaning of Ritual: The British Monarchy and the "Invention of Tradition", c. 1820–1977.' In *The Invention of Tradition*, ed. Eric Hobsbawm and Terence Ranger, 101–64. Cambridge: Cambridge University Press, 1983.

Castelnuovo, Guido. 'Principati regionali e organizzazione del territorio nelle Alpi occidentali: l'esempio sabaudo (inizio XIII–inizio XV secolo).' In *L'organizzazione del territorio in Italia e Germania: secoli XIII–XIV*, ed. Georgio Chittolini and Dietmar Willoweit, 81–92. Bologna: il Mulino, 1996.

Celâlzâde Mustafa. *Selim-nâme*, ed. Ahmet Uğur and Mustafa Çuhadar. Ankara: Kültür Bakanlığı, 1990.

Cervantes, Pedro and Miguel Ángel. *Recopilación de las Reales Ordenanzas y Cédulas de los Bosques Reales del Pardo, Aranjuez, Escorial, Balsaín y otros*. Madrid: Oficina de Melchor Álvarez, 1687.

Chatenet, Monique. *La cour de France au XVIe siècle: Vie sociale et architecture*. Paris: Picard, 2002.

Chaves Montoya, María Teresa. *La gloria de Niquea: Una invención en la Corte de Felipe IV*. Aranjuez: Doce Calles, 1991.

Checa Cremades, Fernando. 'Monarchic Liturgies and the "Hidden King": The Function and Meaning of Spanish Royal Portraiture in the Sixteenth and Seventeenth Centuries.' In *Iconography, Propaganda and Legitimation*, ed. Allan Ellenius, 89–104. Oxford: Oxford University Press, 1998.

Checa Cremades, Fernando. *Tesoros de la Corona de España: Tapices flamencos en el Siglo de Oro*. Brussels: Fons Mercator, 2010.

Checa Cremades, Fernando. *Los inventarios de Carlos V y la familia imperial*, Madrid: Fernando Villaverde Ediciones, 2010.

Coreth, Anna. *Pietas Austriaca*. West Lafayette, IN: Purdue University Press, 2004.

Croly, George. *The Coronation: Observations on the Public Life of the King*. London: J. Warren, 1821.

Csapodi, Csapa, and Klára Csapodi-Gárdonyi. *Bibliotheca Corviniana, 1490-1990: International Corvina Exhibition on the 500th Anniversary of the Death of King Matthias: National Széchényi Library, 6 April – 6 October 1990*. Budapest: Országos Széchényi Könyvtár, 1990.

Cziráki, Zsuzsanna. 'Das Siebenbürgen-Konzept der Kriegspartei in Wien von 1611 bis 1616 anhand der schriftlichen Gutachten von Melchior Khlesl.' *Ungarn-Jahrbuch* 32 (2014): 139–79.

Cziráki, Zsuzsanna. 'Szemelvények Melchior Khlesl és a bécsi Titkos Tanács 1611 és 1613 között keletkezett, erdélyi vonatkozású írásos véleményeiből.' *Levéltári Közlemények* 83 (2012): 319–69.

Dandelet, Thomas J. 'Searching for the New Constantine: Early Modern Rome as a Spanish Imperial City.' In *Embodiments of Power*, ed. Gary B. Cohen and Franz A.J. Szabo, 191–202. New York: Berghahn Books, 2008.

Dittelbach, Thomas. *Rex imago Christi: Der Dom von Monreale: Bildsprachen und Zeremoniell in Mosaikkunst und Architektur*. Wiesbaden: Reichert Verlag, 2003.

Duchesne André. *Les Antiquitez et recherches de la grandeur et Majesté des Roys de France*. Paris: Jean Petit-Pas, 1609.

Duerloo, Luc. *Dynasty and Piety: Archduke Albert (1598-1621) and Habsburg Political Culture in the Age of Religious Wars*. Farnham–Burlington: Ashgate, 2012.

Duindam, Jeroen. *Myths of Power: Norbert Elias and Early Modern European Court*. Amsterdam: Amsterdam University Press, 1995.

Duindam, Jeroen. 'Rulers and Courts.' In *The Oxford Handbook of Early Modern European History, 1350-1750*, vol.2, *Cultures and Power*, ed. Hamish Scott, 440–77. Cambridge: Cambridge University Press, 2015.

Duindam, Jeroen. *Vienna and Versailles: The Courts of Europe's Dynastic Rivals, 1550-1780*. Cambridge: Cambridge University Press, 2003.

Elliott, John H. 'A Europe of Composite Monarchies.' *Past and Present* 137 (1992): 48–71.

Elliott, John H., and L.W.B. Brockliss, eds. *The World of the Favourite*. New Haven, CT–London: Yale University Press, 1999.

Engel, Pál. *The Realm of St. Stephen: A History of Medieval Hungary, 895-1526*. London–New York: I.B. Tauris, 2001.

Ertman, Thomas. *The Birth of Leviathan: Building States and Regimes in Medieval and Early Modern Europe*. Cambridge: Cambridge University Press, 1997.

Ertuğ, Zeynep Tarim. 'The Depiction of Ceremonies in Ottoman Miniatures: Historical Record or a Matter of Protocol?' *Muqarnas* 27, no. 1 (2010): 251–75.

Evans, Robert J[ohn] W[eston]. *The Making of the Habsburg Monarchy 1550-1700: An Interpretation*. Oxford: Oxford University Press, 1979.

Fantoni, Marcello, George Gorse and Malcolm Smuts, eds. *The Politics of Space: European Courts ca. 1500–1750*. Rome: Bulzoni Editore, 2009.

Feridun Ahmed Bey. *Nüzhet-i Esrârü'l-Ahyar der-Ahbâr-i Sefer-i Sigetvar: Sultan Süleyman'ın Son Seferi*, ed. H. Ahmet Arslantürk and Günhan Börekçi. İstanbul: Zeytinburnu Belediyesi Kültür Yayınları, 2012.

Fetvacı, Emine. 'The Production of the Şehnâme-i Selim Ḫân.' *Muqarnas* 26, no.1 (2009): 263–316.

Fiorentino, Carlo M. *La corte dei Savoia (1849–1900)*. Bologna: il Mulino, 2008.

Fisher, Geoffrey. *I Here Present Unto You. . .: Addresses Interpreting the Coronation of Her Majesty Queen Elizabeth II*. London: SPCK, 1953.

Fleet, Kate. 'The Ottomans, 1451–1603: A Political History Introduction.' In *The Cambridge History of Turkey*, vol.2. *The Ottoman Empire as a World Power, 1453–1603*, ed. Suraiya N. Faroqhi and Kate Fleet, 19–43. Cambridge–New York: Cambridge University Press, 2013.

Fodor, Pál, ed. *The Battle for Central Europe: The Siege of Szigetvár and the Death of Süleyman the Magnificent and Nicholas Zrínyi (1566)*. Leiden–Boston–Budapest: Brill–Research Centre for the Humanities, Hungarian Academy of Sciences, 2019.

Gal, Stéphane. *Charles-Emmanuel de Savoie: La politique du précipice*. Paris: Payot, 2012.

García Bernal, José Jaime. *El fasto público en la España de los Austrias*. Seville: Universidad de Sevilla, 2006.

Garipzanov, Ildar. 'David, Imperator Augustus, Gratia Dei Rex: Communication and Propaganda in Carolingian Royal Iconography.' In *Monotheistic Kingship: The Medieval Variants*, ed. Aziz Al-Azmeh and János M. Bak, 89–118. Budapest: Central European University, Department of Medieval Studies, 2004.

Gaude-Ferragu, Murielle. *Queenship in Medieval France, 1300–1500*. New York: Palgrave Macmillan, 2016.

Gentile, Luisa C. *Riti ed emblemi. Processi di rappresentazione del potere principesco in area subalpina (XIII–XVI secc.)*. Turin: Zamorani, 2008.

Gibson, William. *The Church of England 1688–1832: Unity and Accord*. London: Routledge, 2001.

Giesey, Ralph E. *Cérémonial et puissance souveraine: France, XVe–XVIIe siècles*. Paris: A. Collin, 1987.

Giesey, Ralph E. 'Inaugural Aspects of French Royal Ceremonials.' In *Coronations: Medieval and Early Modern Monarchic Ritual*, ed. János M. Bak, 35–45. Berkeley: University of California Press, 1990.

Giesey, Ralph E. *Le rôle méconnu de la loi salique. La succession royale, XIVe–XVIe siècles*. Paris: Les Belles Lettres, 2007.

Giesey, Ralph E. *The Royal Funeral Ceremony in Renaissance France*. Geneva: Librairie E. Droz, 1960.

González Cuerva, Rubén, and Alexander Koller, eds. *A Europe of Courts, a Europe of Factions: Political Groups at Early Modern Centres of Power (1550-1700)*. Leiden: Brill, 2017.

Grew, Nehemiah. *Cosmologia Sacra: or a Discourse of the Universe as it is the Creature and Kingdom of God*. London: W. Rogers, S. Smith and B. Walford, 1701.

Guarino, Gabriel. *Representing the King's Splendour: Communication and Reception of Symbolic Forms of Power in Viceregal Naples*. Manchester: Manchester University Press, 2010.

Gustafsson, Harald. *Political Interaction in the Old Regime: Central Power and Local Society in the Eighteenth-century Nordic States*. Lund: Studentlitteratur, 1994.

Hagen, Gottfried, 'Legitimacy and World Order.' In *Legitimizing the Order: The Ottoman Rhetoric of State Power*, ed. Hakan T. Karateke and Maurus Reinkowski, 53–83. Leiden: Brill, 2005.
Harai, Dénes. *Gabriel Bethlen, prince de Transylvanie et roi élu de Hongrie, (1580–1629).* Paris: L'Harmattan, 2013.
Hatton, Ragnhild. *George I: Elector and King.* Cambridge, MA: Harvard University Press, 1978.
Hatton, Ragnhild. 'In Search of an Elusive Ruler: Source Material for a Biography of George I as Elector and King'. In: *Fürst, Bürger, Mensch: Untersuchungen zu politischen und soziokulturellen Wandlungsprozessen im vorrevolutionären Europa*, ed. Friedrich Engel-Janosi, Grete Klingenstein and Heinrich Lutz, 11–41. Vienna: Verlag, 1975.
Hausenblasová, Jaroslava, Jiří Mikulec and Martina Thomsen, eds. *Religion und Politik im frühneuzeitlichen Böhmen: Der Majestätsbrief Kaiser Rudolfs II. von 1609.* Stuttgart: Franz Steiner, 2014xs.
Hennings, Jan. *Russia and Courtly Europe: Ritual and the Culture of Diplomacy, 1648–1725.* Cambridge: Cambridge University Press, 2016.
Hortal Muñoz, José Eloy, Pierre-François Pirlet and África Espíldora García, eds. *El ceremonial en la corte de Bruselas del Siglo XVII.* Brussels: Palais des Académies, 2018.
Hortal Muñoz, José Eloy. 'El personal de los Sitios Reales desde los últimos Habsburgos hasta los primeros Borbones: de la vida en la periferia a la integración en la Corte.' In *Siti Reali in Europa: Una storia del territorio tra Madrid e Napoli*, ed. Lucio d'Alessandro, Félix Labrador Arroyo and Pasquale Rossi, 75–95. Naples: Università suor Orsola Benincasa, 2014.
Hortal Muñoz, José Eloy. 'La integración de los Sitios Reales en el sistema de Corte durante el reinado de Felipe IV.' *Libros de la Corte* 8 (2014), 27–47.
Hortal Muñoz, José Eloy. *Las Guardas Reales de los Austrias hispanos.* Madrid: Polifemo, 2013.
Hortal Muñoz, José Eloy and Gijs Versteegen, *Las ideas políticas y sociales en la Edad Moderna.* Madrid: Síntesis, 2016.
Ila, Bálint. 'Az 1614-i linzi egyetemes gyűlés.' *A Gróf Klebelsberg Kuno Magyar Történetkutató Intézet évkönyve* 4 (1934): 231–53.
Il festino della felicità nel cuore, nella bocca, en ella pompa di Palermo, sulla trionfal acclamazione di Carlo VI Imperatore, III Re delle Spagne, e di Sicilia. Stretto in breve relazione d'ordine dell'Illustrissimo Senato Palermitano. Palermo: Regia Stamperia di Antonio Epiro, 1720.
Ingram, Robert. *Religion, Reform and Modernity in the Eighteenth-century: Thomas Secker and the Church of England.* Woodbridge: Boydell & Brewer, 2007.
Jackson, Richard A. *Vive le Roi! A History of the French Coronation from Charles V to Charles X.* Chapel Hill: University of North Carolina Press, 1984.
Jespersen, Knud J.V. *A History of Denmark.* Basingstoke–New York: Palgrave Macmillan, 2004.
Jespersen, Knud J.V. 'Absolute Monarchy in Denmark: Change and Continuity.' *Scandinavian Journal of History* 12, no. 4 (1987): 307–16.
Jespersen, Knud J.V. 'The Rise and Fall of the Danish Nobility, 1600–1800.' In *The European Nobilities in the Seventeenth and Eighteenth Centuries*, 2 vols.: *North, East and Central Europe*, ed. Hamish M. Scott, 41–70. London: Longman, 1995.
Kafadar, Cemal. 'Janissaries and Other Rifraff of Ottoman Istanbul: Rebels without a Cause?' In *Identity and Identity Formation in the Ottoman World: A Volume of Essays in Honour of Norman Itzkowitz*, ed. Baki Tezcan and Karl K. Barbir, 113–34. Madison: University of Wisconsin Press, 2007.

Kantorowicz, Ernst H. '"Deus per Naturam", "Deus per Gratiam": A Note on Mediaeval Political Theology'. In *Selected Studies*, ed. Ernst H. Kantorowicz, 121-37. Locust Valley, NY: J.J. Augustin Publisher, 1965.
Kantorowicz, Ernst H. *Laudes Regiae: A Study in Liturgical Acclamations and Mediaeval Ruler Worship*. Berkeley-Los Angeles: University of California Press, 1946.
Kantorowicz, Ernst H. *The King's Two Bodies: A Study in Mediaeval Political Theology*. Princeton: Princeton University Press, 1957.
Kertzer, David I. *Ritual, Politics, and Power*. New Haven, CT: Yale University Press, 1988.
Knecht, Robert J. *The French Renaissance Court, 1483-1589*. New Haven, CT-London: Yale University Press, 2008.
Koenigsberger, Helmut G. *Estates and Revolutions. Essays in Early Modern Europe History*. Ithaca, NY-London: Cornell University Press, 1971.
Krischer, André. *Reichsstädte in der Fürstengesellschaft: Zum politischen Zeichengebrauch in der Frühen Neuzeit*. Darmstadt: Wissenschaftliche Buchgesellschaft, 2006.
Kuchař, Karel. *Early Maps of Bohemia, Moravia and Silesia*. Prague: Ústřední Správa Geodézie a Kartografie, 1961.
Kunt, Metin. 'A Prince Goes Forth (Perchance to Return).' In *Identity and Identity Formation in the Ottoman World: A Volume of Essays in Honor of Norman Itzkowitz*, ed. Karl Barbir and Baki Tezcan, 63-71. Madison: University of Wisconsin Press, 2007.
La Placa, Pietro. *La Reggia in Trionfo per l'acclamazione, e coronazione della Sacra Real Maestà di Carlo Infante di Spagna, Re di Sicilia, Napoli e Gerusalemme, Duca di Parma, Piacenza, e Castro, Gran Principe Ereditario della Toscana ordinata dall'Eccellentissimo Senato Palermitano*. Palermo: Regia Stamperia di Antonino Epiro, 1735.
Leppert, Richard. 'Imagery, Musical Confrontation and Cultural Difference in Early 18th-century London.' *Early Music* 14, no. 3 (1986): 323-45.
Lowth, Robert. *A Sermon preached before the Lords Spiritual and Temporal, in the Abbey-Church, Westminster; on Friday, January 30, 1767: being the Day Appointed to be Observed as the Day of the Martyrdom of King Charles I*. London: A. Millar, T. Cadell and J. Dodsley, 1767.
Lunger Knoppers, Laura. *Constructing Cromwell: Ceremony, Portrait, and Print, 1645-1661*. Cambridge: Cambridge University Press, 2000.
Mączak, Antoni, ed. *Klientelsysteme im Europa der Frühen Neuzeit*. Munich: Oldenbourg Verlag, 1988.
Maiden, John. *National Religion and the Prayer Book Controversy, 1927-1928*. Woodbridge: Boydell & Brewer, 2009.
Marguerite de Navarre, *Heptaméron*, ed. Renja Salminen. Geneva: Droz, 1999.
Marguerite de Valois. *Mémoires et autres écrits, 1574-1614*. ed. Éliane Viennot. Paris: Honoré Champion, 1999.
Martínez Ruíz, Enrique, and Magdalena de Pazzis Pi Corrales, *Protección y seguridad en los Sitios Reales desde la Ilustración al Liberalism*. Alicante: Universidad de Alicante, 2010.
Martineau, Harriet. *Autobiography*. London: Smith, Elder, 1877.
Maskell, William. *Monumenta Ritualia Ecclesiae Anglicanae or Occasional Offices of the Church of England according to the Ancient Use of Salisbury the Prymer in English and other Prayers and Forms with Dissertations and Notes*. London: William Pickering, 1846-7.
Merlotti, A. 'Il "sacro" alla corte sabauda di Vittorio Emanuele II da Torino a Roma (1849-1878).' In *Stato sabaudo e Curia romana*, ed. Jean-François Chauvard, Andrea Merlotti and Maria Antonietta Visceglia, 155-74. Rome: Ecole française de Rome, 2015.
Merlotti, Andrea. *L'enigma delle nobiltà: Stato e ceti dirigenti nel Piemonte del Settecento*. Florence: L.S. Olschki, 2000.

Michel, Eva, Maria Luise Sternath and Manfred Holleger, eds. *Emperor Maximilian I and the Age of Dürer*. Vienna: Prestel, 2012.
Mikó, Árpád. *The Corvinas of King Matthias in the National Széchényi Library*. Budapest: Országos Széchényi Könyvtár, Kossuth Kiadó, 2008.
Milhous, Judith, and Robert D. Hume. 'Opera Salaries in Eighteenth-Century London.' *Journal of the American Musicological Society* 46, no. 1 (1993): 26–83.
Mínguez, Víctor, and Pablo González Tornel. 'La reggia in trionfo, 1735: La coronación de Carlos de Borbón en Palermo y "gli splendori della magnificenza".' *Reales Sitios*, no. 188 (2011): 50–67.
Muir, Edward. *Civic Ritual in Renaissance Venice*. Princeton: Princeton University Press, 1981.
Muir, Edward. *Ritual in Early Modern Europe*. Cambridge: Cambridge University Press, 1997.
Muir, Edward. *Ritual in Early Modern Europe*. 2nd revised edn. Cambridge: Cambridge University Press, 2005.
Nieto Soria, José Manuel. *Ceremonias de la realeza: Propaganda y legitimación en la Castilla Trastámara*. Madrid: Nerea, 1993.
Norman, Edward R. *Church and Society in England 1770–1970: A Historical Study*. Oxford: Clarendon Press, 1976.
Nussdorfer, Laurie. *Civic Politics in the Rome of Urban VIII*. Princeton: Princeton University Press, 1992.
Nussdorfer, Laurie. 'The Politics of Space in Early Modern Rome.' *Memoirs of the American Academy in Rome* 42 (1997): 161–86.
Nussdorfer, Laurie. 'The Vacant See: Ritual and Protest in Early Modern Rome.' *The Sixteenth Century Journal* 18 (1987): 173–89.
Olden-Jørgensen, Sebastian. 'Ceremonial Interaction across the Baltic around 1700: The "Coronations" of Charles XII (1697), Frederick IV (1700), and Frederick III/I (1701).' *Scandinavian Journal of History* 28 (2003): 243–51.
Olden-Jørgensen, Sebastian. 'Statsceremoniel, hofkultur og politisk magt i overgangen fra adelsvælde til enevælde – 1536 til 1746.' *Fortid og Nutid* (1996): 3–20.
Oresko, Robert. 'The House of Savoy in Search for a Royal Crown in the Seventeenth Century.' In *Royal and Republican Sovereignty in Early Modern Europe*, ed. Robert Oresko et al., 272–350. New York: Cambridge University Press, 1997.
Pálffy, Géza. 'Heraldische Repräsentation der Jagiellonen und der Habsburger: Die Wappen des königlichen Oratoriums im Prager Veitsdom im mitteleuropäischen Kontext.' *Historie – Otázky – Problémy* 7, no. 2 (2015): 176–90.
Pálffy, Géza. 'Kaiserbegräbnisse in der Habsburgermonarchie – Königskrönungen in Ungarn: Ungarische Herrschaftssymbole in der Herrschaftsrepräsentation der Habsburger im 16. Jahrhundert.' *Frühneuzeit-Info* 19, no. 1 (2008): 41–66.
Pálffy, Géza. 'The Bulwark and Larder of Central Europe (1526–1711).' In *On the Stage of Europe: The Millennial Contribution of Hungary to the Idea of European Community*, ed. Ernő Marosi, 100–24. Budapest: Research Institute for Art History of the Hungarian Academy of Sciences–Balassi Kiadó, 2009.
Pálffy, Géza. *The Kingdom of Hungary and the Habsburg Monarchy in the Sixteenth-century*. New York: Columbia University Press, 2009.
Pálffy, Géza, and Ferenc Tóth. 'Les couronnements en Hongrie à l'époque moderne (1526–1792): Représentations et outils politico-diplomatiques.' *Revue d'histoire diplomatique* 131: no. 3 (2017): 253–75.
Papp, Szilárd. 'Mátyás emlékezete Bautzenben.' In *Rex invictissimus: Hadsereg és hadszervezet a Mátyás kori Magyarországon*, ed. László Veszprémy, 213–36, Budapest: Zrínyi Kiadó, 2008.

Paravicini Bagliani, Agostino. *Il corpo del papa*. Turin: Einaudi, 1994.
Pascual Molina, Jesús F. *Fiesta y poder: La corte de Valladolid (1502-1559)*. Valladolid: Universidad de Valladolid, 2013.
Piech, Zenon. 'Die Wappen der Jagiellonen als Kommunikationssystem.' In *Hofkultur der Jagiellonendynastie und verwandter Fürstenhäuser*, ed. Urszula Borkowska and Markus Hörsch, 13-34. Ostfildern: Thorbecke, 2010.
Pisan, Christine de. *The Book of the City of Ladies*. Translated by Rosalind Brown-Grant. London: Penguin Classics, 1999.
Polišenský, Josef. *Tragic Triangle: The Netherlands, Spain and Bohemia, 1617-1621*. Prague: Charles University, 1991.
Potter, John. *A Sermon preach'd at the Coronation of King George II. and Queen Caroline, in the Abbey-Church of Westminster, October 11. 1727*. London: R. Knaplock, 1727.
Raeymaekers, Dries and Sebastiaan Derks. 'Repertoires of Access in Princely Courts, 1400-1750.' In *New Perspectives on Power and Political Representation from Ancient History to the Present Day*, ed. Harm Kaal and Daniëlle Slootjes, 78-93. Leiden: Brill, 2019.
Raeymaekers, Dries, Sebastiaan Derks, eds. *The Key to Power? The Culture of Access in Princely Courts, 1400-1750*. Leiden--Boston: Brill, 2016.
Rangström, Lena. *Kläder för tid och evighet: Gustaf III sedd genom sina dräkter*. Stockholm: Livrustkammaren, 1997.
Reinhard, Wolfgang. *Geschichte der Staatsgewalt: Eine vergleichende Verfassungsgeschichte Europas von den Anfängen bis zur Gegenwart*. Munich: C.H. Beck, 2000.
Relación de la orden que se tuvo en el bautismo de la señora Infanta, hija primogénita del Invictísimo Rey Don Felipe III, nuestro Señor, en Valladolid a siete de octubre de mil y seiscientos y un años. Valladolid: Herederos de Bernardino de santo Domingo, 1602.
Rodrigues-Moura, Enrique. 'Religión y poder en la España de la Contrarreforma: Estructura y función de la leyenda de los Austria devotos de la Eucaristía.' In *Austria, España y Europa: Identidades y diversidades*, ed. Manuel Maldonado Alemán, 11-30. Seville: Universidad de Sevilla, 2006.
Rodríguez Moya, Inmaculada. 'La esperanza de la monarquía: Fiestas en el imperio hispánico por el nacimiento de Felipe Próspero.' In *Visiones de un Imperio en Fiesta*, ed. Inmaculada Rodríguez Moya and Víctor Mínguez Cornelles, 93-119. Madrid: Fundación Carlos de Amberes, 2016.
Roosen, William J. 'Early Modern Diplomatic Ceremonial: A Systems Approach.' *The Journal of Modern History* 52 (1980): 452-76.
Rosand Ellen. *Opera in Seventeenth-Century Venice: The Creation of a Genre*. Berkeley: University of California Press, 1991.
Rosenthal, Earl. 'The Invention of the Columnar Device of Emperor Charles V at the Court of Burgundy in Flanders in 1516.' *Journal of the Warburg and Courtauld Institutes* 36 (1973): 198-230.
Ruiz, Teofilo F. 'Unsacred monarchy: The Kings of Castile in the Late Middle Ages.' In *Rites of Power: Symbolism, Ritual, and Politics Since the Middle Ages*, ed. Sean Wilentz, 109-44. Philadelphia: University of Pennsylvania Press, 1985.
Russell, Nicolas, and Hélène Visentin. 'Introduction: The Multilayered Production of Meaning in Sixteenth Century French Ceremonial Entries'. In *French Ceremonial Entries in the Sixteenth Century: Event, Image, Text*, ed. Nicolas Russell and Hélène Visentin, 15-26. Toronto: Centre for Reformation and Renaissance Studies, 2007.
Schnath, Georg. 'Neue Forschungen zur ältesten Geschichte des Welfenhauses.' *Niedersächsisches Jahrbuch für Landesgeschichte* 31 (1959): 255-63.

Schramm, Percy. *A History of the English Coronation*. Translated by Leopold Wickham Legg. Oxford: Clarendon Press, 1937.

Selaniki Mustafa Efendi. *Tarih-i Selaniki*, ed. Mehmet İpşirli. Ankara: Türk Tarih Kurumu Yayınları, 1999.

Shaw, Dougal. 'Thomas Wentworth and Monarchical Ritual in Early Modern Ireland.' *The Historical Journal* 49, no. 2 (2006): 331–55.

Shils, Edward, and Michael Young. 'The Meaning of the Coronation.' *Sociological Review* 1 (1953): 63–81.

Snickare, Mårten. *Enväldets riter: Kungliga fester och ceremonier i gestaltning av Nicodemus Tessin den yngre*. Stockholm: Raster förlag, 1999.

Spangler, Jonathan. 'Holders of the Keys: The Grand Chamberlain, the Grand Equerry and Monopolies of Access at the Early Modern French Court.' In *The Key to Power? The Culture of Access in Princely Courts, 1400–1750*, ed. Dries Raeymaekers and Sebastiaan Derks, 153–77. Leiden–Boston: Brill, 2016.

Spielman, John P. *The City and the Crown: Vienna and the Imperial Court 1600–1740*. West Lafayette, IN: Purdue University Press, 1993.

Stock, Paul, ed. *The Uses of Space in Early Modern History*. New York: Palgrave Macmillan, 2015.

Stollberg-Rilinger, Barbara. 'Die Wissenschaft der feinen Unterschiede: Das Präzedenzrecht und die europäische Monarchien vom 16. bis zum 18. Jh.' *Majestas* 10 (2002): 1–26.

Stollberg-Rilinger, Barbara. *The Emperor's Old Clothes: Constitutional History and the Symbolic Language of the Holy Roman Empire*. New York–Oxford: Berghahn, 2015.

Stollberg-Rilinger, Barbara. *Rituale*. Frankfurt am Main–New York: Campus, 2013.

Stollberg-Rilinger, Barbara. 'Zeremoniell als politisches Verfahren: Rangordnung und Rangstreit als Strukturmerkmale des frühneuzeitlichen Reichstags.' In *Neue Studien zur frühneuzeitlichen Reichsgeschichte*, ed. Johannes Kunisch, 91–132. Berlin: Duncker & Humblot, 1997.

Strohmeyer, Arno. *Konfessionskonflikt und Herrschaftsordnung: Widerstandsrecht bei den österreichischen Ständen (1550–1650)*. Mainz: Zabern, 2006.

Strong, Roy. *Art and Power: Renaissance Festivals, 1450–1650*. Berkeley: University of California, 1973.

Strong, Roy. *Coronation: A History of Kingship and the British Monarchy*. London: Harper Collins, 2005.

Stock, Paul, ed. *The Uses of Space in Early Modern History*. New York: Palgrave MacMillan, 2015.

Sturdy, David. '"Continuity" versus "Change": Historians and English Coronations of the Medieval and Early Modern Periods.' In *Coronations: Medieval and Early Modern Monarchic Ritual*, ed. János M. Bak, 228–44. Berkeley: University of California Press, 1990.

Symcox, Geoffrey. *Victor Amadeus II: Absolutism in the Savoyard State, 1675–1730*. Berkeley: University of California Press, 1983.

Szathmáry, Tibor. *Descriptio Hungariae: Magyarország és Erdély nyomtatott térképei 1477–1600*. Fusignano: Grafiche Morandi, 1987.

Thiemann, Manfred. 'Mathias Rex anno 1486: Das Matthias-Corvinus-Denkmal in Bautzen.' *Ungarn-Jahrbuch: Zeitschrift für interdisziplinäre Hungarologie* 29 (2008): 1–32.

Thomas, Bruno. 'Die Augsburger Funeralwaffen Kaiser Karls V.: Ein Beitrag zur 400. Wiederkehr des Tages seiner Totenfeier.' *Waffen und Kostümkunde* 3, no. 1 (1959): 28–47.

Thuróczy, János. *A magyarok krónikája*. Facsimile edn. Budapest: Helikon Kiadó, 1986.
Tillyard, Stella. *A Royal Affair: George III and his Troublesome Siblings*. London: Chatto & Windus, 2006.
Timms, Colin. 'George I's Venetian Palace and Theatre Boxes in 1720.' In *Music and Theatre: Essays in Honour of Winton Dean*, ed. Nigel Fortune, 95–130. Cambridge: Cambridge University Press, 2005.
Timms, Colin. *Polymath of the Baroque: Agostino Steffani and His Music*. Oxford: Oxford University Press, 2003.
Tiozzo, Clauco Benito. *Le ville del Brenta da Lizza Fusina alla città di Padova*. Venice: Cavallino, 1980.
Toajas Roger, María Ángeles. 'La heredad de la Zarzuela: Nuevos documentos de su historia.' *Anales de Historia del Arte* 17 (2007): 85–116.
Tobia, Bruno. *Una patria per gli italiani: Spazi, itinerari, monumenti nell'Italia unita (1870-1900)*. Rome–Bari: Laterza, 1991.
Varey, John E. 'Processional Ceremonial of the Spanish Court in the Seventeenth Century.' In *Studia Iberica: Festschrift für Hans Flasche*, ed. Karl-Hermann Körner and Klaus Rühl, 643–52. Bern–Munich: Francke Verlag, 1973.
Vester, Matthew, ed. *Sabaudian Studies: Political Culture, Dynasty, and Territory, 1400-1700*. Kirksville, MO: Truman State University Press, 2013.
Viennot, Éliane. 'Masculinité et francité du monarque des lis: le débat sur la loi salique et la construction du consensus national pendant la dernière guerre du XVIe siècle.' *Proslogion: Studies in Medieval and Early Modern Social History and Culture* 13, no. 1 (2016): 212–29.
Visceglia, Maria Antonietta. 'Cérémonial et politique pendant la période moderne.' In *Cérémonial et ritual à Rome (XVIe-XIXe siècle)*, ed. Maria Antonietta Visceglia and Catherine Brice, 1–19. Rome: Ecole française de Rome, 1997.
Visceglia, Maria Antonietta. *Guerra, Diplomacia y Etiqueta en la Corte de los Papas (Siglos XVI y XVII)*. Madrid: Polifemo, 2010.
Visceglia, Maria Antonietta. *Riti di corte e simboli della regalità: i regni d'Europa e del Mediterraneo dal Medioevo all'età moderna*. Rome: Salerno Editrice, 2009.
Vocelka, Rosemarie. 'Die Begräbnisfeierlichkeiten für Kaiser Maximilian II, 1576/77.' *Mitteilungen des Instituts für österreichische Geschichtsforschung* 84 (1976): 105–36.
Wallbrecht, Rosemarie E. *Das Theater des Barockzeitalters an den welfischen Höfen Hannover und Celle*. Hildesheim: August Lax Verlag, 1974.
Wanegffelen, Thierry. *Catherine de Médicis: Le pouvoir au féminine*. Paris: Payot, 2005.
Ward, Anthony, and Cuthbert Johnson. 'John Wickham Legg (1843-1921): A Contribution Towards the Rediscovery of British Liturgical Scholarship.' *Ephemerides Liturgicae* 97 (1983): 70–84.
Warf, Barney, and Santa Arias, eds. *The Spatial Turn: Interdisciplinary Perspectives*. London: Routledge, 2009.
Watanabe-O'Kelly, Helen. 'Early Modern European Festivals – Politics and Performance, Event and Record.' In *Court Festivals of the European Renaissance: Art, Politics and Performance*, ed. John R. Mulryne and Elizabeth Goldring, 15–25. Aldershot: Ashgate, 2002.
Watanabe-O'Kelly, Helen. 'The Early Modern Festival Book: Function and Form.' In *Europa Triumphans: Court and Civic Festivals in Early Modern Europe*, 1 vols., ed. John R. Mulryne, Helen Watanabe-O'Kelly and Margaret Shewring, 3–17. Aldershot: Ashgate, 2004.
Weber, Matthias. *Das Verhältnis Schlesiens zum Alten Reich in der Frühen Neuzeit*. Cologne–Weimar–Vienna: Böhlau, 1992.

Wickham Legg, Leopold G., ed. *English Coronation Records*. Westminster: Archibald Constable, 1901.
Williamson, Fiona. 'The Spatial Turn of Social and Cultural History: A Review of the Current Field.' *European History Quarterly* 44, no. 4 (2014): 703-17.
Wilson, Peter H. *Europe's Tragedy: A New History of the Thirty Years War*. London: Allen Lane, 2009.
Woolley, Reginald Maxwell. *Coronation Rites*. Cambridge: Cambridge University Press, 1915.
Wolffe, John. 'Protestantism, Monarchy and the Defence of Christian Britain 1837-2005.' In *Secularisation in the Christian World: Essays in Honour of Hugh McLeod*, ed. Callum G. Brown and Michael Snape, 57-74. Farnham: Ashgate, 2010.
Woolley, Reginald Maxwell. *Coronation Rites*. Cambridge: Cambridge University Press, 1915.
Wrede, Martin. 'The House of Brunswick-Lüneburg and the Holy Roman Empire: The Making of a Patriotic Dynasty, 1648-1714.' In *The Hanoverian Succession: Dynastic Politics and Monarchical Culture*, ed. Andreas Gestrich and Michael Schaich, 43-72. London: Routledge, 2016.
Wünsche-Werdehausen, Elisabeth. '"La felicita in trono": l'entrata di Vittorio Amedeo II a Palermo nel 1713.' *Artes* 13 (2005-7): 361-88.
Yates, Nigel. *Anglican Ritualism in Victorian Britain 1830-1910*. Oxford: Oxford University Press, 1999.
Zalama Rodríguez, Miguel Ángel. 'The Ceremonial Decoration of the Alcázar in Madrid: The Use of Tapestries and Paintings in Habsburg Festivities'. In *Festival Culture in the World of the Spanish Habsburgs*, ed. Fernando Checa Cremades and Laura Fernández-González, 41-66. Farnham: Ashgate, 2015.
Zelfel, Hans Peter. 'Wappenschilde und Helme vom Begräbnis Kaiser Friedrichs III: Ein Beitrag zum Begräbniszeremoniell.' *Unsere Heimat: Zeitschrift des Vereins für Landeskunde von Niederösterreich und Wien* 45 (1974): 201-9.
Zorzi, Alvise. *Venetian Palaces*. New York: Rizzoli, 1991.

Index

Page numbers in **bold** refer to figures, page numbers in *italic* refer to tables.

absolutism, 7, 10
    performance of, 213–25
access, 10–1
    culture of, 6
    to Royal Household, 89–90
accession gratuities, 27
administrative arrangements, 93
Albert II, king of Germany, 176, *176*, *179*
Alfonso X 'the Wise', King of Spain, 87–8
Alienor (Eléonore) de Poitiers, 73
Alm, Mikael, 10
Anglo-Catholic restoration, 54–8, 59
Anne de Beaujeu, 71–2
Anne of Brittany, 72, 74
anthropology, 3
architecture, 198–9, **199**, **200**
Arciszewska, Barbara, 12
Ariosti, Attilio, 202
Asterix (comic series), 134
audiences, 132

Baillie, Hugh Murray, 5
Bak, János, 50
baptisms, royal, 11, 105–16
    Bourbon ceremonies, 112–3
    canopies, 114–5
    ceremonial customs and etiquette, 105, 105–8, **109**, **110**
    crystal chair, 114
    fonts, 114
    godparents, 108, 111, 112, 113
    location, 106, 111
    magnificence, 114–5
    music, 114
    participants, 105, 107, 108, **110**, 111–2
    procession, 108, **110**, 111–2
    ritual objects, 105, 107, 113, 114–5, 115–6
    and space, 105
    tapestries, 115

Bayezid, Prince, 23
Bayezid II, Sultan, 19
Benfield, Barker, 205
Bernadotte, Jean-Baptiste *see* Charles XIV John, King of Sweden
Besztercebánya, Diet of the Kingdom of Hungary, 7, 135, 143–52
    the arguments, 147–9
    blame, 150
    context, 146–7
    participants, 143
    precedence negotiations, 144–6
    precedence struggle, 143–4
    solution, 150, 152
    stakes, 149–52
Bethlen, Gábor, 144–6, 145, 146, 149–50, 151, 152
body politic, the, 2–3
Bonaparte, Joseph, 162
Bregnsbo, Michael, 7
bureaucratization, 5
Burgundy, 73

Cannadine, David, 4–5, 50
Carlo Emanuele I, Duke of Savoy, 9
Caroline Mathilde, Queen of Denmark, journey across Funen, 7, 213–25
    arrival in Denmark, 217
    background, 213–7
    conditions, 221
    etiquette, 220, 221, 223–4
    expenses, 224–5
    meals, 220, 221, 223–4
    meaning, 222–3
    Middelfart, 220
    Nyborg, 221–2
    Odense, 220–1
    retinue, 217–20, 223
    Roskilde, 222

Index

Castelnuovo, Guido, 158
Castle, Terry, 205–6
Catherine de Medici, 72, 73, 76, 79–80, 80
ceremonial, definition, 3–4, 69
ceremonial debates, Besztercebánya, Diet of the Kingdom of Hungary, 7, 143–52
   the arguments, 147–9
   blame, 150
   context, 146–7
   participants, 143
   precedence negotiations, 144–6
   precedence struggle, 143–4
   solution, 150, 152
   stakes, 149–52
ceremony and ritual, historians approaches to, 2–6
Champier, Symphorien, 157
Charles Albert, King of Sardinia, 158, 163
Charles Emmanuel III of Savoy, 161
Charles Felix of Savoy, 161, **162**
Charles II (III of Sicily), King, 33, 34
Charles IX, King of France, 74
Charles V, Emperor, 89–90, 94, 164, 172, 177
Charles VI of Habsburg (IV of Sicily), 33, 37–8, 43
Charles VIII, King of France, 71–2, 74
Charles XIII, King of Sweden, 121, 122, 123, 124, 125, 126, 127, 128, 129, 130, 133
Charles XIV John, King of Sweden, 10, 121–35
   accession, 128
   Act of Adoption, 127
   arrival in Sweden, 121–2
   Bernadotte's elevation to Prince, 122–7
   coronation, 128–30
   death, 132
   entry into Stockholm, 123–5
   funeral, 132–5
   the homage, 130–2
   integration into the royal family, 124
   Oaths of Allegiance, 125–7, 130–2
   proclaimed Prince Charles John, 126
   royal presentations, 123–4
   succession, 135

Charles of Bourbon (V of Sicily), Duke of Parma, 33, 38–9, 39, 41, 42, 43
Charlotte, Queen, 51
Checa, Fernando, 115
Christian VII, King of Denmark, 215, 222
chronological scope, 12
Church of England, 9
Cichè, Francesco, 36, 38
civic rites, 43–4
civil power, sacralization of, 40–1
Clement XI, Pope, 35
coats of arms, 11, 172–3, **173**, **174**, 175, 175–7, *176*, 186
coins, heraldic representation, 175, **175**, **185**
Coke, Sir John, 1–2
collective political bodies, 144
Cöln, Johannes von, 150–1
communication, 7
   limitations, 132
   ritualized, 12
   symbolic, 11, 171 *see also* heraldic representation
Contarini, Marco, 201–2
continuity, 35
Cook, Richard, 80
coronations and coronation rites, 7–9, 157
   accession ceremonial, 20–1
   accession gratuities, 27
   Anglo-Catholic restoration, 54–8, 59
   benediction, 52
   British, 8–9, 49–59
   civic rites, 43–4
   Danish, 49–50, 214
   enthronement, 20–1
   French queens, 75
   heraldic representation, 181–3, **181**, **183**
   Hungary, 181–3, **181**, **183**
   justification by faith, 51–2
   monarchic rites, 43–4
   Oaths of Allegiance, 130–2
   Protestant Reformation, 50–4, 59
   role of Providence, 52
   Savoy, 157–60, 161, 163–4
   Selim II, 7–8, 19–28
   shortening, 53
   Sicily, 8, 33–44
   Sweden, 128–30

Cosandey, Fanny, 72, 75
court, the, definition, 87–8, 89, 90–1
court ceremonial, Queen's Household, France, 69–81
  bedroom, 77
  court festivals, 80
  evening meal, 79
  honour guard, 78
  ladies' entourage, 78–9
  midday meal, 79
  morning *toilette*, 77–8
  private spaces, 79–80
  queen's carriage, 78
  Regulations of Henry III, 75–80, 81
  rights and duties, 76–80
  royal legislation, 69–81
  and Salic Law, 70, 70–3, 81
  tradition and influence, 70–3
The Court Society (Elias), 3
court studies, 5–6, 87
Covarrubias, Sebastián de, 89
Croly, George, 49
cultural patterns, 7
culture of access, 6
Cuzzoni, Francesca, 201, **201**

Davidson, Randall, Archbishop, 55–6
Dávila, Gil González, 89
Denmark
  absolutism, 213–5, 222–3
  Caroline Mathilde, Queen of Denmark, journey across Funen, 7, 213–25
  clergy, 215
  coronation rite, 49–50
  coronations and coronation rites, 214
  Middelfart, 220
  Nyborg, 221–2
  Odense, 220–1
  Queen Caroline Mathilde's arrival in, 217
  rank system, 223–4, 225
  Roskilde, 222
  royal appointments and promotions, 214
  Royal Law, 213
  royal power, 7, 213–25
  social order, 223–4
descriptive approach, 2–3
dignity, 127, 129
diplomatic self-representation, 144

Divine Providence, 52
Dixon, Nicholas, 8–9
Dohna, Abraham von, 144–6, 148–9, 151
Dornau, Caspar (Dornavius), 144–6, 148–9, 151
dual corporality, 39–40
Dublin, 1–2
Duchesne, André, 69, 75
Duindam, Jeroen, 3, 6
Dürer, Albrecht, 172
dynastic representation, 11, 182, 183–5, **184**, **185**, 186

Edward VII, King, 54–5
Elias, Norbert, *The Court Society*, 3
Elizabeth II, Queen, coronation, 56, 57–8
enthronement, 8, 20–1, 34, 41
Ernest Augustus, Elector of Hanover, 193, 194–5, 196, **197**, 198
etiquettes, 93–5, 105, 105–8, **109**, **110**, 220, 221, 223–4
Eurocentric perspective, 4–5

family networks, 105
Fantoni, Marcello, 5
female households, France, 10
Ferdinand I, Emperor, 178, *179*
Ferdinand II, Emperor, **183**
Ferdinand III, Emperor, 183
Feridun Ahmed Beğ, 22, 23, 25–6, 26, 27
festival books, 42–3, **43**
Florence, 95
France
  ceremonial customs and etiquette, 95
  continuity of women's power, 72
  court ceremonial tradition and influence, 73–4
  court festivals, 80
  definition of ceremonial, 69
  detachment of space, 95–6
  female households, 10
  laws of succession, 72
  limitation of the power of the Queen, 70–3
  queen's carriage, 78
  queens foreign origins, 73–4
  Queen's Household, 69–81
  queenship, 75–80
  règne des femmes, 71–2

Regulations of Henry III, 75–80, 81
royal guards, 95–6
royal legislation, 69–70
Salic Law, 70, 70–3, 81
Francis I, King of France, 71
Francolin, Hans, 172
Franz Joseph, Emperor, 164
fratricide, 19
Frederick III, Emperor, 172, 176, *176*, 177, *179*
Funen, 215
    etiquette, 220, 221, 223–4
    impact of Queen Caroline Mathilde's journey across, 224–5
    meaning of Queen Caroline Mathilde's journey across, 222–3
    Middelfart, 220
    Nyborg, 221–2
    Odense, 220–1
    Queen Caroline Mathilde's journey across, 7, 213–25
    Queen Caroline Mathilde's retinue, 217–20, 223
    Roskilde, 222
funerals, 132–5
    Habsburg emperors, 175–8, *176*, *177*, *179*, 180–1, **180**, 186

Geertz, Clifford, 3
Geijer, Erik Gustaf, 134
geographical scope, 12
George I, King, 198–206
George II, King, 215
George III, King, 9, 12, 51–2, 193, 215
George IV, King, coronation, 9, 49, 52–3
George V, King, coronation, 55–6
George VI, King, coronation, 56, 56–7
Giesey, Ralph, 39, 69, 75
Glorious Revolution, the, 9, 51
Godefroy, Théodore, 95
Gómez de Mora, Juan, 95
Goths, 134
Grandee of Spain rank, 105, 107–8, 108, 111–2
Grandis, Vincenzo de, 198
Great Britain
    Abdication Crisis, 56
    Acts of Union, 51
    Anglo-Catholic restoration, 54–8, 59
    coronation rite origin and early development, 50–1
    coronations, 8–9, 49–59
    the Glorious Revolution, 9, 51
    Hanoverian, 193, 195, 198–206
    impact of Venetian culture, 12, 201–6, **201**, **203**, **204**
    masquerade in, 203–6
    opera in, 201–3, **201**
    Protestant Reformation, 50–4, 59
    Royal Academy of Music, 202
Greenblatt, Stephen, 3
Grew, Nehemiah, 52
Grünenberg, Conrad, 185
Guistiniano, Marino, 71
Gustav IV Adolf, King of Sweden, 121, 124, 129, 130

Handel, Georg Friedrich, 198
Handelman, Don, 3
hand-kissing, 9, 161–3
Hanover, 193–8
    dynastic history, 193–5
    Herrenhausen, 195–6, **197**
    impact of Venetian culture, 193, 195–6, **196**, 198
    Leine Palace, 196, **197**
    opera in, 196, **197**, 198
    Venetian Carnival, 196
Heidegger, Johann Jacob, 202–3, 205
Henry III, King of France, 10, 74
    Regulations of, 75–80, 81
heraldic flags, 11, 171–2, 177–8, *177*, *179*, **180**, 181–3, **181**, **183**, 186
heraldic representation, 11, 171–86
    coats of arms, 11, 172–3, **173**, **174**, 175, 175–7, *176*, 186
    coins, 175, **175**, **185**
    coronations and coronation rites, 181–3, **181**, **183**
    dynastic, 182, 183–5, **184**, **185**, 186
    errors, 184–5, 186
    flags, 11, 171–2, 177–8, *177*, **180**, 181–3, **181**, **183**, 186
    funerals of Habsburg emperors, 175–8, *176*, *177*, *179*, 180–1, **180**, 186
    Habsburg and Jagiellonian, 171–3, **173**, **174**, 175, **175**
    Prague, 172, 173, **174**, 184–5

high politics, 3
historians, approaches to ceremony and ritual, 2–6
Hogarth, William
   The Bad Taste of the Town, 193, **194**, 205
   Berenstadt, Cuzzoni, and Senesino, **201**
   Taste: The Gate of Burlington House, **204**
holistic approach, 6
Holy Roman Empire, 40, 144
holy unction, 157
honour, defending, 152
Hortal Muñoz, José Eloy, 10–1
Howley, William, Archbishop of Canterbury, 9, 53
Hundred Years War, 73
Hungary, 172
   coronations and coronation rites, 181–3, **181**, **183**
Hungary, Diet of the Kingdom of, 7, 143–52
   the arguments, 147–9
   blame, 150
   context, 146–7
   participants, 143
   precedence negotiations, 144–6
   precedence struggle, 143–4
   solution, 150, 152
   stakes, 149–52

Ireland, Wentworth's inauguration as Lord Deputy, 1–2, 4, 12
Istanbul, 19, 21, 22, 23, 23–4, 26, 27
Italy, Kingdom of, 10, 35, 163, 164

Jäger, Clemens, 172
Janissaries, 20–1, 26–7, 27, 28
Jenkins, Claude, 55
Jones, Inigo, *Designs*, 199, **200**

Kantorowicz, Ernst, 39
   The King's Two Bodies, 2–3, 4
Kármán, Gábor, 7
The King's Two Bodies (Kantorowicz), 2–3, 4
Koeppen, Adolphus Louis, 163

La Placa, Pietro, 38, 39, 42
language, symbolic, 5

Lefebvre, Henri, 88
legitimacy, 8, 11–2, 20, 41, 44, 148
Leibniz, Gottfried, 198
Leopold I, King of Hungary, 181–2, **181**
lineage, dilution of, 40
Loschi, Sertorio, 78–9, 80
Louis II, King of Hungary and Bohemia, 175
Louis XII, King of France, 74
Louis XIV, King of France, 2–3
Louise de Savoie, 71, 80
Lowth, Robert, Bishop, 52
Loya, Diego de, 34, 34–5
loyalty, 39

Madrid, 89, **91**, 96, 97, 98
Manners-Sutton, Charles, Archbishop of Canterbury, 9, 53, 59
Marguerite de Navarre, 71
Marguerite de Valois, queen of Navarre, 72, 76, 79
Martineau, Harriet, 49
Mary of Habsburg, Queen of Hungary, 173
Mary Stuart, Queen of Scots, 74
Maskell, William, 54
masquerade, in Great Britain, 203–6
Matthias Corvinus, King of Hungary, 172, **173**, 176–7, *177*, 186
Maximilian I, Emperor, 172, 175, 176, 177
Maximilian II, Emperor, 178, *179*, 182
Mehmed II, Sultan, 21
Merlotti, Andrea, 9–10
modernization, 193
Mohács, Battle of, 175, 178
Monarchia composita, 9
monarchic rites, 43–4
monarchical power, 10
monarchy
   dual corporality, 39–40
   and the individual, 39
   legitimacy, 41
   sacred character of, 39–41
   Sede Vacante, 44
Mongitore, Antonino, 34
Mortensen, Christen, 213, 225
Moya, Inmaculada Rodríguez, 11
Muir, Edward, 3, 4, 6
municipal powers, 44

Index

Murat, Joachim, 161–2
Mustafa Selaniki Efendi, 19

Naples, 161–2
Napoleon, 121–2, 164
National Library of Russia, Saint
 Petersburg, 76
National Library of Spain, 106
nobility, the, position of, 6
Núñez de Castro, Alonso, 89
Nussdorfer, Laurie, 44

Oaths of Allegiance, 125–7, 130–2
oath-taking, 9, 160–1, **162**, 165
Olivares, Count-Duke of, 92, 97
opera
 in Britain, 201–3, **201**
 in Hanover, 196, **197**, 198
Order of the Iron Crown, 164
Ottoman Empire
 accession gratuities, 27
 army homage ceremony, 25–6
 coronation of Sultan Selim II, 7–8,
  19–28
 enthronement, 20–1
 fratricide, 19
 location of throne, 27–8
 long sixteenth century, 19
 Selim II claims throne, 22–3
 Selim II's accession, 19–20
 Selim I's enthronement, 21
 succession of 1566, 22–6
 taxes and taxation, 26

pageantry, 4–5
Palermo
 coronation of Charles of Bourbon (V
  of Sicily), Duke of Parma, 38–9
 coronation of Victor Amadeus II of
  Savoy (I of Sicily), 35–7, **37**, 158–9,
  161
 coronations, 33–44
 festival books, 42–3, **43**
 Piazza Marina, 34
 proclamation of Charles VI of
  Habsburg (IV of Sicily), 38
 Sede Vacante, 44
Pálffy, Géza, 11
Palladio, Andrea, *Four Books*, 199, **199**

Palma, Nicolò, 38
papal power, 44
patrimonialization, 90
patronage, 87, 198
Paul, St, 70–1
Pertev Pasha, 23
Philip II, King of Spain, 94, 95, 106, 108,
 115, 177
Philip III, King of Spain, 111, 115
Philip IV, King of Spain, 89–90, 94, 95, 98,
 106, 111–2, 115
Philip V, King of Spain, IV of Sicily, 33,
 34–5, 43, 105, 112–3
Piccioli, Maria, 201–2
Pisan, Christine de, 69, 71
Pius IV, Pope, 73
political harmony, 93
politics, and religion, 40–1
power
 exertion of, 222
 transitions of, 34, 41–2
Prague, heraldic representation, 172, 173,
 174, 184–5
precedence, Besztercebánya, Diet of the
 Kingdom of Hungary
 argument, 143–4
 the arguments, 147–9
 blame, 150
 context, 146–7
 negotiations, 144–6
 solution, 150, 152
 stakes, 149–52
proclamations, 39
Protestant Reformation, 50–4, 59

Queen's Household, France, 69–81
 autonomous political space, 72–3
 bedroom, 77
 continuity of women's power, 72
 court festivals, 80
 evening meal, 79
 honour guard, 78
 influence, 70, 71
 ladies' entourage, 78–9
 midday meal, 79
 morning *toilette*, 77–8
 private spaces, 79–80
 queen's carriage, 78
 Regulations of Henry III, 75–80, 81

rights and duties, 76–80
and Salic Law, 70, 70–3, 81
significance, 78–9
status, 70, 75
tradition and influence, 73–4
queenship, France, 75–80

Ragusa, Giambattista, 34, **37**
Ratcliff, Edward, 56–7
Reinhard, Wolfgang, 4
relics, 164
religion, and politics, 40–1
representatives, participation, 9
Rich, John, 205
Ripart, Laurent, 158
ritual
definition, 3–4
typology of, 4
ritual objects, 11, 105, 107, 113, 114–5, 115–6
Robinson, J. Armitage, 55–6
Royal Academy of Music, Great Britain, 202
royal exaltation, instruments of, 36–7
royal guards, 95–6
Royal Household, access to, 89–90
Royal Law, Denmark, 213
royal power, 3
staging, 7, 213–25
royal presentations, 123–4
royal promenades. *see* Caroline Mathilde, Queen of Denmark, journey across Funen
Royal Stables, Spain, 94
Rudolph II, Emperor, 184–5

Saint Bartholomew's Day Massacre, 77
Saint Petersburg, National Library of Russia, 76
Salic Law, 70, 70–3, 81
Sartorio, Antonio, 198
Savoy, House of, 9–10, 35–7, 157–65
age, 163
corona ferrea (Iron Crown), 164
coronation of Victor Amadeus II of Savoy (I of Sicily), 158–9, 161
coronations and coronation rites, 157–60, 163–4
dynasty, 158, 163

hand-kissing ceremony, 161–3
hegemonic role, 163
oath-taking ceremony, 160–1, 161, **162**, 165
states, 158
Schramm, Percy, 49
Secker, Thomas, Archbishop of Canterbury, 8–9, 51–2, 55–6, 57, 59
secularization, 41, 71
Selaniki Mustafa Efendi, 22, 23, 24
self-representation, diplomatic, 144
Selim I, Sultan, 21, 23–4
Selim II, Sultan
accession, 19–20, 22–6
accession gratuities, 27
claims throne, 22–3
coronation, 7–8, 19–28
enters the Imperial Palace, 27
entry in Istanbul, 23–4, 27
legitimacy, 20
location of throne, 27–8, 28n8
return to Istanbul, 26
takes command of army, 24–6
Shaw, Dougal, 1–2
Shils, Edward, 58
Shishkin, Vladimir, 10
Sicily, Kingdom of
coronation of Charles of Bourbon (V of Sicily), Duke of Parma, 38–9
coronation of Victor Amadeus II of Savoy (I of Sicily), 35–7, **37**, 158–9, 161
coronation ritual, 34, 40
coronations, 8, 33–44
expulsion of the Habsburgs, 33, 38
festival books, 42–3, **43**
kings, 33
nature of the monarchy, 39–41
proclamation of Charles VI of Habsburg (IV of Sicily), 38
proclamation of Philip V, 34–5
Sede Vacante, 44
succession, 33
transitions of power, 34–9, 41–2
social mobility, 193, 202
Sokollu Mehmed Pasha, Grand Vizier, 22–3, 24–6
Sophia Madeleine, Queen Dowager of Sweden, 124–5

Sorel, Agnès, 69–81
Sørensdatter, Bodil, 213, 225
sources, 6
sovereign authority
    and enthronement, 20–1
    succession of 1566, 22–6
    transference of, 8, 19–28
sovereignty
    accession to, 8
    dual nature of, 39–40
space, 5–6, 10–1, 87–98
    boundaries, 97
    control over, 97
    court space, 98
    detachment, 95–6
    importance of Royal Sites, 91–2
    influence over, 97
    infrastructures, 96–7
    institutional development, 88
    political, 97
    reconfiguration, 89–90
    regulation, 93–5
    role, 87, 88, 98
    and royal baptisms, 105
    Royal Stables, 94
    spatial turn, 88, 99n9
    theatres, 96–7
    transformation of court space, 95–7
Spain
    Bourbon baptism ceremonies, 112–3
    ceremonial customs and etiquette,
        93–5, 105, 105–8, **109**, **110**
    court space, 89–92, **91**, **92**
    definition of the court, 87–8, 89, 90–1
    governorships, 92
    Grandee of Spain rank, 105, 107–8,
        108, 111–2
    importance of Royal Sites, 91–2
    institutional development, 88
    patrimonialization, 90
    reconfiguration of space, 89–90
    ritual objects, 11, 105, 107, 114–5, 115–6
    royal baptisms, 11, 105–16
    royal guards, 95–6
    Royal Site infrastructures, 96–7
    Royal Sites, 10–1, 87–98
    Royal Stables, 94
    Spanish court, 89–92, **91**, **92**
    transformation of court space, 95–7

Spanish Succession, War of the, 33, 35,
    37–8
spatial turn, 88, 99n9
spectacle, 4–5
stability, 35
Starkey, David, 5
state, the
    personification of, 8
    supra-regional, 158
state formation, 147
statues, 34
Steffani, Agostino, 198
Stockholm, Bernadotte's entry into, 123–5
Stollberg-Rilinger, Barbara, 5
Süleyman, Sultan, 22, 23–4
Sweden, 10, 121–35
    Act of Adoption, 127
    Bernadotte arrives in, 121–2
    Bernadotte's elevation to Prince,
        122–7
    Bernadotte's entry into Stockholm,
        123–5
    Charles XIV John's accession, 128
    Charles XIV John's funeral, 132–5
    coronations and coronation rites,
        128–30
    Oaths of Allegiance, 125–7, 130–2
    royal presentations, 123–4
    succession, 121–2, 135
symbolic communication, 11, 171. *see also*
    heraldic representation
symbolic language, 5

taxes and taxation, 26
Temple, Frederick, Archbishop, 55
theatres, 96–7
Thurzó, Count Imre, 151
Tornel, Pablo González, 8
Tractarian movement, 54
treason, 152
Turin, 35, 37

Utrecht, Peace of, 33, 38

Venetian culture, impact of, 12, 193, 195–6,
    196, 198, 201–6, **201**, **203**, **204**
Victor Amadeus II of Savoy (I of Sicily),
    King, 33, 35–7, **37**, 39, 41, 42, 43, 44
    coronation, 49, 158–9, 161

Victor Emmanuel II, King of Italy, 163, 164
Victoria, Queen, coronation, 9, 52, 53–4, 54–5
Vienna, Congress of, 122
Viennot, Éliane, 72
Villeparisis, Henri Clutin de, 73
Visigoths, 134
Vitale, Pietro, 36, 42, 43

Wanegffelen, Thierry, 71–2
Wars of Religion, 95
Watanabe-O'Kelly, Helen, 42
Wentworth, Thomas, inauguration as Lord Deputy of Ireland, 1–2, 4, 12
Wickham Legg, John, 54
Wickham Legg, Leopold, 54–5

William IV, King, coronation, 9, 52, 53, 54
Wilson, H.A., 54
Władysław II, King of Hungary, 172–3, **174**
women
  autonomous political space, 72–3
  husband's power over, 70–1
  inheritance, 70
  and Salic Law, 70–3
women's activism, 71
Wünsne-Werdehausen, Elisabeth, 36

Yelçe, Zeynep, 7–8
Young, Michael, 58

Zasius, Johann Ulrich, 177–8

www.ingramcontent.com/pod-product-compliance
Lightning Source LLC
Chambersburg PA
CBHW062133300426
44115CB00012BA/1910